The Napoleonic Era in Europe

THE
NAPOLEONIC ERA
IN EUROPE

Jacques Godechot
Université de Toulouse

Beatrice F. Hyslop
*Emeritus, Hunter College of the City University
of New York*

David L. Dowd
Late of the University of Kentucky

Holt, Rinehart and Winston
*New York Chicago San Francisco Atlanta
Dallas Montreal Toronto London Sydney*

*To Irene
and Alexandra Dowd*

Cover illustration: Napoleon in His Study. Painting by
Jacques-Louis David. (National Gallery of Art,
Washington, D.C. Samuel H. Kress Collection)

Copyright © 1971 by Holt, Rinehart and Winston, Inc.
All Rights Reserved
Library of Congress Catalog Card Number: 71–114155
SBN: 03–084166–6
Printed in the United States of America
1 2 3 4 090 9 8 7 6 5 4 3 2 1

Preface

The year 1969 was the bicentennial of the birth of Napoleon I. Although a voluminous literature on Napoleon and his times exists—in 1908–1910 Kircheisen assembled over 100,000 titles—French scholars are continuing to add new volumes. Research by American historians has been less on the career of Napoleon than on the French Revolution era that preceded it. Although some excellent volumes have appeared recently in French and in English, it is appropriate to publish this work, which embodies the latest research and is designed not only for the general reader but for the historian as well.

Special exhibits of Napoleonic memorabilia were organized to mark the bicentennial. In Paris, at the Grand Palais the exhibit was entitled *La Gloire de Napoléon;* at the Bibliothèque Nationale, the *Napoleonic Legend;* at the Archives Nationales, *Napoléon tel qu'en lui-même;* and an exhibit was held at the Museum of the Legion of Honor, which Napoleon founded. The permanent exhibit at Malmaison, the home of Josephine, was enlarged and rearranged. There were two exhibits in Corsica and one at the Île d'Aix, the last French soil touched by Napoleon. The new studies and the exhibits may well stimulate further research and publication, and perhaps development of a new legend.

In 1964 Professor Jacques Godechot, of the Université de Toulouse, and Professor David L. Dowd, then professor at the University of Florida but subsequently at the University of Kentucky, agreed to write a book on the French Revolution and the Napoleonic era with special focus on the interaction between France and Europe. Professor Dowd was to write the first part, on the Revolutionary era, and Professor Godechot the second, on the Napoleonic era, which would be translated by Professor Dowd. Professor Godechot's text was completed in 1964.

In 1967 Professor Godechot published a volume in the Clio series entitled *L'Europe et l'Amerique à l'époque napoléonienne,* demonstrating in addition to the interaction between France and Europe their interaction with America—the Atlantic Revolution interpretation associated with Professor Godechot and Professor Robert R. Palmer. This volume, designed for university students, provided a detailed annotated bibliography and a final part suggestive of research still to be done.

In the autumn of 1968, Professor and Mrs. Dowd were killed in an automobile accident. The projected volume was unfinished. Although Professor Dowd had translated much of Professor Godechot's part on Napoleon, only a few chapters on the Revolution had been written.

When Holt, Rinehart and Winston signed a new contract with Professor Godechot and me, it was decided to publish the work as two books. One, on Napoleon, was to be published as soon as possible, and a companion volume, on the Revolution, which I would write, would be published later. It had been hoped that the volume on Napoleon would appear before the end of 1969, but that proved impossible for a variety of reasons. Although the task I undertook with regard to the volume on Napoleon was to complete the translation, it was agreed that I would adapt Professor Godechot's text for the American reader. Parts in the original manuscript on the interaction with America were omitted as too brief to be satisfactory for the American historian. It was agreed that I would write an introductory chapter (Chapter 1) on France and the European world in the decade of the Revolution, to 1799, the year of Napoleon's *coup d'état,* and a final chapter (Chapter 14) on Napoleon, the man and the legend. Chapters 2 to 13 have been altered or expanded where new research has been published since 1964. Material on culture in the Napoleonic period, originally included in Chapter 12, has been separated from this chapter and with new material added now forms Chapter 13.

Much of the additional material for the present volume has been drawn from Professor Godechot's *Napoléon* in the series *Le Mémorial des siècles,* edited by Gérard Walter, published early in 1969. Some issues of the *Annales historiques de la Révolution française* have been useful since they present new research or evaluations. The issue of April–June 1969 was entirely devoted to "L'abolition du régime féodal dans le monde occidental," and that of January–March 1970, to Napoleon. In both numbers there were articles by Professor Godechot. In the latter he wrote a chapter on "Sens et Importance de la Transformation des Institutions révolutionnaires à l'Époque napoléonienne," in which he reveals succinctly his general view of Napoleon. In many respects, Napoleon carried on changes and institutions begun during the Revolutionary era, reduced liberty, but conserved equality before the law. Napoleon's real innovations, according to Professor Godechot, were in the relations of church and state and in secondary and higher education. He gives less credit to Napoleon for the Codes in this article than in the present volume. In editing the translation and writing the new chapters, an attempt has been made to bring the 1964 text up to date on publications through 1969.

The present author wishes to thank the daughters of Professor Dowd, Irene and Alexandra, for permission to bring out this work of their father's in conjunction with Professor Godechot. I wish to express appreciation for help given by Dr. Kenneth L. Culver, formerly with Holt, Rinehart and Winston, who had worked with Professor Dowd; to various typists, including Miss Alberta Kanya, and to Mr. Clifford L. Snyder and others of the staff of Holt who have assisted in production of the volume.

January 1970   Beatrice F. Hyslop
                                  Professor Emeritus, Hunter College of
                                  the City University of New York

                                  Visiting Professor: Spring 1969, Univer-
                                  sity of Kentucky; Spring 1970, Winthrop
                                  College, South Carolina

Contents

MAPS

ILLUSTRATIONS

1

EUROPE IN 1799

On 18 Brumaire, Year VIII (November 9, 1799) Napoleon Bonaparte carried out a *coup d'état* that overthrew the French Directory and led to establishment of the Consulate. A Corsican by origin, trained in French military schools, and already renowned for his role in the recapture of Toulon and in the Italian and Egyptian campaigns, he was to occupy the center of the European stage until his downfall in 1815. What was France in 1799? What was the situation in the British Isles and on the continent of Europe?

FRANCE

There had been a decade of revolution in France, revolutions in Switzerland and Holland, and war accompanying changes from 1792 on elsewhere. France had tried a limited monarchy under the Constitution of 1791, which contained the Declaration of the Rights of Man, voicing democratic ideals of the early revolutionaries. This was followed by the First French Republic, under a succession of regimes, culminating with the Consulate of 1799.

During the elections to the Estates General called for 1789 in order to remedy the financial situation, extensive pamphlet literature spread ideas of reform derived from the Enlightenment of the eighteenth century. Electoral assemblies, in addition to electing their deputies, drew up instructions called *cahiers de doléances*. These documents are both descriptive of conditions on the eve of the Revolution, and also voiced the reforms that the particular electoral assembly wanted the Estates General to make. The *cahiers* ranged in views from conservative to progressive reform; only a few could be called radical. Although Louis XVI had allowed double the number of deputies from the third estate compared with those of the clergy and nobles, there would be no advantage unless voting was by head. The *cahiers* of the third estate insisted on vote by head, and not by order.

When the Estates General met, a deadlock ensued for over a month while the privileged classes insisted on vote by order, backed by the king and court party, and the third estate on individual votes irrespective of order. After declaring the third estate the National Assembly, with or without the other two classes, the members took the Oath of the Tennis Court, binding them not to separate until a constitution and reforms had been voted. The king gave in and ordered the deputies of the privileged classes to join the third estate. By the end of June, the National Assembly could proceed to organize its committees and to start debate on reform.

In the meantime the economic crisis continued to worsen, especially in Paris. After the capture of the Bastille on July 14, 1789, an event henceforth symbolizing freedom and celebrated each year on this day, the National Guard with Lafayette in command, and a new elected government in Paris were set up. After a wave of fear and destruction in the provinces, the National Assembly voted the abolition of feudalism. Actually, only serfdom was ended by the law of August 11–15, 1789. Laws in February and March 1790 did away with seignorial dues and contractual services, but with indemnities to the seignorial lords payable by the peasants. It was not until 1792 and 1793 that all survivals of feudalism were completely suppressed.

Confiscation of properties of the Catholic Church in 1789 and the issuance of assignats (paper money) based upon their sale alleviated for a time, the critical financial situation that had led to revolution, but later, with war and inflation, these measures contributed to further economic crises. Although the organization of France into departments helped to equalize taxation regionally, new measures for individual taxes were brought into operation slowly. The wealthy could not easily avoid payment, but the common people often ignored the new laws, which aimed to spread the tax burden according to the ability to pay.

Abolition of titles of nobility in 1790 and the Civil Constitution of the Clergy in 1791 after its condemnation by the Pope, split the nation and led to widespread emigration of those opposed to these measures, the émigrés seeking the aid of foreign rulers in reestablishing the Old Regime. Following the attempted flight of Louis XVI in June 1791, the rulers of Austria and Prussia signed the Declaration of Pilnitz promising aid to the royal family, but after Louis XVI took the oath to uphold the Constitution of 1791 (September 14, 1791), the emperor Leopold and Frederick William II took no overt steps to fulfill their promise.

The Constitution of 1791 was preceded by the Declaration of the Rights of Man, inspired by the Enlightenment and the bills of rights in the state constitutions of the thirteen states. This declaration voiced liberty, equality, security, as the reformers of 1789 conceived these individual rights, affirmed popular sovereignty as the source of law, equality before the law for trials and taxation, and implied an equal right to vote to all citizens, a statement later broken by the division of citizens into active and passive citizens. The document also asserted the right to overthrow the government, but when this 'right' was included, the drafters were thinking of the government of the Old Regime, and not the new reformed one of the constitution that took nearly two years to complete. The Constitution of 1791, as it is called, and not of 1789, provided for a limited monarchy, legislative power to a unicameral legislature, a long suspensive veto to the king, an elected judiciary, and decentralized departmental governments.

The Legislative Assembly, elected by the active voters (a tax requirement was adopted both for office-holding and for elections to the Assembly), began to function in October 1791. It was an entirely new body of representatives, for on the eve of its closing in September of the same year, the National Assembly had voted that none of its members should be eligible to sit in the next legislature. Fairly soon, representatives from the department of the Gironde and some neighboring departments formed a group that came to be known as Girondins, under the leadership of Jacques Pierre Brissot(de Warville) and Pierre Vernignaud. The group became influential in the Legislative Assembly and developed into a war faction, suspecting the royal family and rulers of monarchical states of plotting against the French government. It was only to be expected that letters would be exchanged between the queen Marie Antoinette and her brother Joseph II of Austria as well as with his successors Leopold II and Francis II (all children of the Empress Maria Theresa); the Girondins became increasingly suspicious that the ruler of Austria was aiding the French émigrés, plotting with the queen through correspondence, and encouraging the princes of the Holy Roman Empire who possessed lands within France to resist the application of French decrees in their holdings, particularly those pertaining to the abolition of feudal rights.

After a brief diplomatic crisis, the Legislative Assembly declared war on Francis II as king of Bohemia and Hungary rather than emperor of the

Holy Roman Empire. If the Assembly had declared war on Francis as Holy Roman emperor, all the princes of the Empire might have been at war with France. The declaration of war on April 20, 1792, gave as reasons collusion between the Bourbons—both the royal family and the Bourbon émigrés—and the Austrian Hapsburgs with a view to the overthrow of the French government and encouragement of opposition to revolutionary legislation within and outside of French borders.

The revolutionaries, especially the Girondin leaders, were optimistic that soldiers fighting under the banner of "Liberty, Equality and Fraternity" would soon defeat the heterogeneous armies of Austria, joined by Prussia, and that the French king would reveal where his loyalties lay. They overlooked, however, the fact that many officers had emigrated, that there had been opposition in 1789 to militia service, and that the regular army was not only ill fed and ill equipped but also lacked discipline. Provision for the election of army officers by the common soldier had not ensured good training or even obedience to commands. The mobilizing of resources for war put a further strain on economic production and distribution, especially in the cities. Initial successes against the Austrian Netherlands soon turned to defeat and retreat. The threatening manifesto of the Duke of Brunswick, commander of the invading forces, led to an insurrection in Paris on August 10, 1792, and the overthrow of the monarchy.

A provisional government, in which Georges Danton played an important role, imprisoned the royal family, issued a call for elections based on universal suffrage to a National Convention to replace the Legislative Assembly, and asked for volunteers to fight the enemy. Panic seized the Parisians at the news of the fall of Verdun and the departure of men for the war. The provisional government was unable to prevent the infamous September massacres during which 1000 to 1300 prisoners, noblemen, priests, middle class, and common criminals were assassinated by mobs at the prisons. The day before the first meeting of the National Convention, the Republican army fought a battle at Valmy in eastern France to a draw; the Prussian commander had decided to order winter quarters instead of continuation of the battle. This was considered a victory for the French; even the young Goethe, secretary to the Prince of Württemberg in the invading army, wrote from the battlefield that this was a great day for liberty. Although Goethe revised this statement after 1815, the fact that the Prussians did not press on toward Paris gave the National Convention a respite in its beginning days.

One of the first acts of the Convention was to declare France a republic and to appoint a committee to draw up a new constitution, as the Constitution of 1791 was no longer satisfactory in many of its provisions. In addition to taking measures for the defense of France, the Convention brought Louis XVI to trial—much as the English Parliament had Charles I in 1649.

He was condemned for treason and ordered executed. The sentence was carried out on January 21, 1793.

During the trial of the king the National Convention, which felt confident of its republican ideals, issued two decrees known as the Propagandist Decrees. The first, issued on November 19, 1792, was a Declaration of Assistance and Fraternity to Foreign Peoples. It asserted briefly in a single article the willingness of the French to aid oppressed people to "regain" their liberty. When writing this decree, the members of the Convention had the Austrian Netherlands particularly in mind. An attempt by the Belgians to gain control of their own affairs in 1790 had failed. Some leaders of the revolt considered the French as friends and were ready to collaborate with them against the Austrians. The decree promised assistance and protection from harassment.

The second decree promulgated on December 15, spelled out instructions for French generals to follow in conquered (or liberated) territory. The generals were immediately to declare the sovereignty of the people, abolish existing governments and taxes, and do away with survivals of feudalism and the privileges of the clergy and nobility. In other words, the French promised the same kind of reforms that had been achieved in France since 1789. The generals were to announce to the people that the French brought them "peace, assistance, fraternity, liberty and equality," that property and security of persons would be assured, and that new governments based on universal suffrage would be set up. The property of the former government, however, would be confiscated and administered by the new popular government.

The rest of the December declaration set a different tone. French commissioners would be appointed to advise the new governments on matters of common defense, the meeting of expenses for the aid given by France (Article 7), and methods of obtaining provisions and munitions for the army. Although Article 11 promised aid until the new government was firmly established, the French would consider as enemies and treat accordingly, anyone "refusing liberty and equality," or trying to restore former privileges and the Old Regime. Then came a list of the institutions to be abolished, including the salt tax (gabelle), town tolls (octroi), and clerical privileges. The decree ended with a reassertion of the altruistic ideal of promoting the welfare and fraternity of people. Unfortunately, the territories where the policy would be applied did not always see eye to eye with the French armies and their program of reform. The Belgians were strongly clerical and objected to measures against the Catholic Church. The decree did not foresee and hence provided no safeguards against the possibility that a French soldier would seek to line his own pockets rather than carry out the liberal policy outlined by the National Convention.

After the death of Louis XVI, the war had been extended to include

England, Spain, and Holland, and by the spring of 1793, the situation of the French army had become critical. The desertion of General Dumouriez, head of the Revolutionary army, precipitated a crisis in the National Convention. The Committee of General Security, the Committee of Public Safety—in a sense an executive cabinet responsible to the elected body, and the Revolutionary Tribunal to try cases of treason, were set up to formulate and execute policy. Throughout their functioning, membership on these bodies was elected by the Convention and renewable by it. A struggle for control ensued between Girondins, responsible for the war and for recent defeats, since Dumouriez had been appointed by a Girondin ministry, and accused of monarchism by their opponents, and the more radical Jacobins, who emerged victorious. Following the expulsion of the Girondins from the Convention, May 31–June 2, the Jacobins controlled the Convention and the Committees. Robespierre, a leader of the Jacobins, became a member of the Committee of Public Safety and remained so until his own downfall in July 1794.

The republican Constitution of the Year I (1793), the most democratic of the Revolutionary decade, was completed, approved by a plebiscite, and then suspended until peacetime. Throughout the Reign of Terror, as this period has been called, the government was provisional and revolutionary. From the summer of 1793 until the fall of the Robespierrist government, there were really four centers of power in Paris: the National Convention, the great Committees, the municipal government of Paris or the Commune, and the popular assemblies in the sections of Paris. One might add, the Jacobin Club which served as an unofficial steering committee for all of these bodies. In the departments, Jacobin Clubs played a vital role in law enforcement, and the Convention appointed, on nomination of the Committee of Public Safety, deputies *en mission* to supervise local application of revolutionary legislation. In all the larger towns or cities, there were sectional assemblies comparable to those in Paris. These assemblies were a key to charges against suspected traitors, supplied reports of price evasion, located necessary supplies for the army, and provided for the production of munitions. Today's tourist can still see holes in pillars and vaults of famous public buildings made by republicans seeking saltpeter for the production of gunpowder.

Centralization of power was adopted during the Terror in order to win the war, and many laws were passed by the Convention to insure success. Conscription was voted in August 1793 in order to distribute military duty equitably. A levy of soldiers, intriguing *émigrés*, revolutionary anti-Catholicism, and local factors caused the uprising of the peasants in the west, known as the Wars of the Vendée. Atrocities occurred on both sides of this civil war, and it was not till 1796 that General Hoche was able to bring peace to the area—but only after the failure of a royalist expedition to

Quiberon Bay on the Brittany coast, which had been undertaken by *émigrés* and financed by England. Thus, the Jacobins had civil war as well as foreign war to fight.

To remedy the financial and food crises in the cities, the Convention under pressure from the Enragés and the Paris Sections, representing the sans-culottes, adopted price regulation (Law of the Maximum), taxes on the rich, and measures against currency speculation. It also provided for punishment for evasion of conscription. Breaking these laws might bring one before the Revolutionary Tribunal. The vagueness of the Law of Suspects of September 1793 and later abbreviation of self-defense by the law of 22 Prairial (June 10, 1794) denied the accused the full safeguards of the law introduced into the judicial system under the Constitution of 1791.

In September and October of 1793 the Republican army was able to stem the British, Austrian, and Prussian advances, and the National Convention passed sterner legislation at home to assure loyalty to the Revolution. Marie Antoinette, the duke of Orleans, and the Girondin leaders were tried and executed. A wave of dechristianization encouraged by the radicals swept Paris from November to January 1794. Even a mass in honor of the Goddess of Reason was held in the Cathedral of Notre Dame. The anti-Christian movement was also observed in some of the provincial cities where deputies had been sent to carry out the laws passed by the Convention, to combat federalism—emphasis on departmental government and loyalty rather than upon the national government—and to obtain supplies for the French armies. The tyrannical actions of some of these deputies led subsequently to their trial and punishment. Among them were Joseph Fouché (later minister of police under Napoleon), Louis Marie Fréron, and Jean Baptiste Carrier, notorious for his cruel methods of execution at Nantes.

Although Toulon, the important naval base on the Mediterranean which had fallen to the British in August 1793, was recaptured in December, the war situation was acute. Danton, one of the most important Jacobin leaders of the Convention, and especially Lazare Carnot, a member of the Committee of Public Safety, exerted every effort to obtain men, supplies, and munitions.

The Enragés, who sponsored a radical economic program and dechristianization, were eliminated by the Hébertists, who had first supported them, and in March 1794, the Hébertists were brought before the Revolutionary Tribunal, tried, condemned and executed. A quarrel then developed between Danton and Robespierre and their respective followers. Danton had been the most influential of the Jacobins in arousing patriotic spirit after the fall of the monarchy. When the friction between these two leading Jacobins erupted, Danton was busy with the defense of France. He thought that the Terror could be attenuated, whereas Robespierre was convinced that treason and the enemies of the Republic would triumph if the condemnations by the Revolutionary Tribunal were relaxed. Robespierre also suspected Danton of receiving English money to advocate peace with England and moderation of the Terror—charges later proven, but not at the time. In April 1794, Danton and his friends, who had speculated in assignats and in stocks of the Company of the Indies, were charged with treason, tried and executed. Danton, the most eloquent of the Jacobins, was prevented from arguing in his own defense at the trial.

The period from April until 9 Thermidor (July 27, 1794) was a time when Robespierre, seconded by Léon de Saint-Just and Georges Couthon led the Committee of Public Safety and the various agencies of political power. Robespierre came to be considered the champion of the sans-culottes. The stronghold of sans-culottism was in the sectional assemblies of Paris and other big cities. The introduction of the Law of the Maximum and the Ventôse decrees—distribution of confiscated property to the propertyless—had been aimed to assure the loyalty of sans-culottes before the Robespierre period.

Robespierre had opposed the dechristianization movement, and soon after he became dominant, he arranged for a festival of the Supreme Being, which was a form of eighteenth century deism. Robespierre's rivals made great fun of him, and opposition newspapers reported that he wished to be pope. Although not so intended at the time, this measure actually became a step toward the restoration of Christianity. Robespierre's name is also associated with the law of 22 Prairial, which speeded up trials of the Revolutionary Tribunal, and concentrated them in Paris rather than in the departments. The greatest number of condemnations had coincided with the dechristianization period, but the figures increased again in June and July 1794.

In June, rivalry developed between the Committee of General Security and the Committee of Public Safety. The latter, under the leadership of Robespierre took more and more authority upon itself. The austerity program sponsored by Robespierre was unpopular with members of the Convention who were well off. Robespierre began to suspect a plot to overthrow his regime, and to hint at the withdrawal of immunity from arrest for members of the Convention. Members who feared Robespierre plotted to overthrow him before he could denounce them in the Convention. The group of deputies that overthrew Robespierre and his party on July 27, were less public spirited than he, but feared his power, especially with the sans-culottes. Robespierre was not given a chance to defend his ideas, and his opponents engineered a decree of outlawry against him and his supporters. Robespierre refused to call upon the sections of Paris in his defense, and those who had come to the City Hall expecting orders went home. Robespierre and his immediate followers were executed, virtually without trial.

Following the downfall of Robespierre, the Thermidorian government, led by those who had brought about his downfall, blackened his reputation by portraying him as a bloodthirsty dictator—a reputation that has been refuted but which still is portrayed by conservative historians and popular literature. The Thermidorians repealed the laws establishing the Terror, such Girondins as had survived in hiding returned to the Convention, but legislation against *émigrés* and non-juring clergy was kept. It was not possible to carry out the Constitution of the Year I, and a new, less democratic constitution, that of the Year III (1795), was drawn up providing for government by a bicameral legislature, elected by a limited suffrage, and a Directory of five men chosen by the legislature. The new government was inaugurated on November 2, 1795.

Meanwhile, French armies had begun again to win victories, starting with the battle of Fleurus in June 1794 and had initiated aggressive invasion. The success of the armies led to a series of peace treaties. In February 1795 one was signed with Tuscany (a former Austrian Duchy) and another with the Vendéans; in April, a treaty with Prussia; in May, with Holland; in June, with Spain. On the last day of December 1795, after the Directory had taken office, an armstice was signed with Austria.

Despite internal turmoil, instability of the government and lack of continuity in its leadership, civil and foreign war, many reforms had been initiated since 1789 that were to become a permanent part of French institutions. Some were only temporary, as for example, the abolition of titles of nobility. The Civil Constitution of the Clergy, rejecting the power of the Pope, placed the clergy under the authority of the state, which had already taken over Church property. The state was to pay clerical salaries. During a delay in the papal denunciation, the French annexed Avignon, which had been papal territory since the fourteenth century, after a plebiscite that was favorable to annexation. The requirement of an oath to this constitution and the condemnation by the Pope, split the clergy and led to the emigration of many nonjuring clergy. After the dechristianization experiment and the Robespierre period, a troubled religious situation ensued, even for the Constitutional Church, until a temporary separation of church and state during the Directory, which nevertheless attempted to promote its own brand of deism (Theophilanthropy, sponsored by Louis Marie La Revellière-Lépeaux, one of the Directors). Protestants had been granted full citizenship in the early Revolution; this was later extended to Jews. Toleration was practised. Protestants came under the same law of civil registration as did Catholics. Jewish worship was not interfered with. Subordination of the church to the state continued until 1906.

Under the Old Regime education had been the responsibility of the Catholic Church. Measures against the Catholic clergy led to a crisis in education. The Enlightenment had brought forward reform ideas, and the

Revolutionary assemblies appointed a committee on public education. This body debated thoroughly the diverse ideas of the eighteenth-century philosophers. Antoine Nicolas Condorcet, a member of the Education Committee, presented a famous report to the Legislative Assembly on April 20–21, 1792, at the very time that war was declared on Austria. The basic ideas of this report were subsequently adopted and, although modified, became a part of the French public school system that has prevailed ever since. Education was to be secular, aimed to promote happiness and good citizenship. By its teaching of good morality, education would contribute to the progress of mankind. There was to be universal opportunity to learn, and the educative process was conceived to last throughout the life of the individual. Condorcet described five gradations of schools: primary, secondary, institutes, lycées, and a national society of arts and sciences. Subjects to be taught throughout the years of school would include not only literature, history, and mathematics, but also geography, economics, political science, the natural sciences, and physical training. The higher in the system one mounted, the more emphasis was put on philosophy, morality, and science. Although the Education Committee would allow the study of Latin, the emphasis would be on modern languages and literature. Provision was also made for vocational training. The approach was to be universalism, as regards religion and national sentiment, and human potentialities were to be developed. The plan spelled out details for the primary and secondary schools both with regard to the progression of studies and the teaching staff.

Obviously, this plan was an ambitious one, when the legislature was concerned with war and crisis in daily life, and the financial situation was growing increasingly acute. Successive Revolutionary assemblies wrestled with the problem of putting state-controlled education along these lines into operation. The absence of trained teachers other than those of former religious orders or of the secular clergy was one of the main difficulties. Laws were passed providing for parts of the system, but in actual practice a confused situation existed, with private schools continuing along with the establishment of new state schools. Shortly before the closing of the National Convention, on October 25, 1795, that body did pass an important education law, providing for primary schools, at least in each canton, and a central school (école centrale) in each department. The central schools were really secondary schools, with a curriculum including literature, the arts, mathematics and other science, history, and law. The education law also provided for special schools for various subjects, such as natural history, medicine, rural economics, art, music, political science. Title IV of the law set up a national institute of arts and sciences. Public prizes and rewards were to be awarded as a stimulus to achievement, and on certain national holdiays there were to be celebrations in honor of youth, marriage, agriculture, liberty, the aged, and other common ideals.

The former universities were suppressed in 1794, but new advanced training was provided in institutions that still exist today: the Polytechnic School for military and civil engineering, the École normale for teacher training, the Conservatory of Arts and Crafts, the Conservatory of Music, and the School of Public Administration. These schools were all established between October 1794 and October 1795.

The French language was promoted at the expense of local patois within French frontiers by Revolutionary educational reforms. French had been the language of the European ruling classes and had been the official tongue of diplomacy since the time of Louis XIV. Now the French armies and administrators undertook to spread its use to the people in occupied territories.

Equality before the law, despite temporary setbacks, became a permanent part of French law. Feudalism was finally abolished, and seignorial dues and liens on peasant property were ended. The purchase of nationalized properties increased the number of property holders at the same time that it augmented the size of many holdings, as it was primarily the wealthy who could buy land. Guilds, which had become monopolistic under the Old Regime, were abolished, but simultaneously the Loi Le Chapelier forbade the formation of masters' and of workmen's associations. Uniform weights and measures—the metric system—were introduced on August 1, 1793. The Directory was successful in efforts to check inflation and its economic consequences by curtailing government expenditure, by repudiating one third of the public debt (with payment in bonds of the other two thirds), and by establishing an agency in each department for tax collection. As an additional measure to meet the government deficit, the Directory instituted taxes on licenses, stamps, registration fees, and land and personal property that have endured, although with modification, to this day.

Shortly before the closing of the National Convention, the insurrection of 13 Vendémiaire (October 5, 1795) occurred. This is usually considered a royalist uprising, but it was the pro-Jacobins and republicans who suffered most from the repression after its suppression by Napoleon (by his "whiff of grapeshot"), who was put in command. His success on this occasion contributed to his meteoric rise.

During the four-year rule under the Directory, the government was rendered unstable by successive *coups d'état,* now from the Left, now from the Right. The Directory proceeded against the Jacobins and in 1796 broke the conspiracy of Francois Emile Babeuf (more commonly known as Gracchus Babeuf) and his followers, the Society of the Equals. Babeuf, a collector of seignorial rents before the Revolution, was a minor official and until the Thermidorian period eked out an existence for his large family by journalism. He then began to organize groups with the most radical social and economic programs, demanding an equal right to property and advocates of a democratic republic. Many former Jacobins joined his ranks. "The Manifesto of the Equals," drafted by Sylvain Maréchal, a playwright and publicist, was adopted by the Babeuvists. This manifesto when viewed from the twentieth century seems relatively mild but not so in the eyes of the Directory. The Babeuvists also were conspiring to overthrow the Directory and to bring into operation the Jacobin Constitution of the Year I (1793), which had been overwhelmingly approved in a referendum but suspended until peacetime. The plans of the Babeuvists, which included a form of agrarian communism, were betrayed by spies of the Directory who had penetrated into the group. Babeuf and Auguste Alexandre Darthé, one of his followers, were tried by a special court at Vendôme and executed on May 27, 1797. Filippo Buonarotti, a Babeuvist leader and descendant of Michelangelo, was imprisoned—first at Cherbourg, then Oléron, then Sospello, near the border of Piedmont. From his prison, he continued to agitate for revolution. In 1806 he was allowed to go to Geneva, but was subsequently transferred to Grenoble. Buonarotti founded a secret order, and was leader in north Italy against Austrian rule. He lived for some time in Brussels and died in Paris. He was a lifelong revolutionary and historian of the Babeuf movement.

After the fall of the Babeuvists and the further purging of the Jacobins from the government, the Royalists and émigrés made an attempt to overthrow the Directory on 22 Floréal, Year VI (May 11, 1798). The Clichiens, as the conspirators were called, wished to decrease the power of the Directory, increase that of the Council of Ancients and Council of Five Hundred, and repeal laws against émigrés and deported priests. As a result of the elections in 1797, a new two-thirds majority was returned to the councils. This group of moderate revolutionaries was strongly anti-Jacobin. Carnot attempted to conciliate Jacobin and moderate factions, but he failed, and three directors appealed to Napoleon, who threatened to return from Italy. The three directors moved quickly; they brought in troops under General Augereau, who purged the Councils. Over 200 elections were annulled, and supporters of the Constitution of 1795 elected or appointed. Legislation against émigrés and priests was reinforced. The press was censored, and persons who had illegally returned to France were arrested.

On 30 Prairial, Year VII (June 18, 1799), the republican majority in the Councils forced the resignation from the Directory of Merlin de Douai (former Jacobin) and Louis Larevellière-Lépeaux, both staunch revolutionaries, and replaced them with General Moulin and Roger Ducos, both rather colorless figures. Abbé Siéyès replaced Jean François Reubell, Alsatian patriot, as president of the Directory. Thus, Barras alone of the original five directors still held office. The Directory, by now a middle-of-the-road group, was caught between both Jacobin and royalist pressures. Siéyès succeeded in parrying Jacobin power on the Council of Five Hundred and began to look around for a republican general who could be trusted to uphold the civil government without dominating it. Hoche had died, and Joubert had been killed in the fighting in Italy. Moreau was unreliable, and Bernadotte and Jourdan might be too revolutionary. Siéyès considered Napoleon but hesitated. Napoleon had won laurels first in Italy and then presumably in Egypt. Instead of accepting the task of renewed pacification in the west of France, Napoleon had persuaded the Directory that an effective way to combat England was to strike at its route to India—hence, to attack Egypt—and that he was the one to conduct this campaign.

When, following the defeat of the French fleet by the English at Abukir and by the Syrians at Acre, Napoleon heard of unrest and danger of collapse of the government at home, he left command of French troops in Egypt to General Kléber and hurried home to France. He was lucky enough to escape the English fleet and landed in the south of France on October 9, 1799. His march to Paris was triumphal, for the failures of the Egyptian campaign had not been reported in the French papers. The conquering hero contrasted with the discredited directors. After stormy explanations concerning her infidelity while he was in Egypt, Napoleon was reunited with Josephine, who seconded his efforts. He conferred with all the important figures of the day and finally decided to unite efforts with Siéyès. Ducos, Talleyrand, Fouché, Jean Jacques Cambacérès, and Lucien Bonaparte, Napoleon's elder brother, developed a plot to overthrow the government. The Council of Ancients, fearful of a Jacobin plot, was persuaded to move its sessions to Saint-Cloud, safe from Parisian street uprisings, and was to vote military powers to Napoleon, who would then displace the directors and set up a provisional rule by three consuls—himself, Siéyès and Ducos.

On 18 Brumaire the plans worked well: the Council of Ancients chose Napoleon to protect the government from a presumed Jacobin conspiracy. But on 19 Brumaire both Councils realized that Napoleon and his soldiers were not there to protect them, but rather to force their acquiescence in a new government under his direction. He succeeded in winning over the Council of Ancients, but, despite the chairmanship of Lucien Bonaparte, the Council of Five Hundred resisted. It was necessary for Napoleon to use his soldiers to clear the hall (the Orangerie). Lucien saved the day for his brother, who showed both weakness and confusion during a tumultuous session of the Council that tried to outlaw him. After the use of force, the two Councils met. By appointing Napoleon, Siéyès, and Ducos consuls and providing for two commissions to draft a new constitution, they gave some semblance of legality to the new government. The former directors had either resigned or fled.

EUROPE

By the end of 1795 France was at war only with Austria and England. Napoleonic victories in Italy, despite setbacks in Austrian German lands, led to preliminary peace at Campo-Formio in 1797, but an end to war with Austria did not come until the Treaty of Lunéville in 1801 after Napoleon defeated the Austrian forces at Marengo. War continued with England until 1802.

The decade of revolution in France affected other countries. In England parliamentary government under George III was influenced in domestic policy by events on the other side of the Channel. Edmund Burke's *Reflections on the French Revolution,* published toward the end of 1790, became the bible of the Tories, who defended the king, Anglican Church, and aristocracy against real or supposed subversive influences from France. English liberals had reacted favorably to changes in France in the first years of the Revolution, and the congratulations of the Society for the Revolution—formed to celebrate the English Revolution of 1688—on the capture of the Bastille linked events in France with English liberties gained a century earlier. By November 1789 English reform societies, notably the Revolution Society, heard addresses by men such as Richard Price who joined changes in France with the demand for suffrage and religious reform in England. His famous sermon entitled "A Discourse on the Love of Our Country" implied broadly that the Revolution of 1688 had not gone far enough. It was published for all to read. Price also recommended the formation of societies for parliamentary reform throughout England and that these groups actively communicate with one other about their activities and possible joint action.

The Society for Constitutional Reform which had failed prior to 1789 to achieve suffrage reform and had languished after the Gordon riots in June 1780, regained importance under the influence of Price. It asserted the principles of popular sovereignty, universal suffrage, abolition of the slave trade, and legislation favorable to the dissenters. In a congratulatory message to the French government, the society endorsed John Cartwright's efforts for the extension of the suffrage in England. When Thomas Paine and Burke started to debate changes in France and their lessons for England, the Pitt government began to regard the various reform societies as unpatriotic and their efforts to extend suffrage and individual freedoms as threats to the government. William Pitt was prime minister from 1784 to 1801, and his brand of patriotism (bolstered by the aristocracy and the Anglican Church), so ably defended by Burke, led to persecution and suppression of persons and societies that desired reform. These reformers did not envisage rioting and bloodshed as the means to achieve their goals. Nevertheless, the leaders were prosecuted and some were imprisoned after trial. The reform clubs were closed by 1794, and efforts to bring about reform through Parliament failed. The unrest and sporadic violence that followed led to the suspension of the writ of *habeas corpus* in 1794.

The English press was well developed in 1789, and had good coverage of news on the Continent. Its own agents and government sources, such as the duke of Dorset, the English ambassador to France, who reported favorably on the capture of the Bastille, kept it abreast of events in France. At first the press commented favorably on the Revolution. However, French *émigrés* began to come to England and actively organize for a return of the Bourbon monarchy and the Old Regime. Their unfavorable accounts and violence reported in French papers greatly influenced the English papers, and the outbreak of war in 1793 between France and England naturally affected the bias of the news and its sources on the Continent. Insofar as the English navy continued to control the seas, communication between *émigrés* in England and in the Rhineland, where their center was at Coblenz, as well as in other centers of *émigré* activity, strengthened the denunciation of the Revolution already voiced so effectively by Burke.

Furthermore, unrest and uprising in Ireland complicated British politics and made British leaders suspicious of French aid to Irish rebels. During the Directory, a mutiny occurred in the English fleet operating in the Channel. Although it was crushed, and the leader Richard Parker executed, France failed to take advantage of this weakness in English defense. French aid to the Irish against England was part of French help to oppressed peoples. General Hoche had been unable to land a French force in Ireland in 1796, and when a rebellion broke out in 1798, only a small expeditionary force under General Humbert actually landed. Ignorant of the Irish terrain (especially the Irish bog) and poorly seconded by Irish recruits, the French forces were defeated and captured. Subsequently, Wolfe Tone, the Irish patriot who had been influential in obtaining help from France, was captured. He committed suicide while awaiting trial. Irish rebels were tracked down and killed. By the Act of Union of 1800, Ireland was annexed to England, lost its former parliament, and Catholic disabilities were restored. Thus, Ireland, which looked to the French revolutionaries for help in establishing its freedom, lost the degree of political independence it had enjoyed.

The Scotch were also inspired by French democratic ideas. They tried to obtain a wider suffrage and more voice in the British Parliament, to which Scotland had sent representatives since the Act of Union of 1701. They too were unsuccessful in applying the aims of the French Revolution to their situation.

The need to defend British commerce in wartime led to trade regula-tions and the strengthening of the navy. England soon ruled the seas. The French fleet was virtually kept prisoner at Brest, and the British held Tou-lon for half a year in 1793. British ships roamed the Mediterranean, and following the victory at Abukir Bay during the Egyptian campaign Britain further handicapped French rule and prosecution of the war. The French West Indies were also a theater of naval warfare with England victorious. In all the continental coalitions England was a key member.

England's control of all the British Isles was strengthened by the reac-tion to the French Revolution, and extension of the suffrage and liberal measures for religion and labor were postponed a quarter century.

Holland had experienced an abortive revolutionary movement in the 1780s, in which the House of Orange supported the aristocracy and federal-ism, whereas the revolutionaries advocated a unitary but more democratic government. This revolution was put down by English and Prussian forces, and leaders of the uprising took up residence in France. When the French Revolution began to encourage revolution elsewhere, it helped these self-styled exiles to plan changes in their own country. French campaigns in the Austrian Netherlands exerted pressure on Holland, and after the execution of Louis XVI, the French Republic in February 1793 declared war on the House of Orange and its aristocratic followers. Following the French vic-tory of Fleurus, on June 25–26, 1794, General Pichegru invaded Dutch territory in December. The Dutch revolutionary Jacobin clubs that had sprung up after the French declaration of war aided the French army along its route. Pichegru captured Amsterdam in January 1795. William V fled to England and a republic was declared. The Netherlands henceforth was to be known as the Batavian Republic. The first constitution that the vic-torious revolutionaries drafted was rejected by a plebiscite. Peace was signed with France on May 16, and the French attempted to conciliate the various Dutch factions. While the Dutch argued over constitutions, the French army occupied Holland, and it aroused less opposition by its poli-cies there than in some other areas. In 1798, after the *coup d'état* of Fructi-dor in France brought a more conservative Directory to power, General Daendels, who distrusted the Dutch democrats, brought a republican consti-tution to Holland that would provide a government patterned after the Directory in France. This constitution was in operation in Holland in 1799. William V chose to live in exile in England.

The Austrian Netherlands, which had been invaded when war broke out in 1792, suffered from the war on its soil. It had opposed some of the enlightened reforms of Joseph II before 1789, but its two factions failed to set up an autonomous regime and Austria continued to rule it. After war broke out with France its inhabitants were powerless to take effective measures against the antifeudal and anti-Catholic measures of the occupying French army. The nobles bided their time to get back their former power. The battle of Fleurus marked the last major encounter on Belgian soil, and the fighting passed to other theaters of war. French occupation, however, continued to be onerous. In 1795, France annexed Belgian territory and organized it into French departments similar to those within France.

Switzerland, like Holland, had experienced a revolution prior to 1789, and some of its leaders, like their Dutch counterparts, went to live in France. The movement in Switzerland had been, however, within certain cantons, some were democratic and some were aristocratic (often bourgeois) in leadership and the revolutionary efforts were put down by foreign intervention, invited in some cases by the opposition leaders. In addition to a Helvetic Club in Paris, by 1792 Jacobin clubs were forming in the major cities. In Geneva Jacobins were successful in bringing about a regime similar to that in France. In 1798 Zurich and Bern temporized and a Helvetic Republic was set up. Some cantons approved the constitution of this union, and some rejected it. Valais and the forest cantons were forced to acquiesce after the invasion by French troops. Thus, in 1799, Switzerland was a sister republic to France.

Portugal, after its separation from Spain in the seventeenth century, had been ruled by the House of Braganza. Maria I came to the throne in 1777 and ruled with her husband Pedro III until his death in 1786. She then ruled alone until 1792, when she was considered insane; her son, known as the Prince Regent, ruled until 1816, when he took the title of Jean VI. The minister, Marquis de Pompal (Sebastian Joseph de Carvalho et Mello) had provided Portugal with an enlightened rule from 1750–1777 until the accession of Maria, who dismissed him. The French Revolution affected Portuguese trade because of its treaty with England, but the Portuguese government and society were little influenced by events north of the Pyrenees.

Spain, which had enjoyed a short period of Enlightened Despotism under the ministry of Aranda and Charles III, declined under the weak monarch Charles IV. The real rulers of Spain were the queen and her lover Manuel Godoy. They were supported by the Catholic Church, the military, and the landed aristocracy. When the French Revolution began, Spain and France were allied since 1761 by the Family Compact. However, during the controversy over Nootka Sound (on the coast of Vancouver Island, Canada), in 1790, the National Assembly declined to aid Spain against England, and the alliance lapsed. The Spanish monarchy felt threatened by the French revolutionaries and reacted strongly against the changes in the status of the Catholic Church. Strict laws excluded French revolutionary pamphlets from Spain, while French *émigrés*—nobles and priests—were welcomed.

War broke out between France and Spain after the execution of Louis XVI, and the fighting surged back and forth along the Spanish border. By 1795 Spain was willing to sign a peace with France, regaining the territory that French armies had occupied, but ceding the Spanish part of Santo Domingo to France. The internal situation changed little before 1799.

The House of Hapsburg held Austria proper plus the Hapsburg crown lands, which included Bohemia, Hungary, the Tyrol, and parts of north Italy. Ever since the thirteenth century the head of the house had been successful in obtaining the election to emperor of the Holy Roman Empire. The Hapsburg power in the empire had declined as the empire itself became weaker and its constituent parts grew in importance. Prussia, which was rising in the seventeenth century, became a kingdom in 1701 with only nominal allegiance to the Emperor. In the eighteenth century, the father of Frederick II and Frederick the Great himself built up Prussia's army and gained Austrian Silesia by the War of the Austrian Succession and the Seven Years' War; other principalities, such as Baden, Württemberg, Bavaria, and Saxony, also successfully wrested control of their own affairs from the emperor, and the Imperial Diet. The Czechs in Bohemia had been subordinated to Hapsburg rule since the Thirty Years' War. Maria Theresa, wife of Emperor Francis I, that astonishing woman who ruled rather than her husband, over such extensive domains and diverse peoples, had won many Czechs by her charities and patronage. Similar actions in Hungary gained her support there. Maria Theresa bore Francis I sixteen children of whom Marie Antoinette, Joseph II, and Leopold II were the most famous. In Austrian territory, Cameralism, as Austrian government through councils was called, prevailed. Local representative bodies in the various provinces or parts of the empire exercised very little power. The throne was supported by the great landed magnates and by the army, officered chiefly by German-speaking Austrians. It was before Maria Theresa's death that the first Partition of Poland was carried out by Russia, Prussia, and Austria but she regretted the action; Austria received the greater part of Galicia.

The French Revolution period saw three successive Holy Roman Emperors, all sons of Maria Theresa: Joseph II, Leopold II, formerly duke of Tuscany, and Francis II. Joseph's rule that coincided with the period, 1765–1790, is considered that of an enlightened despot in Austrian lands. Differing from his mother, Joseph took measures after her death in 1789 against the property of the Catholic Church, closed the monasteries, and attempted to institute secular education. He abolished serfdom but met opposition from both the landowners and the serfs. He attempted tax reform and started work on a reformed code of law. In view of the existing decentralization, carrying out of such measures in the sprawling territory under the Hapsburgs required centralization. Joseph did not consult his subjects as to whether they wished these reforms. Opposition was so great that, along with difficulties arising out of the French Revolution, he withdrew most of his reforms before his death.

When Leopold, who is considered a successful enlightened despot for his reforms in Tuscany (before his accession), came to the Austrian throne, and became emperor of the Holy Roman Empire in 1790, not only did a confused state of Austrian affairs exist, but Marie Antoinette, his sister, was exerting increased pressure for aid to the royal family in France against the French Revolution. Both Joseph and Leopold had been critical of their sister's role in France, and Leopold temporized while establishing his authority in the diverse Austrian principalities. He did, however, sign the Declaration of Pilnitz with Prussia assuring the French royalty of aid. He died at a critical point in negotiations with the French, and his brother Francis succeeded him in March 1792.

A little more than a month later, the French revolutionaries declared war on the king of Bohemia and of Hungary. Throughout the revolutionary wars, Austria had to defend distant territory—Belgium and north Italy—and curb revolution in Austria and in Hungary. The war in the Rhineland and western Germany was supported by those principalities but, as we shall see, Napoleon transferred the center of attack from Austrian territory in Germany to the Italian provinces and won a preliminary peace at Campo-Formio in 1797 and a more durable treaty at Lunéville in 1801. By the use of secret police, revolutionary movements were severely suppressed in Vienna, the Tyrol, and Hungary.

The preoccupation of Austria, Prussia, and Russia with the partitions of Poland may have given respite to the French revolutionaries in the west. In the second partition, in 1793, Austria was ignored by Prussia and Russia, but in 1795 Austrian forces aided in the defeat of the Polish Jacobins. Austria was then invited to participate in the final partition dismembering Poland as an independent political nation. Poland as such disappeared from the map of Europe for over a hundred years.

Prussia under Hohenzollern rule had risen rapidly in the eighteenth century and had progressed under the Enlightened Despotism of Frederick the Great (II). Frederick William II, nephew of Frederick II, ruled from 1786 until 1797. His successor, Frederick William III, outlived all other monarchs of the period, remaining on the throne until 1840. From the reforms of Frederick the Great until the Age of Stein, during the war of liberation from France under Napoleon, the internal regime of Prussia changed little. Centralization had been increased by Frederick II, but the Rhineland sections remained detached from Brandenburg, and it was only following the partitions of Poland that Prussian territory formed a land mass in the east.

Like other monarchs, the Prussian kings felt themselves threatened by events in France, but in the fighting the Prussian army with a large number of mercenaries could not boast of the exploits of Frederick II and was no match for the French Revolutionary army. Defeat, withdrawal and fighting in its Rhineland territory, led to a separate peace with France in 1795 and Prussia did not again take up arms until 1806.

Italy, as Metternich was to say early in the nineteenth century, was "a geographic expression," a congeries of kingdoms, republics, dukedoms, and the Papal States, with a large section of the north a part of Austria. For centuries Italy had been the theater of warfare between foreign powers or had been invaded by a foreign power seeking to control it. Venice had declined, but was still an important maritime power. Tuscany underwent reform under Archduke Leopold, who left it to become ruler of Austria, and the Kingdom of Naples was a decadent territory under incompetent Bourbon rulers. French intervention in 1792 brought cessation of attacks on French shipping but no reform. Only a few Italians had begun to feel the need of reform and been touched by a spirit of Italian patriotism. The Italian campaigns under the Directory, at first unsuccessful and then brilliantly successful under Napoleon, aided by Italian Jacobins, kindled sparks of nationalism. The Cisalpine, Ligurian, Roman, and Parthenopian republics were established, and reforms inspired by those of the French Revolution instituted.

The ideology and events of the French Revolution exerted a negative and temporary influence north, east, and south of the Danube. Scandinavian countries, which had experienced Enlightened Despotism, responded little to French ideas. They attempted to uphold the rights of neutrals in the warfare. The help given by Count Fersen, Sweden's ambassador to France, in planning the unsuccessful flight of the royal family in 1791 was a personal matter and not a policy of the Swedish government.

Catherine the Great (II) of Russia turned from her liberal reform ideas of the early years of her rule, even before the Revolution, but as the Revolution ensued, she became even more defensive than before of existing monarchical institutions and the power of the aristocracy. She no longer showed concern for the peasantry or the city worker, and the partitions of Poland and the Turkish wars showed the same Old Regime type of aggression that existed before France voiced the principle of self-determination of peoples.

Turkey, which in 1789 ruled the Balkans, Syria, and Egypt and exercised suzerainty eastward in Asia Minor and westward in northern Africa, was a Muslim sultanate, upheld by autocratic power, exercised through a tightly controlled civil service, the Turkish army, and the famous corps of the Janissaries. The Christian peoples of the Balkans and the Greeks suffered only when the sultans needed extra men and subsidies to fight their wars against Russia or against revolting Turkish principalities. The Greek, Rhigas was imbued with ideas from the French Revolution, but the impact of the Revolution came after 1799 rather than before. The Egyptian campaign of Napoleon likewise shook the Turkish empire, but influence from French ideas was delayed.

All of continental Europe, except Switzerland and some areas of Italy, had monarchies in 1789, supporting a state church or Catholicism and upheld by a powerful aristocracy. By 1799, boundaries had changed; France had helped to organize sister republics and had annexed territory extending her boundaries beyond the "natural frontiers"; and the great states had weakened under French pressure. Where there was a substantial bourgeoisie, it was often politically weak and dissatisfied. The peasants made up the bulk of the population of all states and, except in France, their lot had been little changed by the Revolution and the war. The Hanseatic cities, Italian ports, and the merchants of England, Holland, Portugal, Spain, and France were all affected by English and French sea warfare, but much less before 1799 than after 1806, when the Continental System was instituted. The urban worker may have suffered more than any other sector of the population in the face of food shortages and high prices, but there was no unemployment. If a person was not serving in the army or engaged in his usual craft or occupation, he would probably be engaged in war industries. An increase in population in most countries throughout the eighteenth century provided civilian workers as well as soldiers but increased the pressure on food supplies, always subject to good and bad harvests in addition to the stresses and demands of war.

SPECIAL BIBLIOGRAPHY

Insofar as this chapter is introductory to the present volume on Napoleon, a highly selective list of reference works on the decade of the French Revolution is given here. Many more items can be found in Jacques Godechot, *Les Révolutions* (Clio series, Presses universitaires, 1963), which in many ways was the volume preceding his *L'Europe et l'Amérique à l'époque napoléonienne,* in the same series (1967). In *Les Révolutions,* the bibliographical list and analysis are found on pages 11–75, chapters 1–4.

Only a few works in French are given in this selective list.

Aulard, Alphonse, *The French Revolution, a Political History of the French Revolution* (London, 1910).

Brinton, Clarence Crane, *A Decade of Revolution, 1789–1799* (Rise of Modern Europe series, vol. 12, New York: Harper and Row publishers, 1934).

Cambridge Modern History, vols. VII, VIII (London: Macmillan and Sons, 1904).

Gaxotte, Pierre, *The French Revolution* (London: Scribners, 1932).

Gershoy, Leo, *The French Revolution and Napoleon*, (2d edition, New York: Alfred A. Knopf, 1964). Bibliography brought up to date, over 1st edition of 1934.

Godechot, Jacques, *La Grande Nation*, 2 vols. (Paris, 1956).

———, *Les Institutions de la France sous la Révolution et l'Empire*, revised edition (Paris, 1969).

———, *Les Révolutions (1770–1799)*, (Paris: Presses universitaires, 1963), and *France and the Atlantic Revolution*, a translation by Herbert H. Rowen (New York: The Free Press, 1965).

Gottschalk, Louis, *The Era of the French Revolution and Napoleon* (Boston: Houghton Mifflin Company, 1929). Chronological table useful.

Kaplan, Jeffry, *New Perspectives on the French Revolution* (New York: John Wiley and Sons, 1965).

Lefebvre, Georges, *Quatre-Vingt-Neuf* (Paris, 1939); published in English as *The Coming of the French Revolution*, trans. by R. R. Palmer (Princeton, N. J.: Princeton University Press, 1947); in paperback (New York: Alfred A. Knopf, Vintage, 1947). Several editions of each.

———, *The French Revolution*, 2 vols.; vol. I translated by Elizabeth M. Evans, vol. II by John H. Stewart and James Friguglietti (New York: Columbia University Press, 1962, 1964).

Madelin, Louis, *The French Revolution* (New York: Oxford University Press, 1916).

Mathiez, Albert, *The French Revolution*, trans. by Catherine Alison Phillips (New York: Alfred A. Knopf, 1929).

New Cambridge Modern History, vol. VIII, *The American and French Revolutions* 1763–1793 (London: Cambridge University Press, 1965), vol. IX, *War and Peace in an Age of Upheaval, 1793–1830* (London: Cambridge University Press, 1965).

Palmer, Robert R., *The Age of the Democratic Revolution*, 2 vols. (Princeton, N. J.: Princeton University Press, 1959, 1964).

Rudé, George, *Revolutionary Europe, 1783–1815* (New York: World Publishing Co., Meridian Books, 1964).

Soboul, Albert, *Précis de la Révolution francaise* (Paris, 1962).

Thompson, J. M., *The French Revolution* (London: Oxford University Press, 1945).

2

THE CONSULATE

What was the new regime instituted in France by Napoleon Bonaparte, Abbé Siéyès, and Roger Ducos on the day after the *coup d'état* of 18 Brumaire, year VIII (November 9, 1799) going to be? The French had only a vague idea. They were certain that the Republic would continue. A few moderates wondered whether Bonaparte would agree to play the role of George Monck (the English general who had brought back the Stuarts after the Puritan Revolution) and lend himself to the restoration of Louis XVIII. But the vast majority of Frenchmen refused to believe that a man who had shot down the Royalists on the steps of the Church of Saint Roch four years earlier, on 13 Vendémiaire, Year IV (October 5, 1795), might reestablish a Bourbon on the throne. Moreover, had not his two colleagues—the other two provisional consuls, Abbé Siéyès and Roger Ducos—voted in the Convention for the death of Louis XVI? The Republic would certainly continue.

What Republic? A republic whose executive power would undoubtedly be stronger than in the past. Since the Constitution of 1791, which had greatly reduced executive power, constitutional law as well as governmental practice had constantly tended to strengthen this power. There would be, then, a strong executive, strong to the point of dictatorship. But was dictatorship anything really new? Since 1792 the French had lived under dictatorial regimes, that is, regimes in which the minority imposed its will on the majority. Undeniably the republicans had been only a small group on August 10, 1792. The Girondins, the Montagnards, and the Thermidorians, who had successively dominated the Convention, had been even less numerous. The Directory, elected by a minority that came to power only by the Two-Thirds Law, under a constitution voted by a feeble minority of electors, had been able to maintain itself only by two *coups d'état*. Would the government that emerged from the *coup d'état* of 18 Brumaire last longer than that which had been installed on 18 Fructidor? Its success would undoubtedly depend on how well it would fulfill two basic hopes held by the great majority of Frenchmen: the reestablishment of peace and the end of civil discord.

The *coup d'état* of 18 Brumaire had even less significance abroad. It was hardly to be distinguished from the fourteen *coups d'état* that since 1797 had punctuated the history of the French, Batavian, Helvetic, Cisalpine, Roman, and Neapolitan republics. Would Napoleon give France a more stable regime than that which General Joubert had given to Holland or General Brune to the Cisalpine Republic? How could this be foreseen? Brune and Joubert had been companions of Bonaparte in the Army of Italy. Would their leader succeed better than they?

What was really known about General Bonaparte? The great victories he had won in Italy in 1796 and 1797 were common knowledge—but the forced contributions and requisitions paid by "liberated" Italian states to support the French military victories were not. Already Napoleon practiced a policy of severe reprisals as an example to prevent future insurrection; he burned an entire village as a warning to the Milanese. This was not known, however, to the French, at that time. It was generally believed that the victories in Italy had forced the last continental adversaries of France— Austria and the Italian states—to lay down their arms.

Bonaparte's Egyptian campaign had struck the popular imagination, but only the minor victories had been publicized. The French newspapers had hardly mentioned his defeats. The impression created by his victories, therefore, obliterated any negative effect. In England, however, he was remembered chiefly for the defeats he had suffered at sea at Abukir and on land in Syria. These became known in France only later. Bonaparte's unexpected return to France on October 9, 1799, had appeared miraculous, and seemed to designate the rise to power of the prestigious hero of Italy and Egypt. In England the *coup d'état* realized by a French general who had just been defeated in the eastern Mediterranean did not merit much attention. On the whole, Napoleon Bonaparte was not particularly well known either in France or elsewhere. Even his triumphal journey from Frejus to Paris and the remaining three weeks before the *coup d'état* of

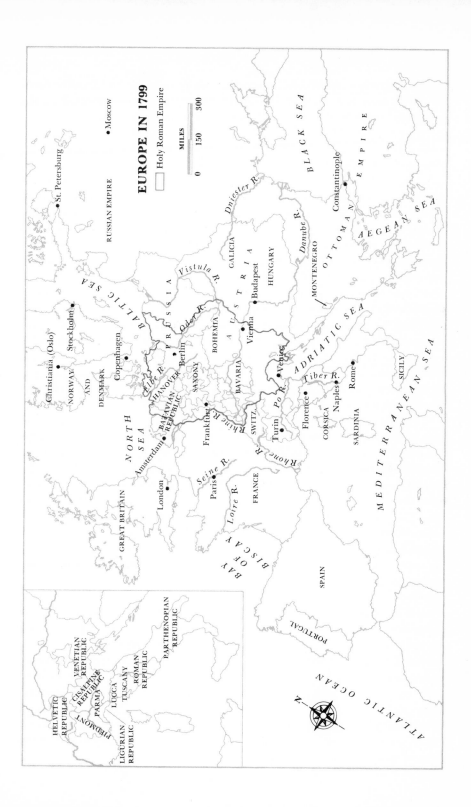

EUROPE IN 1799

☐ Holy Roman Empire

MILES

0   150   300

• Moscow

• St. Petersburg

RUSSIAN EMPIRE

BLACK SEA

OTTOMAN EMPIRE

Constantinople

AEGEAN SEA

Dniester R.

Danube R.

MONTENEGRO

GALICIA

AUSTRIA

HUNGARY

Budapest •

Vienna •

BOHEMIA

Vistula R.

P R U S S I A

Oder R.

BALTIC SEA

Christiania (Oslo) •

Stockholm •

NORWAY

AND

DENMARK

Copenhagen •

Elbe R.

Berlin •

HANOVER

SAXONY

BAVARIA

Venice •

Po R.

ADRIATIC SEA

Tiber R.

Rome •

Naples •

SICILY

SARDINIA

CORSICA

Florence •

Turin •

SWITZ.

Rhine R.

Frankfurt •

BATAVIAN REPUBLIC

Amsterdam •

NORTH SEA

London •

GREAT BRITAIN

Seine R.

Paris •

FRANCE

Loire R.

Rhone R.

BAY OF BISCAY

SPAIN

PORTUGAL

MEDITERRANEAN SEA

ATLANTIC OCEAN

N

HELVETIC REPUBLIC

PIEDMONT

LIGURIAN REPUBLIC

PARMA

CISALPINE REPUBLIC

VENETIAN REPUBLIC

LUCCA

TUSCANY

ROMAN REPUBLIC

PARTHENOPIAN REPUBLIC

18 Brumaire were hardly time enough for him to provide a great deal of favorable self-publicity, although he had already become aware of the value of propaganda.

NAPOLEON BONAPARTE

Napoleon Bonaparte at the time of the *coup d'état* of 18 Brumaire was just over thirty years of age. Today such youthful commanding generals or statesmen are a rarity. But in the Europe of 1799 this was not the case. Monarchs were often very young when they succeeded to the throne. Louis XVI was just twenty when he became king. The emperor Francis II was twenty-four when he was crowned at Frankfurt in 1792 and personally took over direction of the government. In France politicians who had headed the revolutionary movements since 1789 were not much older: Barnave was twenty-eight in 1789, Brissot was only thirty-eight in 1792 and was considered almost an old man, but Robespierre at that same time was only thirty-four, and Barbaroux and Saint-Just were twenty-five. As for thirty-year-old generals, France had known them under the *ancien régime* and had dubbed them "colonels in bibs." The Revolution had promoted many of them: Joubert had been named general at twenty-six, Desaix at twenty-five, Jourdan at thirty-one, such examples are numerous. But it was Bonaparte's career rather than his age that made him "the extraordinary man whom one would be tempted to describe as great"—these are the words used by a secret agent of the Bourbons in France. Moreover, it was his career during the Revolution that accounts for his greatness, for his childhood was similar to that of many other sons of the lesser nobility at the end of the *ancien régime*. His father, Charles Bonaparte, had been a lawyer at Ajaccio, Corsica. He claimed to belong to an illustrious Italian noble family established in Corsica since the sixteenth century, but the proofs that he presented are disputable. Charles died young, probably of cancer, at Montpellier, in 1785.

Napoleon, though he was only the second of eight children, immediately assumed the role of head of the family, eclipsing his less intelligent elder brother Joseph. Napoleon was then a "gentleman cadet" at the École militaire in Paris. He had been living in France since 1779, thanks to royal scholarships that had enabled him to study at the Collège d'Autun for three months and then at the military preparatory school of Brienne. He proved to be a fairly good student in the sciences and was sent to the École militaire in 1784.

The following year he graduated forty-second in a class of fifty-eight, as a second lieutenant of artillery. Named to the La Fère Regiment, Napoleon spent four years at Valence; then, after a leave of twenty-one months in Corsica, he rejoined his unit in its new garrison at Auxonne, near Dijon. What had young Napoleon done during these garrison years? After all, he was only sixteen when he went to Valence in 1785. He undoubtedly learned the profession of artilleryman, for the La Fère Regiment was a sort of regimental school. But he also spent a great deal of time reading Classical history and literature, French history and literature, and works of the Enlightenment, and thinking about his future. He was ambitious and dreamed of glory. Would he find this glory in France where he was now an ordinary second lieutenant, one among hundreds of others, or in Corsica, his motherland? Should he not be helping Pasquale di Paoli to restore the independence of Corsica? He put his ideas and dreams on paper. He wrote novels, *Clisson and Eugenia, The Masked Prophet, The Earl of Essex,* in which he set forth his desires for either glory or oblivion.

> What is to be done in this world? Since I must die, wouldn't it be better to kill myself? . . . My life is a burden to me—all torment and no pleasure. It is a burden because the men with whom I live and with whom I will probably always live, have mores as different from mine as the light of the moon differs from that of the sun. I cannot follow the only way of life which would permit me to endure living, from which follows a disgust with everything.

Such were Napoleon's reflections when the Revolution broke out in France. Then new and vast perspectives opened before him. In Corsica, at any rate, the sons of well-known families might occupy the numerous elective positions that had just been created by the new laws. Bonaparte rushed back to Corsica, and put himself at the head of the "national" movement that demanded the complete integration of the island with France. He had his elder brother Joseph Bonaparte elected to the directory of the district of Ajaccio in 1791, and he himself was elected lieutenant colonel of the National Guard. But all this strained the relations of the Bonaparte family with Paoli, who was still a partisan of Corsican independence. On the whole, Corsican politics involving France, Genoa, Piedmont, Sardinia, and Austrian territory in north Italy, could be of great importance at a time when all of Europe was in turmoil, when the Revolution and the counterrevolution were confronting each other at every turn. Nevertheless, young Lieutenant Bonaparte could see that his dreams of glory would not be realized in Corsica but on the Continent.

It was time to return to France. It was already getting late. On January 1, 1792, Lieutenant Bonaparte was listed as "absent without leave" from his unit; and on April 20, 1792, France declared war on the king of Bohemia and Hungary. Napoleon Bonaparte finally arrived in Paris on May 28. He witnessed the days of June 20 and August 10. The fall of Louis XVI did not particularly move him: he had nothing but contempt for such a weak ruler.

Still without orders, on October 10 he left again for Corsica where Paoli, recalled from exile by the Constituent Assembly, had been named commander of the twenty-third Military Division at Bastia and had stepped up his efforts to make the island independent. The war against the Kingdom of Sardinia aggravated the differences between Paoli and the Bonapartes. Bonaparte, who had reentered the French military service, participated in the occupation of the Sardinian island of San Stefano. Paoli, thinking of the help that Sardinia might provide for an independent Corsica, wanted to end hostilities. The conflict, a parallel to that between the Girondins and the Montagnards on the mainland, came to a head in April. On April 2, 1793, the Convention, acting on a report of the commissioners it had sent to Corsica, decided to arrest Paoli. Christopher Saliceti, deputy of the Convention and friend of the Bonapartes, was to carry out the order. Paoli replied at Corte on May 29 by having an assembly condemn the Bonaparte family "to perpetual execration and infamy." The Bonapartes were forced into exile, under threats from Paoli's partisans. Napoleon, his mother Letizia, and his brothers and sisters landed at Toulon on June 10.

Nine days earlier, twenty-nine of the principal Girondin deputies in the Convention were arrested in Paris. France was deeply divided. Though the "Mountain" (the Montagnards) had been victorious in Paris, more than sixty departments had supported the Girondins. In Corsica Napoleon Bonaparte had sided with France against the separatist tendencies of his province; on the mainland he could not help but come out for the Montagnards, for Paris and for the central government and against the "federalist" tendencies of the peripheral departments. He set forth his ideas in a pamphlet, *Le Souper de Beaucaire* (The Supper of Beaucaire), which he had printed at Avignon.

This profession of faith by Captain Bonaparte drew favorable attention from the national representatives combatting federalism in the departments of southern France. Napoleon was made artillery commander of the Army of the Midi, September 16, adjutant brigadier general October 7, and chef de battalion, October 28. In the capacity of artillery commander he participated in the siege of Toulon where the Royalists, relieving the Federalists, had called in the English and the Spaniards on August 23. Bonaparte accomplished his first military success at Toulon. With remarkable certainty of judgment, he pointed out the best battery positions to General Dugommier, the army commander. With an astonishing air of decision, Bonaparte directed the work of the siege artillery. Because of his strategy and organization, the Republican troops on December 17 were able to seize the forts commanding the harbor. The English and Spanish ships were forced to evacuate. Next day, the troops of the Convention were in control of the town. On December 22 Napoleon Bonaparte, at the age of twenty-four, was named brigadier general.

Portrait of Napoleon, unfinished, by Jacques Louis David. (The Louvre. Photo from Giraudon)

The logic of his actions, rather than ideological considerations, had brought him into the camp of the Montagnards among the partisans of a democratic republic. It was also the camp in which a courageous and talented officer could advance most rapidly. After the capture of Toulon, Bonaparte maintained his political views and linked himself with the Montagnard representatives to the Army of Italy, Saliceti and the younger Robespierre (Augustin). As a result of this association, he was dismissed from the army after the fall of Robespierre and placed under house arrest from August 9 to 20, 1794. Thereafter, the Thermidorians distrusted him. However, Napoleon was named general of infantry in the Army of the West, but the guerrilla war in the Vendée would have been a professional dead end. He refused the post and went to Paris, where he was deprived of his rank on September 15, 1795.

Bonaparte was in the capital, unemployed, when the Royalists marched against the Convention on 13 Vendémiaire, Year IV (October 5, 1795). Barras, who was in charge of the defense of the assembly, had known Bonaparte in Provence and had not forgotten his success in Toulon. Aware that he was in Paris, Barras asked him to repulse the Royalists. Bonaparte did not hesitate. He sent for cannon from the military camp at Grenelle, lined them up hub to hub, and mowed down the Royalists, who had been driven back toward the Church of Saint Roch. The Republic was saved! Napoleon was named General of division by the Convention and ten days later, on October 16, commander in chief of the Army of the Interior. He was twenty-six years old.

Was Napoleon Bonaparte going to remain a political general? The capture of Toulon and 13 Vendémiaire were victories against Frenchmen rather than against foreign troops. Until then Napoleon had always defended the most radical party of the Convention. Was he going to continue? In March 1796 the Directory, which had succeeded the Convention, felt itself threatened less by the Royalists than by the democrats. The Equals (Égaux), as they were called—the disciples of Babeuf and of Buonarroti—wanted to replace the bourgeois republic with a radical socialist regime. Barras, then the most influential man of the Directory, ordered Bonaparte to close the Pantheon Club where the Equals were meeting. The operation was carried out without difficulty on February 28, 1796. On March 2 Napoleon was named commander-in-chief of the Army of Italy. This was his chance to show what he could do at the head of a real army, against a large number of well-equipped enemy forces. Following a brief courtship, on March 9, the day before leaving Paris for Nice, Napoleon married Josephine Tascher de la Pagerie, a creole (colonial-born white woman) of Martinique, widow of General Beauharnais and mother of two children, Hortense and Eugène.

The Army of Italy was the weakest of the three French armies then operating against Austria and her allies. It numbered only about 40,000 men, while the armies on the Rhine had more than 100,000 each. In the plan of operations Carnot presented to the Directory, the Army of Italy was merely supposed to divert the enemy's attention by a feint; the armies on the Rhine were to strike the decisive blow in the fight against the Hapsburgs by marching on Vienna. For the first time Bonaparte was about to demonstrate to the world his strategic genius and his great political talents. His army of Italy would assume the primary role in the war with Austria, and would become the heart of Europe's problems.

When the three French armies opened the offensive in the spring of 1796, they were initially successful. However, two armies on the Rhine were soon checked and forced to retreat to their initial bases. The Army of Italy, on the contrary, consolidated its success and frustrated all Austrian counter-offensives designed to regain control of the Po valley. The various Italian city-states in their desire to be free of Austrian rule at first aided whole-heartedly in the battles against the Austrians, but as Napoleon demanded more and more supplies and subsidies, the richer cities either rose in rebellion or furnished what was demanded out of fear of reprisal. Napoleon issued proclamations announcing "Liberty, Equality, Fraternity" and the benefits of the French Revolution as the goal for Italians.

His great victories on the Italian peninsula, unexpected and almost miraculous, were won against superior forces. Bonaparte had transformed a bedraggled, ill-provisioned remnant-force that had been demoralized by successive defeat into a strong, patriotic fighting army. His victories allowed him to make his first affirmation of authority vis-à-vis the French government. Until then, he had not realized his own value. Not until the evening of the battle of Lodi, he said, did he become conscious of "the ambition to execute the great things which, until then, had occupied his mind like some fantastic dream." Disobeying the commissioner of the Directory, Salicetti, even though he was his old friend from Corsican days, Napoleon signed an armistice with the Kingdom of Sardinia. Instead of revolutionizing this state, the pact allowed the monarch to remain on the throne.

Now, aware of his value to the French government and his goals and considering himself indispensable, Bonaparte decided to offer his resignation rather than march on Rome as the Directory had ordered. Since he was filling the coffers of the French treasury, always in a desperate condition, the Directory no longer dared tell him what to do. Although many of Napoleon's requisitions of this early period were for supplies to feed and clothe the French army, after the battle of Lodi opening the way to Milan he demanded from the Milanese 20 million French francs, horses and clothing and a part of an armistice with Modena required that principality to furnish twenty paintings. When insurrection occurred, punishment was swift. Napoleon threatened rebels at Milan and himself saw to the shooting of "assassins" at Tortona. He announced to the Directory that he was shipping 2 million francs in gold to Paris. By an armistice signed with the Pope at Bologna, June 22, the Papal States were to pay 21 million French francs. At the same time, he ordered the confiscation of English, Russian, and Austrian stores at Leghorn. Napoleon aimed to close Italian ports to English trade.

In 1797 his demands on the Italians increased. Venice was not only to pay money, but send ships, twenty paintings, and five hundred manuscripts to France. While promising freedom to Venice, he wrote to the Directory that his terms would render Venice powerless. Verona was required to turn over all silver treasures in public buildings and churches.

In this same period Bonaparte set up sister republics in conquered Italian territory. Free to move as he desired, he asserted himself by creating republics whose control he gave to the moderates, eliminating from power both conservatives and democrats. The latter he regarded as anarchists, for there was a strong element of Babeuvism among them. In 1797 once again he saved the republican regime in France by sending troops to Paris, thus enabling the Directory to execute the *coup d'état* of 18 Fructidor, Year V (September 4, 1797). This permitted him to impose his own peace terms at Campo-Formio on October 18, 1797. Thus it was Napoleon who formulated French foreign policy — not the Directory. The treaty settled Italian affairs according to Bonaparte's wishes but left those of Germany hanging in the balance, even though they were of greater interest to the French government.

Germany was to be discussed at the Congress of Rastatt in December. The Directory appointed Bonaparte as its representative. But after spending several days in the little Baden town, Napoleon realized that the Congress was a hornets' nest and that he was unlikely to secure anything to his advantage there. He asked to be put in command of the struggle against England, the last enemy of France. After being named commander in chief of the army of England, he quickly realized that he could not successfully invade the British Isles as long as the French fleet lacked control of the seas. He advised that England be attacked at the source of its power and wealth: in the Near East, in Egypt, and beyond that in India. The Directory was only too happy to consent, for this twenty-nine-year-old general who constantly gave advice that sounded like orders was becoming annoying. Such a venture would place the authoritative general far from the seat of national decision. Consequently, the Egyptian expedition was authorized.

This expedition, which had begun so successfully with the capture of Malta — the most important fortress in the Mediterranean — and the occupation of Egypt, was soon marked by reversals: the destruction of the French fleet at Abukir (August 1, 1798) and the retreat from Syria. Bonaparte became the prisoner of his conquest, but he was free to organize it. Acting as head of the government, he established new institutions in Egypt. There he learned from the English what had been going on in Europe. The Second Coalition had been formed; French troops had evacuated Italy; the republicans had been defeated in Germany. Bonaparte felt that the moment had come for him to play the role to which he aspired. Without waiting for an order of recall, he turned over his army command to General Kléber and "miraculously" slipped by the English cruisers. He disembarked at Frejus on the south of France on October 9, 1799. He was in Paris by October 14, and less than a month later, on November 10, became the head of the government, following the *coup d'état* of 18 Brumaire.

Most Frenchmen were undoubtedly reassured by what they knew of Bonaparte's career and ideas. Always victorious as far as the ordinary Frenchman then knew, he had been able to impose peace on Austria in 1797. Was he not, therefore, the logical choice to reap the ultimate consequences of the victories that had just been won by General Brune in Holland and General Massena in Switzerland and to restore peace once more? His role at Toulon in 1793, his actions on 13 Vendémiaire and 18 Fructidor could not miss being appreciated by revolutionaries. His intervention at the time of the closing of the Pantheon Club, his attitude with regard to the anarchists in Italy, even the appearance that he had just given to the operation of 18–19 Brumaire (an action against the Jacobins of the Council of Five Hundred) were reassuring to the moderates and even gave some hope to Royalists. Bonaparte seemed just the man to reestablish domestic and foreign peace and, "to end the Revolution," a goal of the majority of Frenchmen.

That was how the French judged Napoleon Bonaparte on the morrow of 18 Brumaire. But what do we think of him today, basing our judgment on his entire career, his acts, and his writings and on the testimonies of his contemporaries? Undeniably, he was exceptionally intelligent and he was capable of making split-second decisions. He had an almost unlimited capacity for work. He was possessed by insatiable ambition. As soon as he had attained his goals, he pressed on to exceed them.

Napoleon never forgot that he owed his fortune to the Revolution. However, more than a man of the Revolution, more than a man of the nineteenth century, he was a disciple of the *philosophes* of the eighteenth century, a disciple of Montesquieu and particularly Voltaire rather than of Rousseau. Napoleon was to become an enlightened despot—no doubt the most enlightened of the line, and the last.

Napoleon did not believe in the sovereignty of the people, or in the popular will, despite his plebiscites. He scorned parliamentary assemblies, whose unending debates he described as mere "prattle." He had great confidence in Cartesian logic and in mathematical reasoning rather than in "reason." He commanded in preference to using reason to persuade. He chose men with talent as mathematicians, jurists, and political technicians, even if they were cynical and venal. He thought that "enlightened" but firm determination could accomplish anything, especially when supported by bayonets. He despised and feared the crowd, which he had seen in action on June 20 and on August 10, 1792. As for public opinion, he had no doubts that he could mold and direct it as he saw fit. While in Italy and in Egypt he learned from experience the power of the press, and later was able to manipulate the press as a marvelous propaganda tool. He suppressed papers that printed hostile news and inserted favorable reports in others. Bonaparte has been called one of the most "civilian" of generals. But beneath his various costumes and titles he remained a soldier, and he left a strong military imprint on the authoritarian regime that he established following the *coup d'état* of Brumaire.

THE NEW CONSTITUTION

The Constitution of the Year VIII (1799) differed in structure and in design from the other three constitutions that France had drafted since 1789 (1791, 1793, and 1795), none of which remained in force for more than two years. The Constitution of 1795, setting up the Directory, could no longer serve after 18 Brumaire. Since Government after that *coup* was provisional, Napoleon was in a hurry to provide a new instrument. A first draft, influenced chiefly by Abbé Siéyès, providing for a weak three-man executive was turned down not only by Napoleon, who wished to assure his own predominance, but also by the surviving legislative bodies.

The new constitution was drafted by two commissions of twenty-five members, one from the Council of Ancients and the other from the Council of Five Hundred, and produced the text in less than a month. In reality, Bonaparte, Siéyès, and Pierre Daunou exerted the decisive influences as to the content of the articles. The new document did not represent a clean break with its predecessors, however. Its writers had been inspired not only by the earlier French constitutions, but also by those that had been written during the previous four years in the sister republics in Italy and Switzerland, whose merits and defects could be evaluated at the time.

The governing principle of the Constitution of the Year VIII had been expressed by Siéyès: "authority," he said, "comes from above and confidence from below." Constitutional speculators had wished to see a Caesarean regime. It was based on a pyramidal organization, having at its base the entire citizenry provided with illusory powers and at its summit, a chief dictating orders to subordinates. The Directory was replaced by the Consulate as the executive branch of the government.

Unlike its predecessors, the Constitution of 1799 made no provision for a Declaration of Rights. Some guarantees, though, were scattered through the text. Article 46 provided for a watered down *habeas corpus,* with a delay of ten days, not the twenty-four hours of earlier constitutions, and this was a guarantee only in case of conspiracy. Inviolability of domicile and assurance against nocturnal searches were stated in Article 76, while Article 77 provided for a warrant for arrest. Article 83 allowed the individual right of petition. Guarantees of persons and property were implied in

Articles 93 and 94, which promised the irrevocability of the laws against *émigrés* and confirmed the sales of nationalized property. Not a word was mentioned about Liberty, Equality, Fraternity.

The text of the new constitution actually began with a definition of French citizenship. All males born in France upon reaching the age of twenty-one were citizens. Foreigners could acquire citizenship by ten years' residence—a generous policy initiated during the Revolution. Despite Article 93, laws against *émigrés* were to be modified, and under the articles on citizenship, *émigrés* could regain French citizenship by returning to France.

The chief of state, called the First Consul, was given immense powers, both legislative and executive. He was to be assisted by two other consuls. Of course, Bonaparte was invested with this office. Instead of Abbé Siéyès and Roger Ducos, who had formed a provisional consulate with Napoleon, Jean Cambacérès, former member of the National Convention, deputy from Montpellier, distinguished jurist, and Charles Lebrun, former secretary to Maupéou, Chancellor of Louis XV, were made second and third consuls. They had only consultative powers, and were mere figureheads. It was the First Consul who initiated legislation, named magistrates and the members of the Council of State, and, in accord with the special provision for the Year VIII, chose the members of the three legislative assemblies: the conservative Senate, the Legislative Body *(corps législatif)*, and the Tribunate.

In order to compensate for the enormous power that had been entrusted to a single man, the delegates to the constitutional assembly reestablished universal male suffrage, but in actuality, universal suffrage was rendered largely illusory by the complicated composition of national lists of eligible voters *(notables)* by an eliminatory scheme in three stages—parish, department, national. In view of the appointments made the first year to the legislative bodies by Napoleon, advised by his Senate, this system was never put into effect, and in 1802 it was replaced by electoral colleges. Again, the composition of the colleges was by an eliminatory process, from canton, to district or arrondissement, to department. To those elected by department, ten to twenty life members were named by the First Consul. All members of the electoral colleges held office for life. These notables selected candidates for the Legislative body, the Tribunate, and for General Councils of the departments. The Senate chose from the list submitted by the electoral colleges for the legislative bodies. The Senate itself was recruited by cooptation from names submitted by the First Consul, the Tribunate and the Legislative Body.

Although the principle of universal suffrage and of representation of the citizens seemed to be maintained, it was merely window dressing. Universal suffrage, in fact, was exercised only rarely since the members of the electoral colleges were chosen for life. Even then, it was not really free suffrage since the members of the departmental electoral college had to be chosen from among the "600 plus imposés," the 600 paying the highest taxes. Clearly, the representative character of the assemblies was more an illusion than a fact.

The legislative process was divided between the initiative of the First Consul and the Council of State, on the one hand, and the three assemblies on the other. Only the Senate had some degree of independence of executive pressure, since its members were named for life. It was charged with preserving the constitution by indicating when a proposal of a law was unconstitutional. In addition, the Senate could, with the agreement of the consuls, modify the constitution by means of special decrees called *senatus-consulta*. Since the constitution contained no specific method of amendment, these powers were similar to the judicial review that was beginning to be exercised by the United States Supreme Court. In France, however, the review was prior to the passage of a law.

The function of the Tribunate was to debate bills introduced by the government. Because of some opposition to Napoleon, this body was purged in 1807. As for the Legislative Body, it was supposed to enact or reject bills submitted by the Tribunate, but without debate or modification. It rejected only a few, and until 1814, it proved submissive to executive pressure.

The First Consul chose the members of the Council of State. This was a new creation somewhat comparable to the Conseil du Roi, which had disappeared in 1790. It was composed of about fifty councillors, some in "ordinary service" and others in "special service." Later on auditors and masters of requests were added. The functions of a *maître de requêtes* derived from the Old Regime: such an officer presented petitions, was sent out to an area to supervise law enforcement and might be assigned additional duties. Bonaparte handpicked the members of the Council of State from among the talented men about whose merits he had learned through his experience in the army or in personal relations. In the mind of the First Consul, the Council was to serve a dual purpose. It would draft bills to be sent to the Tribunate; its great activity in this area is demonstrated by its examination of 3300 bills in 1804. Thus, it was through the Council that Bonaparte exercised legislative initiative. Secondly, the Council would serve as a court in judging administrative disputes, thereby creating a jurisprudence that would have a regulatory value of the first order. As the French civil service grew, the Council of State has served as a key organ in the administrative structure. At the beginning of the Consulate, Bonaparte attended meetings of the Council of State. Individual council members were often given important missions and functions. Since its sessions were secret and it operated quietly, the Council was often misunderstood. In actual fact, its composition assured impartial consideration and legal integrity in its operations. The Council was an important instrument of Napoleonic rule, and it has continued to be important ever since.

The ministers were given subordinate roles. Napoleon never called them to meet as a cabinet. He dealt with each separately and only in regard to his particular ministerial jurisdiction. Since the ministers were appointed and dismissed by him, each was responsible to the First Consul and not in any way to the assemblies. Bonaparte made a distinction between the executive power, confined to the First Consul, and the "government," carried on by the ministers and the Council of State. The number of ministers was not specified in the constitution, but in practice there were generally ten.

As soon as Napoleon had accepted the new text, it was put into effect, despite provision for a referendum. Registers for recording approval of or opposition to the new constitution were opened at departmental centers for two months, the results of which were announced in January, 1800. The majority of Frenchmen were in favor of it. However, in order to weigh the significance of the vote of 3,011,007 for and 1562 against, one must remember that citizens had to enter their opinion publically on a register in the presence of the municipal authorities. One should also not overlook the fact that 4 million Frenchmen abstained. Nevertheless, many revolutionaries as well as a large number of conservatives voted "yes," in the hope that the new constitution would bring the Revolution to an end and restore peace in France. Their vote was more a show of confidence in Bonaparte than in the text itself.

THE NEW INSTITUTIONS

The constitution was obscure, leaving a great deal of room for interpretation. It was also short, because Bonaparte wanted it promulgated quickly, and differed from the detailed Constitution of the year III. This text of 1799 did not even precisely set up the administrative organization of France. This was regulated by organic laws published mainly from 1800 to 1804, some of which were subsequently modified. These laws were more important than the constitution itself, which, having been extensively amended in 1802 and 1804, was to disappear ten years later, in 1814. However, the administrative institutions introduced at the beginning of the Consulate, under the new constitution, were "granite blocks"—to use Napoleon's expression—upon which contemporary France was to be built. In fact, the revolutionary assemblies had already prepared the administrative work of Napoleon and his advisers. For the most part, the new administrators updated the existing institutions introduced during the Revolution, in the light of experience, improving or discarding what appeared to be unsound and retaining what worked out satisfactorily. Under the Consulate French institutions took on the appearance they were to keep for one hundred and fifty years. Consequently, the credit for the stability of the French government machinery has been attributed, often excessively, to Napoleon.

Local administration was centered in the departments that had been created in 1790. Within present-day France, their number has remained nearly the same. The only important addition was the department of Tarn and Garonne, formed in 1807 and designed to make the city of Montauban a seat of government. But with his successive conquests and annexations, Napoleon created new departments outside of France proper. These numbered 130 under the *Grand Empire* of 1810. The districts, which had disappeared in 1795, were restored under the title of *arrondissements.* These were larger than their predecessors and hence fewer in number. The cantons were likewise enlarged and reduced in number.

The great innovation at the local level was the appointment of prefects and subprefects to head the departments and the districts. Named by the government, they were removable at its pleasure (law of 28 Pluviose, Year VIII, February 17, 1800). The prefectural system was the culmination of a slow but logical evolution. The Constitution of Year III reversed the decentralization of the early Revolution and the special deputies *en mission* of the Terror in placing government-appointed central commissioners with all the departmental administrations. Commissioners, chosen from citizens who had resided in the department for one year, could do little more than request the departmental administrations to execute the law. The Helvetic and Roman constitutions had given the name of prefects to these commissioners and had given them greater authority than in France. The prefect of the Year VIII emerged from these experiments, but his powers were infinitely greater than those of the central commissioner, for, as the law stated, "the prefect alone will be entrusted with the administration." As the departmental representative of the chief of state, he was not only charged with administration, with respect to taxes, law, justice, public works, appointment of town officers of towns of less than 5000 population (the first Consul for those over 5000), and police, but he was also expected to advance the ideas of the central government and to control what was then referred to as "the public spirit." Within a territory that was smaller and hence more easily watched over and administered, the prefect was the heir of the *intendant* of the Old Regime. He was responsible for ensuring rapid law enforcement in even the most remote corners of the department. The newspaper *Le Publiciste* wrote on February 19, 1800, about the effectiveness of the prefectural system:

> From the First Consul to the village mayor in the Pyrenees, everything
> is holding firmly—all the links in the great chain are well connected
> together. Power will move rapidly because it reaches all points of the
> network. Power will be enforced everywhere, opposed nowhere. It will
> always find implementation rather than obstacles against it.

The prefectural system meant an even greater increase in the centralization
that, since the Year II, had once again characterized French administrative
organization. Napoleon said later, at St. Helena, that this extreme centralization had been essential in order to "overcome the immense difficulties"
that then confronted the government.

The prefect did not work alone. He was assisted by an innocuous General Council, made up of wealthy and reliable people originally appointed
by Napoleon but to be elected by the Constitution of the Year X, elected
for fifteen-year terms, and by a Prefectural Council, which was an administrative tribunal at the department level. The subprefects, who headed the
arrondissements and were agents of the prefect, also had a council to aid
them—the District Council *(conseil d'arrondissement)*, which was even less
encumbering. Mayors were named by the prefect in communes with fewer
than 5000 inhabitants and by the chief of state in the others. The municipal
councils of communes with a population over 5000 had been appointed by
the prefect for three-year terms in 1800; but in 1802 the law specified that
councillors would be nominated by cantonal assemblies and the government, selected for twenty years, and that half of the positions would be ro-
tated in ten years. The ones to cease office would be indicated by lots. In
1812, the first renewal took place, and a drawing of lots decided which councillors were to retire. In communes whose population exceeded 5000, the
councillors were chosen for the same length of time from among candidates
proposed by the cantonal assemblies with two nominees for each seat.

The judiciary was extensively reorganized by the government. The new
constitution had devoted only eight articles to it, chiefly to the High Court
of Appeals. The court system established by the Constituent Assembly was
maintained, but one fundamental principle of the judicial organization of
1790, the election of judges, was abandoned, and another principle, that of
trial by jury, was broken down. Henceforth, only justices of the peace were
elected. The other judges belonged to the body of magistrates *(corps de la
magistrature)*—one of those intermediary bodies so important to Montesquieu that Bonaparte wanted to multiply. These judges were named by the
executive, but their independence was guaranteed for they could not be
removed—a principle that was often violated between 1800 and 1815.

The hierarchy of courts was reestablished. At its base was one lower
court or court of first instance *(tribunal de première instance)* for each
arrondissement. Next in the hierarchy were twenty-eight appellate courts

(tribunaux d'appel) which became *cours d'appel* in 1804. To a certain extent, these courts of appeal recalled the former *parlements,* but their jurisdiction was generally more limited and their functions remained purely judicial. To handle criminal matters, each department had courts of correction *(tribunaux correctionnels)* and a criminal court *(tribunal criminel),* which was called the assize court *(cour d'assises)* after 1811. The criminal courts continued the two-jury system (grand jury and trial jury) instituted by the Constituent Assembly, but the assize court used only a trial jury. A special judge was assigned to handle the inquiry. A Supreme Court or High Court of Appeal *(tribunal de cassation),* named *cour de cassation* in 1804, capped the hierarchy.

Justice, however, hardly ever functioned normally between 1800 and 1815. The police, which became highly developed in this period, were all-powerful and omnipresent. Arbitrary arrests were numerous, and special courts *(tribunaux d'exception)* multiplied, rendering judgments without jury or right of appeal. "Administrative" imprisonments were unpleasant reminders of the *lettres de cachet* and the Bastille of the *ancien régime.*

The Directory had already greatly improved the financial organization created by the Constituent Assembly by entrusting the tax assessment of the departments to a direct tax agency *(agence des contributions directes)* made up of public officials. Bonaparte continued along these lines but increased the number of finance officers *(fonctionnaires des finances).* The most useful reform was the creation of *percepteurs permanents,* or state-appointed tax collectors. Formerly, the municipalities had controlled the collection of direct taxes and had awarded the job to the highest bidder. This system sometimes produced incompetent and dishonest tax collectors. Beginning in 1803, however, tax collectors received a flat fee of 4 percent of the taxes that they were able to raise. They were also required to post bond. These tax collectors were headed by one special collector *(receveur particulier)* for each *arrondissement,* and one general collector *(receveur général)* for each department. The treasury administration was also reorganized: a director general of the treasury *(directeur général du Tresor)* stood at the head; general inspectors in the rank below. In addition, there was one paymaster general *(trésorier payeur général)* for each department. In 1807 an audit office *(cour des comptes)* replaced the commission of *comptabilité nationale,* created in 1795, which had not proved satisfactory. The new audit office, which checked the records of all department accountants, rapidly became one of the great organs of the nation.

There was no change in the system of direct taxes that the Revolution had set up. But there was a considerable increase in indirect taxes, which had been light and few in number before 1800. The extremely unpopular tax on the use of highways was abolished, but tolls at city entrances multiplied, and taxes were gradually levied on salt, alcoholic beverages, tobacco, playing cards, and public vehicles. Beginning in 1802, these taxes were consolidated under the general title of excise taxes *(droits réunis)*. These were detested by all throughout the Empire period.

In order to compete with the British economy, Bonaparte effected some sorely needed changes in the French currency and credit systems. The law of 7 Germinal, Year XI (March 28, 1803), fixed the monetary status of France for 123 years and established the *franc de germinal* (which weighed 4.5 grams of fine silver and in which the ratio of gold to silver was 11:15.5). New coins were struck according to the decimal system, in denominations of one half, one, two, and five francs in silver; and ten, twenty, and forty francs in gold. The new French currency, sound and practical, rapidly proved to be the best in all of continental Europe.

Bonaparte wanted to strike at the Bank of England, which had been financing the hostile alliances. Aided by the bankers who had backed the *coup* of 18 Brumaire, he created the Bank of France. Its statutes were approved as early as January 6, 1800. The bank rendered great services to the state by supplying it with money in the form of bank notes *(billets)* and by discounting bills for the principal Parisian merchants. But the Bank of France remained a purely Parisian bank whose influence did not extend throughout the whole of France until the second half of the nineteenth century.

Napoleon's educational measures were based upon the system that had been partially established by the Revolution. He had little interest in primary schools. Lacking funds, they were insufficient in number and had to depend on private and municipal backing. Thus, little progress was made in primary education in the rural areas. Only this first degree of schooling required no fee from the parents. Secondary schools, on the other hand, interested Bonaparte, for they could supply the many functionaries and officers needed to run the government and the armies. The *écoles centrales,* created by the Convention and judged to be too progressive in their programs and methods, were replaced by *lycées* and *collèges.* These schools combined the curriculum of the *ancien régime,* plus a little mathematics, with the military training that was characteristic of the period. The bourgeoisie balked at these institutions, too military and too laic for its taste. In 1806 Napoleon granted the teaching monopoly to the state. Teaching came to be an important part of public service. Although private secondary schools did not disappear, they had to pay heavy taxes and submit to strict control. Napoleon was not concerned with schools for girls. He considered education in the home was the best for them.

In the field of higher education, the university faculties were reinstated, but they were not very active: the *grandes écoles* (École polytechnique, Conservatory of Arts and Crafts, and others) created by the Convention continued to attract the best students who graduated from the *lycées* and *collèges*. In 1808 secondary and higher institutions were combined to form the Imperial University.

Developments were made in the structure of the social welfare program, which remained a public service. Charity boards *(bureaux de bienfaisance)* took charge of relief in the home. Hospitals and asylums *(hospices)*, administered by commissions named by the minister of the interior, took in the destitute sick, the invalid, the old, and abandoned children. Vagrancy and begging were prohibited and severely punished. Beggars were placed in temporary prisons *(dépôts de mendicité)* or employed on public works projects by charity workshops *(ateliers de charité)*.

THE CODES

Bonaparte was anxious that the French people be provided as quickly as possible with a statute recording the "conquests of the Revolution"—especially those of 1789. He thereby proved that he intended to consolidate the work of the assemblies of the Revolution. Since 1790 these bodies had been trying to draw up a law code that would insure uniform civil law in all French provinces (something that the monarchy had never been able to accomplish) and that, at the same time, would transcribe into precise articles those revolutionary innovations that they wanted to preserve. In order to speed up work on this code, Bonaparte entrusted it to a commission of four jurists, Felix Bigot de Préameneu and Francois Tronchet, well-versed in the common law tradition, and Jean Portalis and Jacques de Maleville, specialists in statutory law. The commission completed the project in four months and sent it to the Supreme Court and to the appellate courts for examination. Then, in the course of 102 meetings, the text was debated by the legislative committee *(commission de législation)* of the Council of State. Napoleon personally presided at fifty-seven of these meetings, and he often imposed his own solutions, dictated by logic and common sense instead of judicial precedent. The proposed code was next sent to the Tribunate, but the majority of the members of this body felt that it was too conservative and that it had sacrificed too many revolutionary "conquests." Its report to the Legislative Body reflected this opinion. The project was, therefore, rejected by the Legislative Body—one of the few bills that it did not approve. This opposition infuriated Bonaparte, leading him to reorganize the Tribunate and finally to abolish it. The code was again submitted for study. The civil code that was approved by the purged Tribunate and promulgated on March 21, 1804, was even more conservative than its predecessor. It was given the name under which it has remained famous—the Napoleonic Code.

Despite the many transformations it had undergone, the Code Civil, expressed the great social upheavals of the Revolution and consolidated its great conquests: individual liberty, the right to work, freedom of conscience, and the secular character of the state. As for equality, it proclaimed all men equal before the law, but it protected acquired wealth.

The Code dealt at length with the family, the institution upon which French society was based. The authority of the father was restored. Napoleon's views were particularly influential in lowering the status of women under the Code. The wife was put under the authority of the husband—a situation not modified until after World War II. No clause provided for the possibility of a woman working, receiving salary, or engaging in commerce. Divorce was introduced at the express wish of Napoleon, but the rules were more favorable to the husband and were less liberal than the law of September 20, 1792, in that incompatibility was not a legal cause for divorce. Only divorce by mutual consent and for the reasons of adultery, violence, bodily injury or conviction for crime were allowed. Hindrances were put in the way of divorce in order to maintain the family and avoid scandal. Bodily separation was reestablished to satisfy Catholic scruples. Neither plaints nor fines were equal for the husband and the wife. Woman was rendered inferior. A distinction between legitimate and illegitimate children was reintroduced. Children were under the authority of the father.

Most of the Code is concerned with property—particularly landed property. In order to prevent feudal revivals of this kind, the code sanctified the abolition of the feudal system and the freedom of land ownership. It gave concrete form to Article 17 of the Declaration of the Rights of Man of 1789, which had declared that "property is inviolable and sacred." In so doing, the Code sanctioned the irrevocable character of the sale of nationalized property. Due process was written into the Code, limited by the right of eminent domain. On the other hand, the law of inheritance was a compromise between the testator's wishes, which Roman law had long taken into account, and the interests of the family and of society, which revolutionary legislation had striven to safeguard.

Contracts, safeguards against bankruptcy, the sale and exchange of property, and mortgages were considered at length, but little attention was paid to labor. Life contracts for labor were forbidden—in other words, serfdom was abolished, thereby confirming the freedom of labor. However, greater freedom was given to employers in their dealings with labor, under the pretext of allowing economic laws to operate. The Code even violated the principle of equal treatment before the law by specifying that only the employer's word was to be credited in wage disputes. It should be remembered that the Loi Le Chapelier forbidding economic associations remained on the statute books until 1884, but its operation during the Napoleonic regime was enforced against labor rather than against businessmen.

The proclamation of equality before the law was ignored in the lower position assigned to women. It also did not prevent Bonaparte from reestablishing slavery in the colonies. Despite its imperfections, the Napoleonic Civil Code was generally viewed as superior to the body of laws previously in force. It harmonized reason, tradition, and revolutionary experience and provided a clear, readable uniform code of civil law, comprehensible to the ordinary citizen. Actually, it introduced a stable basis of law during the subsequent changes of constitutions and forms of government. On the whole, it seemed to perpetuate the essential conquests of the Revolution. It was adopted *in toto* or formed the basis of reformed national codes in a large part of Europe and the Americas and even influenced certain American states, notably Louisiana.

The Civil Code was only one of the codes promulgated by Napoleon. The Code of Civil Procedure was completed in 1806, the Code of Commercial Law in 1807, the Code of Criminal Procedure in 1808, and the Penal Code in 1810. The later codes were less liberal than the Civil Code. The jury was eliminated from civil procedures and from the preliminary hearing in criminal cases. However, in the latter, the trial was public and required a jury and counsel for the defense. The Penal Code was a step backward from the humanitarian influence of the eighteenth century in the severity of punishments and in the retention of branding, deportation, and confiscation of property. The Commercial Code reflected the strength of the agricultural economy as did a Rural Code. It omitted many modern items, such as prices, copyrights, weights and measures (uniform since 1793 but revised during the Napoleonic regime), shipwrecks, ports. The Commercial Code underwent more modification during the nineteenth century than all the other codes combined.

Wherever the armies of Napoleon went, the codes were introduced, either voluntarily or under Napoleonic pressure. Just as the Declaration of Rights of Man of 1789 had exerted an influence within France and upon reformers in many European states, the codes introduced liberal principles into ordinary practices. This should be considered under the French Empire rather than the Consulate.

The Civil Code served as an excellent propaganda tool, and Bonaparte was very conscious of the value of good propaganda. He subjugated the press, the theater, letters and the arts in order to use them for his purposes. Two months after the *coup d'état* of Brumaire, at the beginning of the operation of the Consulate, the majority of newspapers in the department of the Seine were suppressed. Only thirteen of them were allowed to publish, and this number was reduced to four in 1811. In 1800 the *Moniteur* became the official paper, later complemented by the *Bulletin de la Grande Armée.* The entire press was rigorously censored. Writers who refused to sing the praises of the regime were ousted or at least publicly disgraced. The theater as well was forbidden to voice criticism, while the fine arts were used for Napoleonic propaganda.

Napoleonic authoritarianism came into being very gradually. Under the Constitution of 1799 the consuls were to be elected for ten years, but measures taken from May to August 1802 transformed the office of First Consul into life tenure. Since Napoleon dominated his two colleagues from the beginning and *senatus consulta,* after the Constitution began to operate, increased his power, Bonaparte's powers were evolving into a dictatorship without however destroying the fiction of the constitution. Under the Consulate Napoleon held the confidence of the French, for he appeared to have consolidated many changes of the Revolution and to have restored general peace.

3

GENERAL
PACIFICATION

The main hope of the 3 million Frenchmen who had approved the plebiscite of the year VIII was that Bonaparte and the new constitution would restore peace—peace at home, ending political and religious conflicts and bringing a solid and lasting peace abroad. In less than two years it appeared that these objectives had been reached.

POLITICAL CONCILIATION
WITHIN FRANCE

Bonaparte came to power at a moment when internal political clashes seemed more intense than ever. The *coup d'état* of 30 Prairial, Year VII (June 18, 1799) had brought the Jacobins back into power. They were only able to maintain this power for two months, however. On August 13, the recently reopened Jacobin Club of Paris was shut down once again. During this time the Jacobins had enacted several "public safety" measures: the law of hostages, a special forced loan on the wealthy on a graduated scale, and a decree that called up all conscripts without exception. There was no guarantee that the Jacobins would not return to power later.

46

The *coup d'état* of 18 Brumaire had used as a pretext, a so-called Jacobin plot.

On the other hand, the Royalists made an exceptional effort to overthrow the republic during the summer of 1799. In early August they revolted in the southwest and nearly seized Toulouse. In September insurrection resumed in Vendée, in Brittany, in Perche, in Maine, and in Normandy. For several hours on October 21 the Royalists were in control of Nantes and on October 26—two weeks before the *coup d'état*—of Saint-Brieuc. The Royalist threat was immediate, and the first to which Bonaparte turned his attention, but he also took steps to eliminate the Jacobins as quickly as possible.

The mere report about the *coups d'état* had dampened the fervor of the counterrevolutionaries. Abbé Bernier, who had been one of the moving forces of the uprisings in the west, but who no longer believed that the Royalists could win, wondered if it might not be better to rally to Bonaparte. He wrote at the end of November: "I believe that Bonaparte and Monck are much alike." Monck, an English general, had supported the Cromwells, but became leader of the restoration of the Stuarts with Charles II in 1660. The uprising eventually sputtered out, and on November 24 General Hédouville, the commander of the repression, proclaimed the end of hostilities. On December 2, several Royalist leaders signed a truce at the chateau of Angrie, near Angers. On December 19 a general armistice was proclaimed for the regions north of the Loire. January 18 and 20, 1800, peace agreements were made with the Marquis d'Autichamp and Châtillon for the regions of the left bank of the Loire. Only a few bands still resisted, but Louis Auguste Bourmont, Comte de Ghaisne, surrendered on February 4, followed by Georges Cadoudal on February 14. Comte Louis de Frotté, the last to hold out, was captured the next day, court martialed, condemned to death, and executed on February 18. It seemed as though the counterrevolution had been crushed.

Actually, the most ardent Royalists had yielded only in the hope that in the near future Louis XVIII would be restored by Bonaparte much as Charles II had been by Monck. Other Royalists thought that in the absence of Louis XVIII, who was too uncompromising, Bonaparte might call on Louis Philippe d'Orléans to rule the French. The more moderate, or the more weary, Royalists felt that, all things considered, the Consulate would be better for them than the Directory. "Bonaparte isn't liked," they said, "he's preferred," and they resigned themselves to submission.

Louis XVIII shared the illusions of his most fanatical supporters. On February 20 he wrote to Bonaparte:

> No, the victor of Lodi, of Castiglione, and of Arcole, the conqueror of Italy and of Egypt cannot prefer empty fame to glory. You are losing

precious time, however. We can insure peace for France. I say we, because I need Bonaparte, and because he would not be able to do without me. General, Europe is watching you, glory awaits you, and I am impatient to restore peace to my people.

Bonaparte was in no hurry to reply. He was undoubtedly waiting for new victories that might consolidate his situation and increase his fame. It was not until after his victory at Marengo and his new triumphs in Italy that he decided to reject brutally the pretender's proposition. On September 7, 1800, Bonaparte wrote as follows:

Sir (Monsieur), I have received your letter. I thank you for the courteous things which you say to me. You must not hope to return to France, for you would have to march over one hundred thousand corpses. Sacrifice your self-interest to France's repose and happiness. History will reward you for it. I am not insensitive to your family's misfortune. I will gladly contribute to the comfort and tranquility of your retirement.

As early as December 26, 1799, Bonaparte had had an interview with two of the leaders of the Chouans—rebels in Brittany and Normandy—d'Andigné and Baron Jean-Guillaume Hyde de Neuville, and told them: "The Bourbons haven't a chance. You have done all that you could for them. You are brave men. Come over to the winning side. Yes, come under my banners. My government will be one of youth and vitality." They were not convinced. Hyde de Neuville and Cadoudal, who had also spoken to the First Consul, decided to take up the fight again. In the fall of 1800 new attacks were launched against the republicans in the west. Senator Clément de Ris was kidnapped under mysterious circumstances that remained unexplained for a long time, but today we know that the Royalists had organized the attack. The constitutional bishop of Finistère, Yves Marie Audrein, a former member of the Convention who had voted for the execution of Louis XVI, was murdered November 19. Finally, on December 24, 1800, an attempt was made against Bonaparte himself. As his carriage drove down the rue Saint Nicaise on the way to the theater, a machine infernale (bomb) exploded. At the time, the police were unable to identify the perpetrators of the attack. Jacobins and "anarchists" were blamed. The republican opposition, in fact, had been rallying its forces for a year in an effort to prevent the consolidation of the consular regime. Without waiting for evidence, Bonaparte made an immediate decision to purge France of every remaining Jacobin. About a hundred of them, chosen from those who had been active in most of the Jacobin movements since 1792, were arrested and without being tried were deported to the Seychelles Islands in the Indian Ocean.

Officials who were suspected of Jacobinism were dismissed. Thus deprived of its leadership, the left-wing opposition was crushed.

Investigation of the attack on Bonaparte continued. Before long it was discovered that the Chouans, rather than the Jacobins, had been responsible. Two Chouans, Carbon and Saint-Réjant, were arrested, sentenced to death, and executed on April 20, 1801. D'Andigné and Bourmont were imprisoned without trial in the citadel of Besançon. Hyde de Neuville and Cadoudal fled to England. Internal peace returned to France, facilitated to a great extent by the negotiation with the Holy See of a concordat that ended the religious conflict, the main cause of civil disputes.

RELIGIOUS PACIFICATION

At the time of Bonaparte's *coup d'état* of Brumaire, the throne of Saint Peter was vacant. The previous pope, Pius VI, had been driven from Rome by the French in February 1798. He was removed from Florence, where he had taken refuge, deported to France, and died at Valence on August 20, 1799. The most anticlerical of the counterrevolutionaries had hoped that Pius VI would be the last of the popes. Before his death, however, Pius had arranged for a conclave to be held, in spite of the circumstances of the moment. It took place at Venice, Austrian territory since 1797. Barnabé Chiaramonti, the bishop of Imola and the candidate of France's ally Spain, was elected pope following three and one-half months of debate. He took the name of Pius VII. The new Pope could hardly be considered an enemy of the Revolution. In 1797 in Imola—then a city of the Cisalpine Republic—he had delivered a Christmas homily concerning the relationship between religion and democracy. Among other things, he stated that "democracy was not incompatible with the Gospel" and that the republic "demanded virtues which could only be learned through the teachings of Jesus Christ." This text may be considered as one of the early formulations of Christian democracy.

In order to reestablish peace in France, Bonaparte had to negotiate with the Pope. As early as 1796 Bonaparte had been sent to Bologna as an intermediary between the Directory and Pius VI. There he had tried in vain to persuade the Pope to retract bulls that condemned the constitutional church. Since that time the religious situation in France had gone from bad to worse. The constitutional church, separated from the state since 1795, had tried to establish itself, but despite the moral leadership of its head, Bishop Grégoire, it appealed to only a minority of believers. The rationalist religions, such as the *culte décadaire* ("the tenth day worship") and Theophilanthropism, had even fewer members. In the face of persecution, the Roman Church continued to be the church of the majority, but its organization was seriously affected by the death of many of its bishops and by the exile of virtually all of those who survived. The Roman clergy had been sympathetic to the counterrevolution since 1792. In order to restore peace within France, religious conciliation was essential and to achieve that negotiations with the Pope were necessary.

Did Bonaparte reestablish the preeminence of Catholicism in France because he was a believer or simply so that he would be in a better position to dominate the French people? The question is extremely interesting in terms of Napoleon's psychology, but less so from the point of view of general history. There is a mass of absolutely contradictory evidence concerning Napoleon's religious views, ranging from the famous declaration that "the day of his first communion had been the most wonderful day of his life" and the preamble to his will: "I am dying in the apostolic, Roman religion in which I was born," to Voltarian affirmations such as: "Society cannot exist without religion. When one man is dying of hunger next to another who is glutted, it is impossible to make him accept this difference if there is no authority there to tell him: 'It is God's will that there be both poor and rich in this world, but later, and for all eternity, the situation will be different.'" or, again, "My political belief is to govern according to the will of the majority. By becoming a Catholic, I ended the Vendéean War, by becoming a Muslim I established myself in Egypt, and by espousing Ultramontanism I won over the Italians. If I had to govern a nation of Jews, I would rebuild Solomon's temple." In any case, everything happened as if considerations of a social order and *raison d'état* greatly outweighed the religious aspects of the problem.

Bonaparte himself made the first advances. When French troops reoccupied northern Italy in the summer of 1800, following the victory of Marengo, he lavished honors and esteem on the Italian clergy. On June 5, 1800, at Milan, he addressed an assembly of 200 priests, including two bishops. "Now that I have full power," he said, "I have decided to use all appropriate means to assure and protect this religion." And he immediately opened negotiations with the Pope. Certainly Pius VII was suspicious. As soon as he arrived in Rome from Venice, he learned of the French victory at Marengo and of the return of Republican troops to the Legations, that is, to the northern provinces of the states of the Church. He had good reason to fear the reestablishment of the Roman Republic and his own expulsion from Rome. However it may have been, it was better to negotiate. On September 21, Pius VII sent Bishop Spina and the monk, Caselli, to Paris to confer with France.

The negotiations were long and difficult. Bonaparte had imposed two essential conditions: the French episcopate was to be completely renovated by the resignation of all bishops, "Roman" as well as constitutional; and the sale of former Church lands was to be acknowledged. To represent him in the negotiations, Bonaparte appointed Abbé Bernier, a former Chouan, who had just rallied to the general's ranks and appeared to him to be the man for the job. The talks were slow, first because, according to the Roman maxim, "A misunderstanding or lack of deliberation in anything which emanates from the Seat of Truth can never be justified by haste," but also because at the beginning, the points of view were poles apart. The Pope became more and more conciliatory as Bonaparte's victories consolidated his power. After ten months of negotiation, the treaty — it was not referred to as the Concordat until a later date — was signed on July 16, 1801.

This treaty was of great importance, for it reconciled the Church and the Revolution. The Pope recognized the French Republic, ordered the resignations of all bishops, both refractory and constitutional, and provided for the appointment of new prelates, named by the First Consul and installed by Rome. The Pope sanctioned the sale of confiscated ecclesiastical property, and the French government, in turn, promised to pay the salaries of the priests, who were to take a loyalty oath to the state. The dioceses were to be reorganized to fit France's new administrative divisions. The regular clergy were not mentioned. The Concordat of 1801 implicitly sanctioned religious freedom and the registration of births, marriages, and deaths by the state.

At first glance, and this was probably Bonaparte's feeling as well, it seemed that the Pope had made the most important concessions. Royalists and traditionalists were enraged. Certain bishops of the *ancien régime* resisted for a long time before finally resigning. Anticlerical revolutionaries were not much happier. The Concordat actually left the Pope with a great deal more power over the French bishops than he had had before 1789: the resignation of all French bishops at the request of the sovereign pontiff meant the end of their former independence; the nomination of all the parish priests by the bishops (instead of the local landlord or lay authority) also placed the lower-ranking clergy in direct dependence on Rome. Former Gallicanism appeared to receive its deathblow from the Concordat, and Ultramontanism was on the verge of rapid development. It is unlikely, however, that many men of the time foresaw all the consequences of the Concordat.

The objections of anticlerical revolutionaries were mainly a matter of principle. They had hoped to see Catholicism disappear and were greatly disappointed at witnessing its restoration by the First Consul himself. Because of their attitude, Bonaparte did not dare to promulgate the treaty when it was signed. It was not published until seven months later, accompanied by the Organic Articles intended to affirm the state's position of superiority and to dissipate ambiguities and implications in the Concordat that both parties had more or less intentionally allowed. The Organic

Articles revived a certain number of Gallican traditions: the government retained control over the reception and publication of papal bulls and briefs as well as the publication of conciliar and synodic decrees, the meetings of national or metropolitan councils, the nomination of bishops (although consecration was left to the Pope), the formation of cathedral chapters, the setting of religious holidays, and the creation of new parishes. All seminary professors had to adhere to the famous Gallican Declaration made by the French clergy in 1682 and were supposed to teach its doctrine. Rights and duties of bishops and archbishops were precisely defined by the Organic Articles. The number of dioceses was established at ten archbishoprics and sixty bishoprics, one third less than those existing in 1790. The number of parishes was fixed at 3000—one per canton—and, in theory, included one branch church per commune. The Organic Articles also fixed the salaries of the clergy, to be paid by the state. The Concordat had been silent on the monastic orders. Napoleon gradually allowed some to form, especially teaching orders.

The nature of these Organic Articles was certain to annoy the Pope, but since it appeared that the application of the Concordat was contingent on these articles, he protested only for form's sake. For all practical purposes, the schism between the Pope and Napoleon disappeared in the following two years. The reestablishment of Catholic unity heralded a period of renewed religious fervor. The publication of Chateaubriand's *Le Génie du Christianisme* was the first manifestation of the new spirit. However, the dechristianization of 1793 and the ten years of religious struggles had left deep scars that resulted in both the decline of religious practice and the rise of anticlericalism at the end of the century. Later, in 1806, Napoleon composed a catechism to be used in all Catholic churches in France.

Although Catholicism was declared the religion of the majority of the French, Bonaparte decided to regulate the other faiths as well. The Reformed (or Calvinist) Church and the Lutheran Church were given a charter in 1802. Protestants were grouped into consistorial churches (one for every 6000 faithful), and the ministers were paid a salary by the state.

The Jewish faith was not organized until 1808. Napoleon and his advisers looked upon the Jews less as a religious group than as a people. There had been approximately 40,000 in France in 1789. Although the Revolution had granted them a civil status and allowed them to enter all offices and types of business, they turned from their prior methods of earning a living only slowly. They continued to be animal traders and loan dealers. Their loan business often led to hostility on the part of the Christian population. Napoleon's aim was that of assimilation. He called Jewish leaders together in 1806 to learn their views on marriage, divorce, and military service. When the answers to his queries were considered favorable to assimilation, he convoked a great assembly to meet February 9, 1807, called the Great

Sanhedrin. This body agreed to divorce and military service for Jews, denounced usury but was ambiguous on intermarriage.

Napoleon issued regulations for the Jews, following the meetings of the Sanhedrin. The decree of 1807, with additions in 1808, organized the Jews into groups, comparable to the dioceses and consistories for Catholics and Protestants. Each consistory supervised affairs within the area and the execution of imperial laws, including conscription. All the local units were governed by a Central Consistory in Paris, headed by Napoleon. Thus he held a position in Jewish affairs similar to the one he held in both French Catholic and Protestant circles. In actual fact, he interfered less with the internal affairs of the Jewish groups than with those of the Catholic.

In economic matters, in part because of complaints against interest rates charged by the Jews in eastern France, French Jews with the exception of those of Paris and of the southwest, were the object of special legislation relating to loans. Borrowers were granted recourse to the courts to obtain debt reduction. The legislation apparently achieved its goal of easing terms on loans, since it was not renewed at its normal expiration date in 1818. Any Jew engaged in business was required to obtain an annual licence from the prefect. Any foreign Jew settling in France was required to purchase land, and no new Jews would be allowed to settle in Alsace. Napoleon thought to encourage assimilation by requiring the Jews to adopt last names, but this was not entirely successful. Many continued to be distinguished from Christians by the name chosen.

Even though Napoleon's legislation concerning the Jews was discriminatory and sometimes irritating, it must be recognized that it did contribute to internal pacification by removing any pretext for a peasant uprising of an antisemitic nature, such as had occurred in Alsace at the beginning of the Revolution. The Jews considered Napoleon their friend, and assimilation was furthered.

PEACEMAKING ABROAD[1]

The victories at Zurich and in Holland in the autumn of 1799 had stopped the allied offensive and had brought about the retreat of Russian troops. In order to achieve a peace that would safeguard the conquests of the Revolution, Bonaparte still had to conquer Austria and England.

He devoted the winter and spring of 1800 to preparing his offensive. War was unavoidable since neither King George III of England nor the

---

[1] Consult the section of the bibliography entitled "Napoleon and Europe." See also Georges Lefebvre, *Napoléon,* (Paris, 1965), pp. 88, 89, 96, 100, for specific bibliography. The bibliography is not given in the English-language edition.

Bonaparte Crossing the Alps, by Jacques Louis David. This is an idealization of Napoleon, who is reputed to have crossed the Alps on a mule, not a prancing white horse. The picture in no way suggests the hardships of the journey through the Great Saint Bernard Pass used by Napoleon. (Château Malmaison. Photo from Giraudon)

Emperor Francis II had answered the peace overtures addressed to them by Bonaparte in two open letters. Bonaparte wanted to begin the campaign under the best possible conditions. This meant that he would have to prevent the coalition from enlisting allies; at the same time he would have to win friends for France. France had traditionally sought an alliance with Prussia, but Siéyès had failed in this purpose when he was sent to Berlin in 1798. In the winter of 1800 Bonaparte sent Beurnonville and Duroc to Berlin. Although they were no more successful than Siéyès, at least Prussia remained neutral. Bonaparte had better luck with Russia. He succeeded in completely disengaging Tsar Paul I from the coalition.

From the military point of view, the rigorous application of the 1798 Jourdan-Delbrel universal conscription law permitted Bonaparte to assemble an army of 60,000, designated as a reserve army, in the Dijon region. With his usual insight, Bonaparte understood the strategic importance of Switzerland: as long as he controlled this country, he could outflank the Austrian armies in Germany and Italy. The most pressing danger was in Italy, where General Massena, besieged in Genoa, was at the end of his resources and would soon be forced to surrender.

Bonaparte entrusted the command of the Army of Germany to General Moreau, and made Marshal Berthier, who was then the minister of war, the nominal commander of the reserve army, for under the terms of the Constitution of the Year VIII, the First Consul could not personally direct an army. Napoleon did accompany this army, however, not as its official head. He took it across the Great Saint Bernard Pass, still snowbound (May 15–20) into Italy, and unexpectedly attacked the rear of the Austrian army that was besieging Genoa. The Austrians did an about-face and met the French at Marengo on June 14, 1800, near the fortress of Alessandria. The battle nearly ended in defeat for the French army, but the arrival of General Desaix and his troops at the end of the day reversed the situation. Desaix himself was killed in the battle, but the French emerged as masters of the entire Po valley, as far as the Adige River.

The Cisalpine Republic was restored, and General Jourdan was named governor of Piedmont, although the fate of this area was not clearly spelled out. The victory at Marengo had great importance for the political situation, for it consolidated the powers of the First Consul and permitted him to hasten the establishment of domestic peace by opening the way to the negotiation of the Concordat, as has already been noted, and by allowing thousands of *émigrés* to return to France, despite the terms of the constitution.

The Austrian army in Italy was beaten, but Austria was not vanquished. Contrary to what had occurred in 1797, the Army of Germany played the principle role in the march on Vienna. On December 3, 1800, General Moreau won a great victory over the Austrians at Hohenlinden in Bavaria. The emperor asked for an armistice, which was concluded at Steyer on December 25. Since July, negotiations between France and Austria had been entered into on several occasions. On August 24 it was decided that a peace congress should be held in 1801 at Lunéville, in Lorraine. England was invited but refused to participate. The kingdom of Naples, threatened by Murat's troops, capitulated and signed the armistice of Foligno, February 18, 1801.

The Congress of Lunéville lasted for more than a month and resulted in the peace treaty of February 9, 1801. Perhaps Bonaparte could have imposed on Austria the unification of an independent Italy, which he now controlled, just as the deputy from Doubs, the Jacobin Briot, had demanded so eloquently at the tribunal of the Council of Five Hundred in August 1799. But Bonaparte, as he had at Campo-Formio, remained the enlightened despot, faithful to eighteenth-century policies of partitions and exchanges. His only stipulation was that the Cisalpine Republic be restored. He thought about annexing Piedmont to France. In the spring of 1799 a hotly contested referendum had favored this annexation. If he did this, he would have abandoned the policy of "natural frontiers," without adopting that of "nationalities." He also wanted to maintain the Papal States while he was negotiating the Concordat. He envisaged territorial changes in Tuscany that would benefit the Spanish Bourbons in exchange for colonial expansion in America, and he left Venice to Austria. The Italian patriots, who had once again placed their trust in Bonaparte and had again been disappointed, were driven into opposition.

Bonaparte, now Chief of state, was more concerned about the Rhine at Lunéville than he had been at Campo-Formio. This time, Austria formally recognized Belgium and the left bank of the Rhine as French possessions. France, in return, promised to help her to secure compensations on the right bank, thus succeeding where the Congress of Rastadt had failed in 1799. Under the pretext of distributing these territorial compensations, Bonaparte secured a permanent means of intervention in the German part of the Holy Roman Empire.

Peace still had to be concluded with England. As in 1798, preparations were made for a landing on English shores, but these were carried out only partially. Before attacking England, Bonaparte wanted to be sure of assistance from the chief maritime powers of the Atlantic and Baltic. In the Atlantic, this meant Spain and the United States. On October 1, 1800, he signed the Treaty of San Ildefonso with Spain. In return for the promise of a Tuscan kingdom created for the son of Louis, Duke of Parma, son-in-law of King Charles IV of Spain, Spain ceded to France the part of Louisiana that she had annexed in 1763. By the terms of another treaty, signed at Aranjuez on March 21, 1801, Spain promised to declare war on Portugal, an English ally. The Treaty of Mortefontaine between France and the United States (September 30, 1800) reestablished good relations between the two countries—relations that had been compromised in 1797 by the XYZ affair. The two republics acknowledged two fundamental principles of international maritime law respecting neutral trade that England refused to accept: the flag covers the merchandise, and any ship escorted by a warship is exempt from the right of search.

In the Baltic, Bonaparte hoped to obtain the adherence of Russia to a league of neutral powers directed against England, similar to the one that had been formed in 1780. Since his recall of his armies from central Europe and his departure from the Austrian-English coalition at the end of 1799, Paul I annoyed with England had developed a great admiration for Bonaparte. Consequently, negotiations were an easy matter. Bonaparte skillfully directed the tsar's ambitions toward the Balkans. At the same time, he showed a disposition to grant Paul I the title of Grand Master of the Order of Saint John of Jerusalem along with the possession of Malta. Paul I, thereupon, decided to form a League of Armed Neutrality with Sweden, Denmark, and Prussia (December 1800), which reacted unfavorably on English trade.

England's position became serious, now that she was seemingly isolated in the world. She reacted with a vengeance. On the night of March 23, 1801, Paul I was assassinated by disgruntled Russian nobles, whose conspiracy was aided by an English subsidy. England next ordered her Baltic squadron (in which Lord Nelson was serving) to bombard Copenhagen and to destroy the Danish fleet (April 2). As the result of these two actions, the neutral coalition was dissolved. Alexander I, son and successor to Paul I, did not share his father's admiration for Bonaparte. The neutrals, disconcerted by the death of Paul I and the attack on Copenhagen, were afraid to continue their threat of excluding English shipping from the Baltic. Denmark abandoned the league on April 9, 1801.

England's position, however, still remained precarious. Despite the gains that the war had brought her, England was battle-weary. Her economy was suffering too. The issuance of paper money, although in moderate amounts, gradually increased the cost of living. Two poor harvests, in 1799 and in 1800, accentuated the rise even more. England was forced to increase her imports of food products—fish from Canada and Sweden, rice from India, cereals from the United States, Sicily, north Africa, and even from France. Despite these efforts, riots broke out, and demands were made for the resignation of Prime Minister Pitt, who was held responsible for the rising prices and the continuing war. Pitt sent troops against the rioters. The middle classes began to fear for their property. In addition, they were bewildered by the discovery that the English soil could no longer provide enough food for its inhabitants. They had not envisioned clearly the economic consequences of demographic pressures that had increased England's population from 5 to 10 million between 1700 and 1800. The union of Ireland and Great Britain, voted on February 5, 1800, and entailing certain concessions to the Catholics, increased opposition. Pitt was forced to resign on February 3, 1801; thus, the man who had advocated war to the death relinquished his power. The last obstacle to peace between France and England was removed.

Pitt was replaced by Henry Addington, a liberal Whig, pacificist, and anti-Catholic. Addington, however, was not supported by a party in the modern sense. According to estimates, his followers in Parliament varied between twelve and sixty. He had only two really well-known men in his ministry: Lord Saint Vincent (Admiral Jervis) in the admiralty, and Lord Hawkesbury (son of Charles Jenkinson, Earl of Liverpool) in the foreign office. The other ministers were second-rate men, either Addington's friends or relatives. He was able to win a majority only because he sought peace.

Negotiations begun in February 1801, lasted for more than seven months, responding to the repercussions of military operations, notably those in Egypt. There the French army, commanded by General Menou, resisted foot by foot the advance of British and Turkish forces up the Nile valley. As in the case of the negotiations at Lille in 1796 and 1797, debate concentrated on the Dutch colonies that England wanted to retain, but the possession of Malta and Egypt also figured prominently in the discussions. Preliminary peace terms were finally signed at London on October 1, 1801. Hostilities were to stop immediately, and negotiations for a definitive peace were to begin at Amiens. Peace was signed in this city on March 25, 1802.

England returned to France all of her colonies. Of those colonies belonging to France's allies, she kept only Ceylon, taken from the Dutch, and Trinidad, won from Spain. She implicitly recognized the provisions of the Treaty of Lunéville. With regard to Egypt, the English had the advantage since the French army had capitulated during the summer of 1801. Bonaparte, however, arranged to have Egypt returned to Turkey. As for Malta, in order to prevent the English from installing themselves there, the First Consul demanded that the island be given back to its former rulers, the Knights of Saint John of Jerusalem. But England introduced a provision that delayed the evacuation of the fortress by her troops for three months following ratification of the treaty. During this period the Order of Malta was to be reorganized and its integrity guaranteed by the six great European powers.

The conclusion of peace with Russia and Turkey did not entail any great difficulties. Russia had specifically hoped that Bonaparte would restore the king of Sardinia over whom the tsar was protector to Turin. The First Consul refused, consenting only to the insertion in the treaty of a clause recognizing the Kingdom of Naples. Peace was signed under these terms on October 8, 1801. With the tsar serving as mediator, a treaty was made with Turkey on the following day (October 9). France gave Egypt back to Turkey and allowed the Ionian Islands to be organized into a Republic of the Seven Islands under Turkish sovereignty. Finally, Spain made peace with Portugal at Badajoz on June 6, 1801, and retained the city of Olivenza. France received only a few customs advantages for the export of cloth to Portugal but not the closing of Portuguese ports to the English, as she had hoped.

Thus, the pacification of 1801 encompassed all of Europe and covered political, civil, and religious quarrels alike. It appeared that the conflicts that had begun in 1789 had finally been resolved and that, despite the concessions made by France, the victory of the Revolution was acknowledged everywhere. Now that peace prevailed in the Western world, it seemed that Bonaparte had kept the promises he made when he declared, after the *coup d'état* of Brumaire: "Citizens, the Revolution is now settled in the principles which started it: it is completed."

Was it really over? Would the peace attained in 1801 be lasting? That would depend on Bonaparte himself (Would he be able to control his ambition?) and on England (Would she accept a peace which seemed to diminish her importance in the world?). Above all, it would depend on the revolutionary and counterrevolutionary forces that had been confronting each other in the west for thirty years, and that were far from losing their dynamism.

4

RESUMPTION OF WAR AND CREATION OF THE FRENCH EMPIRE

At the close of 1801 it was certainly difficult to foresee that Napoleon Bonaparte planned to transform the power that he held in France into a monarchy for his own benefit, and then to extend the limits of this monarchy to the remotest parts of Europe. Within two years he had restored peace, both within and outside of France, as he had promised. He had been elected First Consul for ten years, and he was "reeligible indefinitely" for an indeterminate period. Any transformations of the power of the First Consul, which, by the terms of the constitution, was already vast, and now coupled with incomparable prestige, could only indicate an alarming ambition whose limits were difficult to perceive. The change from a decennial Consulate to a life Consulate was, in fact, the first striking manifestation of Napoleon's insatiable ambition. It was accompanied by political actions that quickly proved to the world that as far as the First Consul was concerned, the treaties of 1801 were not final. These treaties, in Napoleon's view, did not mark the end of the Revolution or the recognition of the existence of the "Great Nation." Rather, they established the starting point for a new line of expansion—an expansion that would entail a resumption of war, a war that would not end until the fall of Napoleon fourteen years later. Europe would then emerge from the ordeal deeply shaken, and at last, despite the apparent victory of the counterrevolution, it would be the Revolution and its ideology, institutions, and economic and social structure that would be firmly established throughout most of western and central Europe.

THE CONSULATE FOR LIFE

Bonaparte took advantage of the indisputable increase in his popularity brought about by his peacemaking efforts to have the First Consul's term of office extended from ten years to life. At his instigation Cambacérès planned a "scenario" to meet the First Consul's demands. Immediately after the reading of the Amiens peace treaty in the Tribunate, a member of this body—in agreement with the Second Consul and the president of the Tribunate—suggested that congratulations were in order for the First Consul. The president of the Tribunate, Chabot de l'Allier, extolled Bonaparte and asked that the Senate be invited to "prove to the consul the gratitude of the nation." The Tribunate sent two delegations to present this resolution, one to the Senate, the other to the First Consul. The Senate thought that Bonaparte would be satisfied with a ten-year extension of his power, and it adopted a resolution accordingly. But Napoleon wanted more and made no attempt to hide his disappointment, declaring that he intended to secure a prolongation of his powers from the whole French nation and not merely from the Senate. Therefore, he brought before the Council of State a proposal for a referendum, at that time called a plebiscite. The Council of State, following the suggestions that Bonaparte had transmitted through Pierre Louis Roederer, drafted the questions to be submitted to the people: (1) Should Napoleon Bonaparte be elected Consul for life? (2) Should he be allowed to name his successor? Sensing that the time was not yet ripe for such action, Bonaparte had the second question withheld. A plebiscite was conducted similar to that of the Year VIII for the approval of the Constitution of 1799. There were 500,000 fewer abstentions than in 1800, and although some of the former abstainers voted against the life Consulate, most of them gave their approval. The negative votes numbered 8374 (1562 had been cast in 1800), a small figure but one that proved that an opposition still persisted despite police measures taken against Jacobin and Royalist leaders. Generals and soldiers voted against the life Consulate. It appears that the excess of affirmative votes entered in 1802 came from the conservative element.

The *senatus consultum* of 16 Thermidor, Year X (August 3, 1802) recorded the people's decision. In addition, it made several modifications in the Constitution of the Year VIII. These were aimed at strengthening the executive power at the expense of the legislative. Henceforth, the First Consul, during his lifetime, would be allowed to choose his successor. He had the power to convene the Senate and to convene and adjourn the Legislative Body. He presided over the Senate and named the presidents of the Legislative Body, cantonal assemblies, and electoral colleges. He could dissolve the Tribunate and the Legislative Body with the consent of the Senate. He could grant clemency after hearing a commission composed of three ministers (including the minister of justice), two senators, two councillors of state, and two judges from the highest court of appeals. Finally, he was no longer compelled to have the assent of the Legislative Body to peace treaties and alliances that he negotiated.

The First Consul's stipend was increased considerably, from 500,000 francs to 6 million francs (the two other consuls received only 600,000 francs). The First Consul was to have an entourage of four generals, and his wife was to have four *dames du palais* (ladies-in-waiting). Thus, the First Consul was becoming a veritable monarch. Already "Napoleon was piercing through under Bonaparte."

The Constitution of the Year X abandoned the system of lists of notables, created by Siéyès, and adopted the system of electoral colleges. This organization was more "representative" than that of Year VIII, but it did nothing to strengthen the legislative assemblies, whose power, on the contrary, was reduced. The Tribunate was divided into 3 sections that deliberated separately. In addition to the members that it chose by cooptation, the Senate was to include several members by virtue of their offices. Its powers were increased. It could dissolve the two other legislative bodies. It could override judgments of the tribunals when they appeared to endanger the security of the state. The senators also profited individually, for within the jurisdiction of each appellate court a *sénatererie* was set up — that is, a domain whose revenues, estimated at 20,000 or 25,000 francs per year, were allotted to a senator.

The founding of the Legion of Honor marked another step toward the return to traditional institutions. The *ancien régime* in France, as in all of Europe, had had its chivalric orders, which by the end of the eighteenth century had become mere honorific decorations. They were all abolished on July 30, 1791, with the exception of the Cross of Saint Louis, a decoration awarded to officers for distinguished service in the army. This, in turn, was eliminated on July 28, 1793. The Republic rewarded courageous military men with *armes d'honneur* and crowns of oak leaves.

Bonaparte wanted to create in a new form an order that would include as members both soldiers who had demonstrated heroism and the most meritorious civilians. Although the bill was bitterly opposed in the Council of State, it did pass — but only by a hairbreadth. The assemblies approved it next by a slight majority vote. This law of May 19, 1802, created the Legion of Honor. It was a legion (a corps) composed of fifteen cohorts, each of which included seven chief officers, twenty commanders, thirty officers, and 350 legionnaires. Each cohort represented a territorial *arrondissement*, in which it was to establish a hospital for disabled legionnaires. An administrative Grand Council, named by the First Consul, headed the Legion. Two years passed before the decoration itself was instituted (July 11, 1804). More and more, the Legion of Honor took on the trappings of the chivalric orders that had been suppressed in 1791.

The French, pleased with the new-found peace, paid little heed to the direction in which the regime had evolved between 1801 and 1802. Not even the foreigners who flocked to France in large numbers for a firsthand look at the Republic that had been the object of so many disparaging remarks in their own country were conscious of the movement to the right. Life seemed to be going along on its normal path, enhanced by celebrations lavishly given by a popular, young government head.

Foreigners were warmly welcomed. France, the victor, was generous with its former enemies. The English, in particular, came in large numbers, and many wrote accounts of their trip that were published at home. The English did not regard themselves as a defeated nation, since they had emerged from the conflict with several colonial acquisitions. The leader of the opposition in the House of Commons, Charles Fox, came to Paris and was received by Bonaparte, who had busts of both Fox and Nelson placed in his office. English visitors were amazed at the ease with which money circulated in France and at the abundance of hard cash. Jean Bernard Trotter, Fox's secretary, wrote: "In London, one had a hard time trying to get a few guineas out of a banker who conceded them as a favor. In Paris, the banker gave you a choice of gold or silver; both were abundant." The English were also astonished at the low cost of living in France in comparison with Great Britain. They remarked about the small number of beggars and unemployed, but they also observed the ruined chateaux and churches that had been left abandonned for ten years. In general, they were not shocked by the power of the police in the Republic, but they did comment that French police did not have the same role as the police in Great Britain. Sir John Carr wrote:

> The English police force seems to be more concerned with arresting the thief than preventing the theft. . . . In France, the police is highly esteemed, and combines strength with vigilance. . . . Despite jealous rumors which have spread on its account, it deserves the constant admiration of the sincere stranger who may, under its protection, safely wander through all the quarters and suburbs of Paris."

The English were undoubtedly aware that the police were keeping a watchful and spying eye on them, but they judged that freedom of speech was greater in France than in England. They especially admired the religious freedom—notably in regard to the Hebrew worship—and the secular nature of the civil state. To the English, equality was the Revolution's greatest achievement. It was chiefly in this area, they thought, that France differed from England. Anyone could have access to and actually attain the highest office in the state, whereas in England, public office was regarded as the birthright of noble and wealthy families, and was inaccessible to religious dissenters to the Anglican religion. The democratic character of society, the attitude of the servants, of the tradesmen who spoke to employers or clients on a tone of equality, seemed to them to be very different from the British way of life. Commentators on France's economy noted the large number of small and medium-sized landowners that had emerged during the Revolution. The British landed gentry viewed this with alarm and regarded Bonaparte as one of the worst enemies of humanity for having condoned the division of the great noble estates.

The English were impressed by the high esteem in which French learning and those who pursued it were held by the state. They noted the eminent position accorded to scholars in the government; Pierre Simon Laplace and Jean Antoine Chaptal were ministers of the interior. The visitors delighted in the honors bestowed on the renowned English naturalist Joseph Banks, twenty-six times president of the Royal Society of London, who was named to membership in the Institute of France on January 21, 1802.

It seemed as if an era of lasting peace founded on Franco-British collaboration was about to open. But for this to come about, there had to be an entente not only in the area of personal feelings, but also in the economic arena. It is on this field that the two countries, both in the throes of the Industrial Revolution but in different stages of development, were to clash.

PEACETIME EXPANSION OF FRANCE

The war had fostered a surge in the iron metallurgy industry in France, but had reduced activity in the textile industry, which had been paralyzed by a lack of cotton. As Bonaparte saw the situation, the iron industry would maintain itself and would even improve during peacetime, while the textile industry would return to its former position now that peace was restored. He considered it essential that the great French ports of Le Havre, Nantes, Bordeaux, and Marseilles, whose prosperity had been severely compromised by the war, regain their former traffic. This was not only a question of economics, but also of politics, for it was probable that the basis for the political attitudes held by people of Bordeaux and Marseilles in 1793 were traced to the interruption of their commerce. Bonaparte's policy, therefore, was aimed at challenging England's economic dominance on the sea, while at the same time conserving the markets that France had acquired through conquests on the Continent.

However, one should not overemphasize that Napoleon was preoccupied with considerations of an economic nature, especially in 1801 and 1802. Basically, he was motivated by an extraordinary thirst for power, which led to his desire for constant domination in all areas. Now that peace had been attained, there were several areas in which France, and therefore Bonaparte, might exercise power more or less freely. Within France, first of all, he was free to set customs tariffs as he saw fit, except for the threat of eventual reprisals. He was also free to reorganize France's former colonies—such as revolt-torn Saint Domingue—where intervention had heretofore been impossible because of the English blockade. He also had a free hand in reorganizing those newly acquired possessions of Spain—the western part of Saint Domingue and Louisiana. Next, there were the sister republics, where for six years French intervention had been more or less traditional. An opening for French intervention had also been established in Germany, as we have said, in consequence of the Treaty of Lunéville. In all these areas Bonaparte could legitimately manipulate affairs, but the only justification for French intervention in the remainder of the world was a pure quest for power—a quest that would undoubtedly clash with England's ambitions.

Indeed, in these various areas, Bonaparte's first thoughts were never toward sparing England. Did he purposely want to start another war? This is not very likely. Did he underestimate England's strength? Possibly. But it is more likely that these questions never entered his mind. He pursued a political course aimed at the grandeur of France and, therefore, at the augmentation of his own powers. He never conceived that the coalition that he had just beaten down would pull itself together and rise against him. On the whole, his foreign policy followed the trend set by the *Grande Nation*,[1] which from 1794 to 1799 had spread throughout the world and had increased its power without ever having devised a clearly defined plan for expansion. Napoleon made his plans as the situation called for them, quickly substituting one plan for another even before the first had been completely executed.

Bonaparte's prime objective within France was to revitalize commerce and industry, to prevent a decline in certain manufactures that had prospered during the war, to combat unemployment, and, to use an expression not known at that time, to do everything in his power to avoid an "economic crisis." Furthermore, there was a favorable combination *(conjoncture)* of economic, political, social, and demographic conditions in the west

---

[1] Jacques Godechot entitled his two-volume work on France and Europe, 1789 to 1799, *La Grande Nation,* because that was the name given to France by the people of the areas conquered or cooperative with the French Revolutionaries. After 1799, and even before the Empire, the word *empire* was substituted for *nation.*

that permitted such policies. Following a period of fluctuation during the years 1774–1792, and especially 1788–1792, the main curves of the *conjoncture* showed the demographic curve with an excess of births, and the slow, economic curve with a steady rise in prices and wages.[2]

STEPS LEADING TO WAR

To avoid a crisis, Napoleon had recourse to the classic technique of the *ancien régime:* protectionism. As soon as the peace treaties were signed, he concluded commercial treaties, favorable to France, with Naples (March 28, 1801), with Spain (March 21, 1802), with Portugal (September 28, 1801), with Russia (October 8, 1801), and with Turkey (June 25, 1802). England was also eager to negotiate a commercial treaty, but only on terms similar to those of the Treaty of Eden of 1786. This treaty had given British manufactured products an advantage on the French market, and had elicited marked discontent in France, as can be seen in the *cahiers de doléances* of 1789.[3] Advantages for French wines had been forgotten by the French. Bonaparte, backed by a large majority of French merchants, refused to bargain on these terms, and in 1803 he introduced a new customs tariff that put a heavy tax on manufactured products—especially cotton goods—as well as on refined sugar. English merchants were greatly disappointed for the new duties shut doors to anticipated markets resulting from France's aggrandizement, as well as on the Dutch, Swiss, and Cisalpine markets bound to France by treaty.

In addition, France set out to challenge Britain's control of the seas. As soon as peace had been restored, France showed unmistakable signs of seeking colonial expansion. Even before the Treaty of Amiens was signed, Bonaparte had sent an expeditionary force commanded by his own brother-

---

[2] A school of historians in France led by Ernest Labrousse has done extensive research on social and economic history for the Revolutionary period, using statistical methods, and primary sources. (See Labrousse, *Esquisse du mouvement des prix et des revenus en France au XVIIIe. siècle* (Paris, 1933), also his *La crise de l'économie francaise à la fin de l'ancien régime et au début de la Révolution* (Paris, 1944). The word *conjoncture* is used a great deal by this school to designate the simultaneous combination of political, social, and economic factors in development.

[3] The *cahiers de doléances* were the instructions drawn up by the electoral assemblies that chose deputies for the Estates-General of 1789. All three classes—clergy, nobles, and the third estate—drew up instructions. Therefore, the *cahiers* provide an indication of conditions and of programs of reform on the eve of the Revolution. See Beatrice F. Hyslop, *French Nationalism in 1789 according to the General Cahiers* (New York: Columbia University Press, 1934; revised edition, New York: Octagon Press, 1968).

in-law, General Leclerc (Pauline Bonaparte's husband), to regain the former French colony of Saint Domingue. On May 9, 1801, Pierre Toussaint L'Ouverture, a former Negro slave who had become a general in the service of France, had promulgated a constitution that for all practical purposes made the island autonomous. The Leclerc expedition landed at Cap François on February 4, 1802, and Toussaint L'Ouverture was arrested on June 7. Success seemed to be achieved. At the same time, the French took over the eastern part of Saint Domingue, which Spain had ceded by the Treaty of Basel, but which had not yet been occupied. This foothold made by France on one of the first Spanish colonies of America was more important than it seemed at first glance. It heralded the revolutionary storm that was soon to shake these colonies and would end in their gaining independence. But it was also an attack on England's economic hegemony in the Spanish empire in America, and it was certain to produce bitter resentment in London.

Bonaparte also planned to occupy Louisiana, the former French possession ceded to Spain in 1763 but returned to France in 1800 by the Treaty of San Ildefonso. On the North Sea, preparations were made for transporting General Victor to Louisiana, but his departure was postponed. Instead, General Decaen was sent to the French tradingposts in India with a large military staff apparently to recruit a large army of sepoys for the expedition to Louisiana. Certainly France had legitimate reasons for re-entering her former colonies and those ceded to her by Spain. But the aggressive and frankly imperialist guise of this occupation gave England legitimate cause for alarm.

This anxiety was aggravated by French policy in the sister republics. Under the Directory, France had treated the "sister republics" more as satellites than as equals, but this attitude had been justified by the war. With peace it would seem that sister republics would become truly independent. Nothing of the kind took place. Bonaparte had at least two good reasons for intervening in the republics' internal affairs. The sister republics in Italy (Cisalpine, Ligurian, Roman, Parthenopean) had been destroyed by the Austro-Russian conquest and the power of reaction, before Napoleonic reconquest. Those that had been restored by the peace treaties needed assistance in their reorganization. In 1799 the two other republics (Batavian and Helvetic) had devised constitutions inspired by the democratic French Constitution of the Year III. How could Bonaparte, who had struck down this constitution in France on 18 Brumaire, tolerate a related form to persist in the sister republics as a living reproach? Although Bonaparte's constant intervention in the domestic affairs of these new states was, therefore, logical, here, as in the colonies, to onlookers it appeared as acts of aggression and "imperialism," which further disconcerted Great Britain. By terms of the Treaty of Lunéville, the boundaries of the Cisalpine Republic in Italy were restored to nearly those it had held in 1799. The same treaty also implicitly recognized the former Republic of Genoa, which had become the Ligurian Republic in 1797.

When Bonaparte entered Milan on June 2, 1800, he had established a provisional government for the Cisalpine Republic. A legislative assembly met in July but was unable to draw up a new constitution for the republic. Other proposals elaborated during the summer of 1801 also came to naught, mainly because of opposition from Bonaparte. Bonaparte then decided to convoke a constitutional assembly in Lyons for the purpose of adopting a draft written by a liberal Milanese noble who held Bonaparte's confidence — Count Melzi d'Eril. The assembly met in Lyons on December 29, 1801, and remained in session until January 26, 1802. After making a few criticisms and modifications, the assembly did adopt Melzi d'Eril's draft, which Bonaparte had reexamined and approved. In its broader lines the constitution resembled the French Constitution of the Year VIII. Instead of placing the executive power in the hands of a group such as the Consulate, however, it was entrusted to a president of the republic who had enormous powers at his disposal, including a monopoly on legislative initiative.

The Lyon assembly gained fame and created an international stir not because of having adopted a constitution for the Cisalpine Republic but, rather, because of Bonaparte's intervention and because of the two significant measures that he put through. The First Consul arrived in Lyons on January 11, 1802, just when the assembly was choosing a president for the republic under the new constitution. Melzi d'Eril was elected but declined when it became obvious that Bonaparte was not pleased. Another politician, Antonio Aldini, was elected, but he too declined for the same reason. By now it was apparent that the only person acceptable to Bonaparte for the presidency would be Bonaparte himself. His associates, especially Talleyrand, tried to sway the deputies to offer him the presidency, and finally Bonaparte was elected by acclamation on January 25. No one dared count the votes. Witnesses claimed that he received less than a third. Melzi was elected vice-president. Bonaparte's election to the presidency of the Cisalpine Republic revealed to the entire world his insatiable ambition. It also disclosed his intention to keep this republic under French rule. In order to obliterate the bad impression that his "election" had created in Italy, Bonaparte chose the solemn closing session of the assembly on January 26 to proclaim theatrically the transformation of the Cisalpine Republic into an Italian Republic. He thereby took the first step in fulfilling the desire of the most ardent patriots since 1796. The call for Italian unification had been most fervently expressed in Briot's petition to the Council of the Five Hundred during the summer of 1799. The term Italian Republic reverberated meaning and hope to the Italians. It suggested that this republic would constitute a nucleus for a state that would gradually incorporate all of the Italian peninsula.

The great powers of Europe recognized its significance. Archduke Ferdinand of Austria wrote: "The new order of events which has issued from Lyon . . . entails grave consequences for all of Europe if it should really take shape, and of this I cannot yet be entirely persuaded." For quite some time, the Austrian ambassador to Paris, Philippe de Cobenzl, entertained the hope that the proclaiming of an Italian Republic would mean a rupture in peace negotiations with England, which were then taking place in Amiens. Whatever its result, the proclamation of the Italian Republic marked an important date in the history of the *Risorgimento,* but it was only an illusory declaration—one not followed by action.

Bonaparte's attitude with respect to Piedmont, Genoa, and Tuscany revealed what little importance he attached to these unifying intentions. It did not take long for people to realize that if he had plans for Italian unification, he was relegating them to a far distant future. If he had entertained the idea of Italian unity in June 1800, he could have joined the then Cisalpine Republic and Piedmont, which was under French occupation. He did nothing. On September 11, 1802, Bonaparte decreed that Piedmont would be incorporated into the French republic and divided into six departments. His pretext was the hotly contested referendum of February 1799. His true reasons were the need to counterbalance Austrian power on the peninsula to the extreme east of the Po Valley by its control of Venetia and economic—for Piedmont furnished raw silk for the Lyonnais silk industry. Piedmontese patriots, including the future historian Carlo Botta, protested. International reaction was aroused. Piedmont was only a step. Napoleon's plans for further personal aggrandizement continued to increase.

The Republic of Genoa, restored in 1800 as the Ligurian Republic, was provided in 1802 with a new constitution based on that of the Italian Republic. The constitution did not guarantee the independence of this Italian state. Bonaparte viewed the port of Genoa as a French arsenal and all of Liguria as Piedmont's natural outlet to the Mediterranean Sea. As early as 1803 it became obvious that France would soon annex the Ligurian Republic which did take place on June 30, 1805.

Nor was Parma destined to be joined to the Italian Republic. After the death of the duke of Parma, Ferdinand de Bourbon, in 1802, the little state was administered by a Frenchman, Moreau de Saint-Méry, who had been an important figure in the revolution in Saint Domingue earlier, and who now introduced French laws and institutions in Parma. Annexation to France took place in 1808.

Nor did Tuscany become a part of the Italian Republic. Under the terms of the Treaty of Lunéville the Hapsburgs, who had controlled the duchy, relinquished their claims to this Italian region. Bonaparte made it the kingdom of Etruria for the benefit of Louis de Bourbon, son of Duke

Ferdinand of Parma and son-in-law of King Charles IV of Spain. The neighboring principality of Lucca was administered by Bonaparte's old Corsican friend, Saliceti, and then by General Hédouville, until June 23, 1805, at which time Bonaparte's sister Elisa and her husband Félix Bacciocchi were named princess and prince of Lucca and Piombino.

After having filled Italian patriots with great hope by his early measures in Italy, Bonaparte quickly ended their dreams of unity—at least so long as he was at the helm. Furthermore, he disquieted Europe, especially England, by treating Italy as his personal domain.

Bonaparte's intervention in the two other sister republics (Helvetic and Batavian) confirmed their alarm. Switzerland (the Helvetic Republic) had been deeply shaken by the war of the Second Coalition. More than half of its territory had been occupied by Austro-Russian troops during the summer of 1799. Aristocrats and conservatives had hoped that the invaders would be victorious and that the *ancien régime* would be restored. The Jacobins, on the other hand, supported the French. In November 1799 Frédéric César de La Harpe, a moderate Jacobin was about to execute another *coup d'état* when he learned of 18 Brumaire and he dropped his plan. In January 1800, however, the legislative councils learned of the plot, dissolved the Helvetic Directory, and formed an executive commission presided over by Jean Rodolphe Dolder. This began a long period of instability in the Swiss republic, during which the "unitary" Jacobins and the more conservative "federalists" alternately sought Bonaparte's aid. In answer to the Swiss pleas for help, Bonaparte presented a draft for a federalist constitution entitled the Act of Malmaison (April 29, 1801). This compromise between unitary and federalist tendencies satisfied no one. Disturbances intensified and the French army, under the command of General Chevin de Monchoisy and Raymond Verninac, a representative of France, intervened. On their own initiative, these two emissaries of Bonaparte set up a government headed by Alois Reding, a well-known aristocrat, who on February 26, 1802, promulgated a new constitution that for all practical purposes restored the *ancien régime*. Those supporting a unitary state were furious and again called on Bonaparte. He annulled Reding's constitution. An assembly of notables called together by Verninac, approved the Act of Malmaison.

French troops evacuated Switzerland in the spring of 1802, and it seemed that peace had been restored. But the French had no sooner departed, than Reding aroused the forest cantons of Schwyz, Uri, and Unterwalden and seized Zurich, Bern, and Fribourg. The legal head of government, the *Landamann* Dolder, who had fled to Lausanne, again appealed to Bonaparte, who imposed his mediation by a new army sent into Switzerland to enforce the settlement. The army dispersed the insurgents and arrested Reding. Bonaparte then convened a Helvetic Council in Paris to amend the Malmaison Act of April 29, 1801. From this council emerged the Mediation Act of February 19, 1803, reorganizing the republic. The Helvetic Confederation now consisted of nineteen autonomous and equal cantons. The Diet, the legislative body, was a simple conference of the cantonal delegates. Executive power was exercised by the head of one of the six "directing" cantons. Bonaparte named Louis d'Affry, a former officer in the service of France from the canton of Fribourg, to this position. On September 27, 1805, France and the Helvetic Republic entered into a fifty-year defensive alliance that permitted France to recruit four infantry regiments in Switzerland. In reality, the Swiss republic became a French dependency. Since August 30, 1802, the neighboring Valais had been an independent republic held in tight control by France. Although the French exercised less control on Switzerland than in the Valais, it was apparent in 1803 that the Helvetic confederation was also a dependency of the French Republic.

The Batavian Republic's constitution of 1798 had worked out no better than the Constitution of the Year III had in France. Two *coups d'état* had taken place in January and June 1798 and a third was being planned, as in Switzerland, when news of the 18 Brumaire *coup* arrived. The French representative in the republic, Charles Louis Huguet, Marquis de Sémonville, believed that it would be relatively easy for him to have a new constitution, modeled on the French Constitution of the Year VIII, ratified by referendum. But the Dutch legislative councils declared Sémonville's measures illegal and void. General Augereau, a veteran of the *coups d'état* and a supporter of the French, forcibly dissolved the councils. The referendum was held—a handful of citizens voting "yes" and the great majority abstaining, but the abstentions were deemed approvals, and the constitution became official on October 6, 1801. The new government, headed by twelve regents, chose the members of the legislative councils, and in line with Bonaparte's dictates, eliminated democrats. The Batavian Republic was now more than ever a vassal of France.

Bonaparte's intervention in Italy, Switzerland, and Holland merely perpetuated a policy that had begun with the Convention and the Directory. Europe was indignant, certainly, but at least she was more or less accustomed to French meddling in these areas. But Napoleon's policies in Germany and in the Mediterranean basin were another matter.

France's intervention in the affairs of Germany was the direct consequence of the Treaty of Lunéville and had been foreseeable since the Rastatt Congress of 1797–1799. German princes had to be compensated for possessions they had lost in the Rhineland and in Italy. As soon as the treaty had been concluded at Lunéville, negotiations were opened in Paris with the princes. These meetings resulted in the distribution of considerable "favors." The principal beneficiary was France's minister of foreign affairs, Talleyrand, who became in 1807 a vice-general elector, and who would thus have cashed in on from 10 to 15 million francs. As in the days of the Reformation, church property was acknowledged as belonging to the state, and it was this property that the French offered as compensation to the lay princes. The archbishop of Mainz, Karl Theodor von Dalberg backed Talleyrand's proposal and persuaded the German prelates to accept.

On June 3, 1802, France and Russia invited the German Diet of Ratisbon to ratify the plan adopted in Paris. A series of long and bitter debates ensued. For a long time Austria had remained firm in her refusal, but she finally gave in on December 26. After Austria had accepted, the Diet had no choice but to bow down. The plan was promulgated in the form of a recess (Recès, the name used for an important order issued by the Diet) on February 25, 1803.

The Recess of 1803 abolished the remaining ecclesiastical estates in the Holy Roman Empire that had not been secularized in 1555 and 1648. There were only three exceptions: the master of the Teutonic Order, the Grand Prior of the Order of Malta, and the seat of the archbishopric of Mayence (Mainz) was transferred to Ratisbon (Regensburg). The first two were permitted to retain their estates. The Recess also did away with forty-five free cities. Only six free cities remained: the three Hanseatic cities of Bremen, Hamburg, and Lübeck and the three commercial centers of Nuremberg, Augsburg, and Frankfurt-am-Main. The states of Prussia, Bavaria, and Baden gained the most from the terms of the Recess. Prussia received the bishoprics of Paderborn, Hildesheim, Erfurt, and a section of Münster. Bavaria was enlarged by the bishopric of Freising and a part of Passau. The duchy of Baden annexed the free cities of Mannheim and Heidelberg as well as portions of the bishoprics of Constance, Speyer, Strasbourg, and Basel. Hanover was given a bishopric of Osnabrück; Austria, the bishoprics of Brixen and Trent and a section of Passau. The duke of Tuscany received the bishopric of Salzburg and the city of Eichstädt. These were the most important territorial changes.

The Recess dealt a severe blow to the Catholic Church in Germany, for it lost 2½ million subjects and 21 million florins in revenue. Eighteen universities were secularized, as well as many convents. The number of electors of the Holy Roman emperor increased from six to ten when the princes of Salzburg-Tuscany, Baden, Württemberg, and Hesse-Cassel were promoted to this title. Since there was only one remaining ecclesiastical elector (Dalberg, transferred from Mayence to Ratisbon) and since three of the new electors (Baden, Württemberg, Hesse-Dassel) were Protestants, the latter commanded a six-to-four majority in the electoral college. There was a chance that the imperial crown would be taken away from the Catholic House of Hapsburg at the next election. The Recess of 1803 rocked the Holy Roman Empire and heralded the beginning of an hereditary empire for Austria in the following year. The state that actually benefitted most from the Recess was France, for she gained all the power that Austria had lost. Austria had been weakened; her preponderance in the Empire replaced by that of France, who gathered the enlarged states of southern Germany— Bavaria, Württemberg, and Baden—into her sphere. Napoleon claimed sovereign power to dispose of German territories. Accordingly, he offered Hanover to Prussia, who refused the offer in order to avoid displeasing England. Dalberg, who had become archbishop of Ratisbon, chancellor of the Holy Roman Empire, and president of the Diet, was responsible for the triumph of French politics in Germany. On April 27, 1803, Emperor Francis II accepted the Recess, but viewed it as a defeat. This decision precipitated the resumption of hostilities between France and England.

RESUMPTION OF WAR

Although Bonaparte's tariff and colonial policies, as well as France's peacetime expansion in Italy and constant intervention in the domestic affairs of Switzerland, Holland, and Germany had elicited England's indignation, these actions alone probably would not have been enough to entail the breaking of the Treaty of Amiens if Napoleon at the same time had not seemed to be threatening England's maritime interests in the Mediterranean. Since the Egyptian campaign and the occupation of Malta, the British government realized that control of the Mediterranean area was essential to protect her interests in the East.

Bonaparte increased the number of missions in the Mediterranean countries. General Brune was sent to Turkey as an ambassador on September 11, 1802. Colonel Sébastiani, whom he had met during his Egyptian campaign, was given a mission in Egypt, an apparent indication that France had no intention of renouncing her influence in this country. Louis Eugène Cavaignac, former member of the Convention, was named consul to Muscat in Arabia, and it appeared that he was also destined to play a role in the great undertaking against British interests in the Levant. On August 7, 1802, a naval division, commanded by Admiral Leyssègue, along with the famous Colonel Hulin—the most famous of the "conquerors of the Bastille"—appeared in the harbor of Algiers. Hulin sent a threatening letter to the dey, whose privateers had captured two French vessels. The dey assured the French of his good faith and saw to it that the captains of the guilty privateers were punished. It was probably because of this action that a French landing was avoided.

It was Malta that became the battleground for France and England. The Maltese question was at least the pretext, if not the cause, for the resumption of war.

Article 10 of the Treaty of Amiens specified that the Maltese archipelago would be returned to the Order of Saint John of Jerusalem and that the takeover would occur "as soon as the exchange of ratifications would have taken place." The order was to be reorganized and would no longer include either French or British *langues,* or sections; it would only be Maltese. British forces were to evacuate the island "in the three months following the exchange of ratifications, or sooner if possible." The independence and neutrality of the Maltese archipelago were to be guaranteed by the six great European powers: France, Great Britain, Austria, Spain, Russia, and Prussia. Maltese ports were to be open to international trade, and the Order of Malta was to make peace with Muslim powers. Article 11 of the treaty seemed the very counterpart of the preceding article. According to its provision, French troops were to leave the ports of the Kingdom of Naples and of the Papal States, which she had occupied in 1800. The evacuation was to be a parallel to the English evacuation of Malta. As it turned out, neither of these two articles, which seemed so essential to the treaty, were executed.

Who was responsible for the refusal to carry out the treaty? Was France at fault for maintaining her garrisons in southern Italy, or did the blame fall on England, who continued to occupy Malta? If Bonaparte bore heavy responsibility for the general problems of political economy and imperialist expansion reviewed above, and if he was completely responsible in the case now in question, which was, we must remember, the *pretext* for the break, then it seems that the blame lay on England, who had done everything possible in Malta to evade compliance with the Treaty of Amiens.

As soon as the treaty had been signed, the British government made it clear that it would not be easily dispossessed. Alexander Ball, the man whose efforts had led to the English occupation of the Maltese archipelago, was named royal commissioner to Malta on June 5, 1802. As soon as he arrived Ball tried to elicit expressions of pro-English sentiment from the Maltese. On June 15, a Maltese National Congress published a *Declaration of Rights* of the people of Malta, a curious blending of the revolutionary ideas brought by the French, and of British constitutional principles. This declaration acknowledged the king of England as "sovereign lord" of the archipelago and denied him "the right to cede the islands to any other power." However, in case he wanted to abandon his sovereignty, the Maltese people proclaimed their right "to elect another sovereign," or to govern themselves "without control." For all practical purposes, this prevented any restitution of Malta to the Knights of Saint John of Jerusalem, whom the majority of the population detested. These knights had reorganized, however, and on September 16, 1802, the Pope selected a new grand master from the candidates whose names had been submitted to him. His choice was a Roman bailiff, Bartolomeo Ruspoli, who was then staying in England and who enjoyed the good graces of the British government. But he refused. He did not believe he could institute order under the conditions imposed on him by the Treaty of Amiens. On February 9, 1803, Pius VII designated a new grand master, Neapolitan Gianbattista Tommasi, who accepted and prepared to go to Malta. But Alexander Ball, the commissioner, raised every imaginable obstacle in his path. At the same time, Ball persecuted the knights who were still in Malta. One was even arrested and then expelled. British troops remained on the island despite the treaty. The British government explained that it would not leave until all the powers had ratified the Treaty of Amiens. Russia, disturbed by French policies in the Near East, and Prussia had not yet submitted their formal approval.

On February 9, 1803, the British minister of foreign affairs (Hawkesbury) demanded "reassuring explanations" from Bonaparte, before going ahead with the execution of Article 10 of the treaty. Annexation of Italian territory and Napoleon's intervention in Switzerland led Lord Hawkesbury to a more hostile attitude. Then on March 16, he demanded English occupation of Malta "for ten years," in compensation for France's aggrandizement on the Continent. The First Consul offered to negotiate, but within the framework of the Treaty of Amiens. He even went as far as to solicit the mediation of the Tsar Alexander I, suggesting that England might keep Malta for one or two years, after which time the island would be handed over to Russia. England asked for an explanation from Napoleon of France's policy on Malta. Alexander accepted to mediate, and exchanges ensued. Napoleon knew that France was not ready for war. Henry Addington (Viscount Sidmouth), English prime minister, said that Bonaparte's proposals were unsatisfactory and withdrew the British ambassador from France, May 12, 1803. Without a declaration of war, the British began to seize French ships. England, having lost confidence in Bonaparte and having decided that from the economic point of view war would bring more advantages than peace, precipitated a crisis. England demanded a ten-year occupation of Malta and French evacuation of Holland. On May 18 England declared war, a war that was to last for eleven years.

Although it has often been debated, the question of responsibility for the breach is very clear. It was England who was incontestably at fault in the Malta affair. If the situation is examined in a broader perspective, it must be conceded that all of Bonaparte's foreign, colonial, and economic policies had been of a provocative and aggressive character since 1801. Bonaparte lacked the prudence that Louis-Philippe, Guizot, Napoleon III, and Delcassé later demonstrated in their dealings with England. Napoleon Bonaparte was the leader of the *Grande Nation* and for seven years he had been successful in most of his undertakings. Could he have envisioned defeat? If the France that had emerged from the Revolution were finally to remain in peace, did not the whole counterrevolution behind England have to be beaten down for once and for all? The English were equally convinced that they had to defeat Bonaparte, who in their eyes personified those features of revolutionary France that many of them abhorred—the principle of equality that allowed no consideration to birth, and which meant that anyone could attain the highest positions; the rationalism that cleared the boards of tradition and experience; and finally, the dictatorship of a general whom this nation of manufacturers and merchants could not view without hatred. Henceforth, between Bonaparte and England, there would be a duel until death—terminated only twelve years later by the fall of Napoleon.

CREATION OF THE FRENCH EMPIRE

Peace had led to the establishment of the Consulate for life; war was to provoke the creation of the French Empire. Since England had taken the initiative in hostilities, it was easy for Bonaparte to accuse the prime minister of Albion of perfidy and treason. War justified, furthermore, reenforcement of the dictatorship. A renewal of action by the Royalists accompanied the renewal of war. Networks, organized in the interior of France, informed foreign powers and *émigrés* of French plans. Bonaparte succeeded in unmasking the English agent, Francis Drake, who operated a central clearing office for all Royalist bulletins of information. The Comte d'Antraigues served as an intermediary for Drake. After the recall of Drake, d'Antraigues arranged to have his bulletins from France arrive in England from Russia. The most interesting of these were signed by "The Friend of Paris." It has been suggested that Pierre Daru, general secretary of the French ministry of war was "the friend," but there has been no substantiation of this identification. The point to be made here is that the "underground" would shortly manifest itself in France in a concrete manner.

Cadoudal and Hyde de Neuville, Royalists who had escaped the Consular police in 1801, returned to France. Their objective was not another uprising such as the Vendée in 1793, of which Cadoudal had been a leader, but rather the assassination of Bonaparte. The two fugitives and their colleagues were convinced that the only way to effect a lasting change of regime was to strike at the head.

They were joined by General Pichegru, who, after the *coup d'état* of 18 Fructidor, had been deported to Guiana, had escaped, became an exile in England, and returned to France shortly after Cadoudal and de Neuville. The conspirators included General Moreau, former friend of Pichegru who had already had contacts with Royalists during the campaign of 1796. Moreau considered himself wronged by Napoleon because he had not received the material recognition that he felt was due him for his great victory at Hohenlinden, December 3, 1800. French police quickly learned of the conspiracy. In January 1804 minor figures in the plot were arrested, and they revealed the identity of their leaders. Moreau was imprisoned in the Temple on February 15; Pichegru captured thirteen days later; and Cadoudal arrested in Paris on March 9 after a veritable manhunt in the Latin Quarter where he had taken refuge. The last accomplices were imprisoned by the end of March. Their interrogation revealed that they anticipated the arrival of a prince of the House of Bourbon in France. Bonaparte became convinced that this must be the son of the last Condé, the Duke of Enghien, who lived in Baden at Ettenheim, several kilometers from the French border. Other information received by the police and the constabulary at this same time seemed to confirm these suspicions. Without taking time to verify the facts, for he wished to strike quickly and definitively in order to terrorize the Royalists, Bonaparte had the duke of Enghien kidnapped in neutral territory and brought immediately to Vincennes as a prisoner. There, in one night he was judged by a court martial presided over by General Hulin, condemned to death, and executed in the moat of the fortress, on March 21, at 2 A.M. It was a veritable assassination. "Worse than a crime, it was a mistake," someone said.

The execution achieved for the time being its objective and struck terror into the Royalist party. Pichegru committed suicide in prison on April 16. Had he been killed by the police to prevent him from speaking or had he really killed himself? This mystery has not yet been solved. Cadoudal and his accomplices were put on trial on May 28 before a special court with no jury. Moreau was given the lenient penalty of two years in prison. Bonaparte, furious, had wanted to have him shot, but could one shoot the victor of Hohenlinden? Under pressure from Moreau's friends, Bonaparte commuted the sentence to perpetual exile. Moreau left for the United States and only returned to Europe in 1813 to take up arms against Napoleon. He died at the battle of Dresden, killed by a French bullet. Cadoudal and several of his accomplices were condemned to death. Others, notably Polignac, were acquitted, but kept in prison. They were not freed until the Restoration in 1814.

The violent repression of this plot consolidated the passive resistance of the old aristocracy and a part of the bourgeoisie, but it also served as a pretext for the police to act with new vigor. Its chief, the former Terrorist Joseph Fouché saw his influence increasing. To establish it firmly, he began to flatter the master with the suggestion that the best way to discourage plots in the future was to transform the Consulate for Life into an hereditary empire: the principle of inheritance would avert assassination since it would be powerless to bring about a change in the form of government.

The Senate, inspired by Fouché, sent a message to Bonaparte incorporating essentially the same line of reasoning. But only the question of heredity was considered. Bonaparte desired more. He invited the Senate "to make known its entire thought." The Tribunate, however, entirely submissive to the First Consul expressed the wish that "Bonaparte be proclaimed hereditary emperor of the French" (May 3, 1804). The very next day the Senate joined the Tribunate, and the Private Council was requested to make the necessary modification of the Constitution. The Council deliberated from May 16 to May 18. These modifications formed the *senatus consultum* of 28 Floreal Year XII (May 18, 1804). They were submitted for popular ratification. The French people were called upon to reply to the following question: "Do the people want inheritance of the imperial dignity in direct, natural, legitimate or adoptive descent by Napoleon Bonaparte and in the direct descent of Joseph Bonaparte and of Louis Bonaparte? . . ."

The plebiscite was held under the same conditions as those of the years VIII and X (1799 and 1801). There were about the same number of "yeas" as in 1801 (3,572,328 as against 3,568,885), but there were only 2569 "nays" as compared with 8374 in 1801. Opponents, recognizing the futility of their gesture of voting "no" and fearing the all-powerful police, took refuge in a prudent abstention.

The organization of the government underwent few changes. "The government," declared the amended constitution, "is entrusted to an hereditary emperor." If the emperor had no male child, he could designate as his successor an adopted child; in default of this, the imperial dignity was to devolve on Joseph or on Louis, brothers of Napoleon. A regency was provided for in case of the absence of the emperor. The emperor was required to take an oath indicating that he pledged to respect "equality of rights, political and civil liberty, the irrevocability of the sales of nationalized property." He was to enjoy a civil list similar to that granted to Louis XVI in the Constitution of 1791: 25 million francs. In general, the emperor's powers were greater than those of the First Consul, powers of the assemblies were again reduced, and the influence of the Council of State weakened.

Napoleon I quickly embarked on a plan for establishing institutions reminiscent of the Old Regime. First of all, he wanted to be consecrated by the Pope himself, thereby overshadowing the Bourbons while simultaneously relating the new monarchy to the Carolingian empire. Pius VII hesitated for a long time. He was concerned about the tenuous Concordat, but he finally consented. The ceremony took place with great pomp in the Cathedral of Notre Dame in Paris, on December 2, 1804. The grandiose painting by Jacques Louis David portrays well the importance of the occasion. Following a precedent set by Charlemagne, Emperor Napoleon took the crown from the Pope's hands and placed it on his own head. Royalists were indignant. Old republican soldiers, along with General Delmas, thought, "Fine words! *(Belle capucinade!)* The only thing lacking is the hundred thousand men who gave their lives so that hereditary power would

Napoleon Crowning Himself, sketch by Jacques Louis David. Compare David's sketch of Napoleon with the less dictatorial stance in the finished painting on page 275. (Caisse Nationale des Monuments Historiques. Archives Photographiques)

be abolished." Patriots in other countries were abashed. Beethoven withdrew the dedication for the *Heroic Symphony*, which he had composed in Bonaparte's honor.

Henceforth, the Roman eagle surmounted the tricolor and appeared in the armorial bearings of the new dynasty, along with golden bees. The

Legion of Honor became more like previous knightly orders. The emblem created on July 11, 1804, followed the same form and the ribbon was the same color (blue) as the former order of Saint-Louis. Noble titles were revived for members of Napoleon's family. In 1808, an hereditary imperial nobility was created, including great feudatories, princes, dukes, counts, and barons. The nobles were granted the privilege of creating the right of primogeniture in favor of their oldest son; but, in contrast to the former nobility, they were allowed no judicial or fiscal privileges. As powerful as Napoleon was, there were limits that not even he could transcend. He was obliged to honor the most important of the conquests of 1789. Napoleon hoped to entice the old royal nobility to join with the new, but the recently returned *émigrés* merely jeered at these men of recent peasant origin who "disguised themselves as great lords" while retaining the language and manners of their youth.

Contrary to the emperor's expectations, royalist opposition had not died. At the same time, republican opposition made itself more clearly felt. The emperor perfected his propaganda machinery, that new effective weapon that he had borrowed from the Revolution. He turned to periodicals—the four Parisian newspapers and the official departmental journal—to songs, to imagery, to sculpture, to painting, to speeches, to books of all kinds, to the theater to advance his image and that of his regime. But opposition still persisted despite the new propaganda measures. The police and constabulary tracked down enemies of the regime and locked them up in state prisons or even in insane asylums, often without the benefit of a trial. Those who were simply suspect—still another reminder of 1793—were forced to reside in strongholds, were put under police surveillance, or were compelled to deliver one or two of their sons as hostages to the state, which then placed the boys in a lycée, a military school or in a regiment.

The whole system of authoritarianism coupled with police surveillance formed the basis of Napoleon's dictatorship, which was as indispensable to carrying on the war in 1804 as it had been ten years earlier. When the war began, France was confronted only by England. Soon France would be opposed by a European coalition as in 1794. What potential, then, did France and Europe hold around 1805?

5

FRANCE AND EUROPE IN 1804

When France and England resumed war, Europe was divided into three camps: Great Britain, which had initiated the renewal of hostilities; the neutral powers, that is, all of central and northern Europe as well as a portion of Mediterranean Europe; and France and her satellites. Each of these groups had characteristics that could have permitted a certain degree of prediction as to the course of subsequent events.

ENGLAND

As astonishing as it might appear, Great Britain had emerged from eight years of war stronger than when she had entered it. In 1801 pressure from a battle-weary public had forced the British government to negotiate a peace. Although France had certainly been acknowledged as victor, Britain's position was in no way viewed as a defeat. British public opinion was more or less clearly aware of the country's strength and was not disposed to allow France a monopoly in exploiting the advantages of peace. It refused to admit that peace, for Great Britain, might be more unfavorable than war—which, as it turned out, was the correct appraisal of the times. In economic, social, and political matters, Great Britain was much better prepared to face a long war in 1803 than she had been in 1793.

THE ECONOMY—THE INDUSTRIAL REVOLUTION   England's Industrial Revolution, which had begun around 1760, had received impetus from war production and had developed further than continental Europe's— which had not started until nearly twenty years later. The margin of advance that the British Isles held over the Continent, therefore, was greater in 1804 than it had been in 1794. Industry began to locate in about ten clearly discernible regions. The principal area included London and its suburbs. London, an immense agglomeration, with its nearly 860,000 inhabitants, was then the most heavily populated city in the world. The principal industry in the London area was silk. From 10,000 to 15,000 machines employing nearly 30,000 workers produced mainly for the domestic market.

The Norwich region, to the northeast of London, had traditionally been a center for the production of carded wool. It was one of the few English regions that had made no progress since the start of the Industrial Revolution. Production from the 10,000 textile machines in the region had fallen from £ 1,200,000 in 1770 to 800,000 in 1805. The same situation existed in the woolens factories of the West Country, that is, the area around Gloucester, Bristol, and Plymouth, to the west of London. But the woolen industry in this region had been supplanted by sugar refining (in Bristol) and by tin works and iron works (in Bristol and in Cornwall).

The Newcastle region on the North Sea had already been ranked among the great producers of coal and the related by-products of chemicals and glass. The Birmingham region in the Midlands also became a great coal and metal producer, claiming forty-two blast furnaces and twenty-five factories in 1806. The city of Birmingham, with a population of 74,000, ranked fourth among English cities, following London, Liverpool, and Manchester. It was the great center for arms production and had shown considerable development since 1793.

The cotton industry was centered in Lancashire, particularly in the two great English cities of Liverpool and Manchester. In 1811 the Lancashire area boasted 3,400,000 of Great Britain's 4,600,000 spindles. Manchester was the principal center for cotton spinning in all of England.

The pottery district extended around Derby, Nottingham, and Leicester, the area to the northeast of Birmingham. The district was not only the headquarters for earthenware and porcelain fabrication, but for various other industries as well—notably silk and lace manufacturing.

Like the regions of Newcastle and Birmingham, southern Wales was another coal area (often called the black country) and the metallurgy industry flourished there. Cast-iron production rose from 10,000 tons in 1788 to 76,000 in 1806. There were thirty-six active blast furnaces.

In Scotland industry was concentrated around Glasgow. At the outset of the Industrial Revolution Glasgow already was important for the spinning and weaving of linen and cotton, and for a metallurgy industry in the process of expansion. In 1805 it would have been difficult to oppose a "black England" to a "green England," as became possible in later years. The industrial centers could still be represented by just a few small dots on the map of the British Isles, but at the time they overshadowed those of any country on the Continent both in numbers and in importance.

These industries had not undergone equal development. Those which held first place had been renovated by the Industrial Revolution, that is, by the introduction of steam engines and new machinery and, in metallurgy, by blast furnaces. Some industries had been stimulated by the war, while others had retained their traditional form.

The cotton industry in England had been the one most affected by the Industrial Revolution. The practice of spinning and weaving cotton in the home had all but disappeared by 1805. These operations were transferred to large factories where there was a heavy concentration of workers, both male and female. One of these factories had nearly 100,000 spindles and employed 1500 workers, but this was an exception. On the average, the mills would draw together only 200 to 300 workers.

The introduction of the blast furnace and the use of coal instead of wood charcoal had caused an upheaval in heavy metallurgy. In 1806 Great Britain had 222 blast furnaces, owned by 122 companies producing an average of 250,000 tons per year. This was 75 percent more than France for the same period.

Development in the area of ship construction was the result of the war rather than of the Industrial Revolution. Essentially, the industry was based on the utilization of wood. An enormous quantity of lumber was needed since both war and merchantships were constructed exclusively of wood. British shipyards had built 100,000 tons of warships and merchant vessels between the years 1803 and 1805, which meant an annual demand for 224,000 cubic meters (approximately 340,000 cubic yards) of wood. Great Britain was nearly deforested at the beginning of the nineteenth century and could no longer meet her own requirements. Instead, she purchased lumber from the Baltic countries. This explains that region's importance both to the British economy and to her national defense. It also explains England's reactions when the League of Armed Neutrality was formed in 1801, when Tsar Paul I was assassinated, and when Copenhagen was bombed. British concern about events in the Baltic region was destined to increase as the tonnage of annual construction rose. In 1805, 450,000 cubic meters of wood were consumed in new ship construction and maintenance and repair of ships already in service. England certainly could have purchased the necessary wood elsewhere, especially in the United States and Canada. These regions were even more richly forested than Scandinavia, but their exploitation still remained to be organized: trees had to be selected, woodcutters chosen, arrangements made for stockpiling and shipping. The process could not be improvised. In addition, shipyards could hardly utilize green wood. In order to be really useful, the wood had to undergo a long period of immersion. Great Britain did have important wood reserves, so the consequences of the break in communications with the Baltic were not actually felt for several years. The naval construction industry itself remained completely at the artisan level and out of the stream of the Industrial Revolution.

The same situation characterized the ceramics industry. Although steam engines had begun to come into use, wool and flax spinning, and even their weaving, as well as the minor metallurgy industry, such as the manufacturing of nails and pots and pans, was still artisan.

Taken as a whole, industry required a large segment of the British population. Undoubtedly, 1805 was the year in which the number of Britishers employed in industry, commerce, and various public services surpassed the agricultural population; it was the year in which Great Britain became a modern nation. The figures for 1811 are as follows: 35 percent of the population was employed in agriculture, 45 percent in commerce and industry, and 20 percent in various other functions. The textile industry brought together the largest number of workers—790,000, of which 350,000 were engaged in the cotton industry and 200,000 in wool. Metallurgy as yet employed only 300,000 workers; ceramics and glassmaking, only 40,000. British industrial and agricultural revenues were then nearly equal, in the area of £ 215 million.

To a great extent, the advancement in British industry was linked to foreign trade, since a large part of the raw materials came from abroad and since a large proportion of the manufactured products were destined for export. The textile industry depended entirely on imports for its silk and cotton. Half of the cotton (27,000 pounds) came from the United States; the remaining sources were the Antilles, Brazil (through Portugal), and India (for a minor amount of 1,500 pounds). Half of the silk came from Europe and half from Asia. Even some of the wool worked in England was imported, mainly from Spain and from Portugal (7,000 pounds). Of the products that were manufactured in England, half of the woolen and cotton cloth, one fourth of the linen, hemp, and silk products, half of the metal products, and one fifth of the ceramics and glassware were exported. Thus, a large percentage of British industry was working for the export trade, which around 1805 was divided into three large groups, each of which absorbed nearly a third of Britain's exports: continental Europe (33 percent), the United States (27 percent), and the rest of the world—that is, essentially the British colonies—40 percent.

By 1805, therefore, it seemed apparent that an eventual closing of European markets to British trade would not deprive her industry of essential raw materials, but that it would create a crisis of surplus production by cutting off one third of her export market. Such a blow would be serious but not mortal. The gravity of the situation could be alleviated by the substitution of another export market for Europe—Portuguese and Spanish America, for example, which had theoretically been closed to British products, although they had been entering the countries as contraband for a long while. If free trade with these countries were granted, the volume of British exports would be subject to a considerable increase. On the other hand, if a substitute market were not found, and if the United States market were to close at the same time as the European market, then Great Britain, placed in the impossible position of having to sell two thirds of her usual exports elsewhere, might have to run an extremely serious and perhaps fatal risk.

AGRICULTURAL PROBLEMS   Even though Great Britain had been industrializing since 1760, she still remained an agricultural country. However, the role of agriculture in the British economy was in the process of complete transformation. Because of the increase in population, which had doubled during the eighteenth century, and because of the gradual substitution of animal husbandry for cereal crops, cereal exports, which had still been made at the end of the eighteenth century, stopped completely around 1805. Even in an average year, agricultural production was not quite sufficient to support Great Britain, and she was forced to import foodstuffs. In a bad harvest year the British population was absolutely dependent on imports. In 1803, for example, Great Britain imported approximately 7,500,000 bushels of cereals, including more than 2,800,000 bushels of wheat. Due to insufficient imports, prices skyrocketed. A "quarter" of wheat (8.3 bushels) which had been worth 47 shillings in 1798 had risen to 148 shillings 6 pence in 1801, a period of scarcity that had been aggravated by the League of Armed Neutrality's prohibition on wheat exports from the Baltic countries. Most of Great Britain's grain was imported from the Baltic—three fifths. Holland and Ireland supplied three tenths, and the United States, one tenth. Of the Baltic countries, Prussia furnished the greatest amount of grain, especially Polish wheat exported from Danzig. If the closing of European markets were to coincide with a poor harvest, Great Britain would be gripped by a food shortage and by a catastrophic rise in prices. If this rise were to take place during a period of industrial unemployment, the workers would be thrown into a miserable situation. Another unknown factor at the time was whether American wheat production could permit enough exportation to replace the European wheat exports. In the event of war, therefore, British agriculture represented a very vulnerable point.

THE FINANCIAL SYSTEM   France, however, had persuaded herself that Britain's financial system was the most vulnerable element in her economy. In England the credit system had been more greatly developed than in any other European country. But Frenchmen, remembering their own country's twofold experience with Law's system and the assignats, found it difficult to imagine that English credit could stand up during a long war. Undoubtedly, the British credit organization harbored seeds of inflation and a possible depreciation of currency, but it rested on a solid structure that formed a kind of three-tiered pyramid.

Local banks were at the base of the pyramid. Great Britain had 527 in 1804, whereas France could claim only a few. The number of British local banks was constantly increasing, surpassing 800 in 1809. At that time many towns whose population was under 10,000 had a bank. This situation was inconceivable in France, where there were constant complaints about the lack of banks and the consequent necessity of having to resort to usurers. These local banks received deposits, effected payments and collected debts for their customers, issued bank notes, and, above all, discounted commercial notes. Since the Bank of England limited its operations to London and the surrounding area, the local banks played a prime role in the British economy.

The step between the local banks and the Bank of England was occupied by the private banks of London, which were also on the increase. In 1797 they had numbered sixty nine; in 1804 there were seventy nine. They had various and often specialized functions. The Hoare Bank, for example, specialized in mortgage loans to the aristocracy. These private banks had state funds (exchequer bills) on deposit and had accounts with the Bank of England.

The Bank of England, already over a hundred years old, was a very powerful stock company, which to a certain extent played the role of a state bank. It received on deposit the liquid funds of the Treasury; it assured the management of the national debt; it made short-term loans to the state by purchasing exchequer bills; and it gave advances to subscribers to state loans. It issued bank notes, but they were circulated only in the London area (just as the bank notes of the Bank of France were acceptable only in Paris). This explains why the local banks issued money. The Bank of England also handled business affairs with private citizens for whom it performed the same services as the other banks.

From the time when the Bank of England was created, its bank notes had been easily convertible into either gold or silver, but a financial crisis occurred in 1797. A deficit in the balance of payments and the reestablishment of the circulation of metal money in France led to the flight of British gold. At the same time, the government's short-term debt to the bank increased to a dangerous level, while individuals, fearing a French invasion, held their cash tightly. The gold balance fell from £6 million in 1795 to £1 million on February 28, 1797. Already on February 26 an Order-in-Council had suspended the free convertibility of bank notes. This decision allowed the bank quickly to reestablish its reserves and undoubtedly prevented the bank's failure. But an act of November 30, 1797 (the Restriction Act), stipulated that free convertibility would only be restored one month after a peace treaty was signed. After the Treaty of Amiens was concluded, however, the principle of nonconvertibility was maintained, and as soon as war was resumed a new law specified that free convertibility would not be restored until six months after the conclusion of peace. The British government was thus assured of always having the means to finance the war, short, of course, of furthering inflation.

A moderate inflation, in fact, did develop. The total amount of bank notes in circulation went from £12 million in 1790 to £15 million in 1800 and reached £17.5 million in 1804. Gold disappeared and was replaced by paper, tokens, and Spanish silver dollars. Before 1797 the smallest denomination bank note was £5 (125 germinal francs), but the Bank of England then began to issue £1 and £2 bills. It must be remembered that the smallest denomination issued by the Bank of France during the same period was 500 francs, or £20. The danger of inflation had existed prior to 1808, but it was not a very serious threat. It was reflected in the general price index, however, which rose from 100 in 1790 to 150 in 1807.

The pound sterling was undoubtedly fragile because of the threat of inflation and the deficit in the balance of payments, which, after 1805, was worsened by subsidies granted to England's powerful allies. But the fragility was considerably less than many Frenchmen, and especially Napoleon, imagined. In fact, the strong elements in the British financial system outnumbered the indications of weaknesses, and when all was considered, Great Britain's financial organization was one of the best weapons it had at its disposal.

COMMERCIAL POWER The stability of the pound sterling, as just noted, was closely linked to the balance of payments, that is, to British trade. France was correct in thinking that she would have to ruin Great Britain's trade in order to defeat her. It is to be recalled that one third of this trade was carried on with Europe, one third with North America, and one third with the rest of the world. A closer examination reveals that this trade was quite diversified.

Britain's peacetime commerce with France was important and constituted 6 to 7 percent of her total trade. It had taken on new life after 1801,
but it collapsed as soon as the war began. There was never a complete interruption of commerce, however. Indirect trade by means of neutral inter-
mediaries continued, and smuggling operations expanded, both from the
Channel Islands and across land frontiers. On May 18, 1803, the Privy Council decided to grant licenses to British traders who wished to deal with
France under a neutral flag. These licenses authorized the purchase of wines
and spirits in France. Payments were made by bills of exchange on Amsterdam. The French government closed its eyes to this traffic. French exports into Great Britain were more numerous in 1805 than in 1802, but
Napoleon's government very rapidly took steps to close France to British
products.

England set about developing her trade with Holland as a substitute
market. Even though their country was officially at war with Great Britain,
the Dutch maintained trade relations with the English as long as possible.
Sir Francis Baring wrote in July 1805:

> Anyone who has the latest information about the situation of Holland
> must realize that we can expect favors and even interest from the Dutch,
> as well as every action favorable to us that they dare adopt in their state
> of dependence. . . . In a country where so many people depend on trade
> for their livelihood, and where nature is so stingy with its other re-
> sources, a French general might watch them starve to death, but as long
> as the government is Dutch, it will find a way to deceive its masters and
> to protect trade.

In 1802 trade with Holland reached 10 percent of Great Britain's total trade.
As the port of Amsterdam gradually began to close, British trade shifted to
the German ports of Emden and Hamburg.

British exports into Germany, which had already been considerable in
peacetime, continued on the upswing for as long as Germany remained
free of complete French occupation. In 1802 exports to Germany represented 22 percent of Britain's total exports. The figure rose to 26 percent
in 1803 and reach 32 percent in 1805. The English utilized the port of Tön-
ningen in Schleswig, then under Denmark, instead of Hamburg, which had
been blockaded by the French occupation of Hanover. Germany thus
played an important role in England's European commerce.

Trade with the Baltic countries ranked next. Russia, Sweden, and
Prussia absorbed from 6 to 7 percent of Britain's exports and accounted for
8 to 9 percent of her imports, especially wood, hemp, and cereals.

Britain's trade with southern Europe was less important. Spain sold
mainly wool to England. This trade declined as soon as the war resumed,
but it was taken up by Portugal. Lisbon became the great center for English

trade on the Iberian peninsula. Anglo-Italian trade was minor. Scarcely 1.5 percent of Britain's exports found their way to Italy, and these mainly to Venice and Trieste. The Ottoman Empire had only an insignificant role in Great Britain's foreign trade.

In short, it was necessary for France to close off Holland, Germany, the Baltic regions and Portugal in order to paralyze Britain's trade with the European continent.

The other continents remained open. The position of the United States in regard to British trade was of prime importance and has often been underestimated. Shipments to the United States accounted for 13 percent of England's total exports in 1802; the figure rose to 21 percent in 1805. The main export items were cloth and articles made of iron and cast iron. The United States, on the other hand, sold very little to Great Britain, supplying only 6.4 percent of England's total imports in 1803–1804. Half of these sales consisted of cotton; but later lumber was included which, as we have seen, had a potential for further development in the event that the Baltic was closed to the English.

In the remainder of the world, Britain's colonies and trading companies were important factors—the British Antilles led the list, and then Asia, whose trade was monopolized by the British East India Company. The latter exported cotton and woolen cloth and iron and cast iron articles to the Indies and to China. It imported tea, printed cotton, raw silk, cotton, spices, and other products in smaller quantities from these areas. Trade with Africa consisted mainly of slave traffic. This traffic had declined and had finally been prohibited in 1807, as the result of campaigns by William Wilberforce, others and the Society of Friends of the Blacks.

Trade was also carried on with Latin America and, until 1810, consisted mainly of traffic in contraband and goods in transit through Spain and Portugal. Specific details on this trade are not available, but it is known that the trade was important. The Spanish and Portuguese territories in America had been economic dependencies of Great Britain since the beginning of the nineteenth century, and for the prior two centuries one of the essential goals of English politics had been to open completely these countries to its trade. Britain's exports to the areas included cotton goods, canvas, hardware, tools, ceramics, glass, tallow soap, and, as along as it was possible, slaves. She imported dye products, cocoa, cattle and mules, cotton, hides, tallow, and precious metals. Smuggling operations, which had been organized for two centuries, were centered in Jamaica, the Bahamas, and Trinidad. But after 1804, Great Britain was ready to develop direct trade with Latin America, as soon as its ports were opened to her.

British foreign trade was, therefore, extremely powerful in 1804. It had made steady progress since 1789. If an index is assigned to English exports, with the figure 100 representing exports in 1806, the following pattern may be observed: the figure increased from 72 in 1797 to 104 in 1800, climbed to 113 in 1802, fell back to slightly below 100 in 1803, inched slowly back up to 100 in 1806, and returned to 113 in 1809. What made Britain's commerce so powerful was the fact that she had many possible substitute markets. If Europe were to be closed, Great Britain could orient herself toward North America or Latin America or even toward both countries at the same time. If Napoleon sought to strike Britain down, he would not only have to conquer Europe, but would also have to annex the Americas—a gigantic, if not impossible task.

POLITICAL EVOLUTION   In 1804 Great Britain's position was strengthened not only by its expanding economy, but also by the disappearance of all serious domestic political opposition. In 1793 Great Britain had entered into war despite opposition from clubs and correspondence societies sympathetic to the Revolution and despite the 80,000 Jacobins who, according to Burke, resided in her territory. One by one, the correspondence societies had shut down, and their leaders had been condemned and sent as convicts to Botany Bay, Australia. An Association for the Preservation of Liberty and Property Against the Republicans and Equalitarians had been founded by John Reeves and John Bowles. It had gathered together all the "honest people," the "friends of order," and its propaganda soon surpassed that of the partisans of the Revolution. The mutiny of the squadrons on the English Channel and on the North Sea in the spring of 1797 could have been serious if it had received support within Great Britain. Lacking this, it failed miserably.

Ireland, perpetually in revolt against England, presented a more serious threat to the British government since she could have provided an excellent landing base for French troops. The Irish did revolt in the spring of 1798, but at a time when it was impossible for France to intervene. The revolt was crushed with bloodshed, and Great Britain imposed an Act of Union on Ireland. Despite relentless opposition, the Dublin Parliament, thanks to bribery, approved the act in the spring of 1800 by a vote of 158 to 115. By its terms the Irish Parliament was abolished. Since the Irish deputies to the London Parliament were in the minority, Irish Catholics lost what few rights they had had, and peasants gave up all hope of witnessing a change in the oppressive "colonial" regime under which they lived. The question of Ireland was open to the future, but the immediate danger had disappeared.

Thus, it appeared that around 1804 strength was clearly on the side of Great Britain, and one might well wonder if Addington's policy of peace was really justified. England's image of France, as reported by numerous English tourists, was sometimes favorable and sometimes not. If a number of tourists came back thoroughly enchanted with their visit, others returned convinced that Bonaparte was a dangerous upstart, a dictator with imperialistic aims. Fox, a bitter foe of Pitt and one of the great Whig leaders, was a defender of the French Revolution. Many of his influential friends and supporters abandoned him on this issue and regarded war with France as "just and necessary." This was the opinion of Charles Gray, considered to be Fox's successor. As for the Tories, they had always considered peace to be "foolish and dangerous."

Nevertheless, Addington remained popular because he had effected a considerable reduction in taxes. He had abolished the income tax instituted by Pitt and had partially replaced the revenue derived from it by increasing customs duties, stamp taxes, and indirect excise taxes. He had broadened Parliament's control over finances, and from this he gradually arrived at the idea of an annual budget. He had checked expenditures by reducing the regular army to 95,000 men (in addition to 48,000 militia men, 24,000 reserve soldiers, and 18,000 garrisons in Ireland) and the crews of the fleet to 70,000 men instead of 130,000.

Addington's popularity reached its zenith during the elections of 1802. But soon afterward, French expansion gave strength to the opposition. Addington was vehemently attacked by Pitt, William Grenville, and Henry Dundas. Under fire from these men, he had to change his stand and resolve himself to entering war against France. He drew nearer to war in the spring of 1803 at a time when conditions were unfavorable, for the armed forces had just undergone a reduction. The regular army, composed mainly of German mercenaries and scattered throughout Great Britain, Ireland, and the British colonies, was incapable of sending an expeditionary force to the Continent and even of providing adequate defense for England should the French succeed in landing there. The situation was less serious in regard to the navy, for although many ships had been disarmed, at least they still existed and could rapidly be put back into service, thanks to the importance of the maritime population in England.

Addington, however, wanted to carry on a low-cost war. To his way of thinking, the war was to be wholly naval and defensive. With the Continent abandoned to Napoleon, the British fleet would prevent a French landing. If all attempts to land failed, this would mean that Great Britain was the victor.

The members of Parliament were not confident of Addington's ability to lead the war efforts. To add to his troubles, Addington found at the very outset that the war was more costly than he had calculated. He had to reinstate the income tax. It is true that although the assessment rate was half the former rate, this tax yielded £4.5 million (as opposed to £6 million in Pitt's day) in consequence of improved tax-collection methods. But the restitution of the tax killed Addington's popularity. He lost it completely when Nelson made it known that his squadron had been forced to leave Portsmouth with only its minimum crew. Necessary reform of the army, putting the treasury in charge of furnishing uniforms (in the colonels' names), and calling in English volunteers to complement the regular troops resulted in increased expense, and resentment rose against Addington. Even though he could have mustered twenty-one majority votes, he resigned in April 1804.

On May 7, 1804, Pitt organized the new ministry; the war to the finish against France was to resume. Pitt directed the war effort relentlessly until his death in 1806.

THE NEUTRAL POWERS

No continental power that opposed the French Empire and her satellites (the former sister republics) could be compared to Great Britain in the area of industrial revolution. In the lands outside the French sphere there were only a few industrial centers, separated by great distances: in Germany, the regions of Westphalia, Saxony, Silesia, and Bohemia; in Russia, the Ural region. The main industries were metallurgy and cotton. The wool and linen industries, in the main, were still carried on in the home. Nor did continental Europe have a financial structure that resembled Great Britain's organization. Private banks were rather well developed in Germany, especially in Frankfurt, Nuremberg, and Augsburg, but state finances everywhere were largely dependent on tax revenues. Each state, in fact, had its own problems, and the German states faced Napoleon's imperialism separately.

THE GERMAN STATES   The Recess of 1803, which had reduced the number of German states from 350 to less than 200, created a major problem in Germany. Certain people began to think that German unity might not be a utopia after all. But above all, the extensive redistribution of land had stirred the ambitions of the principal powers that hoped for self-aggrandizement to the detriment of the small states still in existence. British and French politics succeeded in taking advantage of these appetites, especially those of the main German states that had been enlarged by the Recess— Austria, Prussia, and Bavaria.

As soon as peace had been restored, the Emperor Francis II took steps to strengthen the Austrian state. As had been the case in England, danger from subversion seemed to have been eliminated by the severe repression of Jacobin conspiracies in Austria and in Hungary in 1794. It was also of prime importance to reorganize Austria's administrative system and to improve her financial system so that, if necessary, she would be able to resume war with France under the most favorable conditions. Francis II instituted a sort of ministerial council (the *conferenz ministerium*) that would henceforth coordinate the various administrative branches. Rules regarding the subordination of local administration to central administration were clarified. On the financial side, taxes were raised and voluntary contributions were solicited from provinces, corporations, and individuals. Paper money was still in use, however, and in an ever-increasing volume. Since metal reserves were insufficient, the Austrian money situation was precarious, thus making it impossible to enter a war without English subsidies and making it difficult to endure a prolonged war.

The most important action by Francis II to strengthen his state was one destined to increase Austria's influence in Germany. On August 11, 1804, Austria was proclaimed an hereditary empire. Francis II of Germany had decided on this action, by which he became Francis I of Austria, because changes in the German electoral body appeared to have removed all chances for his son someday to be elected Germanic emperor. If the new Austrian Empire were founded on heredity, it would be assured of rule by Hapsburg descendants, who might simultaneously reign over the German Empire as well. Francis II felt that as hereditary emperor he would be on equal rank with Napoleon I and with the Tsar Alexander I, both hereditary emperors, rather than perhaps be treated condescendingly because of having been elected. If he had taken the title of emperor of Hungary, however, the charter of the Holy Roman Empire would not have been affected since this country was not included. By proclaiming himself emperor of Austria, a province of the Holy Roman Empire, he set a precedent for nonnegotiated changes in the Holy Roman Empire's charter. His example was promptly emulated by the electors of Bavaria, Württemberg, and Saxony, who proclaimed themselves kings.

In the face of these important changes, Prussia prudently waited. When war resumed between France and England in the spring of 1804, Napoleon ignored Germany's neutrality, arranged for General Mortier's troops to occupy Hanover (a personal possession of the king of England), and then offered it to the king of Prussia. In order to avoid a tangle with either England or Russia, the latter refused to accept Hanover and made an all-out effort to maintain the policy of neutrality that he had held since his accession in 1797. He hoped to gain more through this policy than through war and some day to obtain for himself, or at least for his heir, the title of emperor of Germany. In order to avoid an incident with Napoleon, he even forbade the court to go into mourning after the execution of the duke of Enghien.

Bavaria was the German state that profited most from the Recess of 1803. The elector, Max-Joseph, was one of the first European sovereigns to recognize Napoleon as an emperor. He himself was furthermore almost more French than German. Duke de Deux Ponts before 1799, he had been a colonel in the Royal-Alsace regiment under Louis XVI. Because of this association, his name had even appeared on the list of the *émigrés*, although Bonaparte had deleted it at the beginning of the Consulate. From the time he succeeded to the throne of Bavaria in February 1799, Max-Joseph had affirmed his good will toward France. "I was brought up in France and I beg you to regard me as French," he declared to the ambassador of the Directory. "Each time I heard that the armies of the Republic had been successful, I felt, to my delight, that I was French." His prime minister, Maximilian von Montgelas, a Savoyard by origin and a friend of the Enlightenment, passed for a man of the Revolution in Germany during the entire Empire period. For a long time, in fact, Max-Joseph and Montgelas had favored an "enlightened" and pro-French party in Bavaria, despite the scheming of the electress, sister to the empress of Russia.

And so in 1804 Germany was oscillating between these three powers: an Austria anxious to safeguard her influence and ready to resume war against France if the opportunity were to present itself; a Prussia firmly neutral despite the many advances and magnificent promises made by England, France, and Russia; and, finally, a Bavaria whose ruler considered himself ruler of the pro-French in the Germanies.

The result was a jockeying for power among the princes. The German people as a whole passively witnessed the political changes and reversals of alliances. For about ten years, however, the populace had been hearing echoes of the great social upheavals taking place in the countries of the west, especially on the left bank of the Rhine. The people still had a vague and confused hope that one day the fate of peasants and workers would improve, that the burden of tithes, duty service, and seignorial privileges would be lightened, if not removed. No matter who their allies were, the German masses were ready to follow those who would accomplish these great reforms.

SCANDINAVIA   Scandinavia in this period comprised two states —Denmark and Sweden. Danish monarchy dominated not only Denmark but also Norway, Iceland, the Faroe Islands, and Greenland. The king of Denmark was duke of Schleswig and Holstein as well, but these two duchies were principalities in the Holy Roman Empire. Denmark also possessed a few small colonies—the Saint Thomas, Saint John, and Saint Croix islands in the Antilles—and a trading post on the coast of Guinea.

The Swedish monarchy united Sweden and Finland under its authority, as well as western Pomerania with the island of Rügen and, until the Recess of 1803, the port of Wismer. In the Antilles, Sweden possessed the tiny island of Saint Barthélemy. The Scandinavian states had a total population of about 6 million, divided nearly equally between the two crowns.

Neither Denmark nor Sweden had been affected by the revolutionary movement. Nevertheless, these two states had been governed by enlightened sovereigns or ministers who had enacted profound political, economic, and social reforms. Andreas Peter von Bernstorff, Danish foreign minister for all but four years in the 1773-1797 period, favored agrarian development. Discoveries of English agronomists were applied in Denmark, and agricultural yields increased. After Bernstorff's death (1797), the king, who had relied heavily on Bernstorff, made it a habit to consult more frequently with the Council of State and with the ministerial colleges. In Norway, governed by a *statthalter* residing in Oslo (Christiania), the small and rather impoverished nobility gradually lost its privileges after 1797. Influenced by the Pietist movement, an extensive program of social assistance developed.

King Gustavus III of Sweden had been assassinated in 1792 because he had wanted to accord a more important position in the state to the bourgoisie and to the peasants. After his death, however, his successor, Gustavus Adolphus IV, continued to follow the same policy. He convoked the Estates, dominated by the clergy and the nobility, on only one occasion during his reign—in 1800. He stubbornly pursued the policy of land redistribution that had been inaugurated by his predecessor so that the very face of Sweden was transformed: the consolidated village gave way to the dispersed or widely scattered village, and peasants gradually became landowners. It has been estimated that when Gustavus IV Adolphus was dethroned by a *coup d'état* in 1809, Swedish peasants owned more than half of their native soil. By that date the nobility had lost all fees from peasant lands and all privileges related to the administration of the state. Without having experienced an actual revolution, the Scandinavian countries had been transformed nearly as much as those of western Europe. This situation explains their policy of neutrality, made manifest by their adherence to the League of Armed Neutrality on December 16, 1800. The assassination of Tsar Paul I and the bombing of Copenhagen quickly tested the League. Although Denmark continued to declare its neutrality in 1804, Gustavus IV Adolphus formed an alliance with the British, and, in January 1805, with Russia. His participation in the conflict was not significant, however.

RUSSIA   In 1804 Russia, with her 35 million inhabitants, was the most heavily populated state in Europe. But she was unquestionably one of the most backward states from the point of view of her social structure. Nearly all the peasants were bound to the land as serfs. There was only a small bourgeoisie in the cities since domestic trade was mainly handled by Jews. The nobility comprised great landowners, and, after Peter the Great, functionaries, since most public offices carried noble titles.

Industry had been developing in the Urals after 1700. The main industry there was metallurgy, set up by the state to subsidize the needs of the army and navy. At the outset, Swedish and German technicians had trained the Russian specialists. Private industry, established by aristocrats, developed alongside the state industry, especially during the reign of Catherine II. Although the majority of workers were serfs, they received wages, nevertheless. Some of the factories were destroyed during the great Pugachev uprising in 1773. They were slowly rebuilt and by 1804 industry in central and southern Russia had surpassed that of the Ural region. If conditions were favorable, this industry would allow Russia to sustain a war against the French Empire.

Russia's administrative organization, far more advanced than her social status, put her on equal footing with the other great states of Europe. This organization had been created by Peter the Great and perfected by Catherine II, who had lent it an enlightened aspect. Although the regime still remained an absolute monarchy, the tsar could consult with a senate that functioned as the chief governmental council and could avail himself of the ministerial councils and of a local administration that, since the time of Catherine II, had been carefully stratified and subordinated to the central power. Alexander I had acquired liberal ideas from his tutor, Frédéric-César de La Harpe, one of the main figures in the Helvetic revolution of 1798. Immediately after his succession to the throne in 1801, Alexander gathered around him a Council of Friends composed of Count Paul Stroganov, Count N. N. Novosiltsov, and Prince Adam Czartoriski. This circle tried to introduce into the Russian regime reforms inspired by their study of the French and English administrations. Thus, the ministerial colleges were abolished, and authority was vested in ministers, as in the west. Alexander I considered emancipating the serfs, but he took only a few very timid and ineffectual steps in this direction. By ukase of 1803 landowners were authorized to enter into contracts by which, under certain conditions, serfs could obtain their freedom. The Council of Friends wanted more. Alexander I had complete confidence in the man whom he asked to draft a constitution—Mikhail Speranski, the son of a Russian Orthodox parish priest. The task was completed in 1809, but circumstances had changed in the interim. The authoritarian tendencies that Alexander I had inherited from his father prevailed over the liberal ideas that he had acquired from Laharpe or Stroganov. Alexander retained only one item of Speranski's proposal—the Empire Council, inspired by Napoleon's Council of State.

Russia was still drawn more closely to England than to France, however. Russia, as previously indicated, was one of Great Britain's best customers; in addition, she was an important source for lumber and other raw materials. With the exception of the Francophile Stroganov, who had been tutored by a member of the Convention—Gilbert Romme—and who had visited France in 1789 and 1790, the Council of Friends was pro-English.

It was to England, therefore, that Alexander I first turned. Napoleon's occupation of Hanover had brought the French armies dangerously close to Russia's borders, and the French troops that had been stationed in Neapolitan ports seemed to threaten Russian interests in the Mediterranean. Chancellor Alexander Vorontzof, whose brother was ambassador to London, persuaded Alexander that Napoleon and Russia had opposing views on the Ottoman Empire. On April 11, 1805, Alexander and Great Britain signed an alliance agreeing that France should be restricted to her 1792 borders and that a European league, or federation, should be established with provisions that "would constitute a new code of the rights of men."

THE OTTOMAN EMPIRE   The Balkans undoubtedly played the most important role in the Anglo-Russian alliance. In 1804 the Balkan peninsula, as yet intact, was an integral part of the Ottoman Empire. But since 1800 the Ottoman Empire had become increasingly weaker. After the French and English troops had left Egypt, the sultan, Sélim III, had not been able effectively to reestablish his authority, for it had been usurped by Mehemet Ali, commandant of the Albanian troops sent to Egypt to fight the French. As early as 1803, Mathieu de Lesseps, the French consul general in Egypt, wrote to Paris that "of all the leaders who are confronting each other, the *bikbachi* Mehemet Ali is the one most capable of pulling Egypt out of anarchy." Two years later the successor, Bernadino Drovetti, noted that Mehemet Ali "had the most important inhabitants on his side and wanted to elevate himself to supreme power by popular demand." As a matter of fact, he had been impressed by Bonaparte's methods at the same time that he was opposing him. Mehemet Ali was carried to power on May 12, 1805 by means of a quasi-plebiscite. Drovetti then wrote:

> The same enthusiasm reigns here as it had in France during the first moments of the Revolution. Everyone is buying arms and even children are following the example. Mehemet Ali and the people have a common cause, which is *his* cause.

From then on, Egypt did indeed escape the sultan's authority.

Arabia was not much more obedient. The influence of the Wahabites continued to grow. In 1803 they seized Mecca and soon dominated the entire Arabian peninsula, from which they even launched expeditions into Syria.

In Europe the Balkans were unsettled. Revolutionary ideas had been penetrating the Balkan peninsula since the French occupation of Venice and the Ionian Islands in 1797. In 1799 the Ottoman government had been forced to recognize the independence of Montenegro. In 1804 a Montenegrin, George Petrovitch, called Karageorge (the Black), incited the Serbs to rise against the sultan. For all practical purposes, Serbia freed itself from Ottoman influence until the year 1812.

In order to prevent the disintegration of his empire, Sélim III introduced a few reforms that, he hoped, would stop the disturbances, but these reforms were either insufficient or poorly executed. If they were favorable to the Christians, they alienated the Muslims and vice versa. Troubles continued. In 1807 Sélim was dethroned and fourteen months later was executed by order of his successor, Mustafa IV.

THE STATES OF SOUTHERN ITALY   In addition to the Ottoman Empire, only the states of southern Italy, the Papal States, and the Kingdom of Naples escaped Napoleon's clutches in 1804 and attempted to preserve their neutrality.

The Papal States had lost the Legations, that is, all of its northern extremity, which had been annexed to the Italian Republic. It was reduced to the area of the Marches, Umbria, and Latium. Umbria was the only rich country from the point of view of agriculture. The Roman countryside, divided into hundreds of immense estates *(latifundia)*, was poorly cultivated. The Borghese prince, for example, held 22,000 hectares (approximately 44,000 acres); Prince Sforza Cesarini held more than 10,000. It has been estimated that within the entire Roman state the great landowners held three tenths of the public property, the clergy six tenths, and the people one tenth. Industry was almost nonexistent, and trade was meager, even though the Roman State had two good ports, Civita Vecchia on the Tyrrhenian Sea and Ancona on the Adriatic. This tiny state was thus incapable either of effectively opposing France or of coming to her aid. Pope Pius VII, who had remained on good terms with Napoleon by signing the Concordat of 1801 and by going to Paris for Napoleon's consecration as emperor on December 2, 1804, found it difficult to maintain his neutrality despite pleas from France and Austria, and above all, from his neighbor to the south, the king of Naples.

In June 1799 the Bourbons had regained the Neapolitan throne with the help of the peasants *(Sanfédistes)* who had revolted against the barons and the bourgeoisie who had rallied to the Italian Republic. The revolt had been organized and directed by Cardinal Ruffo, who advised the king to reward the people by abolishing the feudal system and by lightening the tax burden on the peasants. Lieutenant Colonel de Torrebruna had given the king a detailed memorandum supporting the same solution. But the royal family, as well as their prime minister Sir John Francis Acton, preferred individual vengeance to any general measures that would have entailed a serious reform of the state. They thereby alienated both the nobility and the lower classes as well as a segment of the clergy, for they confiscated the property of monasteries that had supported the republican regime. By the end of 1799 the Bourbons had lost all solid support in the Kingdom of Naples. In addition, they were faced with a serious financial crisis, for the treasury was depleted. The only bills in circulation were those issued by Neapolitan banks—especially by the Bank of Saint James, which gradually assumed the functions of a state bank after 1800. Financial difficulties were aggravated by the renewal of war against France and by the French occupation of Neapolitan ports. Wages were withheld from public officials, soldiers, and the police. The minister of finance, Guiseppe Zurlo, resigned. His successor Luigi Medici, unable to realize certain structural reforms, was powerless to rectify the situation. Criticism directed at the Bourbons reached its height in 1805. The brigandage resulting from the *Sanfédiste* revolt of 1799 continued to spread. In the face of all these factors, King Ferdinand IV, Queen Marie Caroline (Marie Antoinette's sister), and Prime Minister Acton looked to Russia and to England. Although their troops were weak and poorly paid, their only thought was to take up the war against France.

PORTUGAL   The economic and social structure of Portugal closely resembled that of the Kingdom of Naples and Spain. In general, the country was divided into huge estates belonging to a few nobles and wealthy bourgeoisie and cultivated by a mass of wretched peasants. Portugal, like Spain, commanded an important colonial empire, with Brazil as its prize possession. It also had rich trading posts in Asia—particularly in India—and in Africa. Lisbon's trade was important and was comparable to that of Cadiz.

Portugal's internal organization and foreign policy had its own particular characteristics. Whereas Spain had called together the *Cortes* rather frequently, even throughout the eighteenth century (1714, 1724, 1760, 1789), Portugal had not convoked its *Cortes* since 1698. The Portuguese monarchy had thus become more absolute than the monarchy in Spain. Portugal had been enlightened under Pombal's ministry, but the Enlightenment had not extended beyond the closed circle of the aristocracy and upper middle class. Despite the presence of Masonic lodges, Portugal had been even less permeable to revolutionary propaganda than Spain.

Since the Middle Ages Portugal's foreign policy had traditionally allied her to England. These bonds had been strengthened by a treaty concluded by Lord Methuen in 1703. This treaty opened Portuguese ports to British vessels. Portugal had entered into the war against France during the summer of 1793, and had fought alongside the English until peace was restored in 1801. Portugal, like a launch, was once again ready to follow the wake of the battleship.

FRANCE, ITS SATELLITES AND ALLIES

FRANCE   Three years of peace and of administrative reorganization had restored a certain degree of prosperity to France. Landholding
peasants, reassured by the Constitution of the Year VIII that their land
purchases could not be revoked, no longer hesitated to display their com-
fortable circumstances. Lady Morgan, an Englishwoman visiting France in
1803, claimed that she saw peasants who had 150 sets of bed sheets in their
cupboards. This was undoubtedly an exception, but a significant one. Dam-
aged buildings were either repaired or rebuilt in the regions that had suffered from civil war (the west of France and the Rhône valley) or from the
foreign war (the departments of Nord, Pas de Calais, and Bas-Rhin): Since
1796 harvests had been good and had sold well. Landless peasants or small
landholders easily found jobs. Young men entered the armies, either as
draftees or as paid substitutes for those who had "drawn a bad number" and
did not want to serve. Others worked in the newly developing industries.

The material condition of artisans and workers had indeed improved
under the Consulate and at the beginning of the Empire. War had spurred
development in the metallurgy industry, and since Napoleon did not inter-
rupt the manufacture of armaments, there had been no "reconversion crisis"
in 1801. In addition, a new surge in the textile industry was brought on by
peace and the attendant resumption of cotton importation. In 1789 France
had been gripped by a considerable agricultural and industrial unemployment, but in 1804, on the contrary, complaints were voiced about a labor
shortage. Wages also rose. In Paris some workers were earning twice as
much as they had in 1790. During the same period, a middle class woman
complained about having to spend nine francs a day, however, high salaries
were the exception. Wages generally ranged between two and five francs
for men and half of that figure for women. However, locksmiths and gold-
smiths eventually earned seven francs a day.

Industrialists who sought low-priced labor resorted to using women
and even children more and more frequently. Jean Baptiste Boyer-Fon-
frède, the brother of a Girondin member of the Convention, had started a
large factory for the spinning and weaving of cotton at Toulouse, and he
employed 350 children. According to reports from the factory doctor, this
factory was a model of philanthropy and industry: the children were
housed, fed, and even instructed—but received no salary. Although the prefect praised the establishment, the mayor attested that "the children are
undernourished when they are healthy and poorly cared for when they are
sick." They were in fact submitted to rigid discipline and were compelled

to work thirteen hours a day. And in Arpajon, near Paris, Jean François Marie Delaître demanded sixteen hours work per day in his textile mill.

By the provisions of the Loi Le Chapelier of 1791, workers were not permitted to form associations or confederations or to go on strike. In addition, the Empire required each worker to carry a small notebook *(livret)* listing all the places that he had worked. Workers were forbidden to move without a passport. Nevertheless, French workers seldom thought to complain, since, around 1805, jobs were plentiful and wages had gone up.

Industrial development, however, could have been even greater. If the owners of the forges, spinning mills and weaving mills had made the necessary effort, France could have overtaken England in that great race called the Industrial Revolution. But the leading classes in France, whether they stemmed from the nobility or from the bourgeoisie, had not cast off the habits that had been molded by two centuries of Colbertism. They could conceive of economic development only within the framework of a strong protective customs barrier, and they easily persuaded Napoleon to share their views. Bonaparte, accordingly, decided on a course of economic expansion based not on an agreement with England, which would necessarily have been based on free exchange, but on a policy of increased protectionism and the creation of markets on the Continent through subjugation of neighboring nations.

THE KINGDOM OF ITALY   After the Empire had been instituted in France, it quickly became apparent that the Italian Republic would not be able to retain its constitution. The Italian Jacobins and even the French army of occupation were opposed to Italy's being turned into a kingdom. Nevertheless, Napoleon did receive numerous petitions begging him to effect this change. "Let the Emperor of the French be King of Italy!" This was the last sentence of a proposal drawn up by General Pino in the name of the Italian division at the camp of Boulogne.

Napoleon was flattered by these requests. To become king of Italy would complete the analogy with Charlemagne. The *senatus consulta* of the Italian Republic, seeing its imminent doom, finally sent the Emperor a petition analagous to the others but with the additional stipulation that Napoleon was to take the title of king of Italy—and not of Lombardy—for they still hoped that the state, whose capital was Milan, would eventually extend over the entire peninsula. Other demands were also made for the new kingdom. There was to be greater independence and lower taxes, which would be achieved by abolishing the contributions paid by the Italian Republic to France in support of its occupying army. At the same time, however, the vice-president of the Italian Republic, Melzi d'Eril, secretly opened negotiations with Austria, asking her to oppose the creation of a kingdom of Italy. Austria did nothing, but the emperor, Francis, concluded from this overture that if a war were to break out, Italy would readily rise up against Napoleon. This strengthened his desire to resist France.

Napoleon was vaguely aware of the Italian opposition, and for a brief period he thought of "naming" his elder brother Joseph as king of Italy, but Joseph refused. Napoleon decided, on February 5, 1805, to take the "iron crown" of the Lombards for himself, along with the title of king of Italy, at the same time appointing his stepson, Eugène de Beauharnais, to the position of viceroy. The Kingdom of Italy was solemnly proclaimed in Paris on March 17, 1805. Napoleon took this occasion to declare that he had "always thought about rendering the Italian Nation free and independent." In a later speech, he added that the transformation of the Italian Republic into a kingdom would bring nearer "the time when the Italian people will have acquired the energy and the stability without which they are incapable of forming a free and independent state."

Prince Eugène was coldly received in Milan on March 16. Napoleon, on the contrary, was given a warmer welcome on May 8. The coronation was held in the Milan cathedral on Sunday, May 26. Napoleon placed the "iron crown" of the Lombard kings on his own head. He left the capital of Lombardy almost immediately. In August Prince Eugène took up permanent residence in Milan with his young wife Augusta, a Bavarian princess who quickly became more popular than her husband. A small court was organized in Milan, and the impression that the Kingdom of Italy would one day include the entire peninsula was confirmed.

THE ETRURIAN KINGDOM AND THE PRINCIPALITY OF LUCCA   The king of Etruria (former Duchy of Tuscany), Louis de Bourbon, son-in-law of Charles IV of Spain, died on May 27, 1803. As regent, his wife allowed Italian Jacobins who had been persecuted in Milan to seek refuge in Florence, and she also tolerated the presence of numerous English agents and spies. Napoleon was extremely annoyed. It looked as if Tuscany's days under Bourbon domination were numbered.

As for the Republic of Lucca, it was transformed into a principality, joined to the principality of Piombino, and placed under the authority of Elisa (Napoleon's sister) and her husband Felix Bacciocchi (June 23, 1805).

THE HELVETIC CONFEDERATION   France retained a powerful influence on the Helvetic Confederation after the latter accepted the Mediation Act of February 19, 1803 and signed an alliance with France on September 27 of the same year. Louis d'Affry, the *landamann,* or leader, of the confederation, was really Napoleon's underling, and he carried out the Emperor's orders. On January 1, 1804, he was succeeded by Rodolphe de Wattenwyl, an aristocrat from an old family who had been increasingly hostile to the Revolution and to the unitary regime that had controlled Switzerland from 1798 to 1800. Wattenwyl's accession to power coincided with a period of calm in the cantons. French troops evacuated Switzerland on February 14, 1804. Since they had not reentered Switzerland in March 1804 when peasants from the canton of Zurich rose up against the domination of city patricians, the Swiss felt that they had regained their independence and neutrality.

However, France kept a hold on Switzerland. Le Valais remained under French occupation. In 1810 it was to become a part of France and would form the department of Simplon. In March 1806 Napoleon conferred on Field Marshal Berthier the principality of Neuchâtel, at that time a personal possession of the king of Prussia, but which, until 1798, had belonged to the Helvetic Confederation. Thus Napoleon had numerous means of access to Switzerland, by way of Neuchâtel, le Valais or Geneva, which had been annexed to France in 1798. His title of "mediator" permitted him to intervene at will, as much for the purpose of directing the political situation as of regulating the economy.

THE KINGDOM OF HOLLAND   The Dutch constitution had been modified by a *coup d'état* on September 14, 1801, and had been revised along the lines of the French constitution of the Consulate. When war was renewed between France and England in the spring of 1803, however, Holland created obstacles to declaring war on England. After she finally did declare war, she allowed British smuggling to flourish within her borders.

Napoleon attributed this attitude to the constitution. It was too decentralized with the executive power entrusted to a twelve-member Directory. He called Rutger Jan Schimmelpenninck, the Dutch prime minister, to Paris in September 1804 to draft a new constitution that would provide for a single man to head the executive branch. Schimmelpenninck worked out a constitution based on the French Constitution of the Empire. A *Grand Pensionnaire* was to be the executive head. On March 22, 1805, Napoleon named Schimmelpenninck to the newly created post. Legislative power was to be entrusted to *Leurs Hautes Puissances* (Their Highnessess), a chamber whose members were elected by the citizens from among candidates selected by the government, but in 1805 they were chosen directly by the *Grand Pensionnaire* himself.

Napoleon had proposed naming Schimmelpenninck hereditary *Grand Pensionnaire,* but Schimmelpenninck refused, knowing that the Dutch had rebelled from 1783 to 1787 to prevent the *statholder* from becoming a hereditary king. Before long, he was on bad terms with Napoleon. The Emperor demanded the return of 229 million that Holland had borrowed from France. Since the Dutch budget already stood in deficit of 45 million,

Schimmelpenninck refused. He became ill soon afterward. On February 6, 1806, Napoleon seized this illness as a pretext to oust Schimmelpenninck from office. He informed the *Grand Pensionnaire* that since his illness would undoubtedly prevent the exercise of his duties, thus probably forcing him to resign, Holland should be assured of rule by a hereditary king loyal to Napoleon rather than risk having a new *Grand Pensionnaire* chosen from English sympathizers. Schimmelpenninck refused to resign and, instead, sent Admiral Verhuell to Paris to oppose the Emperor's proposal. Napoleon turned a deaf ear to Verhuell's objections. He decided that his youngest brother, Louis, would be king of Holland. His decision was approved by a special Dutch council, which, with one exception—Schimmelpenninck— voted unanimously. The Dutch constitution was retained, with the king assuming the powers of the *Grand Pensionnaire*. Napoleon had made it clear that in the absence of a favorable vote he would annex Holland to the Empire. Under the reign of his brother Louis, however, he felt that Holland would be a docile dependency.

SPAIN   The situation in Spain was different, for Spain had not been conquered by French armies. When the Treaty of Basel was signed in 1795, the French occupied only Ampurdan in the east and Guipúzcoa along the Bay of Biscay. When Spain voluntarily entered into alliance with France in 1796, it was because of hostility against the English, who for three hundred years had been relentlessly trying to preempt Spain's trade with her American colonies. Although Spain was politically allied to France, she remained hostile to the Revolution and even to the philosophical ideas of the Enlightenment. Revolutionary propaganda achieved no success whatsoever in Spain. How could she be of service to France under these conditions?

Spain was still the greatest colonial power in 1805. The mother country itself had only 11 million inhabitants however, in an area as large as France. Madrid, the capital, had a population of only 150,000; Barcelona, Valencia, and Cadiz each had about 100,000. The major portion of the population lived in misery and poverty. The land was parcelled out in a manner similar to that in eastern Germany or southern Italy: huge estates *(latifundia)* were numerous and poorly cultivated. The clergy, equal in numbers to the French clergy prior to 1789 (200,000 members) exerted a great amount of influence. The Inquisition remained a powerful force, and had condemned the great "enlightened" lord, Pablo de Olavide, in 1778. The nobility, numbering around 500,000 and divided into a small number of large gentleman farmers and a mass of wretched squires, held an important position in the state. The nobility and clergy together owned more than half of the lands. The American colonies were still producing great wealth and filling the Mother country's coffers. Mexico alone had sent 45 million piastres in silver from 1800 to 1803.

The Spanish army was a loyal, but small and poorly equipped force. Even though the navy comprised some rather unwieldy old ships and a poorly trained staff, it ranked third in the world, after the British and French fleets. The "strength" of the Spanish fleet accounts for France's desire to make an alliance with her neighbor south of the Pyrenees. With the aid of the Spanish squadrons, the French navy finally began to balance the British maritime forces. This had been proven in 1796. As soon as the alliance of San Ildefonso had been made, the British fleet was forced to evacuate the Mediterranean and the French had been able to regain Corsica without striking a blow. In 1798 the Spanish fleet had made the Egyptian campaign possible. But, it was also through lack of active and intelligent cooperation from Spanish Admiral Mazarredo's squadron that French Admiral Bruix failed to rescue Bonaparte's army, which had been blockaded in Egypt during the summer of 1799. Despite this misunderstanding, the alliance was maintained and resulted in the election of Pope Pius VII (who had no preconceived hostility toward revolutionary France)—at the conclave of Venice. The alliance also led to Spain's attack on Portugal in the spring of 1801. This campaign, the War of the Oranges, ended with the closing of Portuguese ports to the English.

When peace was concluded with England, the Franco-Spanish alliance came to an end, but the cordial relationships between the two countries continued. It was to please Charles IV of Spain that Napoleon named his son-in-law, the duke of Parma, Don Luis, king of Etruria.

The Franco-Spanish alliance produced few repercussions on Spain's internal government. From 1789 to 1796 supporters of the enlightenment had been dismissed from their positions in Spain and had even been subjected to frequent persecution. After 1796 they regained favor. Gaspar Jovellanos was named minister of justice, Mariano Luis de Urquijo (who had translated Rousseau into Spanish) became foreign minister and later prime minister. The Inquisition, meanwhile, relentlessly pursued its activities, including zealous censorship of French books. However, it was required to inform the king of all persons whom it arrested. The government undertook a few reforms, but did so gingerly. A few internal customs duties were abolished, and some church property was sold at auction in small parcels. These mild reforms only served to strengthen the opposition of clergy and nobility. When Manuel de Godoy, the former prime minister who had earned the title of Prince of Peace for his negotiation of the treaty of Basel, returned to power in 1801, he permitted the Inquisition to arrest Jovellanos and Urquijo.

Spain's domestic policies presented no obstacles to the reopening of negotiations between France and Spain in 1803, when war resumed. Neutrality would have been impossible for Spain in view of her location on the Atlantic Ocean. Spain would have had to side with either France or England. Spain did have various grievances against its neighbor: French troops were maintained in the kingdom of Etruria and France had sold Louisiana to the United States (which would ultimately result in the Spanish loss of Florida). Despite these and other grievances as well as ideological differences, Spain chose to side with France. Perhaps this choice was dictated by the King's family interests, for he wanted to keep his relatives on the thrones of Florence and Naples. In addition, he hoped to rule Portugal himself some day. Perhaps, the decision to back France was influenced by Godoy's personal interests and financial subsidies from France. The Franco-Spanish alliance signed on December 14, 1804 was supplemented by a maritime convention in January 1805. The Franco-English war thus became international.

6

TRAFALGAR AND AUSTERLITZ

The war between France and England that resumed on May 13, 1803, would gradually extend to Spain, Austria, Russia, the Kingdom of Naples, and Prussia, until the peace treaties of Tilsit (July 7 and 9, 1807), which would restore only a few months of precarious peace on the Continent. What were the opposing forces?

THE OPPOSING FORCES

The principal forces in the conflict were primarily France's land forces and England's naval forces. The French army was still the army of the Revolution. Recruitment for the army had been vastly extended by the Jourdan—Delbrel law enacted under the Directory on September 5, 1798. This law was a modification of the selective service instituted in 1793, and it introduced the principle of compulsory, universal military service in France. It had the effect of providing the French army with practically unlimited reserves. In 1805, no other country in the world had a comparable system of conscription. In practice, the law was applied with a great deal of flexibility until 1813. Numerous exceptions were made, particularly for married men, and substitution was authorized. Since only the rich were able to afford replacement, obviously, the oligarchic character of the regime was accentuated. Between 1800 and 1812, this law enabled Napoleon to raise more than a million men.

Similar to the practice during the Revolution, the conscripts received their training during campaigns in the regiments that they originally joined. The soldier of the Empire, like the soldier of the Revolution, was not a "barrack" soldier, and he retained a strongly independent spirit, evidenced by a pronounced taste for thievery, if not for pillage, and by his tendency to grumble, even to disobey his superior officers. Napoleon was not too concerned, however: "They grumble," he said, "but they always march." The soldier of Napoleon had the same faults and virtues of those of the Revolution. The rate of desertion in the French army was not excessive and remained at the same level until after 1811 when desertion did increase.

There is no doubt that Napoleon won the loyalty of his army. This can perhaps be attributed in a large measure to his policy of promotions of both commissioned and noncommissioned regulars rather than conscripts. The use of regimental flags, topped by eagles was one means Napoleon used to stimulate bravery and pride in achievement by individual corps. When addressing the army, he would recall the victorious battles fought previously by particular regiments, and he knew their officers by name. He was known to be concerned for the wounded and for the widows and orphans of his soldiers. Napoleon's proclamations to his army during the Italian campaign, 1796–1797, showed psychological insight as well as common-sense appeal. He was lavish with praise for heroic action and victory, but at the same time he challenged his army with unfinished campaigns and future glory.

Requisitions for French armies from the peoples where fighting was taking place affected the wealthy rather than the peasant or urban lower classes. The latter, in fact, frequently found work with the French army. Thus, the masses of people in the countries he fought were not disposed to oppose him. The burden of taxes on the French to support the war was reduced for the French themselves, until later in Napoleon's career. The bad economic conditions of the Terror and Directory in France persisted. The Bank of France tried to alleviate the economic situation by helping finances of the government and of private financiers and merchants. In the days of the Consulate, during which there were greater intervals of peace than before or after, war weighed less heavily on the French. Glowing tales by returning soldiers fired the imagination of new recruits and helped, in many cases, to build the legend of Napoleonic invincibility.

Napoleon introduced few innovations in the organization of the army, but he modified tactics and strategy as the occasion warranted. His training at Brienne as a young man bore fruit in his thorough knowledge of the history of warfare and of the tactics of the great generals of the past. He established new military schools, notably the special military school of Saint Cyr, for officer training, but promotion by rank on the battlefield continued to be practiced. Napoleon, however, awarded promotions on performance, irrespective of past career.

Although Napoleon created no new fighting corps, the Imperial Guard came to be a special corps. Originated during the Directory, suppressed under the Consulate, and revived under the Empire, the Guard increased gradually in numbers until it equaled two regular corps. By several measures, he increased the mobility and maneuverability of his army. Providing food, uniforms, and ordnance for the armed forces was taken out of civilian hands and put under a special army corps, with discipline similar to the fighting corps. This remedied the frequent delay and sometimes failure of the supplies needed to arrive at a particular place in the battle. Napoleon also militarized the war commissioners by organizing the service of the military intendancy. Medical and health services did not receive the same tightening and were often inadequate.

Muskets and cannon in use in 1789 were not replaced. Although they had been extremely modern at that time, they were outclassed by the new weapons put into service by England, Russia and Austria. Napoleon's artillery training and his experience at the siege of Toulon laid the foundations for his military strategy. It was one of his innovations to integrate the artillery in his plans and to develop its corps. Prior to this, the use of artillery had been secondary, but he used it to weaken his enemy before a cavalry or infantry charge and sometimes to divert attention from the real point of attack. Napoleon planned his battles after observation of the enemy and study of the terrain, but he was flexible enough to change as the occasion dictated. He alternated the column attack with a line attack of three rows of soldiers—the third constituting a reserve. He tried hard to flank his enemy and to drive back the weakest part of his opponent's army.

One of Napoleon's greatest weapons was surprise. He won some of his early victories even against superior numbers, by virtue of surprise attack and the mobility of his army. It has been said that Napoleon won his battles "with the legs of his soldiers." Organization of transport, especially for artillery, was another important innovation. Again, it was assigned to a special transport corps of the army rather than to private contract. The cavalry formed another special corps, and its use was integrated with the infantry. On the other hand, Napoleon did not appreciate the potentialities of a balloon corps. He dissolved the one that had been organized during the Revolution and relied on traditional methods of ascertaining the disposition of enemy forces. Rolling country or hills provided observation points. His use of such terrain was eminently successful in Italy and Germany, but less so on the plains of Egypt or Russia.

Although Napoleon's greatest battles were yet to come, he had developed his strategy and his army before Austerlitz.[1] From 1804 on, more foreign regiments were added to the French corps. By the end of the Napoleonic regime, such troops formed approximately 50 percent of the French forces. This undoubtedly constituted one of the weaknesses that brought about his ultimate defeat. There is no doubt, however, that he built a high morale into his fighting forces, including the foreign corps. French *élan* from the Revolution was fostered by Napoleon, and the army spread—by means of the common soldier—ideas and some of the benefits of the Revolution, but these soldiers also served to arouse opposition to France in the conquered lands.

Napoleon never allowed any doubt of his command. His seconds in command were rarely as successful as he, and it was his direction that frequently rescued the army from defeat. Under the Empire, Napoleon planned and conducted his campaigns himself until his fall. He quickly ended the Revolutionary election of officers of the regiments, and by reward for merit and success in battle, he developed the finest officer corps in Europe. Some of the officers raised to the rank of general or marshal had received their initial training under the Old Regime, some during the Revolution, and others under Napoleon. In striving to promote their own careers, they helped bring about Napoleonic victories. Dissatisfaction with Napoleonic rule came from civilians, not from the military who recognized his genius and remained loyal to him to the end, even rallying to him during the Hundred Days.

None of the European armies in 1805 could be compared to the French army. The British army, however, was in the process of being reorganized. The duke of York initiated reform: more soldiers were henceforth recruited from England than from Germany; they were clothed at the expense of the public treasury, and no longer by the colonels. Relationships between officers and soldiers improved; the men were no longer considered as highwaymen who had to be kept in line by a discipline of terror; the duke of

---

[1] Consult the bibliography for the military and the older studies on Napoleon, which tend to place emphasis on Napoleon as a conqueror. See particularly the biographies of Napoleon by August Fournier and by Louis Madelin; G. Six, *Les généraux de la Révolution et de l'Empire* (Paris, 1934); M. Dupont, *Napoléon en campagne* (3 vols., Paris, 1950–1955); Harold T. Parker, *Three Napoleonic Battles* (Durham, N.C., Duke University Press, 1944); David Chandler, *The Campaigns of Napoleon* (New York: The Macmillan Company, 1966); and Robert B. Holtman, *The Napoleonic Revolution (Philadelphia: J. B. Lippincott Co.,* 1967).

York declared that the colonel should be "father to the soldiers." But this innovation, tried out at first in a single regiment, was slow to spread to the rest of the army. In addition, the British army comprised scarcely 95,000 men in regular troops, and until 1815, its organization was irrational. The infantry and the cavalry, for example, were dependent on the War Office, while the artillery and the corps of engineers were under the jurisdiction of the board of ordnance. The first two branches of the army had nothing in common with the latter two; neither uniforms, pay, promotions, nor administration! Arthur Wellesley—the future Lord Wellington who was still an obscure general in the army of India—made efforts to improve the operation of the general staff, communications, and the supplying of provisions and also to increase the infantry's fire power.

Until 1812 the British ground forces played only an auxiliary role in the continental campaigns. The main role was handled by the Russian, Austrian, and Prussian armies. These armies, composed of mercenaries, fighting without ideals, were still organized as they had been prior to 1789. But more important for their future destiny they were poorly commanded.

If the army of Napoleon was superior to that of England, there is no doubt that the British navy was superior to that of France. It was on the sea that the major conflict between France and England would be waged, except as England played a role in the various coalitions against Napoleon. England's greatest strength was her fleet. After 1803 the United Kingdom had 200 large battleships available, many of which were three-decked. In addition, the fleet possessed a large number of frigates and corvettes, all of which were manned by 150,000 crewmen. These crews were still recruited by the deplorable press-gang method, that is, forcible recruitment of sailors in ports. It is also true that the organization, the administration, and the discipline of the navy were poorly handled, as a matter of fact, the great mutinies of 1797 could be largely attributed to these factors. During the Addington ministry Lord Saint-Vincent (Admiral Jervis) took steps to remedy these shortcomings which had been brought to light by a parliamentary investigation. What was important in regard to the effectiveness of the navy was that the commanding admirals, Nelson and Cornwallis, had a doctrine of strategy and tactics (the legacy of Rodney and of Hood) that permitted them to dominate any opposing squadron.

In face of the powerful fleet of Britain, France, who had not replaced the losses sustained at Toulon and Abukir, had only sixty large battleships at the very most at her disposal. Admiral Decrès, the minister of the admiralty, and the commanding officers of the squadrons, Vice-Admiral Villeneuve and Admiral Missiessy, were unable to overcome the inferiority complex from which the French fleet had suffered for more than a century. In order to escape this feeling, they tended to avoid battle and to seek refuge in a war of chase. Napoleon, who transformed the French army into the best army in Europe, while recognizing the importance of the navy to protect French coasts and trade, failed to take comparable measures to strengthen the navy. He did establish naval jurisdictions in the chief port towns, thereby eliminating conflict between naval and civil administrations, and he also applied a form of naval conscription after 1805 in the coastal regions. Similar to Saint Cyr, he established officer schools for naval training, one at Brest and one at Toulon. But these measures could not overcome, in the short time necessary, the eighteenth-century losses topped by the Revolution and defeats between 1798 and 1803 in the Mediterranean.

The Spanish fleet, with about forty vessels, nearly doubled France's maritime forces, but this increment, as we have seen, was of mediocre quality.

Thus, this maritime war that France and England embarked on in May 1804 opened with grave portent for France.

TRAFALGAR

As soon as war broke out, the two great rival nations did indeed confront each other on the Atlantic. England was naturally anxious to secure pawns; so she hurriedly occupied the most poorly defended French and Dutch colonies or trading posts in America—Saint Pierre and Miquelon, Saint Lucia, Tobago, and Dutch Guiana. In order to prevent Louisiana, recently acquired from Spain, from falling prey to the same fate, Bonaparte sold it to the United States for the minimal sum of 80 million francs. Of that sum, 20 million francs were to be used to settle claims of American citizens on France. Little was actually paid for the purchase since France's debts to the United States government had risen to nearly the balance of the millions. France, in turn, occupied Hanover—the personal possession of the king of England on the Continent—without striking a blow.

France's strength lay in returning to the plan for landing on the British Isles, which had been outlined in 1798 and had been taken up again in 1800. England, noting that the purely naval war imagined by Addington could not succeed, saw herself forced to fall back on the system of continental coalition that had been tested and found effective for more than one hundred years. These plans were to preoccupy the two belligerents from 1803 to 1805.

Bonaparte ordered a concentration of flotillas of flat boats, pinnaces, and gunboats on the coasts of the English Channel, as had been done in 1798 and in 1801. The present undertaking was established on a surer footing, since the amount of time and the financial means available were greater than in 1801. More than 2000 small boats, each capable of transporting about a hundred men, were assembled, while the *Grande Armée* — 150,000 men and 400 cannons — was concentrated around Boulogne. Did Bonaparte ever intend, as it was rumored, to have this army transported by surprise on a flotilla to the other side of the Channel from Pas de Calais? It was not likely, more so since Napoleon's competency in naval strategy was hardly to be trusted. Besides, would he have planned this when measures taken by the English had made the execution of the plan nearly impossible?

In reality, it seems that Bonaparte realized, by the end of 1803, that a landing under cover of fog, a storm, or a long winter night was impossible. As he himself had written in his report to the Directory in 1798, mastery of the seas was essential. Absolute mastery of the ocean obviously could only be hoped for after years of work and partial victories. But would it not be possible to obtain a temporary and local mastery of the Channel for a few days? Napoleon exaggerated in order to make himself better understood, when he wrote to Admiral Louis René Madeleine Levassor, Count of Latouche-Tréville: "Make us masters of the strait for six hours, and we will be masters of the world." Would it not be reasonable to keep the British navy out of the Channel for one or two weeks by means of some clever maneuver? That was the estimated length of time required to transport the *Grande Armée* to England and to seize London. Even under these conditions, the undertaking would have been exceedingly risky, for if the slightest delay occurred to slow down the movement of the French army, the army would have been rapidly cut off from its provisions and would have been subject to certain annihilation, much as had been the fate of the expeditionary corps in Egypt. Thus, Admiral Truguet, a man of experience and of courage, formally advised against the landing.

Several successive plans for landings were drawn up despite the advice of experts. The first, signed on May 25, 1804, provided for all French squadrons to concentrate rapidly at Brest. The most delicate operation was to be executed by Latouche-Tréville, commanding the fleet of Toulon. It was thought that France could assemble her squadrons at the entrance to the Channel more quickly than the English. She would thus have numerical superiority, if a fight were necessary, but it was hoped that the English would avoid the battle. The death of Latouche-Tréville on August 20, 1804, his replacement by Pierre de Villeneuve (one of the few survivors of Abukir), and the evolution of the diplomatic situation in Europe caused postponement of the plan.

Tsar Alexander, frightened by French expansion in Germany, had drawn closer to England. Pitt, back in power on May 10, 1804, offered Russia a small subsidy, which she accepted. This marked the beginning of negotiations toward an alliance, which was finally concluded on April 11,

1805. Napoleon, in turn, attempted to renew the old Franco-Spanish alliance. Godoy, motivated by inducements and by even finer promises, brought his country into the war on December 14, 1804.

These circumstances led Napoleon to modify his plans for landing in England. In the future France could count on the help of the Spanish fleet, and especially on her bases on the Iberian Peninsula. The new plan, approved by the Emperor on March 2, 1805, provided for a general concentration of French and Spanish naval forces in the Antilles. Napoleon felt that the presence of sizable naval forces in American waters would draw most of the British squadrons to the area. The French navy would then return at top speed to the Channel and would dominate it for the time necessary for transporting the *Grande Armée* to England. This was a very ingenious plan, which, without a doubt, bore the mark of the illustrious brain that had conceived it.

The vast scheme, which used the entire Atlantic as its theater, had only one defect: it did not take into account the actual condition of the French fleet. For the most part, the ships were in poor repair; provisions were mediocre or insufficient; and crews were incomplete or poorly trained. The leaders, while undoubtedly trained and courageous, were imbued with the defensive spirit of the former navy and were convinced that any plan of attack against the British squadrons was doomed to failure. Villeneuve, the commander of the squadron of Toulon, also viewed the venture with a defeatist attitude.

The orders were given, however. The squadrons of Brest, Toulon, and Rochefort were to meet in the Antilles. Only the squadron from Rochefort departed on the appointed date. Admiral Ganteaume, commander of the squadron of Brest, made the observation that, tightly blockaded by the English, he would not be able to leave without a fight and, consequently, without sustaining losses. He was allowed to remain. Only the squadrons from Toulon and Rochefort would rendezvous at Martinique. They would then meet with the squadron from Brest in the open sea off Ushant Island. Even the simplified plan could not be realized. The squadron from Rochefort returned to its base, after having vainly awaited that of Toulon in the Antilles. Villeneuve's departure from Toulon had been delayed by some necessary repairs. He had not left his port until March 30, but he had been able to pass into the Atlantic without a mishap. Nelson, who had been watching him, thought that the movement involved a new Egyptian expedition, and he deployed his ships between Sicily and Africa to await the French. In the meanwhile the Toulon flotilla was not joined by Spanish squadrons as the original plan called for, and Villeneuve arrived alone in Martinique on May 14. On June 4, Nelson, having finally recognized his error, was at Barbados. Villeneuve had more ships than Nelson, and he could have attempted to beat his adversary in the Caribbean Sea, but gripped by an inferiority complex before the victor of Abukir plus his certainty of failure of the entire plan, he chose to return to France. He left Fort-de-France on June 11. Nelson, informed of this action the following day, set off in hot pursuit. He did not succeed in catching up with Villeneuve, but he was able to advise the British admiralty of Villeneuve's course.

The admiralty then sent a squadron into the open sea along the Spanish coasts in order to block the French route. A battle ensued in a thick fog, on July 22, on the sea near Cape Finisterre. Villeneuve sustained only slight damages, but he used them as an excuse to scatter his ships in the Spanish ports of Vigo, El Ferrol, and La Coruña, where they could be repaired. At El Ferrol, he received new orders from Napoleon, enjoining him to proceed to the entrance to the English Channel as quickly as possible, with all the Spanish ships that could accompany him.

> "I am counting," said the Emperor, "on your zeal for my service, on your love for the country, and on your hate for a nation that has been oppressing us for forty generations and that, with a little perseverance on your part, can be made to enter the ranks of the small powers once and for all."

Villeneuve was dismayed by the emperor's orders. All he could envision were his mastless ships, without rigging, deprived of half of their crews through illness lined up against superior forces in better physical condition. He overestimated the forces with which England could oppose him. Nevertheless, he left El Ferrol on August 13, but upon receiving a report, which turned out to be untrue, on August 15 that a large British squadron was crossing between Ushant and the Cantabrian coast, he took the southern route instead of continuing to the north. Authorizing his actions by a paragraph in Napoleon's orders that permitted him "in the event of a major force" to seek refuge in a Spanish port, he headed toward Cadiz, where he arrived on August 18 without having encountered the enemy. He had no sooner entered the inner harbor when the first ships of an English blockade squadron appeared.

The naval campaign of 1805 was logically brought to a close with the blockade of Villeneuve in the harbor of Cadiz. It had failed in its goal: the concentration of French squadrons in the Antilles and the ensuing evacuation of the Channel for a few days by the British fleet. On the whole, losses were light. The undertaking could have been postponed until the following year, assuming that circumstances on the Continent were to remain the same. This was dubious, however, since Austria (June 16), the Kingdom of Naples (September 10), and Sweden (October 3) had agreed to adhere to the Anglo-Russian treaty of April 11, 1805. Thus, a great coalition (the third since 1793) emerged against France and obliged Napoleon to transfer his *Grande Armée* from Boulogne to Germany. It is, therefore, unlikely that the landing would have taken place even if Villeneuve had been able to join Ganteaume on the sea near Brest at the end of August.

Villeneuve's useless maneuvers seriously compromised the future. Indeed, instead of remaining at Cadiz where, by his very presence he had immobilized an important British blockade squadron, he decided to leave the harbor and to risk a battle that would have been of no value even if he had been victorious. Why did he make this decision? It seems that Napoleon had ordered Villeneuve alone, for reasons of prestige, to return to Toulon (September 16); but two days later, new and slightly different instructions removed Villeneuve from command, entrusted the squadron of Cadiz to Admiral Rosily, and authorized him to act in accordance with the circumstances.

Villeneuve had not only received the instructions of September 16 for him to proceed alone to Toulon but also had heard a rumor emanating from Madrid that he had been dishonorably discharged. In order to save his honor, he decided to leave Cadiz immediately. No decision could have been more pleasing to Lord Nelson, who had taken command of the blockade squadron on September 28. For a long time the British admiral had been considering the plan for a battle to rid England, once and for all of the most threatening squadron that opposed her. Based on the lessons drawn from prior naval victories at Saint Vincent, Abukir and Copenhagen, as well as from battles fought by Admiral Rodney during the American War of Independence, Nelson issued a memorandum to his captains detailing his plan of action. He would abandon the old battle formation for squadrons in use since the sixteenth century—the *ligne de file*, with ships in a single line one behind the other. Instead, his plan called for attacking the enemy in columns, penetrating the French line at the center, isolating enemy vessels, overwhelming them with superior forces, and conducting the assault as closely as possible, by boarding if necessary.

The battle was fought according to this plan on October 20 on the sea near the Cape of Trafalgar, to the east of Cadiz. Even though Villeneuve commanded a numerical superiority with his thirty-three battleships (fifteen of which were Spanish) opposed to Nelson's twenty-seven, he was utterly defeated. Eighteen of his ships were captured by the English, eleven fled to Cadiz in very poor condition, and four, which had escaped, were destroyed by the English on the sea at La Coruña. The English had won a great victory, but they also sustained a great loss, for Nelson met his death in the battle. It was the battle of annihilation as Nelson had planned. The French Mediterranean squadron and most of the Spanish squadron were destroyed. The efforts that France had made since 1798 to reconstruct her navy were wiped out. The French hope of taking up the battle on the sea, and consequently of effecting a landing in England had to be abandoned.

From October 20, 1805 on, England could be certain that Napoleon's army would never enter London. England's victory had not been complete, however. The French Emperor could attempt to defeat them with other weapons, essentially of the economic order. England had only a weak professional army to avert the realization of these designs and to assure herself of total victory over France. She certainly was absolute mistress of the seas. She would be able to turn to the offensive, first against the colonies of France and her allies, and then against continental Europe, after she strengthened her ground army. In the meanwhile, she was forced to resort to the classic method that had so often proved successful for her: she would hurl the coalition armies against France.

In France the stock market was seriously shaken by the news of Trafalgar. The Bank of France decided to reimburse no more than one note per person, and the bank note soon lost 10 percent of its value, but public opinion did not have time to get upset. It quickly became occupied with the victories won on land, and it did not realize at the time that Trafalgar sealed the destiny of the French Empire.

AUSTERLITZ

As soon as he had heard of the formation of the Third Coalition, that is, on August 24, Napoleon ordered the *Grande Armée,* concentrated in Boulogne, to take up a position along the Rhine River. One month later the French Army reached the river between Mannheim and Strasbourg. Its movement had been rapid because the army had made extensive use of carts and wagons for transport. Napoleon planned to crush the coalition forces before they consolidated. And these forces were scattered. In October 1805 the Austrian troops were divided into three corps, one under Archduke Charles in Italy, another under Archduke John in the Tyrol, and the third led by General Mack in the vicinity of Ulm on the Danube. Two Russian armies destined to join the Austrians were only in Galicia as yet. British, Swedish, and Russian corps were operating in north Germany, in the region north of Hanover, and in Swedish Pomerania.

By means of a clever maneuver, with the assistance of a remarkable espionage and information agency, Napoleon isolated and encircled Mack's army, which surrendered in Ulm on October 15, 1805. In Paris and throughout all of Europe, the news of this victory eclipsed that of the defeat at Trafalgar, which occurred five days later. Metternich, then stationed in Berlin, wrote:

> The daily bulletins of the French army that are being published and
> that are flooding Germany and all of Europe, are a new invention and

merit the most serious attention. . . . The gazettes are worth more to Napoleon than an army of 300,000 men. . . . Public opinion is the most powerful weapon.

The news of the surrender of Ulm did indeed deter Prussia from joining with Austria and Russia at that moment, and it served to keep the hesitant Max-Joseph, elector of Bavaria, in the French alliance.

The Viennese route was, therefore, opened. What Bonaparte had been unable to realize in 1797, Napoleon accomplished in 1805. He entered Vienna on November 13, 1805. Austria with whom France had opened negotiations, might have agreed to a peace if France had been able to guarantee her extensive compensations in the Balkans to the detriment of Turkey. The defeat at Trafalgar and the destruction of the French squadron of the Mediterranean prevented Napoleon from offering these inducements to Austria. Thus, Austria decided to continue its alliance with the Russians and thereby hopefully achieve her objectives. Concentrated on the Bohemian plateau, not far from Brno, were 80,000 Russians and 25,000 Austrians. They were numerically superior to the French army that comprised scarcely more than 75,000 men. Action began on December 2, 1805, near the village of Austerlitz (now called Slavkov), on the anniversary of the emperor's coronation. This battle, which was attended by the three emperors—of France, Austria, and Russia—was a brilliant victory for Napoleon. Negotiations between the French and Austrian governments had never been totally interrupted since French troops had entered Vienna. Since the Tsar Alexander had hastily fallen back to the north with his troops and Francis II was isolated, negotiations were resumed with even greater fervor. Peace was concluded at Pressburg (Bratislava) on December 27, 1805.

This time Austria had to renounce all influence in Italy and in the Adriatic Sea. She gave up Venezia, Istria, and Dalmatia, which were incorporated into the Kingdom of Italy. Austria was also excluded from Germany. We have seen that by inaugurating an Austrian Empire Francis II had foreseen the event. The territories of which Austria had had direct possession in Germany were assigned to the electors of Bavaria, Württemberg, and Baden. Bavaria profited most from these spoils. The elector, Max-Joseph, whose loyalty to Napoleon had tottered until the last moment, received important cities such as Augsburg, as well as the Vorarlberg and the Tyrol, totaling more than 600,000 inhabitants. Prince Eugène, the viceroy of Italy, married the Bavarian elector's daughter.

The peace of Pressburg also entailed the removal of the Bourbons from Naples. The Bourbons had participated in the Third Coalition, and they had permitted an Anglo-Russian corps to land at Naples. On December 27, 1805, the same day on which the Treaty of Pressburg was signed, Napoleon proclaimed that "the dynasty of Naples no longer reigns." A few

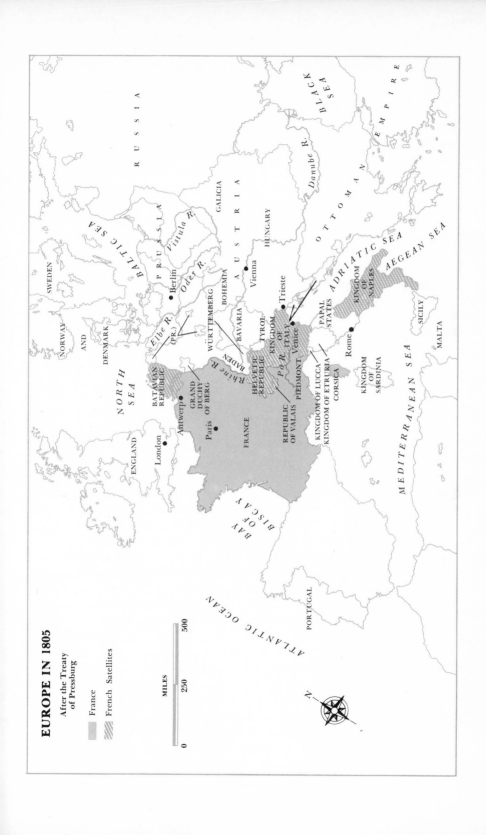

EUROPE IN 1805

After the Treaty
of Pressburg

France

French Satellites

MILES

0   250   500

N

ATLANTIC OCEAN

PORTUGAL

BAY OF BISCAY

NORTH SEA

ENGLAND

London

Antwerp

Paris

FRANCE

BATAVIAN REPUBLIC

GRAND DUCHY OF BERG

Elbe R.

(PR.)

Berlin

Oder R.

Vistula R.

BALTIC SEA

SWEDEN

NORWAY AND DENMARK

P R U S S I A

R U S S I A

WÜRTTEMBERG

BADEN

Rhine R.

HELVETIC REPUBLIC

REPUBLIC OF VALAIS

KINGDOM OF LUCCA

KINGDOM OF ETRURIA

CORSICA

KINGDOM OF SARDINIA

PIEDMONT

KINGDOM OF ITALY

Venice

TYROL

BAVARIA

BOHEMIA

GALICIA

A U S T R I A

HUNGARY

Vienna

Trieste

Danube R.

PAPAL STATES

Rome

KINGDOM OF NAPLES

SICILY

MALTA

O T T O M A N   E M P I R E

BLACK SEA

ADRIATIC SEA

AEGEAN SEA

M E D I T E R R A N E A N   S E A

days later, Napoleon "named" his brother Joseph to be king of Naples. Joseph immediately took over his new kingdom and occupied its entire peninsular portion. The Bourbons sought refuge at Palermo as they had done in 1799, under the protection of the British fleet (February 1806).

The Pope himself was threatened. Ancona, a city of the Papal States, had been occupied by the French in November 1805. Pius VII had called for the evacuation of the city in a tone that led Napoleon to believe that the Pope was hoping for a French defeat. He sent the Pope a menacing reply on January 7, 1806: "I will constantly protect the Holy See," and in the following February he wrote: "Your Holiness is the sovereign of Rome, but I am the Emperor of it. All of my enemies should be Rome's enemies." It was obvious that the slightest insult by the Pope would lead to the annexation of the Papal States either to the French Empire or to the Kingdom of Italy. The Treaty of Pressburg thus resulted in a considerable increase in France's influence on southern Germany and in placing all of Italy (with the exception of Sardinia and Sicily) under the direct or indirect domination of France.

JENA

The victory of Austerlitz and the Treaty of Pressburg had ended the war between France and Austria, but the war against Russia continued. In order to wage a campaign against the tsar's armies without having to fear for his rear lines, Napoleon had to be certain of Germany. Surely, he thought, he could count on the support of Bavaria, Württemberg, and on the duchy of Baden, whose rulers he had gratified. But he also had to assure himself of the states of northern Germany, those lying between the Rhine and the Vistula rivers. The naming of Eugène de Beauharnais as viceroy of Italy and of Joseph Bonaparte as king of Naples seemed to open a new means of domination. Under the Directory the French Republic had had its sister republics; the French Empire then would have its vassal kingdoms, governed by members of the imperial family. When he called Joseph to the throne of Naples, Napoleon had written to him: "I can no longer have relatives in obscurity. Those who will not rise with me will no longer belong to my family. I am creating a family of kings, or rather of vice-kings." And on March 15, 1806, he conferred on his brother-in-law Murat (Caroline's husband), the title of grand duke of Berg, a small state surrounding Dusseldorf on the right bank of the Rhine. On June 5, 1806, Louis Bonaparte succeeded to the Dutch throne.

Napoleon decided that there were enough German states of the right bank of the Rhine dependent on France to constitute a Confederation of the Rhine. Napoleon proclaimed himself the protector of the Confederation on July 16, 1806. In addition to Bavaria and Württemberg, whose sovereigns took the title of king, the Confederation encompassed the Grand Duchy of Baden, the Grand Duchy of Berg, and twelve other small states, including the Grand Duchy of Frankfurt, created for the benefit of Karl T. A. Maria von Dalberg, former archbishop of Ratisbon, future primate, who was transferred to this town with Napoleon's uncle, Cardinal Fesch, as co-adjutant. The Confederation remained open to any German prince who wanted to adhere to it, and several did join (the elector of Saxony, among others) on December 11, 1806. A Diet convening at Frankfurt was to handle affairs of common concern. The formation of the Confederation of the Rhine destroyed the former Holy Roman Empire, which disappeared from the European scene on August 6, 1806, when Emperor Francis II, who had become Francis I of Austria the year previous, laid down the old crown of the Holy Roman-Germanic Empire. The idea of a German empire was to survive, however, and would form the nucleus for a movement for unity that was soon to develop, leading to the formation of a new Germanic empire, a "second Reich."

For the moment, the Confederation of the Rhine resulted in a substantial extension of France's powers, while striking at the very heart of Germany. In a repetition of the operation of 1803, but this time without any consultation with the interested states, Napoleon proceeded with new secularizations, granting the property thus gained to the most loyal members of the Confederation. The same policy of transferring property to loyal followers of Napoleon was carried out for the often minute territories of the knights of the Empire (Reichsritter) who had constituted the traditional supporters of the house of Austria. Napoleon, no longer having any reason to humor them, "mediatized" these principalities and annexed them to the domains of his principal vassals. Thus Bavaria obtained Nuremberg and Württemberg received Ulm. The Confederation of the Rhine simplified the political geography of Germany as Napoleon's Italian policies had simplified that of Italy. It is not surprising that under this impetus the idea of unification made progress in these two countries, whatever the emperor's real objectives might be.

These great French successes seemed to point up the inability of the British to oppose Napoleon's forces with a continental coalition capable of smashing them. In England Pitt, the man who had advocated war, resigned and died on January 23, 1806. Fox, the Whig leader, became foreign secretary, while Addington returned to power as Lord of the Privy Seal. Tories also entered the ministry, with Lord William Grenville heading the treasury and William Windham, the war ministry. It was a kind of ministry of national union and was called "a ministry of all talents." Like the Addington ministry in 1801, it had been formed to deal with France. It did, in fact, dispatch an emissary, Lord Yarmouth, to Paris in June 1806.

Russia, following England's example, also sent a negotiator to Paris, Comte d'Oubril. Once again the Mediterranean problems caused the negotiations to fail. Napoleon demanded that the Bourbons be evicted from Sicily, and that the island be placed under the rule of his brother Joseph, as was the rest of the Kingdom of Naples. Russia consented, in return for important compensations in the East. Yarmouth opposed Napoleon for a long while, but he finally yielded. The British government, even under Fox's direction, however, did not agree with its envoy. Fox knew that if he were to yield on the question of Sicily, he would be overthrown. He therefore refused to ratify the agreement. Ill health forced him to retire from politics that summer, and he died shortly after, on September 13, 1806.

The rupture of negotiations with England also ended the parleys with Russia. War continued with each of the adversaries attempting to recruit allies. Prussia was the only great European power that had not yet taken part in the conflict. Her role was crucial since her land was the only territory separating the Confederation of the Rhine, under French influence, from the Russian Empire. Tsar Alexander tried to draw Prussia to his side, especially through Queen Louise, on whom he exercised a certain amount of influence. Napoleon acted on his own behalf. On December 15, 1805, by the Treaty of Schönbrunn, he had allowed Prussia to occupy Hanover. He presumed that this step would have sufficed to maintain the neutrality of her king, Frederick William III. Frederick William, anxious to avoid involvement, had informed England and Russia that the occupation was only temporary. He had also opened negotiations with France using the services of Count Haugwitz, a minister sent to Paris in the beginning of February 1806. Napoleon had received Haugwitz and requested that Frederick William ratify the Treaty of Schönbrunn at once. He wanted to finalize the transfer of Hanover to Prussia in exchange for an offensive and defensive Franco-Prussian alliance. On March 4 Frederick William signed the Treaty of Schönbrunn, which had been modified in Paris on February 15, and entered the war against England. Napoleon, convinced of the duplicity of the king of Prussia, had not hesitated to propose the restitution of Hanover to England, in the course of the negotiations with Yarmouth during the summer of 1806. Frederick William IV did have conflicting feelings about his French alliance. He was undoubtedly satisfied with holding Hanover, but he regretted the French alliance and the war with England. Thus, at the very rumor of Napoleon's offer—and under Russia's influence—he did an abrupt about-face. On October 1, 1806, he sent Napoleon an ultimatum demanding the immediate withdrawal of all French troops beyond the Rhine.

This was war. Prussia had great confidence in her army, even though it had confronted France only from 1792 to 1795, and although it had retreated at Valmy, this battle had not been viewed as a real defeat. The

Prussian army, nearly 200,000 men strong, well-equipped and well-trained, lived in the memory of the great victories won in the time of Frederick II. Having the support of Russia, the Prussian army felt confident that it could easily beat the French army, even in view of Austerlitz. It was quickly to learn otherwise.

After two weeks of "lightning-war," the Prussian army was on the verge of complete destruction. In Bamberg, on October 7, Bonaparte had received the Prussian ultimatum, which was to expire the following day. Seven days later, on October 14, the Prussian army, which had been resting on the reputation it had acquired at Rossbach and at Leuthen, was crushed at Jena and at Auerstädt. The old duke of Brunswick, the signer of the famous manifesto that had provoked the fall of the monarchy in France on August 10, 1792, was mortally wounded. The Prussian army was completely defeated and demoralized and on October 27, 1806, French troops entered Berlin.

EYLAU AND TILSIT

In the wake of his brilliant victory, Napoleon thought that Prussia and Saxony, which had been dragged into the war, would negotiate. And indeed, Girolano Lucchesini, the Prussian king's minister, signed an armistice with General Duroc on November 16 at Charlottenburg. King Frederick William refused to ratify it. He ordered what was left of his troops to join the Russians, and he placed all of his hope in a victory by the tsar. Only Saxony came to terms with Napoleon. In order to further a split with Prussia, Napoleon not only avoided imposing any onerous or humiliating conditions on Saxony but by the Treaty of Posen (Poznan) of December 11, 1806, he granted the elector the title of king and admitted him to the Confederation of the Rhine. The five dukes of Saxony-Weimar, Gotha, Meiningen, Hildburghausen and Coburg were also admitted. The Confederation of the Rhine now spread extensively to the east of the Elbe, and it very soon comprised other principalities of northeast Germany.

Meanwhile, the Russian army, reinforced by a Prussian contingent, had taken the offensive. The French army went to meet it, and for the first time it entered the vast plains of eastern Europe. The campaign was extremely difficult. Bonaparte's strategy—which had been worked out in the closed fields of northern Italy and then in western Germany, where a normal day's march of 25 to 30 kilometers led the army from one line of defense, waterway, or chain of hills, to another line of defense—proved to be ineffectual in these infinite spaces, where after a day's march the soldier would encounter neither village where he could find shelter and provisions, nor an obstacle behind which he could entrench himself. The battle at

Eylau in eastern Prussia on February 8, 1807, was one of the most murderous of the period. During the fight in the biting cold of the dead of winter, a total of 45,000 men were killed or wounded. Yet it was still indecisive, and the king of Prussia rejected a new peace proposal on April 20, 1807.

French troops gradually advanced into eastern Prussia and into Poland. The port of Danzig (Godansk), whose importance to English trade in the Baltic has already been underlined, surrendered on May 20, 1807. On June 14 a new offensive was pushed back at Friedland, a little to the north of Eylau. Russian forces were still sizable, despite the losses in the campaign of 1806–1807, and the territory of the Russian Empire had not yet been invaded. Alexander would have been able to continue the fight with a reasonable chance for success, but a few of his officers and most intimate advisers, Prince Adam Czartoryski, Count Paul Stroganov, and Count N. N. Novossiltsov, were inclined to seek peace. Besides, the English alliance was becoming more and more burdensome. Its only manifestation was a meager subsidy. It confounded Alexander that British expeditionary forces had not landed in Italy or in Holland, thereby creating new fronts that could have drawn off a part of the French army. After Friedland, Alexander was disposed to negotiate, as was Napoleon. He was worried about the attitudes of Austria, which had not accepted her defeat of 1805, and of Spain, where Godoy was engaged in suspicious intrigues. Napoleon hoped to conquer England now through an economic war supported by the Berlin Decree of November 21, 1806, which had instituted the Continental Blockade, also known as the Continental System. (This system will be examined further in the following chapter.)

An armistice was concluded at Tilsit on June 25. The two emperors met on a raft anchored in the middle of the Nieman River. Two peace treaties were subsequently signed, one with Russia on July 7 and the other with Prussia on July 9. Prussia received the poorest treatment. Napoleon would not forgive her unexpected attack of October 1806, which he considered to be veritable treason. Although Napoleon had won, he had skirted catastrophe, for he had risked the strong possibility that Austria and Spain would join with Prussia. Only the lightning speed of the victories of Jena and Auerstädt had dissuaded Emperor Francis I and the powerful Godoy from pursuing such plans. Napoleon's policies towards Prussia were dictated by a real hatred and deep scorn. Prussia had already felt his wrath, for since October the French occupation—with attendant requisitions and contributions, systematically levied under the direction of Count Pierre A. N. Bruno Daru, intendant general of the *Grande Armée*—had weighed heavily upon her. Prussia emerged from the Treaty of Tilsit in a mutilated condition. She had lost half of her population—5 million out of 10 million—all of her possessions on the left bank of the Elbe River, and all of the territories that she had taken from Poland since 1772—with the exception of a narrow "corridor" linking eastern Prussia to Brandenburg. She was to remain under French occupation until she had effected complete payment of a heavy war indemnity.

The Polish territories ceded by Prussia were placed under the authority of the king of Saxony and became the Duchy of Warsaw. This action revived a Polish state and imbued patriots with the hope that Napoleon might one day reconstitute Poland, in the same way that the Kingdom of Italy had led Italian patriots to the hope of eventually witnessing the unification of their country. The duchy of Warsaw was admitted to the Confederation of the Rhine and so came under the protectorship of France.

The land to the west of the Elbe, which had been lost by Prussia and her allies, became the Kingdom of Westphalia, to the profit of Napoleon's youngest brother, Jerome, who became King. The kingdom was also absorbed into the Confederation of the Rhine, and on August 22, 1807, Jerome Bonaparte married Princess Catherine de Württemberg.

Russia's losses were relatively slight. She ceded to France the Ionian Islands and Cattaro (Kotor), which she had occupied since 1799. She was to return to the Ottoman Empire Moldavia and Wallachia, which had also been under Russian occupation. If the sultan refused to make peace with Russia after this restitution, Russia and France would come to an agreement concerning the seizure of all Turkish European possessions. The Treaty of Tilsit actually did more than restore peace between France and Russia. It outlined a division of Europe between these two empires. In addition, the tsar was supposed to offer his mediation to England. If the British government refused, the two emperors would agree on forcing England to make peace. Napoleon and Alexander were indeed mutually pleased. Before parting, they concluded a secret treaty of alliance. Russia, of course, agreed to adhere to the Continental Blockade. The alliance left Russia complete freedom of action to the east of the Vistula River and allowed Napoleon the same freedom to the west. This apportionment of Europe could only be viable if the Continental Blockade were to succeed in destroying Britain's economy.

7

THE BLOCKADE AND THE CONTINENTAL SYSTEM

After the peace of Tilsit, and for the fourth time since 1793, France and England stood alone as adversaries, face to face across the Channel. Napoleon no longer could contemplate an invasion of England. Ever since the two powers became active foes, each had brandished the usual economic arms. England declared the coast of France in a state of blockade, and France renewed her prohibition against the importation of British goods, a practice that had been decreed as early as 1793 under the National Convention. At the beginning, these measures had not been very effective. However, little by little, war by blockade was perfected.

ORGANIZATION OF THE BLOCKADE, 1803 TO 1806

In France for more than a century the premise had been accepted that the power of Great Britain, based upon its economic organization, was fragile. French economists, and other Europeans as well, considered her system of credit abnormal. Her industry could prosper only by virtue of exportation to Europe. It ought, therefore, to be relatively easy to break down the system by excluding her exports from foreign markets; Great Britain would then be ruined and would not be slow to capitulate. As early as 1800, the Institute of France had announced a competition on the problem of credit. As a result, numerous tracts were published that analyzed the British credit system. All demonstrated its unhealthy character—for example, Charles Saladin in *L'Angleterre en 1800* (1801), Joseph Henri Lasalle in *Des finances de l'Angleterre* (1803), Arthur O'Connor in *L'état actuel de la Grande Bretagne* (1804). German authors appeared to concur; the same premise appeared in the works of Johann Fichte, *L'état commercial fermé* (1800) and *Fondements de l'époque actuelle* (1806) and of Buchholz in *Le nouveau Leviathan* (1805) and *Rome et Londres* (1806). These works all supported the thesis that an effective method of preventing the entry of English merchandise into the European continent and in the British colonies, would bring about the collapse of Great Britain.

Ever since 1793—with the exception of the eighteen months of peace from 1801 to 1803—the two belligerents had taken measures to blockade each other. The British fleet cruised before French ports and seized ships carrying the French flag or that of her allies. The French and the allied governments, in turn, forbade British ships to enter their ports. Such measures were ineffective for traffic continued on neutral ships. Both adversaries tried to catch the neutrals, but each had different conceptions of neutral trade, even diametrically opposed ones. France and the continental states invoked the principles expounded by jurisconsults at the beginning of the seventeenth century, particularly those of Hugo Grotius in his celebrated work *Mare liberum:* goods carried under a neutral flag were free goods. The Treaty of Utrecht of 1713 had already stated the rule that in case of war, "the flag covers the goods." In 1748, in his *Droit public de l'Europe* . . . , Gabriel de Mably had demonstrated that it was forbidden for belligerent ships "to insult neutral trading ships and to seize them."

Great Britain, which possessed the largest maritime fleet in the world, had never subscribed to these rules, and it was in order to assure their observance that the League of Neutrality had been formed in 1780 and 1800. Polemics went back and forth regarding the entry of neutral ships into blockaded ports. If public European law admitted that on the high seas the flag covered the goods, it recognized by contrast, that a blockade would prevent entry of neutral ships into a blockaded port. British naval forces, despite their power, could not effectively blockade all the ports of the continent. The British government disregarded this fact and declared a blockade against numerous ports that she could not effectively carry out. Because of such a declaration she claimed the right to capture, on the high seas, ships whose papers proved that they went to these ports. In 1780 and for the remainder of her regime, Catherine II of Russia protested this practice and in 1800 a *Mémoire sur les Neutres,* published by the Russians with the aid of the French government, had declared: "The right of blockade can only be declared against ports effectively blockaded." Napoleon, in the name of these great principles of the law of nations, was about to protest British methods of blockade. In reprisal, he was forced to close more and more hermetically the Continent to all English goods, even if transported in neutral vessels. Neutrals thus became the victims as much of the English measures as of French reprisals. With the tightening of the blockade, the war would inevitably spread.

After 1803 Bonaparte forbade the entry of colonial goods and manufactured products of English origin into France and required that neutral cargoes be accompanied with a certificate attesting that they were not of English origin. In reply, the British government decreed a blockade of the mouths of the Weser and the Elbe rivers; in 1804 the measure was extended to all French ports on the North Sea and the Channel, and in 1806 to the mouths of the Ems and the Trave (the latter river forming the entry to the important port of Lübeck). This was a paper blockade. Bonaparte decided to reply with extraordinary measures.

THE BERLIN AND MILAN DECREES[1]

Less than a month after the capture of Berlin, Napoleon signed (November 21, 1806) the Berlin Decree that extended considerably the prohibitions against the entry of British merchandise to the continent and stated the bases of what he himself called the Continental Blockade. The decree began by listing Napoleon's complaints against England for not respecting the principles of the law of nations. He asserted that England proclaimed it legal to seize not only goods under the civil jurisdiction of enemy countries but also goods under the jurisdiction of neutrals being transported in commercial ships. In addition, England declared a blockade of those ports where she had not a single warship, although a place can be legally blockaded only when it is so besieged that one cannot enter without imminent danger. The emperor affirmed that these abuses had no other aim "than to raise English commerce and industry on the ruin of continental

---

[1] Two books on the Continental Blockade are especially useful: François Crouzet, *L'Empire britannique et le blocus continental (1806–1813)*, 2 vols. (Paris, 1958) and E. F. Heckscher, *The Continental System* (Oxford: Clarendon Press, 1922). For Spain, see the bibliography under *Napoleon and Europe:* M. Arcola, *Los Origines de la España contemporanea*, 2 vols. (Madrid, 1959); André Fugier, *Napoléon et l'Espagne*, 2 vols. (Paris, 1929–1930); Charles Geoffrey de Grandmaison *L'Espagne et Napoléon*, 3 vols. (Paris, 1908–1931); Gabriel H. Lovett, *Napoleon and the Birth of Modern Spain*, 2 vols. (New York, New York University Press, 1965).

industry and commerce." In consequence, Napoleon looked upon "anyone engaging in trade in English goods as the accomplice of England. . . ." He declared, on his side, a blockade against the British Isles, forbidding all commerce with England, ordering the confiscation of all goods made in England or the English colonies "no matter where seized," the destruction of all letters to or from England, the arrest as prisoners of war of all Englishmen on the Continent. Finally, he forbade entry into any port of ships that had touched England or the English colonies; in case of false declaration, the ship would be declared legal capture. The decree was to be applied not only in France, but also in all allied or occupied countries, that is, Spain, Italy, Switzerland, Holland, Denmark, and Germany. At Tilsit, Russia promised to apply the system, and Napoleon hoped to force Portugal to adhere.

The maritime blockade by England and the Continental Blockade by Napoleon, had different objectives. The British did not envisage starvation for the continent—that was impossible at this time—but to deprive it of colonial products and raw materials that had become essential: tea, coffee, chocolate, indigo, spices, and cotton. In addition, the continent would not have access to machines and maufactured articles that England produced in larger quantities, and cheaper than Europe. The Continental System aimed to deprive England of her commercial sales on the continent in order to create a crisis of industrial overproduction, which would have as probable consequences extensive unemployment, and without doubt would lead to the collapse of credit and money. While the English blockade could at the most handicap France and her allies, the Continental Blockade should lead England to capitulation, and thus a general peace would be reestablished.

As soon as the British government learned of the text of the Berlin Decree, it retorted with a series of Orders in Council. These orders were obscure and confused, but, in a general manner, they declared a blockade against all countries obeying the Berlin Decree, that is all that excluded British goods. In accordance with the orders, only neutral ships that had touched at English ports and paid the same fees that they would have paid if the cargo had been landed in England (about 25 percent *ad valorem*) could trade with European ports against which Britain had declared a blockade. A license delivered by British authorities recognized the payment of these fees and gave authorization to trade with the Continent. England hoped to gain two advantages by such regulation: to hinder continental industry by depriving it of a part of its raw materials and to eliminate from the European continent neutral merchandise to the profit of British goods, which it hoped to pass, thanks to contraband, through the mesh of the Napoleonic net.

It was in order to reduce this contraband that Napoleon issued the Milan Decree (December 17, 1807). All ships having received the British visa or having touched at an English port and paid the fees demanded by the British were declared "good prize." A decree of January 11, 1808 encouraged informing; any sailor certifying that a ship had stopped at a British port would receive a recompense of one-third the net product of the sale of the ship and its cargo, if the declaration was exact.

The Orders in Council and the Berlin and Milan decrees made neutrality an impossibility. Neutral ships with an English license were seized by the French; without license, they were captured by the English. What would be the effects of the blockade on the two groups of belligerents and on neutrals?

THE BRITISH ECONOMY AND
THE CONTINENTAL BLOCKADE

The effects of a blockade are always slow to show themselves. In 1807 England hardly perceived the consequences of the Berlin Decree. Besides, in the period between the issuing of the Berlin Decree and the signing of the Treaty of Tilsit the blockade was barely applied. Napoleon was busy with the war against Russia and paid little attention to the enforcement of the decree. Customs cordons extending all along European shores were very loose and the functionaries charged with enforcing the decrees were corrupt and not zealous. After Tilsit, things changed; the Berlin Decree, then that of Milan, and those that completed them were applied with greater rigor. Northern Europe was closed little by little to English merchandise, while southern Europe, which had only minor markets, was hardly open. The year 1808 was a veritable wasting away for England's economy.

In the Baltic region, Denmark, Russia, and Prussia were forced, after the Treaty of Tilsit, to declare war on England. It was with Sweden, under the protection of a powerful squadron, that England maintained commercial relations. Göteborg became a great port of destination and redistribution—by contraband—of English goods. Despite this, English commerce in the Baltic was considerably diminished. English commercial traffic on the North Sea was almost nonexistent during 1808, and of course, economic relations with France were completely interrupted—except for some trade that trickled into France via smuggling operations. In the Mediterranean trade with Spain and Italy remained extremely weak. By contrast Malta became an important trading post. Here an active trade developed in merchandise, by contraband, and the English commerce of the Levant, soared remarkably. At no time did this compensate for the considerable deficit resulting from the loss of exports to Europe.

The English economy suffered a further blow: the almost complete interruption of commercial relations between England and the United States. The latter was very displeased with the Orders-in-Council announced by England in 1807, which obligated all neutral ships, under threat of seizure, to stop at a British port and there pay sizable fees. In reprisal, the Congress of the United States passed on December 22, 1807, a law forbidding all American merchant ships to leave American ports for foreign ports (the Embargo Act), unless furnished with a presidential license. This embargo was, it should be noted, directed against both England and France. President Jefferson thought that in depriving the belligerents of American cotton, grains, and wood, he would force them to modify their attitude toward neutrals. In addition, American and English merchants fearing war between the two countries, voluntarily reduced their transatlantic commerce, from which resulted great difficulty in financial regulations and settlements. During the first half of 1808 British exports were 60 percent less than in the preceding year.

Thus, the formidable conjuncture of the closing of Europe and of the United States made itself felt in 1808. It was only compensated by an improvement of commerce with Brazil. Portugal had been invaded by the French in 1807, and the Court sought refuge at Bahia. As soon as it arrived there, it opened Brazilian ports to British ships. The increased trade with Brazil could not fill the gap left by disruption of commerce with Europe and the United States. In summary, in 1808 British exports decreased by more than twenty-five percent, which, without being catastrophic, was grave.

What were the consequences in the interior of Great Britain of this lowering? The reexport of colonial products was impaired, stocks of sugar and coffee reached levels until then unknown. The index of the price of coffee fell from 88 for the third quarter of 1807 to 64 in the second quarter of 1808. Sugar was made into rum, and the distillation of grains for the manufacture of British liqueurs *(eaux-de-vie)* was forbidden. The price of pepper and of Indian cottons lowered similarly.

The crisis struck British industry even harder. In the cotton mills piles of unsold goods accumulated. Industrialists MacConnel and Kennedy sold their merchandise at a loss of 3 percent and wrote on March 16, 1808: "Our prospect here is horribly alarming. One can sell neither fabrics nor yarn, and our operations are almost at a standstill." On March 23 they added: "At present we are scarcely working on a half-time basis and we have no intention of buying cotton again while we do not know what the future holds for us." It is difficult, nevertheless, due to the lack of documents, to estimate the number of unemployed and the misery of those who continued to work but at famine wages. The woolen industry was equally affected. An industrialist of Leeds, Rogerson, stated on February 22: "The prospects for commerce are as bad as ever." He noted that there were a great number of workers who accepted employment at 10 shillings per week, while the normal wage was 25 to 30 shillings.

With respect to the silk industry, the crisis was different. The closing of Europe to English commerce led to an abrupt halt of imports of Italian raw silk. It was a lack of raw material that closed the London silk workshops.

The metallurgical industry suffered just as severely. Exports of finished products in wrought iron or in cast iron diminished greatly. A meeting of the iron masters of Yorkshire and Derbyshire adopted the following resolution on June 20, 1808: "The iron masters present, convinced that current production of iron is already sufficient for consumption, judge that production should not be increased before circumstances render it necessary." For the year 1808, the profits of the Foundry of Newtown Chambers and Company were zero; in 1807 they had attained £3,984 (13 percent of the investment).

As Napoleon had anticipated, the economic crisis had social and political consequences for Great Britain. They were, nevertheless, less grave than the Emperor of the French hoped. As in 1780, it was Yorkshire that gave the signal for movement. A petition was circulated there to demand that the government make peace; it received 29,000 signatures. The demand for peace spread to Lancashire, then to other counties. Discontent was everywhere. The workers complained of unemployment or of miserable wages. The leaders of the Whig party demanded the repeal of the Orders in Council, which they blamed for the economic crisis. The British government refused to examine the petitions and declared that they were dangerous and would put the government in a false position if it were engaged in a negotiation. The petitions for peace were not even discussed by Parliament, and by the end of 1808 the agitation subsided. This subsiding was due, first, to the fact that since 1798 there no longer were revolutionary leaders in Great Britain. All those who could have taken the lead of a popular movement were in prison or exiled in Australia. Thus the agitation in Manchester and Lancashire in May and June 1808 did not result in riots. On the continent, the political situation that had evolved allowed hope of an amelioration for the British economy.

THE BLOCKADE AND CONTINENTAL EUROPE

The English maritime blockade disrupted the shipment to Europe of colonial products (sugar, coffee, cocoa, indigo, and cotton) and of products manufactured in England. It posed two problems to the European economy. First, Europeans had to find substitutes for colonial products. Second, they had to develop a European industry that could replace British products on the continental market. In another regard, Napoleon did not forget that in the Continental System that he had instituted, France remained at the center, and it was toward the development of French industry that he brought his principal efforts to bear.

To replace the colonial products that disappeared from the markets, the French government encouraged research by agronomists, chemists, and industrialists. The first step taken was to substitute grape sugar for cane sugar, and in 1808 grape sugar was processed in Piedmont and Languedoc. However, it was a mediocre substitute. In 1810 a certain Foques of Draguignan succeeded in producing grape sugar, the net cost of which was lower than that of cane sugar. The emperor rewarded him with 40,000 francs. The quality of the sugar was still not satisfactory, and the ministry sent the chemist Joseph Louis Proust into the department of Hérault to establish a model grape-sugar factory. The factory was never capable of producing a sugar that could rival cane sugar. Attempts made to manufacture sugar from chestnuts were no more successful.

The researchers then turned to the manufacture of beet sugar. In 1747 a learned German named Margraf had attempted to extract sugar from beets. A Huguenot *émigré* Charles Francois Achard undertook again in Prussia Margraf's experiments, for which he received encouragement from Frederick II. In 1799 Achard produced an excellent beet sugar and sent a memoir on his procedure to the French government. Bonaparte presented the memoir to the Institute of France, which gave a favorable opinion of it. However, peace was established in 1801, and Achard's experiments were abandoned. They were resumed when the Continental Blockade was put into effect in 1808. In 1809, Barruel and Ainard experimented with sugar beets at state expense in the Parisian region and a farmer Scey founded a sugar beet manufacture in Doubs. In 1810 the French government published instructions drafted by Barruel and Deyeux on the manufacture of sugar from beets. By decree of March 25 of the same year Napoleon promised a subsidy of 600,000 francs to anyone who could manufacture sugar from beets equal in quality and in price to cane sugar. On January 15, 1812, the government established five schools to teach the process for manufacturing sugar from beets. They were situated in the Rhineland, Alsace, Picardie, Languedoc, and the Parisian region. Each school was to enroll one hundred students. The sugar-beet factories were granted privileges and were exempt for four years from taxes and town fees (octrois). The total production of beet sugar had not yet reached 2000 tons when the Empire collapsed. Thus a consequence of the Continental Blockade was the development of the manufacture of beet sugar, but its production always remained insufficient to cover the deficit of cane sugar.

The efforts to replace coffee had less important consequences. Roasted chicory roots, which when ground produced a blackish beverage, were tried. Without replacing coffee, it could give the illusion of it.

To alleviate the scarcity of indigo they returned to the use of woad to obtain dye. The government encouraged the culture of the indigo-woad plant, and Languedoc and Tuscany became the center for its cultivation. Instructions for the manufacture of blue dye beginning with woad were drafted by J. A. C. Chaptal, Bardel, Thenard, J. L. Gay-Lussac, and Rodard. On January 14, 1813, a decree set up three imperial factories of indigo-woad at Toulouse, Turin, and Florence. Exemptions from the taxes and subsidies were promised to all those who could prove that they were producing 200 kilos of indigo from woad.

As for cotton, its cultivation was tried in vain in southern France and in Italy. One purchased it in the Ottoman Empire, from which the cotton was transported by land and partially via the Danube and its tributaries. Factories lacked cotton, however, and many were forced to close.

In the domain of industrial production, only metallurgy, stimulated by war manufactures, made progress. The metallurgic industries of central France, east Belgium, and the left bank of the Rhine developed, but these places were situated within the borders of the French Empire.

The "vassal" countries complained of not profiting from the industrial increase resulting from the blockade. In Italy, for example, the manufacture of silk cloth diminished, while the exports of raw silk to France increased. Napoleon wished to favor the Lyonnaise industry (he feared above all a revolt in Lyons similar to the one of 1793 and desired at any price to prevent unemployment in that town). The number of Italian silk factories decreased from 500 to 400 between 1806 and 1811, that of workers employed in this industry from 140,000 to 100,000, and the value of production fell from 14,500,000 lire to 6,200,000 lire. The woolen industry remained a cottage industry. As in the rest of continental Europe the Italian cotton industry was greatly affected. Metallurgy was not well developed, and the blockade did not stimulate any changes in it. On the whole, the Continental Blockade shackled the development of Italian industry and enlarged still more the gap that separated Italy from the industrialized countries of Europe, notably England.

In Germany the principal industrial zone, the basin of the Ruhr River, was found in the Grand Duchy of Berg, of which Murat was the sovereign. The cotton industry, already highly developed in the valley of the Wupper, around the towns of Barmen and Elberfeld, was seriously injured. It only worked with cotton which arrived from the Orient which reached it via the Danube and the Rhine or with contraband cotton. The German looms were mediocre local imitations of English machines and seemed inferior even to those used in France in this epoch. In summary, the manufacture of cotton moved at a slow pace, and was really a depressed industry.

By contrast, the metallurgic industry was booming in spite of the closing of the American market, which before the war already offered a large outlet to the metallurgic industry of the Ruhr. Sales in central Europe, in place of English merchandise, replaced in part the American market. But the industrialists complained because of the very high customs duties that protected the French market. Nevertheless, the manufacture of arms for the French army permitted the maintenance of all factories in full activity. In the valleys of the Sieg and the Ruhr thirty-three blast furnaces operated, six of which worked exclusively in the manufacture of steel. The industry of the Grand Duchy of Berg was far from using all of the coal extracted from the Ruhr basin. Nearly half was exported via the Rhine to Holland. Nevertheless, since the metallurgic industry employed only 5000 workers in Berg, while the textile industry employed ten times more (20,000 of whom were employed in the cotton industry), the net effect of the blockade was detrimental to the economic life of this region. The blockade seriously hurt this most heavily industrialized area of Germany. The grand duchy could only hope for an amelioriation of its situation by annexation to the French Empire, which would eliminate customs barriers and open to it the interior French market. Napoleon refused this, and Berg suffered increasingly from the blockade. It was in this country of the Confederation of the Rhine that hostility to Napoleon manifested itself most rapidly in 1809 and most violently.

THE BLOCKADE AND NAPOLEONIC EXPANSION

The Continental Blockade could only succeed—that is, create a crisis of overproduction in Great Britain and at the same time stimulate continental industry—if it were vigorously applied by all Europe, and above all by the countries of Europe that traditionally served as outlets for British commerce. When Napoleon first instituted the blockade, Russia, Germany, Holland, Spain, and the greater part of Italy closed their ports to the English, but one country Portugal, balked.

Portugal was one of the countries of Europe most hostile to Napoleon's policy for two reasons, as already noted. First, because of its political and social structure, Portugal was one of the European states most hostile to the ideas of the Revolution. Only a very small circle of liberals had expounded these ideas, and its members, some of whom were French in origin had been immediately subjected to government persecution. For the Portuguese government, as for the British, Napoleon continued the Revolution. In addition, the Portuguese government had been economically bound to England for centuries, and above all, since the Treaty of Methuen of 1703.

Portugal refused to apply the measures enacted by the Berlin and Milan decrees. The Spanish prime minister, Godoy, pressured Napoleon to intervene in Portugal. Since the War of Oranges of 1801, which had brought him nothing personally, Godoy considered himself frustrated and desired to carve, to the detriment of Portugal, a personal principality. French intervention in Portugal had, therefore, as its primary reason the application of the Continental Blockade, but the intervention had been precipitated no less by the intrigues of the Spanish government. It would be fatal to the latter and in the long run just as disasterous for Napoleon himself.

In consequence of the attitude of Portugal—which rejected a French ultimatum of July 28, 1807, demanding her to declare war on England—and the intrigues of Godoy, a treaty was signed between Spain and France, at Fontainebleau, on October 29, 1807 that looked forward to the division of Portugal into three parts. The south would be given to Godoy, and the north would be given to the queen of Etruria, whose state would be annexed to the Empire. As for the center region with Lisbon, its fate was reserved. Spain gave the French army the right of passage on its roads with all necessary services included. A French army commanded by General Junot marched through Spain to Lisbon and captured it without difficulty on November 30, 1807. Some days previously the regent Jean de Bragance—the queen, Marie I, was insane—left for Brazil with the entire royal family. The operation seemed eminently successful, but Napoleon was not contemplating the immediate execution of the clauses of the Treaty of Fontainebleau; Godoy was profoundly irritated by this. Could he force the Emperor to keep his promises by relying on the Spanish people? Godoy thought of doing this for a time, it seems. Already in 1806, before Jena, he had published a *Manifesto to the Spanish Nation,* which could have been interpreted as an appeal to insurrection against France. At the announcement of the great victories won by Napoleon over Prussia, Godoy excused himself and explained that his manifesto was directed against Portugal alone. Godoy's policy had differing shades of meaning, but these successive recantations had turned against Godoy the crown prince, Don Ferdinand, who created a "party," and the royal family, as well as Spanish public opinion as far as it existed at that time.

The crown prince Ferdinand in reality detested Godoy who was the queen's lover and the absolute master, it seemed, of Spain. Many of the nobles believed Godoy's policy contrary to the interests of Spain; they counted on Ferdinand to remove the one whom they considered a traitor. Thus, the Party of the Prince (*cuarto del Principe*) was formed. Its leader was a canon of Toledo, Juan Escoiquiez, Ferdinand's former tutor. Godoy and the king were warned and they arrested Ferdinand and some of his accomplices on October 28, 1807, the eve of the signing of the Treaty of Fontainebleau—but this was only a coincidence of date. Prince Ferdinand was found guilty of plotting against the government but he was saved by

Napoleon. He had written to Napoleon asking the hand of the daughter of his stepson, Francois de Beauharnais, ambassador of France to Madrid. Napoleon did not wish the name of a Beauharnais to be compromised in the affairs of the Spanish royal family. Perhaps he saw the family quarrel as the means to involve himself more in internal Spanish politics. He intervened at Ferdinand's request, and Charles IV pardoned his rebellious son on November 5, 1807. Ferdinand and Godoy were reconciled, at least, outwardly. The accomplices were acquitted too.

It was now the Spanish people who accused Godoy of having delivered Spain to the foreigner. In reality, French troops did not restrict themselves to crossing the north of Spain on the great roads leading to Portugal. They spread out from one place to another occupying the towns, fortified places, citadels, and fortresses. Did not the plot of October 1807 prove the weakness of the Spanish government? Was it not necessary to replace Godoy with a man who would form an opposing policy? As for the French, in the case of a quick governmental change in Spain was it not the duty of the French command to assure the security of Junot's army and the security of his lines of communication?

Godoy became more and more unpopular. He was reproached for having "sold" Spain, and his immense fortune, valued at 1.5 million reals, gave some foundation to these accusations. He was reproached for his dissolute life and his numerous mistresses. He was held responsible for the arrest of Ferdinand on October 28. The French government did not ignore these accusations. It considered, furthermore, that they were in great part justified and thought that the solidarity of the Spanish alliance could only be maintained by a change of sovereign, even of dynasty. While Napoleon in France considered what to do, Murat, who had been named commander in chief of the Army of Spain on February 20, 1808, found the country to his liking and thought that the royal throne of Madrid would give him more prestige than the Grand Duchy of Berg. He agitated for intervention and was upheld by the French minister of foreign affairs, Nompère de Champagny, who deemed it impossible to accord confidence to the Spanish Bourbons for much longer.

Napoleon wavered for a time between the diverse solutions. He dispatched several emissaries to Spain, including Count de Tournon, who made reports favorable to a change of dynasty. To prepare for it, Napoleon sent a new army to Spain commanded by General Dupont. In addition he grouped two corps under General Moncey and Marshal Mouton in the Pyrenees, ready to reinforce the troops of occupation. The important cities, Barcelona and Pampeluna, which were not yet in French hands, were occupied in February 1808. At the same time on the orders of the Emperor, the French press released a violent campaign against the Spanish Bourbons and their government. It represented them as base and incapable.

It was in this atmosphere that on March 18, 1808, an uprising broke out at Aranjuez where the royal family was then residing. Godoy was arrested, and Prince Ferdinand acclaimed. King Charles IV abdicated in favor of his son. The uprising extended to Madrid, and to protect French communications with Portugal, Murat and his soldiers entered the Spanish capital. Charles IV and Godoy demanded his protection, and Murat granted it. On the strength of his support, Charles IV withdrew his abdication and placed his fate in Napoleon's hands. But on March 24, Ferdinand was acclaimed triumphantly in Madrid. The Spanish imbroglio seemed inextricable.

It was then that General Savary arrived in Madrid, carrying an order from Napoleon summoning Prince Ferdinand, Godoy, Charles IV, and the Queen to Bayonne. From April 19 to May 10, the tragicomic conversations of Bayonne developed. Napoleon had not yet, it seemed, made up his mind whom he would back when he arrived at Bayonne, but he found Prince Ferdinand "a fool, very malicious and very much the enemy of France." Godoy, whose disgrace had inspired in Napoleon some sympathy, displeased him. Charles IV seemed knavish to him and the queen Marie Louise very ugly. It did not take long for Napoleon to decide on his course of action. He had thought of transferring his brother Louis from the throne of Holland to the throne of Spain, but Louis refused. An attempt at reconciliation between Charles IV and his son Ferdinand failed. Then on May 5 Napoleon received news of the insurrection that had occurred on May 2 in Madrid. He held Ferdinand responsible and decided not to recognize him as king. Since Charles IV refused to return to insurgent Madrid, it followed that the throne of Spain was vacant. Napoleon knew that Murat was a candidate, but Napoleon instead designated for Madrid his eldest brother Joseph, king of Naples, who would be replaced in Italy by Murat. A Spanish constitution based on the French constitution was hastily drafted. It should, Napoleon thought, rally Spanish liberals to the new dynasty.

The "snare" of Bayonne only exasperated the Spaniards. The Madrid revolt of May 2 had been provoked by more and more frequent interventions by the French in Spanish affairs. The tragic comedy of Bayonne was to lead to the revolt of the entire country. Thus, the application of the Continental Blockade had as a consequence the full involvement of France in the Iberian Peninsula; this was to be an extremely serious fact for the French, the consequences of which it was difficult to foresee in 1808.

Napoleon had been led to intervene in the Iberian Peninsula because Portugal constituted a breach in the Continental Blockade through which British merchandise entered the Continent. In Italy, also, similar breaches existed. Tuscany with the port of Leghorn, had maintained longtime commercial relations with Great Britain; the Papal States with the ports of Ancona on the Adriatic Sea and Civita Vecchia on the Tyrrhenian Sea could offer outlets to the English.

Upon the signing of the Treaty of Tilsit, French troops occupied Leghorn and burned the stocks of English merchandise that they found there. On December 28, 1807, a French councillor of state was sent into Tuscany, whose capital had been abandoned by the sovereign, the queen of Etruria. It should be remembered that she was to receive a new kingdom cut from northern Portugal, but, in fact, she obtained nothing. On November 11, 1807, Napoleon had written to his stepson, Prince Eugène, that his intention was to unite Tuscany to the Kingdom of Italy: thus little by little, this kingdom would extend over the entire peninsula. He did not do this. In order to oversee more closely the trade of Leghorn, Napoleon annexed Tuscany to the French Empire on March 15, 1808. He seemed to abandon completely the idea of the unification of Italy that he had manifested in 1796 and 1802. Parma was next to be united to the Empire on May 24, 1808. French troops had occupied Ancona since 1805. They received the order in 1807 to extend their occupation to the entirety of the Marches. To compensate for the bad impression created in Milan by the incorporation of Tuscany and Parma into the Empire, Napoleon decided to annex Ancona and the Marches, a poor region inhabited by an ignorant and fanatic population, to the Kingdom of Italy (May 11, 1808). This would be a source of difficulties for the Kingdom of Italy, for the rural population of the Marches demonstrated its hostility to the new institutions imposed upon them, from the beginning.

The remainder of the Papal States along with Rome and the port of Civita Vecchia were also occupied at the beginning of January 1808. The Pope was menaced not only in his temporal sovereignty but also in his spiritual power. On the day after the Treaty of Tilsit, Napoleon had written to the viceroy Eugène: "I begin to redden from shame and feel humiliated by all the follies that the Court of Rome made me endure and perhaps the time is not distant when I will only recognize the Pope as the Bishop of Rome, as equal and in the same rank as the bishops of my states." Napoleon had then proposed to the Pope a treaty by which the Pope would have obtained a guarantee of his states in exchange for his total submission to the demands of Napoleon. Pius VII refused to sign this treaty, which he judged "hostile to the liberty and the independence of his sovereignty." On February 2, 1808, French troops entered Rome, disarmed the papal guards, and entered the Quirinal Palace where the Pope was residing. One month later most of the cardinals were expelled from the Eternal City. Pius VII only preserved a ghost of his power. The entire Italian peninsula was henceforth directly controlled by French troops. The Napoleonic domination seemed to spread to the entire continent. Was it going to be accepted submissively by the peoples of Europe?

8

THE NATIONAL RESISTANCE TO THE IMPERIAL REGIME

Until 1808, the French army had encountered largely mercenary armies, often numerically inferior and always devoid of the morale that characterized the French soldiers. In part, this explained the French success. To be sure, the French army had had to put down popular revolts, more exactly, peasant insurrections. In fact, the most serious had taken place in France itself, the Vendéean revolt of 1793. In Italy, especially in Calabria, in 1799; in Switzerland, and in Belgium many peasant revolts had erupted against French troops, or rather against certain social groups that had profited from the Revolution that developed with the support of the French soldiers. For example, in Calabria the peasants blamed above all the bourgeoisie and the nobility whose economic situation had been improved by the Revolution, but which had brought no relief to the peasant class. The religious factor had also played an important role in these uprisings: the insurgents revolted against the dechristianizing, impious or atheistic Revolution. Never had the revolts attempted to replace the regime installed by the Revolution with another regime also founded on the ideas of nation, liberty, and equality. They demanded merely the maintenance or reestablishment of the old regime, sometimes with some modifications of the economic or social order.

140

However, after 1808 the popular resistance movements that were to rise against the French armies no longer invoked the Old Regime, but instead demanded the inauguration of the new ideas that for fifteen years had been diffused in part by the French armies. Foremost to be advocated was the national idea—almost unknown in 1789 but which in 1808 became the driving ideal of the principal insurrections. Then came the ideals of liberty and equality applied more to nations than to individuals. Finally the people fought to draw up constitutions similar to those adopted by certain nations. These constitutions were not to be drafted under the aegis of France. More often they were even against the will of France. The year 1808, therefore, marked a great change in the confrontation between France and Europe. It was no longer a revolutionary France struggling against "mercenaries of tyrants," but against national forces issuing from the same great Revolution with which they were coming to blows.

THE SPANISH UPRISING

On May 2, 1808 *(dos de mayo)*, the people of Madrid rose against the French troops. They were provoked by the entry of Murat's soldiers into the Spanish capital and by the French intervention in the quarrel between Charles IV (abandoned by his people) and his son Ferdinand (supported by them) and between Ferdinand (whom they wished to have as sovereign) and Godoy (the detested favorite and prime minister). On May 2, all French soldiers who walked alone in the streets of the Spanish capital were attacked and assassinated to the cries of "Death to the French." Murat organized resistance, and then on May 3, took steps of repression. The number killed on these two days is disputed but it seems that about 200 French soldiers had been killed and 400 or fewer Spanish civilians were massacred in retaliation. These Madrid days of May 2 and 3 were only a prelude and a signal. Three weeks later on May 24 all Spain was in flames.

The insurrection began at the same time in regions very distant from each other, at Oviedo in the Asturias, at Valencia on the east coast, at Málaga on the southern coast, at Seville in Andalusia, and at Badajoz in Estremadura. The simultaneous uprising led to the belief that the rebellion was a planned and well organized undertaking. There is no doubt that since the "plot" of Escorial of October, 1807, Prince Ferdinand or at least his *"cuarto"* had prepared a vast insurrection against Godoy. After Godoy's arrest in March 1808 and the Madrid revolt of May 2, the discontent was directed against the French. From Bayonne, Ferdinand feverishly dispatched orders of insurrection in spite of strict French surveillance. Nevertheless, while certain Spanish historians insist that Ferdinand thus played an active role in spearing the revolt, it is not necessary to exaggerate his action. The Spanish administration was very weak, and, in its entirety, it accepted docilely the monarchy of Joseph Bonaparte.

The insurrection was really born of an immense discontent provoked by the economic, social, and political conditions, and the French actions only triggered it. Economically, the war and the blockade, in interrupting relations between Spain and her rich American colonies, had created a grave crisis. In the ports merchants were ruined; the industries processing raw materials, which had previously developed markedly for about thirty years, were closed, and the workers were unemployed. Barcelona and Cadiz were particularly hard hit. Socially, the nobility, who traditionally governed Spain, were unhappy with Godoy, who systematically deprived them of power according to the principles of enlightened despotism. A large sector of the nobility feared the introduction in Spain of reforms realized in France by the Revolution and its influence on the masses was very strong. The entry of French troops into Madrid and the severe repression of May 3 crowned the latent and hostile discontent of all strata of society. However there is no doubt that the revolt had been coordinated. Circulars sent by members of the high clergy, such as Cardinal Despuig, by the nobles, and by persons of the entourage of Ferdinand, have been found. They call upon the Spanish to rise against the French for the independence of Spain and for the maintenance of religion in its orthodoxy and purity. The clergy were, in great majority, strangely hostile.

The general uprising began on May 24 by anti-French manifestations and the attack of soldiers or small isolated groups at Oviedo—where the peasants descended from the neighboring mountains marching to the cry, "Long live Ferdinand VII"; at Valencia—where 300 French soldiers were massacred; at Málaga, Seville, Badajoz, and other towns of lesser importance. In each province an insurrectional junta formed and took over the local administration. These juntas were composed of prelates, nobles, and sometimes some bourgeoisie. They invested themselves with all power and organized the resistance to the French. At the beginning, the insurrection took a regional form and had no center, which clearly diminished its efficiency.

The juntas considered it expedient to contact France's principal enemy, the British government. First the junta of Asturias, then that of Galicia on June 26, and that of Seville on July 14 sent delegates to London. The delegates were received triumphantly. Charles Francois Dumouriez, a French general who had deserted the army in 1793 after being denounced by the National Convention and now lived in exile in England, drew up a plan of campaign for them. On June 4, Foreign Secretary Canning concluded an agreement with the junta of Asturias. It was soon extended to all the insurgent provinces of Spain. These provinces were regarded as at peace with England; the blockade of their ports was lifted, and commercial relations with England resumed. The British government granted subsidies to the insurrectionary juntas and sent them military counselors to direct the guerrilla bands that attacked the French. More far-reaching operations were foreseen. A British expeditionary corps was to land in Portugal under the command of General Wellesley—the future Wellington. While waiting for the arrival of the British the Spanish conducted uncoordinated attacks against French soldiers, pillaged their supply and munition depots, attacked convoys, and cut communication lines. The part of the regular Spanish army that still remained intact gained the southern provinces, which were not yet occupied by French troops, and regrouped there under the command of General Castaños.

Napoleon was not overly disturbed by these events. He thought that when a French army had installed his brother Joseph on the throne of Spain the resistance would cease rapidly. A French army under the command of Marshal Bessières did open the road to Madrid, and Joseph made his entrance there as the new king on July 20. On the next day another French army commanded by General Dupont, underwent the greatest disaster experienced by France since 1800.

When the insurrection broke out in May, General Dupont, whose troops were grouped around Toledo, had been assigned the mission of marching on Cadiz to raise the blockade of French ships escaped from Trafalgar that were beset by the rebels. He left with his division of 10,000 men, but at Cordova he heard that Castaños was holding the province of Andalusia with an army of 30,000 soldiers, reinforced by 10,000 insurgents. Dupont moved back on Andujar, to wait for General Vedel's division which was to reinforce him. He was able to join up with Vedel; but Castaños, whose forces remained superior, maneuvered skillfully and encircled Dupont at Bailén. A third French division commanded by General Gobert did not arrive to penetrate the Spanish lines as had been planned. Instead Gobert turned back toward Castile. During a month of almost total inaction, between Andujar and Bailén, Dupont had consumed all of his reserve supplies. Furthermore, his soldiers were exhausted by the great heat of southern Spain. He thought that it would be better to negotiate with Castaños who at the beginning of May had seemed obsequious to Murat in Madrid, rather than to try to pass by force. He negotiated a convention at Andujar on July 21. By its terms French troops would be repatriated by sea. First they had to lay down their arms: this was a real capitulation in open country. The junta of Seville and the English had to ratify the convention, but they refused to do so, and the French were then considered as prisoners of war. They were imprisoned on the prison ships of Cadiz and later sent to the island of Cabero, the death camp in the Balearic Isles.

The capitulation of Bailén had immense repercussions in Europe. It showed that the French army was not invincible as everybody believed.

It was an incentive to all the national resistance movements and to all the anti-French uprisings. This encouragement was increased all the more because Dupont's capitulation was followed five weeks later by that of General Junot in Portugal.

On August 1, 1808, an English expeditionary corps of 13,000 men commanded by General Wellesley had disembarked to the north of Lisbon and had been quickly reinforced by an almost equal number of Portuguese. Although the French were numerically superior, Wellesley was able to encircle them near Lisbon, and General Junot was forced to sign a capitulation at Cintra providing for the repatriation of his troops: this time the treaty was executed by the English. Junot's surrender had less repercussions than Dupont's but it proved again that the French army could be (many thought that it must be) vanquished. It was only a question of time.

In reality, after Bailén, all Spain was in revolt. The insurgents held the south; in the north they became masters of the important strongholds of Gerona, Lérida, Saragossa and on the east coast, Valencia. A few days after Joseph took over, the events elsewhere in Spain forced the new king to evacuate Madrid and fall back north of the Ebro River, but the insurrectionists did not profit from his retreat. Each insurrectional junta wished to keep its forces in its own province; therefore, no concentration of troops, capable of driving the French from Spain, could be realized. Even after a central junta composed of thirty-five delegates from the regional juntas was set up at Aranjuez, south of Madrid, on September 25, one single leader did not emerge around whom these forces would rally. The majority, grouped around Gaspar Melchor de Jovellanos, favored a liberal regime, inspired by the British model. The minority led by Count Florida-Blanca, president of the newly formed junta, remained faithful to enlightened despotism. The English army then available on the Iberian Peninsula to aid the juntas comprised two corps—one of 20,000 men in Portugal, the other of 13,000 men at La Coruña. With these conditions of dispersed forces, it was not difficult for Napoleon, who could not rest on a failure, to reconquer Spain. After a victory at Somosierra (November 30), Napoleon entered Madrid and reinstalled his brother there. The towns of the east and north under the insurgents fell one after the other. Saragossa, after an extremely murderous siege, was captured on February 20, 1809.

Henceforth, for three years, Joseph on the one hand, was going to strive to establish his power, to spread his influence, and to pretend to be independent of his brother, the Emperor Napoleon; on the other hand, the war between the French and the Spanish supported by English and Portuguese troops was going to become more and more desperate.

Joseph I settled in Madrid and organized a government that had the outward appearance of solidarity, but not the foundations for it. Joseph, debonnaire and desirous of popularity, hoped to reign without resorting to force.

He desired to win over his subjects rather than constrain them. But he was to wield little influence over them and would be in perpetual conflict with the generals imposed by his brother, and forced, by their mission, to use coercion. In order to win the support of his subjects, he advocated liberalism and sought to surround himself with Spaniards hostile to the former regime. He recruited a certain number of collaborators from all classes of society. These men were despised by the majority of the populace as is readily evident from the term *Afrancesados*. When the French withdrew from Spain in 1812, the 12,000 Spanish families that crossed the Pyrenees with them represented practically all true *Afrancesados*. The many small office-holders who, to save their salary and position, served under the *Afrancesados* were not in sympathy with them. Almost all desired the liberation of Spain from French domination. Among the *Afrancesados* were some of the great men of Spain—Mariano Luis de Urquijo, minister of foreign affairs under Charles IV; Miguel José de Azanza, duke of Santa Fe; Don Gonzalo O'Farrill, François Cabarrus, the great banker for the preceding kings, and others. In general, the Spanish followers of Joseph were older people, who dreamed more of serving an enlightened despot than of instituting a democratic regime. For them, the change of dynasty at Bayonne in May 1808 was comparable to that which Louis XIV had provoked in 1700. For the mass of Spaniards, on the contrary, the cowardly agreement at Bayonne had been counter to the will of the people, and it was necessary to respond to it by revolutionary measures.

Joseph Bonaparte would have preferred to follow the only policy that would have perhaps rallied the Spanish to him—to make peace with England, to send the French army home, to annex Portugal to Spain, and to negotiate with the insurgents. Napoleon opposed this constantly and worked counter to it, taking away from Joseph as much Spanish territory as possible, turning over areas to the administration of the generals, and preparing the annexation of Catalonia to France.

As for the war, it is not necessary to retrace the multiple vicissitudes that marked it from 1809 to 1812. The very geography of Spain forced the dispersal of the forces available to the French commanders. But the French lost their numerical superiority by dividing their troops. Guerrillas were relatively few in number, but they knew the terrain and were extremely effective. They were supported by the great majority of the population, and it found in Wellesley an excellent general. The British army was constantly reinforced in the foray against the French.

The English found on the Iberian Peninsula magnificent terrain for maneuvers which they had lacked until then. With its immense maritime facades, the peninsula lent itself admirably to combined operations. The British expeditionary corps could appear unexpectedly at a given point from the coast. The insurgents aided them in installing themselves defensively. In order to confront them it was necessary for the French troops to execute long and laborious marches under guerrilla fire in a very hilly country without roads that was glacial in winter and torrid in summer. On contact with the English batallions, the French were decimated by a regulated and precise fire. If the French gained the advantage, the British would retreat to the coast where the British naval ships served as base, depart, and some days later reappear at another point on the coast. For the French troops there were then new harassing marches, in the course of which the stragglers and the convoys were pitilessly attacked and often annihilated by the guerrillas. In reprisal, the peasants of the region were massacred and their houses burned. These atrocities, faithful companions of the guerrilla warfare, gave a particularly horrible character to the Spanish war, into which an important portion of the French army sank more and more.

GERMAN RESISTANCE AND
THE WAR OF 1809

In Germany the capitulations of Dupont at Balién and of Junot at Cintra had aroused the hope of prompt liberation. The insurrection of the Spanish people convinced the Germans that a popular revolt could force the French out of their country. In contrast to Spain, in Germany numerous books and pamphlets based on philosophy or nascent Romanticism were published and rapidly diffused, at least among intellectuals, a nationalism imported from France in its origin but adapted to the German state. The writers, praising the Middle Ages and the power of the First Reich, also eulogized the strong state. Only such a state was capable of assuring the free development of the specific character of each people. In 1802 Ernst Arndt, in a book entitled *Germany and Europe,* had set the objects to attain in explaining that the possession of natural frontiers and free access to the sea were indispensible to the full blooming of a people. After the Prussian defeat of 1807, Fichte pronounced in Berlin his celebrated *Discourse to the German Nation,* which, published as a volume, met with extraordinary success. In Vienna August von Schlegel, who had been the tutor of the son of Madame de Stael,[1] conducted at Vienna a literature course in which he

---

[1] Madame de Stael was the daughter of Jacques Necker, Swiss minister of finance on the eve of and at the beginning of the French Revolution. She left France and was later considered an *émigré*. She returned during the Consulate, but was affronted by Napoleon's treatment, for he appeared to take occasions to insult her or belittle her in front of courtiers. He had little respect for intelligent women. She emigrated again. During her stay in Germany, Mme de Stael wrote her famous book, *De l'Allemagne,* which praised features of German history and culture and compared France unfavorably with Germany.

strove to demonstrate the superiority of German letters. Ludwig von Arnim and Clemens Brentano assembled in 1808 German folk songs in *The Marvelous Horn* and by this incited their readers to think of an independent medieval Germany which they opposed to the divided and vassal Germany of their times. Political economist Adam Müller, in his conferences, and above all in his book, *Lessons of Antithesis,* defined the state as the sum of all the material and spiritual wealth of the nation. He multiplied the arguments in favor of its all-powerful nature and fought against the individualism born of the philosophies of the Enlightenment and developed by the Revolution.

All these theories served to justify and fortify the hatred of the occupying foreigner, which was common in all Germany east of the Rhine. The Germans blamed the French for the overwhelming contributions and requisitions that they owed directly to France or to the intermediary of governments that were loyal to it, the interruption of the payment of rents and pensions, and the revocation of numerous functionaries. The discontented began to group themselves into secret societies. The *Tugenbund* was founded at Königsberg in 1808, modeled after the Masonic societies. In 1809 it numbered twenty-five "chambers" and more than 700 members. The association had for its official objective "to exalt civic virtues"; in fact, it sought out, denounced, and punished traitors, those who collaborated with the French, and prepared the great popular revolt against Napoleon. This revolt, if it ought to be made in the name of Germanism, also would have as a consequence the implementation in Germany of the principles of the Revolution—national sovereignty, liberty, and equality. These principles caused fear in many Germans who then looked to Prussia, which was in the process of silently and methodically reforming its army and institutions.

The defeat of 1806 had been a brutal shock to the spirit of the Prussian directing class—that is, the lesser nobility and the cultivated bourgeoisie. They understood that in order for Prussia to achieve victory, later, in a war of revenge, it was first necessary to transform Prussia into a modern state; in other words, it was necessary to revitalize Prussian social structures and to reorganize the army. At the instigation of enlightened men, among whom was Karl von Hardenberg, the Prussian minister dismissed by order of Napoleon, but in correspondence with the king, a commission was charged with reform in eastern Prussia. This commission was composed primarily of Prussians, but there were also west Germans who had seen the transformations introduced by the French in the course of the Revolution in the countries that they administered. They were also influenced by the British institutions that were well known in Germany because of their use in Hanover. This commission abolished at one time the obligation of the lord to restore the farms of his peasants that had been ravaged by the war *(Bauer-*

schutz) and serfdom *(Unterthänigkeit),* which was still the rule in the greater part of Prussia. Only the peasants of the royal domain had been in part emancipated. Bourgeoisie and peasants were permitted to acquire land; landed property was no longer the monopoly of the nobility; reciprocally, the nobles were allowed to enter the professions reserved until that time to the bourgeoisie. The peasants also received the same rights. The rigid Prussian caste system began to become flexible. The reform was soon extended to all Prussian territory. Thus, Prussia was as profoundly transformed as the Kingdom of Westphalia or the Duchy of Warsaw. After 1810 there were practically no serfs in Prussia, but the peasants continued to be indebted for corvées and seignorial dues. The lord preserved his rights of justice and of police; he remained the only administrator of the village. Few of the peasants could acquire enough land to be able to live from it. For the most part, they became agricultural laborers and *brassiers.* [2]

It was the minister Baron Heinrich von Stein who occupied himself with industry, commerce, and administration. He was originally from Rhenish Germany and had read the works of the economists and Physiocrats. While he had signed the edict of October 1807 on the abolition of serfdom, he had not participated in its preparation, for he was not then in the ministry. He abolished a certain number of guilds, suppressed the banalité of mills (fees for grinding grain), proclaimed the equality of towns and countryside in the economic domain. This allowed the peasants to buy and sell on the local markets. He reorganized the executive and divided it among five ministers with precisely defined power. The five ministers were to unite in council. He wanted to create a Prussian national assembly but met with hostility from the country squires of the king's entourage, who opposed his reform. He created in the towns elected municipal governments having at their head an appointed collective "magistrate." The great innovation had consisted of substituting for the election of municipal governments by guilds, traditional in Germany, the election by the citizens paying a certain rent *(cens),* as in France.

The reform of the army, encouraged by Stein, had been accomplished above all by General Scharnhorst, of Hanoverian origin, son of a noncommissioned officer, and by Field Marshal von Gneisenau, who had begun his career fighting for England in North America. They began by purging and reorganizing the high command; the rules of infantry maneuver were changed in the light of lessons learned from the defeats of 1806. The most significant reform was the accelerated incorporation of conscripts *(Krümper)* for a very short term of service of one month at a time. Thus, the army, the effective strength of which had been fixed by a convention of September

---

[2] The word *brassiers* was used in the eighteenth century to designate the rural lower class; the lowest group of the peasantry. The word is rarely used today.

8, 1808, at 42,000 men, could almost instantly triple its numbers. To this army, General von Clausewitz, who had been made a prisoner at Jena, then freed, gave a doctrinaire system that for a long time formed the basis of the superiority of the Prussian army.

AUSTRIAN RESISTANCE

In Austria the effort at renovation had been infinitely weaker. The Austrian government was incapable of making Hungary participate in attempts at reform, nor was it capable of putting its finances in order. Its notes devaluated to 67 percent of their worth before Pressburg. The Austrians were too demoralized to generate strong, overt anti-French feeling. However, anti-French propaganda developed greatly after the Spanish insurrection. Furthermore, it was directed by the minister Count von Stadion, Baron Hormayr, (historian and director of the state archives), and the archduke John. In the intellectual arena Austrian and Hungarian writers aimed their pamphlets, their books, their poems and their plays against France. A state of revengeful spirit permeated the country. In fact this very spirit was responsible for the reorganization of the army in spite of financial difficulties. Regulations were modified; a reserve of more than 150,000 men was instituted; a corps of 23,000 Tyrolian light infantry was created; and an attempt was made to improve the services behind the lines. However, the application of these reforms was slow, and it would require much time before the Austrian army was in condition to combat French troops victoriously.

Events of 1808 seemed to demonstrate that the moment to attack Napoleon had come. Not only had the French troops undergone resounding defeats on the Iberian Peninsula, but the Franco-Russian alliance, signed at Tilsit, appeared weak. The Russian aristocracy, as a whole very hostile to the Revolution, had given the alliance a bad reception. After Tilsit legal disputes between France and Russia multiplied. Russia demanded that France evacuate Prussia on October 1, 1808, as had been provided in the Treaty of Tilsit. She wished thus to deprive France of a base for eventual operations against Russian territory. Napoleon refused, under the pretext that Prussia had not paid the indemnity of war that had been imposed upon her. Russia demanded, therefore, that she be allowed to maintain her troops in the Danubian principalities (the present Roumania). Napoleon only consented on the condition of occupying Silesia himself, an action that dismembered Prussia still more. Then in a celebrated letter written on February 2, 1808, he once again suggested to Tsar Alexander a division of the Ottoman Empire: the Balkans and Asiatic Turkey to go to Russia; Serbia and Bosnia to Austria; and Egypt and Syria to France. Then together they would attack the British power in India. This was an enlarged renewal of the plan that Bonaparte had presented to the Directory in 1798! In order to discuss his grandiose plan, Alexander asked Napoleon for a new interview. At the meeting they would also discuss Finland, where, due to the aid promised by Napoleon against Sweden, Russian troops marked time.

The interview was held at Erfurt on September 27, 1808 after the Spanish and Portuguese disasters. The situation was profoundly affected by them. Needing to send the *Grande Armée* into the Iberian Peninsula, Napoleon was prepared to evacuate Prussia without compensation. But he tried to dazzle Alexander with his power and magnificence. He had the court follow him to Erfurt and the *Comédie Française* played there before an audience of kings. Alexander was not impressed by it; on the contrary, his vanity was wounded. The former minister of foreign affairs, Charles Maurice de Talleyrand-Périgord, Prince de Benevente, who after the defeats of Spain had lost confidence in the durability of the Empire no longer aided his sovereign. Instead he committed veritable treason, for which he must have received important bribes, in addition to a favorable marriage of his nephew with the Duchess of Dino (daughter of the Duke de Courland), because he counseled Alexander to resist Napoleon. Alexander could then maintain his troops in the Danubian principalities and obtain the evacuation of the Duchy of Warsaw by the French army. Moreover, Metternich, the Austrian ambassador in Paris, informed by Talleyrand, made it known in Vienna that Russia would not support France in an attack. Thus Erfurt was a partial failure for Napoleon for he gained only an indemnity from Prussia and release of the army to help in Spain.

After Erfurt, the *Grande Armée* went into Spain and there remained in Germany only two army corps commanded by General Davout. Had not the moment come to attack and inflict on French troops in Germany a defeat similar to those that it had undergone in the Iberian Peninsula. In case of victory it would be the end of Napoleonic power.

In October 1808 Austria asked England for subsidies in order to renew the war against France. The Austrian chancellor, Stadion, negotiated an alliance with Prussia and reached an understanding with the *Tugenbund* in order to launch a vast popular uprising against the French.

It was in the Tyrol that the insurrection broke out. The Tyrol had been annexed to Bavaria in 1805. The union should not have created difficulties since the population of the two regions spoke the same language and had the same customs. The Bavarian administration was, however, tactless. It undertook to name the priests, to submit the convents to considerable taxes, and to close certain abbeys. It reformed the legislation and tried to introduce the Napoleonic Code. Finally, conscription was established at the beginning of 1809. All these measures irritated the people and incidents broke out. Archduke John and Baron Hormayr, who, at Vienna, were at the head of the Austrian war party, decided to profit from the incidents. They contacted three innkeepers: Nessing of Botzen (Bolzano), Huber of Brunecken, and Andreas Hofer of Passeyrthal to organize an uprising. These three men carefully prepared the insurrection, which broke out on April 9, the same day that Austria declared war on France.

Napoleon, well informed of the intrigue, was not caught off his guard. He had reinforced his German army. This army, brought up to the strength of 300,000 men was two thirds composed of foreigners and conscripts. Prussia, judging herself not prepared, refused to move when Austria declared war. Only the corps of volunteers, the Hussards of Death, raised by General Schill and the troops of Katte and General Baron von Dornberg undertook action. Because of the great distances between these Prussian forces, their efforts were poorly coordinated.

Neglecting the insurrections of the Tyrol and of Northern Germany, Napoleon, at the head of the Army of the Rhine, marched on the principal forces of the enemy commanded by Archduke Charles and concentrated in Bavaria. The first engagements took place on April 17. On April 22 the French defeated the Austrians at Eggmühl on the Danube and separated the Austrian armies of Germany and Italy. They entered Vienna on May 12.

However, Archduke Charles was able to retreat with 150,000 men and found himself east of Vienna on the left bank of the Danube. Not as in 1805, the Austrians were able to destroy the bridges of the Danube. Napoleon reconstructed those between the island of Lobau and the villages of Aspern and Essling. These were broken by a flood of the Danube before the artillery and munitions were able to complete crossing to the north bank. The Austrians attacked the French infantry, which was able at great loss to fall back on the island of Lobau (May 21–25). Archduke Charles very nearly achieved a success analogous to that of the Spanish at Bailén or the English in Portugal, but Napoleon arrived to take over the situation himself. He fortified the island and began the offensive again on July 4. This time the French army was able with its artillery and convoys to cross the Danube and defeat the Austrians at Wagram near Essling (July 6).

During this time the insurrection in the Tyrol was checked. Nevertheless, Andreas Hofer was not captured until January 1810. He was shot at Mantua on February 20. In north Germany the insurgents, while dispersed, could have been a threatening force if they had been supported by British troops like the Spanish insurgents. The English, instead of disembarking on the German coasts, landed in Holland. On July 30, 40,000 men were put aground on the island of Walcheren. They took Flushing on August 13. Joseph Fouché, French minister of police and interim minister of the interior, mobilized the national guards of fifteen departments of Belgium and of northern France to repulse them. This gained for him the bitter reproaches of Napoleon, for the English troops commanded by a mediocre

Portrait of Napoleon, unfinished, by Jacques Louis David. This is the more mature Napoleon. (Museum of Bayonne. Photo from Giraudon)

general, Lord Chatham set sail without fighting on September 30. It is possible that Fouché in liaison with Talleyrand and with certain secret societies
such as the *Philadelphes*, had sought to make himself popular in order to
accede, eventually to the supreme power.

The Austrian army was not destroyed by its defeat at Wagram; however, six days later on July 12, Archduke Charles obtained an armistice.
Emperor Francis I always hoped that Russia would intervene. Russian
troops restricted themselves to occupying only Galicia, to prevent the Poles
from entering it. On September 1 Alexander made known to the Austrians
that he would not break with France. The embarkation of the English at
Walcheren succeeded in persuading the emperor Francis I and his entourage that there remained no other course than to sue for peace. A peace
treaty was concluded at Vienna on October 14, 1809, the Treaty of Schon-
brunn.

The Austrian Empire again lost important territories. A part of Galicia
with Cracow was ceded to the Duchy of Warsaw; another area with Tarnopol
to Russia. Salzburg and a part of Upper Austria (the district of the Inn)
were ceded to Bavaria. On the Adriatic, Austria and Hungary lost Croatia,
Carniola, and all their ports, notably Trieste and Fiume. These territories
were joined with Istria and Dalmatia taken from Italy to form the Illyrian
provinces and were united to the French Empire which thus became by a
long frontier adjacent to the Ottoman Empire. The Kingdom of Italy
gained, in exchange for Istria and Dalmatia, the Trentino, ceded by Bavaria. Nevertheless, the frontier was placed to the south of the Brenner
Pass.

ITALIAN RESISTANCE

In Italy the movements of revolt against French domination had
been much less important than in Spain or in Germany. They had been perceptible, however, and had led to important consequences.

In the intellectual life of Italy, in spite of intense Napoleonic propaganda and in spite of the disappearance of freedom of the press, one can see
the attacks against the French increase. This resistance most often took the
form of a return to "Italianism." While the publications in the French language did not cease to multiply, while Italian was invaded by Gallicisms,
and while numerous Italian authors (docile or paid), wrote in French, the
most learned Italians—certain of them enjoyed a wide reputation—persisted in drafting their works in Italian. This was true of the physicists
Alessandro Volta and Luigi Galvani, of the naturalist Lazzaro Spallanzani,
and of the astronomer Barnaba Oriani. Vincenzo Cuoco, historian and

philosopher, published in 1806 a novel entitled *Platone in Italia* (Plato in Italy), in which he gave Italian nationalism one of its bases, calling for unification of Italy. "My book," he wrote "is destined to form the public morale of the Italians, to cause to be born in them that spirit of union, that love of *Patrie*, that love of war which until the present, they have lacked." It was above all Ugo Foscolo who became the hero of the Italian intellectual resistance. In the *Sepolcri*, published in 1807, he took an attitude clearly anti-Napoleonic, wrote a eulogy for Nelson, and justified the British victory at Trafalgar. From his book an ardent Italian sentiment emerged. The dead who slept in Italian soil still divided were the pledges of its future unity. Following these works and many others, the Italians made an effort to purify their language and to free it from local dialects. Napoleon, himself captured by this movement, forbade the use in public acts, other than French, of idioms other than the Tuscan, considered as the purest form of Italian. In 1811 he authorized the reestablishment in Florence of the old Academy della Crusca and charged it with beginning again the publication of the dictionary of the Italian language. While in 1796, French was considered the language of liberty, from 1809 on it was Italian that played that role.

The Italian resistance did not remain on this elevated plane. It expressed itself also by revolts. Much less extensive than those of Spain and Germany, nonetheless they gave French officials cause for concern. When Austria began war in 1809, her troops penetrated Venetian territory through the gap of the mountains at Caporetto on April 11, and the Italian army commanded by the viceroy Eugène retired in haste across the Adige River. Only the victories won by Napoleon were able to force the archduke John to retreat toward Hungary. The Austrians hoped to be aided by popular insurrections as in 1799. The uprisings of the Tyrolian peasants menaced not only the region north of Venice, but also Lombardy, for the Valteline also revolted at the end of April. These revolts and the approach of the Austrian army provoked a veritable panic in Milan, where 10,000 passports were issued in a few days. A peasant revolt broke out also in the Marches, Emilie, and Mantua. Here the peasants complained of the weight of direct and indirect taxes, particularly the town dues *(droits d'octroi)* which slowed transactions with the towns. This was more than a political insurrection—it was a veritable revolt of hunger. The peasants sacked the tax bureaus, registry office, town dues office, and also seized the property of the Jews. They entered Rovigo, Modena, and Bologna and isolated for a brief period Ferrara. The revolt broke out too late to receive aid from the Austrian army which had already made an about-face. After the Napoleonic victory of Wagram many peasants retired to their homes. The return of the Italian army allowed the organization of mobile columns against the insur-

gents. There were 2,700 arrests, numerous house burnings, summary execu-
tions, and 150 condemned to death by tribunals.

In the same period insurrection broke out in Apulia and in Calabria.
It had broken out in 1806 when a corps of 5,000 English coming from Sicily
under the command of General John Stewart disembarked there. These
troops had won at Maida in southern Calabria a striking victory over the
small division of General Reynier (July 4). After their chasing, the English
were driven from the peninsula, the weakening guerrilla action continued,
as in Spain, but in a theater of operations less extensive. After 1809 the guerrilla action diminished and took the form of simple banditry. But it was
always ready to rise again, the more so since members were recruited from
among rebels and deserters who were increasingly numerous, and since it
was supported by a secret society, the Carbonari, or Charbonnerie, whose
objective was the expulsion of foreigners from Italy. Historians are not in
agreement as to the origin of the society. Some believe that it was introduced into the Kingdom of Naples by the English to strengthen the opposition to Napoleon. The hypothesis that today seems most probable is completely different. According to it, the Frenchman Jean-Pierre Briot, who
became intendant of Abruzzi Citérieure at Chieti on August 1, 1806, created
the first Italian *"ventes" (vendite).*[3] Briot born in Franche-Comté in 1771
had indeed belonged to the society of Bons Cousins Charbonniers of the
Jura at the beginning of the Revolution. He had shown the interest he had
in Italy by placing, on August 1, 1799, on the desk of the Council of Five
Hundred the petition of the Italian patriots in favor of the institution of
an Italic Republic. He had shown that he continued to move in the ranks
of Masonry by taking part in the first lodge created on the island of Elba,
where he was a commissioner of the French government in 1801 and 1802.
Besides, one finds no trace of the Italian *vendita* before 1807, which seems
to confirm the role of Briot. It is also possible that the introduction of the
Carbonari into Italy was facilitated by the existence of other secret societies,[4]
also of the Masonic type, such as the Raggi, which provoked the anti-French
insurrection of the Piedmont in 1799. In any case, the combination of the
efforts of the Carbonari and the action of brigandage fostered the development of opposition to the Napoleonic regime and of aspirations toward independence and unity in Italy from 1810 on.

Under these conditions Napoleon could no longer tolerate any terri-

---

[3] *Vendite,* literally "sales," is the word used to designate the branches of the Car-
boneria, similar to the word "lodges" in Masonic terminology.

[4] See Elizabeth L. Eisenstein, *Filippo Michele Buonarroti* (Harvard University
Press, 1959) on the role of this Babeuvist on secret societies in Italy, and her dis-
cussion of the latest Italian scholarship on the subject; and see Armando Saita,
Filippo Buonarroti, Rome, 1951, 2 vols.

tory in the Italian peninsula escaping from his direct or indirect domination. Although Rome was occupied, the Pope continued to "resist." He was angered by the manner in which Napoleon interpreted in France the Concordat of 1801. The Organic Articles published in 1802 without his consent had shocked him. The *Imperial Catechism* (1806), which included loyalty and obedience to Napoleon, irritated him. After the occupation of Rome by French troops (February 2, 1808), Pius VII recalled from Paris the Nuncio Caprara. Napoleon replied by annexing to the Kingdom of Italy the provinces of Urbino and Ancona (May 22, 1808). The Pope then forbade all his subjects to take an oath to the Emperor. In reprisal, Napoleon arrested Cardinal Gabrielli, secretary of state; he was replaced by Cardinal Pacca. When Napoleon ascertained in 1809 that the Tyrol, the Romagna, a part of Venezia, and Calabria were in a state of insurrection, he decided to annex Rome to the French Empire (May 17, 1809). The annexation was proclaimed on June 10. Latium formed the department of the Tiber with Rome as its capital. Nevertheless, the Eternal City was declared an "imperial and a free city, the second of the Empire."

The Pope replied to the violence by excommunicating Napoleon on June 11. The Emperor lost his temper. He wrote to General Miollis, governor of Rome: "He is a furious madman that it is necessary to lock up. Arrest Pacca and the other adherents of the Pope" (June 20, 1809). He wrote to Murat, king of Naples: "If the Pope . . . preaches revolt . . . he must be arrested." Indeed, Pius VII was arrested on July 6, 1809, and taken to Savona as a prisoner. Thus, the Continental Blockade among its consequences led to a grave conflict between the Pope and the Emperor. Had the blockade at least aggravated the economic situation of England?

FAILURE OF THE CONTINENTAL BLOCKADE

While in 1807 and at the beginning of 1808 the British economy seemed seriously hurt by the Continental Blockade, the insurrections on the Continent and the war of 1809 loosened the corset that choked it. Napoleon and Jefferson found themselves unable to enforce the rigorous measures that they had issued against British commerce. Thus, the British economy revived in 1809; as a matter of fact, it knew a veritable "boom," which proved to all how chimerical it was to try to "vanquish the sea by land."

In the Baltic region, the English commerce with Prussia began again, thanks to the negligence and above all to the corruption of the French agents who were charged with overseeing it. Thus in June and July 1809 many ships loaded with colonial products and British manufactured articles were admitted to Königsberg on condition of payment to the consul of a sum equal to 10 percent of the value of the cargo. In Pomerania and Mecklenburg contraband found excellent facilities. Trade flourished here through the intermediary of Sweden, Göteborg being the great neutral center of imports of English merchandise. In Russia, the orders given by the tsar to repulse British merchandise were carried out only rarely. To be sure, when on September 17, 1809, Sweden concluded peace with Russia, she undertook to adhere to the blockade. Sweden renewed her promises of compliance in an agreement with the French negotiated on January 6, 1810. In actual practice the Swedes never applied the prohibition on British merchandise with vigor. The total value of English exports to Sweden had increased by a third, in 1809, as compared to the previous year. Of course, the greatest part of this merchandise was reexported to Central Europe. In 1810 this state of affairs continued. To be sure, the treaty of peace concluded between France and Sweden in January required the king of Sweden to close his ports to English commerce, "to admit no commodities, no English merchandise under any flag that they carried," but this clause functioned only on paper. In total, the number of licenses issued by the English government for trade with the Baltic area was greater in 1810 than in 1809.

English traffic with the countries bordering on the North Sea also increased substantially in 1809 and 1810, particularly with Denmark and Norway and, above all, the island of Heligoland, which became an enormous center of contraband for Germany. For example, in one week, from June 12 to 19, 1809, more than 130 small ships left the island loaded with merchandise valued at more than £300,000, and in depositing it on the neighboring coasts, not one of these cargoes was lost or seized. It was to prevent the flow of contraband that caused Napoleon to establish a line of French customs between the Rhine and Bremen in July 1809. This customs cordon was not effective.

On the west coast of the continent on March 31, 1809, Louis Bonaparte reopened Dutch ports and authorized the import of raw materials, naval munitions, drugs, and spices and the export of agricultural products and canvas. In theory, such commerce could only be undertaken with neutrals. In fact, it was above all the English who profited as the numerous licenses of importation or exportation to Holland delivered by the British government in 1809 proved. Almost normal commercial traffic was conducted with England. Napoleon wrote, very justly, to his brother Louis on July 17, 1809: "All the correspondence of England with the continent is made by way of Holland. Holland is an English province." Napoleon could easily send condemning letters to his brother, but what about his own actions? France herself reopened herself to English commerce. In 1809 the exports of wine, liqueurs, and cereals resumed to England, thanks to special licenses. In exchange France received lumber, wrought iron, and medicinal supplies. The French government accepted the traffic in order to satisfy the provinces of the west, which had been unable to sell, at a good price the produce of the excellent harvest of 1808. This commerce continued and even increased in 1810. It was specified, nevertheless that the merchandise shipped to France must not be English but come from neutral countries or colonies. Beside the official traffic sanctioned by the system of licenses, a clandestine traffic developed via the Channel islands, which played, with respect to France, the same role as Heligoland played with regard to Germany.

With Mediterranean Europe, British commerce was inferior to that of 1808, but very superior to the years before 1808. The occupation of Trieste by the French was the principal reason for this stagnation, but Malta became, like Heligoland and Jersey, a great center of contraband. On the other hand, British traffic with the Ottoman Empire (again at peace with Great Britain) and with Spain (in revolt against Napoleon) marked net progress in 1809 and 1810. The relative stagnation of English commerce in the Mediterranean had little influence on the total European commerce of England. In 1809 Europe absorbed 47 percent of the official value of total British exports, which corresponded to the maximum of the period from 1802 to 1812. This is proof of the failure of the Continental System.

At the same time that English exports to Europe attained this high level, those to the New World also soared. The United States Congress, beginning March 15, 1809, raised the embargo on ships with a European destination. It replaced it by the Non-Intercourse Act, which forbade the access of American ports to ships of the two belligerents and forbade American ships from proceeding to French or British ports. The Non-Intercourse Act was not respected, and commerce between the United States and England began again: American ships that were supposed to go to Lisbon or Cadiz, in fact, sailed to London or Liverpool. On their return, they naturally carried English merchandise. Nevertheless, in 1809 British exports to the United States still remained very low (10 percent of the total official value), but in 1810 they increased considerably to reach 17 percent of the total official value.

Spanish America in this period also opened its doors to England. In effect, the Spanish colonies all refused to recognize Joseph Bonaparte as the sovereign of Spain. They honored only Ferdinand VII, a captive in the chateau of Valençay. While awaiting his liberation, the colonies accepted the orders of the junta of Seville. To be sure, they forced themselves to maintain the "laws of the Indies," that is Spanish monopoly and the prohibition of commerce with the foreigner. Certain governors and captains applied these directives very rigorously (notably in Mexico, in Peru, and in New Granada), but others decided to open their provinces to British commerce: Buenos Aires was the first to welcome the British, then Montevideo, to be followed by Cuba and Santo Domingo.

On April 19, 1810, revolution broke out in Caracas. An insurrectional junta proclaimed a republic there and immediately opened its ports to English commerce. The revolution reached the countries of La Plata (May 25, 1810), New Grenada (July 29, 1810), and Chile (September 18, 1810) all of whom immediately decided to establish commercial relations with Great Britain. Only Mexico, Peru, and Central America remained closed. One must not exaggerate the immediate advantages that England gained from these events. On the one hand, the Spanish authorities decided to blockade Venezuela and Buenos Aires. On the other, the revolution disorganized the economy of the countries of South America. Nevertheless, the index of English exports of the Americas (the United States excepted) went from 153 in 1808 to 167 in 1810 to reach 19,800 pounds, that is 30 percent of the total.

The year 1809 consequently appeared to be for the English economy a year of exceptional prosperity. It marked the failure of the Continental Blockade. Was Napoleon going to admit it? No, he reacted and took rigorous measures. He forced the abdication of his brother Louis, king of Holland, and annexed Holland to the French Empire on July 10, 1810. The Grand Duchy of Oldenburg, the northern part of the Grand Duchy of Berg of the Kingdom of Westphalia, and the Hanseatic towns (the entire German littoral of the North Sea from the frontier of Holland to the north of the Lippe River to the Trave River) were annexed to the Empire on January 22, 1811. To fight against contraband, the Swiss canton of Valais was also annexed (1810) and the canton of Tessin militarily occupied. The Napoleonic empire reached its greatest extension: it was the *Grand Empire*. It is now necessary to study the structure and transformations that this brought to Europe.

9

THE *GRAND EMPIRE*

THE STRUCTURE OF THE *GRAND EMPIRE*

In 1810 and 1811, the French Empire attained its greatest area—130 departments. On the northeast, the boundary line ran from the mouth of the Trave River to the east of Lubeck on the Baltic Sea to the juncture of the Lippe and Rhine rivers at Wesel. On the east from there the line followed the Rhine, then from nearly the present Franco-Swiss frontier (Porrentruy being encompassed in the department of Haut-Rhin) to the north of Geneva. Geneva and its environs, the canton of Valais, were part of France as was Piedmont. The boundary reached the Po River to the east of Turin, then it stretched approximately along the crest of the Apennines just to the north of Naples. Along the Pyrenees there were a few changes. Only the Val d'Aran (the high valley of the Garonne River) was annexed to France in 1812. On the east coast of the Adriatic Sea, the Illyrian provinces and the Ionian Islands were also part of the territory of the Empire.

The French Empire was only the core of the *Grand Empire*. Around the Empire and under French control were the vassal states, some governed by the Emperor Napoleon's relatives and others by foreign princes. The vassal states had succeeded the sister republics created by the Direc-

160

tory. The first among them was the Kingdom of Italy, founded in 1805 by the transformation of the Italian Republic, successor of the Cisalpine Republic. Lastly there were the allied states.

Without doubt, Napoleon was sovereign of the new Kingdom of Italy. He even retained the title of king, but he did delegate a great part of his powers to his stepson, Eugène de Beauharnais. The Batavian Republic was similarly transformed into the Kingdom of Holland in 1806 to the profit of Louis Bonaparte, Napoleon's brother. The kingdom lasted only four years as an "independent" entity. In 1810 it was reunited to the Empire. In 1806 Joseph Bonaparte, another brother of the emperor had been "named" king of Naples; he was transferred to the throne of Spain in 1808 as we have already noted. Joachim Murat, husband of Caroline Bonaparte, Napoleon's sister, succeeded him as king of Naples. For two years he had reigned over a German territory, the Grand Duchy of Berg, which passed under the nominal authority of Napoleon Louis, son of Louis Bonaparte of Holland, with Count Beugnot as imperial commissioner. In 1807, a kingdom of Westphalia was created for Jerome, Napoleon's younger brother. This kingdom was composed of Hanover, Brunswick, and some other adjacent German regions. Finally, Elisa Bonaparte, wife of Prince Bacciochi, in 1805 was awarded the small principalities of Lucca and Piombino in Italy.

The Helvetic Confederation had had Napoleon as a "mediator" since 1803, but it possessed a large amount of internal autonomy. It formed the transition between vassal countries governed by French princes and those which had foreigners at their head. The Confederation of the Rhine was presided over by Charles Theodore of Dalberg, former archbiship of Mainz. The confederation, formed in July 1806 included, besides the Kingdom of Westphalia and the Grand Duchy of Berg, most of southern Germany (notably Saxony), the Grand Duchy of Baden, Württemberg, and Bavaria, the latter having been enlarged from the Austrian Tyrol under the terms of the Treaty of Tilsit in 1807. The Grand Duchy of Warsaw was made a part of it. The king of Saxony became Warsaw's sovereign, but the Duchy of Warsaw was more closely tied to the *Grand Empire* than the other states of the Confederation of the Rhine.

In brief the *Grand Empire* was organized as a federation. At its head was Emperor Napoleon, whose will was all powerful, but not so powerful that he was always capable of imposing it on his relatives who were sovereigns and still less so on sovereigns who were not his relatives. Sometimes he was obliged to take action against them to keep them in line; he even went as far as to dismiss a subordinate if his instructions were not followed, as was the case with Louis king of Holland, in 1810.

Next in the pyramid of rank were the vassal princes, still sovereign and hereditary but whose domains held in "fief," required a new investiture with each mutation. Examples are Elisa Bacciochi in Lucca-Piombino and Marshal Berthier in Neuchâtel. Lower on the ladder were such princes as Talleyrand, the prince of Benevento, the prince Bernadotte, and the prince of Pontecorvo, who could not mint money or maintain an army. Finally, there were the titular heads of "useful" fiefs who were content to take the revenues of immense domains that Napoleon gave them in Venetian territory, in the kingdom of Naples, or in Poland. Such was the hierarchy of the federal imperial system at its height about 1811.

This system never attained a plateau of equilibrium; it was constantly in flux. Several states became, for a short time, part of the *Grand Empire* but then left it. Portugal, for example, who joined in 1808 withdrew in 1809. The *Grand Empire* itself was only the armature of a more vast system —the Continental System. In Chapter 8 it was stressed that the system's goal was essentially economic: to close Europe to English products and to bring about, by the Continental Blockade, the forced capitulation of Great Britain by economic asphyxiation. This Continental System was also in constant evolution. It rested on alliances between Napoleon and the other European states that included a clause of adherence to the system.

The longest standing alliance, the one that had been the basis for the Continental System, was the treaty concluded with Russia at Tilsit on July 7, 1807. The treaty did not demand from the tsar that he modify the archaic internal organization of his vast empire. What it did stipulate was that Alexander close his ports to the English and forbid the importation of English merchandise. The tsar complied with orders to this effect, but they were hardly executed. The interviews that he had with Napoleon at the Congress of Erfurt in September 1808 did not lead him to issue more stringent measures to reinforce the Continental Blockade. His subsequent ambiguous attitude regarding the German insurrections and the Franco-Austrian war of 1809 did not contribute, either, to the consolidation of the alliance. In actuality, the alliance was tottering by 1810.

On October 30, 1807, Denmark, which it will be remembered, also included Norway, became an ally of France and began to apply the Continental Blockade. She entered into a war against Sweden, then involved in a struggle with Russia. Her intervention contributed to the signing of the Russo-Swedish peace treaty of September 17, 1808.

The Russo-Swedish war was to have important consequences. Sweden ceded Finland to Russia. The war had important domestic political implications too. The king of Sweden, Gustavus IV, judged incompetent, had been forced by his generals to abdicate on March 29, 1809, in favor of his uncle the old duke of Södermanland, who took the name, Charles XIII. Charles, sympathetic to France, signed a peace with her and joined the blockade on January 6, 1810. The new Swedish king was childless and Prince Charles Auguste of Augustenburg was adopted as the heir to the throne. Prince Charles died on May 28, 1810, and Charles XIII, under the influence of the French party, accepted as his successor one of Napoleon's Marshals, Bernadotte, elected by the Swedish Diet on August 21, 1810. Joseph Bonaparte and Bernadotte married the two Cléry sisters. Désirée, an early sweetheart of Napoleon, was Bernadotte's wife. At the time it was thought the selection of Bernadotte reinforced the Franco-Swedish alliance.

The most surprising alliance was the one Napoleon concluded with Austria in 1810. In Napoleon's eyes this one would be more solid than all the others since it was going to be founded on family bonds: the marriage of Napoleon with the archduchess Marie Louise, daughter of Emperor Francis I, and, therefore, niece of the former French queen, Marie Antoinette. Napoleon desired this marriage for two reasons. First, he had had no children by Josephine Beauharnais, whom he had married on March 9, 1796, and thus no direct heir. True, the Constitution of the Year XII (1804) had given Napoleon the right to adopt the children or grandchildren of his brothers, and it had allowed, in default of a legitimate or adopted heir, the imperial crown to devolve on Joseph or Louis Bonaparte. However, Napoleon did not favor this solution. He knew that he was capable of having a child, since in 1810 the Polish countess, Marie Walewska, had borne him a son; but he desired to have a legitimate son as a successor. Second, he thought, with reason, that European sovereigns continued to consider his crown as usurped. He reasoned that an alliance with an old reigning family, the Hapsburg, would destroy this impression and he would then be considered an "equal."

Napoleon had thought first of marrying a Russian princess, Anna, sister of Tsar Alexander. Since the war of 1809, the alliance between Russia and France had deteriorated when Napoleon tendered his matrimonial proposal. The tsar refused, arguing that his sister, sixteen years old, was far too young. Napoleon then turned his attention to the Austrian archduchess, Marie Louise, who was twenty years old. The Austrian Chancellor, Metternich, arranged the marriage. He thought that it would give the Austrian empire a respite without pledging to Napoleon as much as he wished and it would also stimulate Franco-Russian disagreements. In France the adversaries of the Revolution favored this marriage, which they thought, would eliminate the regicides who still gravitated around Napoleon. In the course of a celebrated scene on November 30, 1809, Napoleon informed Josephine of his desire for divorce. The divorce was pronounced immediately and the marriage annuled by the *officialité* of Paris. On February 7, 1810, the Austrian government consented to the marriage.

Marie Louise was sent to France. She arrived at Strasbourg on March 22, and the marriage was celebrated in the Louvre on April 2, 1810. On March 20, 1811, Napoleon at long last had the legitimate son he so desired,

Napoleon II, the famous *l'Aiglon* (Eaglet). The *Grand Empire* allied to the old House of Hapsburg seemed to have taken definitive form and appeared, in spite of all, destined to endure. Crowned heads were addressed as "My brother."

THE THEORY OF THE *GRAND EMPIRE*

Did Napoleon wish to realize a pre-established program or to apply a theory or a doctrine in creating the *Grand Empire?* This is a question that must be legitimately settled before approaching the study of the Empire's institutions. The first matter to be considered is if Napoleon had adopted the political doctrine of the traditional French monarchy or the theory of the Revolution, of which he was the heir.

For a long time historians, under the influence of German historian Heinrich von Sybel and the Frenchman Albert Sorel, wrote that the Bourbons had pursued a policy whose end was the acquisition of France's "natural frontiers," that is the Rhine, the Alps, and the Pyrenees. This policy had been described by Cardinal Richelieu in his *Testament politique,* and Louis XIV, Louis XV, and Louis XVI applied their whole lives to realizing it. Gaston Zeller refuted this theory in his works.[1] He showed that the Valois policy had been oriented toward Italy and that Metz was occupied only for strategic reasons—following the brilliant resistance of Francis of Guise to Charles V. It was chance not a premeditated policy that led to the acquisition of Alsace, occupied by the Swedes during the Thirty Years War. In fact, the monarchy under Louis XIV concerned itself with recovering the frontier of the Meuse that the Treaty of Verdun of 843 had given to Charles the Bald, and Louis XIV exhausted himself to acquire Belgium. Under Louis XV the government even abandoned this policy of limited expansion. At the end of the war of the Austrian Succession in 1748, when he could have annexed with a little insistence Belgian territory, Louis XV renounced such annexation. He preferred to obtain Parma and Plaisance for one of his cousins. The foreign policy of the French monarchy had never had for its purpose the acquisition of "natural" frontiers even though certain historians and jurists have said it. Thus it was a policy of "succession," of "inheritances," a dynastic policy, not a national policy.

The French Revolution, of course, had to repudiate the dynastic approach. The Revolution had as its prime political principle the "sovereignty of the people." The *philosophes* particularly Rousseau, had just explained the legitimacy and the working of this basic time of the Revolution. It

---

[1] Gaston Zeller, *Les temps modernes,* vol. II, *De Louis XIV à 1789* ("Histoire des relations internationales"), Paris, 1955, *passim.*

was the sovereignty of the people that Mirabeau invoked in the name of the Third Estate on June 23, 1789, when he explained why the deputies refused to obey the orders of the king. It was also the sovereignty of the people that the National Guard invoked when they formed federations to resist possible feudal reaction. One of the federations, that of the National Guards of Alsace, Lorraine, and Franche-Comté, which was proclaimed at Strasbourg on June 13, 1790, affirmed among other things that Alsace was French not because the treaties concluded among sovereigns had united it to France but because its inhabitants had manifested the "will" *(volonté)* to be French. It was by virtue of this same will, which became the "right of peoples to dispose of themselves" that the inhabitants of Avignon and of Comtat Venaissin (Papal territory), asked to become a part of France on June 11, 1790.

This request greatly embarrassed the Constitutent Assembly. It feared that such an innovation in international public law would provoke war. At that time, the Assembly was very concerned about maintaining peace. The deputy, Merlin de Douai, became the advocate of "the right of peoples to dispose of themselves." It was only after long debates that the Constituent Assembly voted the annexation of Avignon on September 13, 1791. It was by virtue of the right of people to dispose of themselves that the assembly of Allobroges, composed of the deputies of Savoy, demanded the annexation of that province to France. The Convention accepted it on November 27, 1792. After this, the Convention acted less formally and, under conditions often contestible, annexed territories to France. In the county of Nice, in the Rhineland, and in Belgium, it was the Convention that organized plebiscites favorable to annexation. The Directory seemed to have some remorse about such actions, and in the spring of 1799 it organized a referendum on union with France in Piedmont. The result was positive, but this popular vote had taken place under such conditions that the Piedmontese Jacobins revolted against the French. This was the last popular consultation of the revolutionary epoch.

In 1792 another doctrine had arisen beside the theory of the right of peoples to dispose of themselves. It was then that the doctrine of the "natural frontiers" of France emerged as a government policy. It has its roots in the *De Bello Gallico* of Caesar, who stated that nature had fixed the boundaries of Gaul at the Rhine, the Alps, the Mediterranean, the Pyrenees, and the Atlantic Ocean. In diverse restatements by jurists and French historians, notably Eudes de Mézeray, allusion was made to it in the seventeenth and eighteenth centuries, but it was in Germany that it took a consistent form in the second half of the eighteenth century. The Germans contended that the French government desired to attain the frontier of the Rhine. Many were depressed by the possibility, but others rejoiced in it, such as Anarcharsis Cloots, who published in 1785 in Paris his *Hopes of a*

Gallophile (Voeux d'un Gallophile) and Forster of Mainz, who estimated in 1792 that only the annexation of the left bank of the Rhine to France could guarantee liberal institutions to the area. The entry of French troops on the left bank of the Rhine in October 1792 after the victory of Valmy and the reception, sometimes, enthusiastic, but also very reserved, showed that the doctrine of natural frontiers could usefully replace the right of peoples to dispose of themselves to justify annexations. It was by virtue of the theory of natural frontiers that the National Convention decided on the annexation of Belgium in 1795, and the Directory, that of Geneva and of Mulhouse in 1798. It was also in the name of this theory that the Directory prepared for the annexation of the left bank of the Rhine, which was not acquired until 1801 by the Treaty of Lunéville.

The Directory soon abandoned theoretical principles to justify its annexations. Its policies governing such take-overs came to be based on strategic interests of France and the ambitions of certain of its governors, notably Bonaparte. How is it possible to justify for example, the annexation of the Ionian Islands of which the majority of the population spoke the Greek language? Bonaparte who had inspired this strategic policy, followed it when he came to power in 1799, but also let his own ambition guide him. One can say that, during his entire reign, he concerned himself neither with the will of peoples nor natural frontiers. The annexation of Piedmont to France in 1802 is a prime proof of this.

It has been asked if Napoleon did not have as his ambition the design to reconstruct Charlemagne's empire: that he asked the Pope Pius VII to crown him emperor at Paris on December 2, 1804, and that he practically forced the German Emperor Francis II on August 11, 1804, to exchange his title for that of emperor of Austria, could cause one to think for a moment that Napoleon considered himself Charlemagne's successor.[2] If he entertained such a thought, it was soon exceeded. In 1807 Napoleon sought to make Austria and Russia enter the Continental System; thus he, Napoleon, would dominate all of Europe far beyond Charlemagne's frontiers.

Napoleon's ambition was limitless, and his external policy had no other base nor other principle than his own ambition, which went constantly beyond itself to obtain new objectives. Only force was capable of making him renounce his objectives, and it was adverse force from 1812 to 1814 that led to his fall. The *Grand Empire* never represented a stable institution because of Napoleon's ambition. It was only one moment in

---

[2] In the Collection of the Prince Napoléon is a gold medallion, item 369 of the Napoleonic exhibit in Paris at the Archives Nationales (1969), showing the profiles of Napoleon and of Charlemagne, made by François Andrieu, from a design by Dominique Denon, in 1806.

time of imperial politics, and one could not attribute to that ephemeral political construction any rigorous juridical base.

If Napoleon was an ambitious despot, he was also an enlightened despot—the last and doubtlessly the greatest of the enlightened despots. He attached himself, therefore, at the same time to the Old Regime by his despotism and to the Revolution by his Enlightenment. The apogee of the *Grand Empire* and the Austrian marriage marked, at the same time, for metropolitan France a definite turn toward an authoritarian and conservative policy and for the newly conquered countries, and above all for the vassal or allied states, the introduction of new institutions issuing from the Revolution.

THE REACTION IN FRANCE

In France, after 1808, Napoleon had reestablished nobility by creating an "imperial nobility" and an "imperial court."[3] A decree of March 1, 1808, created the titles of prince, serene highness, duke, count, baron, and knight. Certain offices carried with them the rights to these titles. For example, all the great dignitaries were princes and their oldest sons, dukes; every member of the Legion of Honor was a knight. The titles of nobility were hereditarily transmissible if their possessors enjoyed certain conditions of fortune and primogeniture. Many members of the old nobility received titles in the imperial nobility, and Napoleon increasingly recruited high functionaries (members of the Council of State, the Court of Accounts, the courts of justice, subprefects and prefects) from among the old aristocracy.

The renewal of repressive justice in 1808 and 1811 also marked a return to the Old Regime. The Code of Criminal Instruction once again introduced secrecy in the procedure almost with the same conditions as under the Criminal Ordinance of 1670. In the criminal tribunals, which had become courts of assize, the juries of accusation were suppressed and replaced by judges of inquiry. The Penal Code of 1810 was a definite rejection of that of 1791, which it replaced. Severe and unjust penalties (such as gen-

---

[3] The 1969 bicentennial exposition of the birth of Napoleon at the Grand Palais in Paris illustrated well the lavish court established by Napoleon under the Empire: the rich robes of Napoleon and Marie Louise and those of his courtiers, the gold table service for state occasions, the silver, the wall decorations and hangings, the tapestried furniture, the oriental rugs and French imitations of them. Imperial interiors contrasted with the life of the young soldier on campaign.

eral confiscation of property and the death penalty) were frequent. Corporal punishment was reestablished: all parricides condemned to death had their right hand cut off before decapitation. Those condemned to forced labor were exposed to the pillory for an hour and constantly dragged a heavy ball on their foot. They also lost civil rights. All condemned to corporal or degrading penalty were to be branded. Such branding signified the loss of civil rights. The decree of March 3, 1810 reestablished state prisons and gave the Privy Council the right to authorize arrests by administrative process. In 1814 more than 2500 people were arbitrarily imprisoned. The Penal Code of 1810 also judicially repressed beggary and vagabondage, by sentences involving correctional penalties. At the end of their sentence, they were retained in workhouses.

In his relations with the Catholic Church, Napoleon revealed himself more despotic than ever. The Pope had excommunicated Napoleon in June 1809. In a countermove, the Emperor arranged the arrest of the Pope in Rome and his removal to Savona. Pius VII was a virtual prisoner in the episcopal palace and before long deprived of paper and ink, because he forbade bishops to accept appointment from Napoleon. Napoleon intended to force the Pope to make his headquarters in Paris, capital of the *Grand Empire*. As a beginning, he ordered the cardinals to take up residence there. Only twenty-seven cardinals came. Thirteen of those who did, refused to assist in the marriage of Napoleon and Marie-Louise. They were immediately deprived of their property, their pensions, and, the emblems of their office, and were exiled to the provinces. Because Napoleon had unfrocked these cardinals, they were popularly known as the "black cardinals." A year later, the young son of the Emperor was given the title of king of Rome, which seemed to confirm Napoleon's intention to forbid the Pope to return to the Eternal City. Try as he did, Napoleon was unable to prevent orders from the Pope from reaching not only the *Grand Empire* but also the entire Catholic world as well. Resistance of Catholics to Napoleon began to organize and harden. Matters were aggravated when in 1811 the Emperor arranged to tighten the captivity of Pius VII.

The *Imperial Catechism* of 1806 was issued to be used uniformly in all French churches.[4] To the question as to the duties of Christians to the "prince who governs them," the answer was: "Christians owe the prince who governs them and we owe in particular to Napoleon I, our Emperor, love, respect, obedience, fidelity, military service, and the tributes laid for the preservation and defense of the Empire and of his throne; we also

---

[4] The full text of the *Imperial Catechism* may be found in *Napoleon: Was He the Heir of the Revolution?* edited by David L. Dowd for "Sources Problems in World Civilization series" (New York: Holt, Rinehart and Winston, Inc., 1957), pp. 53–54.

owe him fervent prayers for his safety and for the spiritual and temporal prosperity of the state." Another article appeared to define the principle that the Empire was divinely created. Such statements linked religion and loyalty, if not worship, to Napoleon. The *Catechism* was to be taught in the schools.

Basic measures for public education had been taken during the Consulate and Napoleon continued to consider problems of instruction during his campaigns. In the midst of his campaign against Prussia in 1807, at Finkelstein, he took the time to send instructions to the minister of education about some special schools. One letter, dated April 19, 1807, discussed the founding of a faculty of literature and history at the *Collège de France*, in the course of which he indicated his desire for more science in the schools. It was also from Finkelstein that Napoleon ordered the establishment of a school for girls, primarily from the provinces and daughters of his Legionaires.[5] His letter of May 15, 1807, gave details for the buildings, the curriculum and the discipline. Napoleon's attitude on the subordinate position of women was revealed in his instructions. Religion was to be of prime importance, for "what we ask of education is not that girls should think, but that they should believe." All the arts of homemaking, including manual labor, were to be taught; this would make the girls useful, obedient wives "suitable for poor and humble homes." The school was founded at Écouen, near Paris. The original site was destroyed in World War II. Even today there are still two Legion of Honor girls' schools, one located at Saint-Denis and the other at Les Loges in the forest of Saint-Germain-en-Laye, near Paris.

Napoleon attached much importance to the study of history. He himself made its study an ongoing project. On two occasions he even ordered the preparation of a special collection of historical writings (chiefly about antiquity) and of great literature, printed in volumes compact enough to fit in his saddle bags during his campaign. One of these can be seen today at Malmaison. Napoleon was also concerned with contemporary history and the glorification of his exploits.

Napoleon became increasingly sensitive to favorable reporting on the *Grand Empire*. In a letter to Count Emmanuel de Cretet, the minister of home affairs, written from Bordeaux on April 12, 1808, Napoleon discussed old histories of France and the need to bring them up to 1799. "The work must be entrusted not merely to authors of real ability, but also — and this is even more important — to adherents of the government, who will present the facts from their right angle. . . ." Napoleon went on to give some of his interpretations of the past, in which he praised religious tolera-

---

[5] See article by Elvire de Brissac, "The Girls' Schools of the Legion of Honor," *American Society Legion of Honor Magazine*, vol. XXXVI, no. 1, 1965, pp. 11–23.

tion, but linked the September massacres and "horrors" of the Revolution with the Spanish Inquisition. He did not want to bolster reaction, and said "Nobody could oppose the Revolution." He also did not want favorable reports about the Bourbons or the Pope to be published. In a letter to Fouché in 1805, Napoleon spoke of newspapers, and stated "that I shall never tolerate the newspapers to say or do anything against my interests." In 1809, he approved of the *Moniteur Universel,* virtually the official newspaper of the government, but advised it to leave out "everything that it is useless to know." Was Napoleon to be the judge of the utility?

Censorship increased. The decree of August 3, 1810, decided that in the provinces there could be only one "political" newspaper per department and it could only reproduce articles from the official *Moniteur.* A decree of February 4, 1811, allowed only four papers in Paris, the *Moniteur Universel,* the *Journal de Paris,* the *Journal de l'Empire,* and the *Gazette de France.* The *Journal de Paris* and the *Gazette* had existed before the Revolution, but both had changed drastically in the interim. Writers were subjected to a more and more vexatious censorship. In 1810 the celebrated book by Madame de Staël, *De l'Allemagne,* was seized and its author exiled. Chateaubriand was the object of constant surveillance. In 1811, because of him, the class of language and literature of the Institute (the old French Academy) was threatened with suppression as an "evil club." In contrast, the liberal and progressive institutions issuing from the Revolution were diffused in the *Grand Empire.*

THE DIFFUSION OF REVOLUTIONARY INSTITUTIONS IN THE *GRAND EMPIRE*

Under these circumstances, why did Napoleon wish to extend to the *Grand Empire* the most important institutions of the Revolution, those which in France had been created in 1789?

First, Napoleon was a man of the eighteenth century, disciple of the philosophers, admirer of rationalism, and concerned with the effectiveness and simplicity of administration. From this point of view, there was hardly any doubt about the superiority of administrative institutions and social institutions that France had instituted since 1789. Napoleon also thought that the best way to rally the most diverse peoples to the new regime was to suppress the heaviest of the payments that weighed on them, that is, the feudal regime, the tithe, and the corporative organization. He explained his viewpoint in a letter to his brother Jerome.

> What the people of Germany desire with impatience is that the individuals who are not nobles and who have talents have an equal right to your consideration and to positions; it is that every kind of serfdom

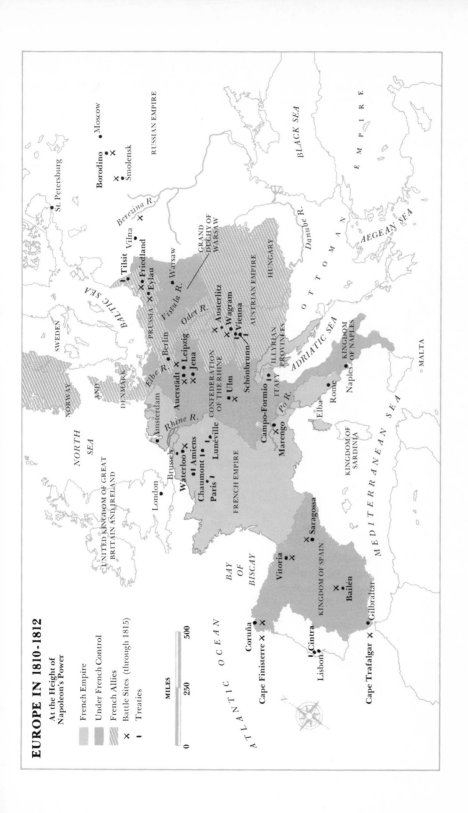

EUROPE IN 1810–1812

At the Height of Napoleon's Power

French Empire

Under French Control

French Allies

✕ Battle Sites (through 1815)

▪ Treaties

MILES

0   250   500

ATLANTIC OCEAN

NORTH SEA

BALTIC SEA

BLACK SEA

AEGEAN SEA

ADRIATIC SEA

MEDITERRANEAN SEA

BAY OF BISCAY

SWEDEN

NORWAY

DENMARK

UNITED KINGDOM OF GREAT BRITAIN AND IRELAND

RUSSIAN EMPIRE

OTTOMAN EMPIRE

HUNGARY

AUSTRIAN EMPIRE

GRAND DUCHY OF WARSAW

PRUSSIA

CONFEDERATION OF THE RHINE

FRENCH EMPIRE

KINGDOM OF SPAIN

KINGDOM OF SARDINIA

KINGDOM OF NAPLES

ILLYRIAN PROVINCES

ITALY

MALTA

London

Amsterdam

Brussels

Paris ▪

Chaumont ▪

Lunéville ▪

Waterloo ✕

Amiens ▪

Rhine R.

Elbe R.

Berlin

Leipzig ✕

Jena ✕

Auerstädt ✕

Ulm ✕

Schönbrunn ▪

Campo-Formio ▪

Marengo ✕

Po R.

Elba

Rome

Naples

Vienna ▪

Wagram ✕

Austerlitz ✕

Oder R.

Vistula R.

Warsaw

Friedland ✕

Eylau ✕

Tilsit ▪

Vilna

Berezina R. ✕

St. Petersburg

Borodino ✕ ▪ Moscow

✕
▪ Smolensk

Danube R.

Coruña ✕

Cape Finisterre ✕

Vitoria ✕

Sarigossa ✕

Bailén ✕

Gibraltar

Cape Trafalgar ✕

Lisbon

Cintra ▪

and intermediary bonds between the sovereign and the lowest class of the people be entirely abolished. If it is necessary to tell you my thoughts completely, I count more on their effects for the extension and strengthening of this monarchy than on the result of the greatest victories.

The abolition of the feudal regime (the suppression of serfdom, seignorial rights, corvées, and the tithe), therefore was the essential feature of his program.[6] It was the fundamental reform of the French Revolution, whose basic principles had been enunciated on the night of August 4, 1789, written into the law of August 11–15, and the Declaration of the Rights of Man also adopted in August 1789. Nevertheless between the principle and the application there was room for innumerable modifications, and Napoleon, who also believed in rallying the nobility to his side, thought of mitigating the rigor by applying his reforms, which in appearance were radical, with much prudence and even reticence.

On this point, furthermore, Napoleon had only to observe what happened in France where the feudal regime had been abolished under the pressure of the popular masses. It is known that the Constituent Assembly, in order to calm the peasant uprising that spread over almost all France, had proclaimed on the celebrated night of August 4, 1789, "the feudal regime is entirely abolished." But the decrees of November 11, 1789, and of March–May 1790 indicated that only serfdom and honorific and personal rights were immediately abolished. Ecclesiastic tithes were suppressed later (April 20, 1790). Real fees,[7] the heaviest, were declared redeemable under conditions often very onerous for the peasants. In fact, the Constituent Assembly had destroyed judicial feudalism, not economic feudalism. When the peasants understood this, they rose again, and it was only after the fall of the monarchy on August 25, 1792 that real fees were abolished

---

[6] Considerable controversy has raged around the meaning of the *régime féodal,* or feudalism, as applied to the French regime. The most definitive data on its abolition in the countries outside France can be found in the *Annales historiques de la Révolution française,* April–June, 1969. The entire number is devoted to the subject and covers Belgium, Holland, Spain, Portugal, Naples, Germany, Bohemia, Hungary, Romania, Poland, Russia, the Scandinavian countries, and Canada. See also Alphonse Aulard, *La Révolution française et le régime féodal* (Paris, 1919); Sydney Herbert, *The Fall of Feudalism in France* (London, 1921); Arthur Cobban, *The Social Interpretation of the French Revolution* (Cambridge University Press, 1964), and his *Aspects of the French Revolution* (New York: Braziller, 1968).

[7] Real fees *(droits)* were those based on a contract, such as the *champart,* land rent *(cens),* inheritance, and mutation fees *(quint, requint, lods et ventes),* and others. The National Assembly debated suppression with and without indemnity from February 11 to March 15, 1790. The issue of reimbursement concerned successive assemblies, and it was not until August 25, 1792, July 17, 1793, and May 18, 1794 that all dues were suppressed without indemnity in France.

without redemption. Still the last payments of a feudal character were not suppressed by the Convention until July 17, 1793 and May 18, 1794.

Legislation abolishing feudalism was introduced without modification in Belgium, only partially at the end of 1792, but systematically in 1794 and 1795. The effect was observable in 1796. Abolition was also put into effect in Holland (the Batavian Republic) in 1795 and 1796, and the last remains of serfdom were abolished in 1795. The tithe remained, under the pretext that, secularized, it constituted a ground rent. Seignorial justice and revenues did not disappear, however, until 1811.

In the greater part of Northern Italy, in the Cisalpine and Ligurian Republics, feudal survivals were suppressed in 1796 and 1797. The republican governments installed when the French troops arrived proclaimed the abolition of seignorial privileges and tithes, and this was confirmed by the constitutions of these two republics. This suppression was definitive. The suppression of the tithes troubled the clergy and incited them to support counterrevolutionary movements.

In Belgium, Holland, and Northern Italy, the abolition of the feudal regime did not bring grave disturbances because it already had almost disappeared. The situation was different as one moved southward and eastward.

On the left bank of the Rhine, although the abolition of the feudal regime had been proclaimed at the time of the entry of French troops, in fact, it was only systematically applied at the beginning of 1798, but then with the greatest rigor. As a consequence, the feudal regime in the Rhineland disappeared more completely than in France itself. In Switzerland, the Helvetic Republic of 1798 abolished without indemnity only personal fees and the "small" tithes, levied on fruits, vegetables and other garden products. The large tithes and the real fees had to be redeemed by the peasants. These reforms profited primarily the bourgeoisie, who had acquired them little by little. The legislative councils, after long discussions, abolished without indemnity only personal fees.

The policies and the methods adopted during the Directory to end feudalism in Europe served as guides for Napoleon. Under the Empire, abolition of the feudal regime was first pursued in Italy. In southern Italy, the feudal regime, which had been brought there by the Norman invaders in the tenth century, was infinitely heavier than in Northern Italy. The nobility there possessed, other than their honorific and onerous rights, important economic monopolies (mills, ovens, presses, mines and salt works). When the French invaded the area in 1798 and 1799, they proclaimed the abolition of the feudal regime, and yet as soon as the French departed, it reappeared again. The Neapolitan Republic, created in January 1799, was preoccupied with suppression, but did not succeed in completely eliminating it. Joseph Bonaparte, who became king of Naples in

1806, took up the task again, and the law of August 2, 1806, applied to the Neapolitan feudal regime dispositions very similar to those decreed for France August 11, 1789: personal fees were abolished without indemnity, but most of the real fees were made redeemable (law of February–March 1790). Judicial privileges were abolished in 1809, and large estates subdivided in the same year. These reforms were definitive, and the feudal regime, at least in its judicial aspect, disappeared from all southern Italy, but only slowly as regards economic features. The peasant of southern Italy remained dependent on the former seigneurs throughout most of the nineteenth century.

Princess Elisa Bacciocchi abolished feudal rights in Lucca, Massa, Carrare and Tuscany. In the Papal States, feudalism was done away with when these territories were joined to the Kingdom of Italy and to the French Empire in 1810, but feudalism was partially restored during the Restoration in 1814.

In Germany affairs were more complex—inevitably so because of the historic development of the many German states under the Holy Roman Empire and their divergent regimes dating back to the Middle Ages. Serfdom was the traditional institution and as one progressed eastward, it was more and more entrenched. However, it was the first feudal institution to receive the death blow. Serfdom disappeared in 1808 in the Kingdom of Westphalia, the Grand Duchy of Berg, the Grand Duchy of Frankfurt and Bavaria. Napoleon tried to manifest a dual policy, sometimes sparing certain princes whose loyalty he desired to retain, and sometimes on the contrary, conciliating the people, in order to arouse them against their rulers. In the Grand Duchy of Berg, serfdom, rents and personal labor obligations were terminated on December 12, 1808, and fiefs on January 11, 1809, but real fees were declared redeemable. The same measures were applied to the Kingdom of Westphalia. The peasants protested against redemption payments, but these were maintained. In the Grand Duchy of Frankfurt, the principalities of Fulda and of Hanau, serfdom alone was ended without indemnity, but real fees and the tithe had to be redeemed in the ducal domain; in the seignorial domains these rights could be maintained. In all these territories personal privileges had been abolished by 1809, and by 1811, personal seignorial rights in most were ended without indemnification. Real fees remained redeemable.

In Württemberg only serfdom was abolished; in all other respects, the feudal regime and tithes were maintained practically in their entirety. In Baden, where serfdom had been suppressed before 1789, feudal fees were maintained. In Hesse-Darmstadt serfdom was declared redeemable; corvées were reduced but maintained. In the Hanseatic departments, annexed to the French Empire in 1810, however, all personal rights were abolished without indemnity as well as a part of the real fees. The others could be redeemed. In Bavaria, serfdom and personal rights were abolished without indemnity in 1808. In 1807 the redemption of real fees had been authorized, but each redemption had to be made the object of a contract with the lord, who could refuse it. Thus, the peasantry was liberated only to a small degree.

Varying degrees of feudalism prevailed, which displeased the peasant, especially in southwest Germany where the greater part of the seignorial fees remained or were to be redeemed. The peasants often refused to pay the fees. When brought by the lords before the tribunals, they were generally condemned to pay; thus justice ranged itself on the side of the proprietors and strove to reduce as much as possible the consequences of the abolition of the feudal regime. The southern states of Germany were clearly behind the states of the left bank of the Rhine and those of northern and central Germany in respect to social institutions.

In the part of Poland that was made the Grand Duchy of Warsaw, the Constitution of 1807 abolished serfdom and Napoleon confirmed this with the introduction of the Civil Code in 1810. All other seignorial fees, the corvées and the tithes were retained. Thus, the greater part of the feudal regime continued.

In Istria, Dalmatia, and the Illyrian provinces, personal fees were abolished, and the corvées and land rents declared redeemable, but the peasants refused to pay or to redeem. Fearing a peasant uprising, many of the nobles emigrated to Austria.

The suppression of the feudal regime even in part, ameliorated the condition of the peasant. Nevertheless, it was only a preface. The elimination of feudal rights should have permitted the peasant to acquire enough land not to be dependent on the proprietor-noble or bourgeois—and to be able to live from his own land. In France, the sale of the lands of the Church and of the émigrés had permitted the increase of peasant proprietorship, although the bourgeoisie had profited more from the sales than the rural classes. In Italy, such was not the case. Several recent investigations provide glimpses for various regions of Italy, but no generalizations for the whole can yet be made. These isolated studies tend to show that in Northern Italy, the bourgeoisie augmented considerably its land wealth to the detriment of the nobility while peasant proprietorship remained unchanged. Thus, in the plain of Bologna bourgeois ownership went from 17 percent in 1789 to 30 percent in 1804, to 48 percent by 1835, while the percentage under peasant proprietorship remained stable.[8] Certain church lands

---

[8] Umberto Marcelli, "La crisi economica e sociale di Bologna nel 1796 . . ." *Atti e Memorie della Deputazione di storia patria per le provincie di Romagna,* vol. III, IV, 1953–1954, and *La vendita dei beni ecclesiastici a Bologna e nelle Romagne 1797–1815,* Bologna, 1961. Also Renato Zangheri, *Prime ricerche sulla distribuzione della proprietà fondiaria nella pianura bolognese, 1789–1835,* Bologna, 1957; and *La proprietà terriera e le origini del Risorgimento nel Bolognese,* t. I, *1789–1804,* Bologna, 1961.

were put up for sale and some communal holdings, some of which were large, such as Tavolière in Apulia, were divided. The peasant who did not have the necessary capital to exploit their newly acquired lands, resold them. In fact, here again the bourgeoisie was the class that profited most from the reforms. In the overall picture, the *latifundia* of the barons did not disappear; on the contrary, they sometimes even increased. In the Kingdom of Naples, an agrarian reform added to the elimination of serfdom. Certain of the Church and communal lands were sold.

An important agrarian reform accompanied the abolition of feudalism in Dalmatia. Here a Venetian law of 1756 had reserved to the state the ownership of the land. The state distributed to each adult male two thirds of a hectare (approximately two acres) with the right to farm it and transmit it to male heirs but with a prohibition against alienation. In exchange, the beneficiary owed military service and paid the tithe to the government. The provincial controller (provediter) Dandolo, named by Napoleon, abolished the law of 1756 and conferred ownership of land on the tenant. The tithe was maintained as a land tax. The peasants immediately sold their lands to speculators. In 1807, the authorities imposed such involved formalities governing the sales that they virtually came to a standstill. Thus a landed bourgeoisie could only become established at the price of liberty of transaction and consequently, contrary to one of the principles of the French Revolution.

In certain regions of Germany, particularly in Westphalia and Bavaria, division of communal lands proceeded. In Bavaria, division of the *hof* (great landed property) was authorized. Once again, the bourgeoisie seems to have been the chief beneficiary of rural reforms.

A peasant problem persisted, especially in the greater part of central Europe, in Poland and in southern Italy. The end of feudalism in the Grand Empire was only one of Napoleon's prime objectives. He was equally concerned with the application of the Civil Code, the Napoleonic Code, of whose promulgation he was very proud. The Code in reality established the facts of civil equality, and so all men of talent were capable, as Napoleon said, for the first time to gain access to judicial and military positions. Until the Empire, it was the nobility in most countries who filled these offices. This was too narrow a base for the needs of the modern state. The Code, based upon the laic state, since it implied a secular civil status, postulated either the separation of church and state or submission of church to the state, by a concordat modeled on the French Concordat of 1801.

It was Napoleon's wish that all the countries of the *Grand Empire* adopt this code without modification. To Napoleon, it was perfect, in keeping with the philosophy of the Enlightenment. The emperor considered men everywhere identical. His correspondence bears witness to these views. To his stepson, Eugène (de Beauharnais) he wrote: "What suits the French is suit-

Portrait of Napoleon by Robert Lefevre. (Museum of Fine Arts, Boston. Bequest of William Sturgis Bigelow)

able for all, because there are very few differences between one people and another." He declared to his brother, Louis, king of Holland, "If you alter the Napoleonic Code, it will no longer be the Napoleonic Code!" and to his brother-in-law, Murat, king of Naples, "I would prefer that Naples belong to the old king of Naples, sooner than allow the Napoleonic Code to be emasculated."

The Code, however, was Napoleonic only in name. It was the Constituent Assembly that had decreed on September 2, 1791, "A code of civil laws common to the entire kingdom will be made!" The Legislative Assembly, the National Convention, and the Councils of the Directory all worked toward the drafting of a code, and if Napoleon is to receive the accolade for hastening its completion, it must not be overlooked that the commission he created for the task profited greatly from the work of the Revolutionary assemblies which took as a base the "principles of 1789."

When the French Civil Code was promulgated on March 21, 1804, it was immediately extended to the entire French Empire. On January 1, 1806, it was introduced into the Kingdom of Italy. There it led to the creation of a secular state, the legalization of divorce, and the institution of the public service for mortgages. In 1808, the Code was introduced without any modification, in the Kingdom of Westphalia and in the tiny principality of Anhalt-Köthen; by contrast, in Hesse-Darmstadt, it underwent some alterations. In 1809, Murat applied it in the Kingdom of Naples under orders from Napoleon. Murat had wished to eliminate the divorce articles, but the Emperor refused to do so. In the same year the Code was applied in the old Papal States, but in 1814, it was abrogated there. The Bourbons who were restored in Naples, preserved the Code.

In the Illyrian provinces and the Grand Duchy of Frankfurt the Code was introduced in 1809 and 1810, but with serious amputations and modifications. In Illyria only the chapters relative to the family, to inheritance, and to the abolition of entails and trust agents,[9] were applied in 1809. The text relative to inheritance introduced important innovations in these countries, since it allowed women the right of inheritance. These measures were well received, and in 1812 the remainder of the Civil Code was promulgated. Nevertheless, while civil marriage became the rule, civil registration was not applied. In the Grand Duchy of Frankfürt, Dalberg proclaimed the Code in 1810, but he curtailed religious liberty in such a manner that Jews remained excluded from common law. They only became citizens in 1812.

On August 15, 1810, Poland received the Civil Code. Although it confirmed the abolition of serfdom, the peasants profited very little, and very slowly, from the dispositions favorable to them. In the same year the Code

---

[9] In the original text of Professor Godechot, the word *fideicommis* was used. According to Pierre A. Chéruel (*Dictionnaire historique des institutions, moeurs et coutumes de la France*, vol. I), this was the practice of willing the whole or part of a property to a person who is charged to give it to another person to whom the person making the will could not have legally willed it. This special trust agent was called a *fideicommissaire*.

was applied in Holland and in 1811 in the Hanseatic departments, which had become an integral part of the French Empire. The grand duke of Baden also adopted it in 1811 but after some modifications. Civil equality in Baden remained theoretical. On the other hand Bavaria and Württemberg refused to adopt the code. In Bavaria the government feared the resistance of the nobility and restricted itself to introducing only the French penal code. Württemberg proceeded with unification of its internal law in this way submitting to a certain extent nonetheless to the influence of France.

Thus, in spite of some gaps, the greater part of the *Grand Empire* was ruled by the Civil Code in 1812, in other words, some of the fundamental principles proclaimed in France in 1789.

Doubtlessly, Napoleon placed more importance and emphasis on the Civil Code than on constitutions. However, philosophes had repeated to such an extent that a state which did not possess a constitution was not a modern state, that Napoleon considered a constitution almost indispensible to every vassal state. But the constitution that was acceptable to him was one that created an all powerful executive and eliminated all possibility of real control by the masses over the conduct of the government. In fact, the constitutions of the states of the *Grand Empire* had been based on the French constitutions of 22 frimaire of the Year VIII (December 13, 1799), 14 thermidor of the Year X (August 1, 1802), and 28 floréal of the Year XII (May 18, 1804). Unlike the constitutions of France, those of the other states of the *Grand Empire* were not submitted to a referendum. The constitution of the Batavian Republic, of October 16, 1801, the constitution of the Luccan Republic of December 23, 1801, the constitution of the Italian Republic of January 30, 1802, the Helvetic constitution of May 29, 1801, as well as that of May 20, 1802, and the constitution of Valais of August 20, 1802, were all inspired by the French Constitution of the Year VIII (1799). The Swiss constitution of February 19, 1803 and the constitutions of the different cantons drafted in the same era were modeled on the Constitution of the Year X (1802). The imperial constitution of the Year XII (1804) served as a model for the constitutions of the Kingdom of Italy of March 17, 1805, of February 16, and August 14, 1806; for that of Lucca of June 1805; for the constitutional texts of the Kingdom of Holland of May 24, and June 9, 1806; for the statute of the town of Frankfurt-am-Main of October 10, 1806; for the constitutional statute of the Duchy of Warsaw of July 22, 1807; for the constitution of the Kingdom of Westphalia of November 16, 1807; for that of the Kingdom of Bavaria of 1808; for that of the Kingdom of Naples of June 23, 1808; for the Spanish Constitution of Bayonne of July 6, 1808, for the constitution of the Grand Duchy of Berg of December 12, 1808; that of the Grand Duchy of Frankfurt of August 16, 1810; and for that of the Duchy of Anhalt-Köthen of December 28, 1810.

These constitutions distributed public powers among the branches of government. All reduced the legislative body to a secondary role. Often the legislative assembly was divided into many houses or sections. For example, in the Kingdom of Italy, deputies were named to the legislative chamber by three colleges—that of the proprietors, that of the learned, and that of the men of commerce. When the chamber convened, the elected of each of these colleges formed three distinct groups. In the Duchy of Warsaw, the Chamber of Nuncios was composed of sixty deputies elected by the nobles and forty elected by the communes. Under the constitution of the Kingdom of Westphalia the character of the Estates of the kingdom (the legislature) was similar. There were one hundred members, seventy chosen from the proprietors, fifteen from the wholesale merchants and manufactureers, and fifteen from the learned men and "other citizens" whose merit had been recognized by the state. The diversity of these bodies reduced considerably the importance of the legislative chambers. Furthermore, they only met rarely and in most states the governments legislated by decree. The constitution of the Grand Duchy of Berg provided for the election of deputies, but they were actually named by the government. This was a tradition that Bonaparte had inaugurated in the Cisalpine Republic in 1797. In Bavaria, a legislative body was provided by the constitution; it was never convoked. Thus, all these constitutions contained various legislative provisions, whose clauses differed even more in their application, and in many cases were never really operative. Napoleon or his representative issued decrees rather than relying on a legislative process.

The constitutions sometimes made allusion to administrative organization. Most of the time, they only sketched the general outlines of the administration, and subsequent laws or decrees created the principle administrative institutions. Napoleon favored a good organization of justice and police so that order was assured in the *Grand Empire.* He demanded an efficient functioning of finances so that taxes flowed rapidly and steadily into the public coffers and he supported a rational organization of the army so that the numerous foreign contingents could be easily incorporated into the French army.

In respect to justice, Napoleon approved of the hierarchy of tribunals and the publicity of debates, but had little use for the jury, which he judged too democratic. Thus, in the reforms of 1808, he had the duties and attributions of the jury reduced considerably. It is not surprising, therefore, that when the Kingdom of Italy accepted the French judicial system, it omitted the jury. In the Grand-Duchy of Frankfurt, judicial tribunals similar to those of France were created, but seignorial justice remained. In Bavaria and Württemberg, justice was reorganized *à la francaise.* In Poland, the functions of the Supreme Court of Appeals devolved on the Council of State.

The French financial system also served as a model for the financial organization of many of the countries of the *Grand Empire*. In this domain, however, Napoleon was more interested in efficient operations than in duplication of the French system. On September 9, 1807, he wrote in the margin of a letter to his brother Louis: "Of what interest is it to France that there are uniformity of taxation in Holland and a thousand other procedures that relate to the opinion one can have of the administration of a country?" Nevertheless, the French land tax and licenses (*patente*) were, in general, adopted. Giuseppe Prina, a very efficient tax administrator and finance minister of the Kingdom of Italy, patterned his organization after the French model. In the Kingdom of Naples, Pierre Louis Roederer, who had been prominent in fiscal matters in the Constitutuent Assembly, was appointed finance minister by Joseph, and he revamped the fiscal organization, along French lines, and established the basis for an orderly system of finances for Naples. The Illyrian provinces, Holland, the Grand Duchy of Berg, the Kingdom of Westphalia, and the Duchy of Warsaw adopted with slight changes the financial organization of France; Bavaria and Württemberg were inspired by it in their reforms.

Napoleon changed the recruitment for the armies of the diverse states of the *Grand Empire* from enlistment to conscription. Access of all to the different ranks was established, more or less, in principle. Thus, the Kingdoms of Italy and Naples, Poland, and some states of the Confederation of the Rhine were able to send sizable contingents to the Grand Army. As a matter of fact, in 1812, at the beginning of the Russian campaign, soldiers from the "satellite" states made up the army of the Grand Empire—310,000 as opposed to 300,000 French. More than any other institution these armies of a democratic character were instruments of national fusion and of diffusion of the new ideas. It was the old soldiers of the imperial armies who after 1815, became the principal elements of the secret societies that fought against the restored governments for the foundation of liberal national states.

Even though other elements of French administration were copied less often than the judicial, police, financial, and military organizations, they too spread into a large section of Europe. The division of territory into departments and *arrondissements,* having at their head prefects and subprefects tightly subordinated to the central power, was adopted in the Kingdom of Italy, in that of Naples (where the departments took the name of provinces and the prefects that of intendants), in the grand Duchy of Berg, the Kingdom of Westphalia, the Grand Duchy of Frankfurt (with however the addition of a new division, the *amt,* between the commune and the *arrondissement*) and the Grand Duchy of Warsaw.

The French organization of bridges and roads was often imitated in the *Grand Empire*. Napoleon pushed this for it gave him numerous well maintained routes for moving his troops. The Kingdom of Italy, the Kingdom of Naples, and the Illyrian provinces had a system of bridges and roads that closely followed the French public service.

Another problem that greatly involved the Emperor was that of relations between church and state. He desired to avoid at any price the clergy's directing the opposition of the masses against his regime. He still recalled vividly the uprisings of the Vendée and of the south of France during the Revolution, and he did not wish to see the Spanish insurrection spread to all Europe. In the religious domain, in other respects, the situation varied according to the country, and Napoleon acted very prudently in regard to each case. The Kingdom of Italy signed a concordat with the Pope in 1802. It reduced the number of parishes, limited the number of seminaries and the number of convents and forbade religious brotherhoods. Nevertheless, the *Imperial Catechism* designed originally for France was imposed on the Kingdom of Italy in 1807.

Elsewhere, no concordat was concluded, but, in general, the Catholic Church was more strictly subordinated to the state. In Westphalia King Jerome himself chose the bishops; the greatest part of the clergy's lands was confiscated and sold; but the civil records (births, deaths, marriages) remained in the hands of the priests. In Bavaria the mendicant orders were suppressed in 1802, all other convents closed in 1803, and the lands of the church confiscated and sold. The same occurred in Baden. In Poland the church was placed under the authority of the state, and the bishops were named by the sovereign. By contrast the church preserved its lands, without, however, recovering those that had been secularized by the Prussian government. The Church also preserved control of the civil records. In Poland too, Catholicism was proclaimed the religion of the state and while freedom of worship and equality of citizens had been proclaimed, the Church obtained the concession in 1809 that political rights would be forbidden to the Jews for ten years.

An effort was made to develop education, with particular emphasis on higher education, throughout the *Grand Empire*. The secularization of education was generalized but in this domain Napoleon did not seek uniformity. Many of the countries of the *Grand Empire* moreover were ahead of France in education. Primary education was developed to a greater extent in respect to the number of schools and in methods in Holland, Switzerland, and Germany. Milan had a public secondary school for girls when France had none. In general, the old universities had survived, and the French organization was only adopted after many modifications and with many reservations. In summary, it seemed that in 1815 intellectual life was more highly developed at the universities of the *Grand Empire* than at those of the French Empire.

While Napoleon's goals in organizing the *Grand Empire* had been neither clear nor precise, it is incontestable that his policy had had as a consequence the accentuation of political, administrative, and social similarities among the different countries of the *Grand Empire* thus in the greater part of the European continent. There was only one area where Napoleon did not succeed, the cultural arena. He did not even seek to impose the French language and culture on Europe.

In a paradoxical manner, it was the Empire, authoritarian and military that gave the greatest expansion to the "conquests of 1789"—the abolition of the feudal regime, civil equality and liberty of conscience. Nevertheless, these conquests were only partial when Napoleon sought to impose them on his conquered neighbors, he necessarily modified their character because to consolidate the grand Empire, he needed the support of the very same local aristocrats who were struggling against him. There was thus, in Napoleon's design, an internal contradiction, which, if the Grand Empire had endured, would doubtlessly have led to a defeat more complete than that which its fall provoked. For if the Grand Empire disappeared, if the political forms which it had established vanished, the social transformation that it imposed continued in most of the countries, and, in general, the administrative and judicial institutions endured. Thus, the *Grand Empire* marked a capital break in the history of Europe; the end of Medieval Europe, the beginning of modern Europe.

10

THE RUSSIAN CAMPAIGN

At the very moment when Napoleon seemed to dominate Europe, he decided to undertake the Russian campaign[1] that was to put an end to the *Grand Empire* and to cause his own fall. Why war with Russia? Undoubtedly, at the bottom of it were the personalities of the two emperors. Alexander had not forgotten that Tilsit consecrated a defeat. He had been irritated by the passive attitude of France and his ally Denmark at the time of the conflict with Sweden, and he dreaded a complete resurrection of Poland. On his side, Napoleon reproached Russia for not having supported the Continental Blockade. At the time of the Erfurt interview the tsar had been very evasive concerning that question. Napoleon reproached Alexander even more for his ambiguous role during the war of 1809. Russia had occupied a part of Poland and had seemed to wish to support Austria. Napoleon, under the influence of his Polish friends, at first, considered a restoration of old Poland, but he knew that Russia would oppose it. It is

---

[1] On the Russian campaign, see *Mémoirs* of Napoleon, *Mémoirs* of General de Coulaincourt, cited in the Bibliography; *Journal* of the Abbé Adrien Surugue and *Relation* by the Count de Rostopchin in Jacques Godechot, *Napoléon (Le Mémorial des siècles)*, Paris, 1969.

184

highly probable that Napoleon would not have undertaken the Russian campaign in 1812 if he had not judged that state to be dangerously weakened by the events occurring in the west as well as in eastern Europe. In the west the economic crisis of 1810–1812 had weakened England and had enhanced the effectiveness of the blockade. At the same time the increasingly hostile attitude of the United States toward England constituted a new threat to the British economy. France's position in Spain seemed to have improved. In the east, Russia seemed involved in Balkan affairs, and Prussia and Austria appeared to have been won over to the French cause.

GREAT BRITAIN AND THE CRISIS OF 1810–1811

Toward the middle of June 1810, in spite of the blockade, the prosperity of Great Britain exceeded all expectations. Lord Liverpool told the House of Lords: "The nation far from finding itself in a state of decline is in the process of ascending . . . higher than ever in commercial prosperity." Several months later, however, the gravest economic crisis that England had undergone since 1789 gripped the country. What were its causes? First, there was a further weakening of the pound sterling, which had manifested itself at the end of 1808 and which was provoked by numerous factors: inflation, imbalance in the balance of accounts, augmented subsidies granted to continental allies, and anxiety of public opinion on the subject of the solidarity of the currency. But the weakening of the pound sterling, although chronologically earlier, was of less effect in unleashing the crisis than the poor harvests of 1808 and, above all, 1809. As soon as the harvest of 1809 ended, the price of cereals began to rise and passed from 88 shillings in July to 106 in October. To prevent an even higher rise of price, the British government decided on importations and granted licenses permitting the purchase of cereals in France and Holland beginning September 28, 1809. In spite of this, the rise in prices continued into the spring of 1810, and the British government had to grant additional licenses for cereal imports. The imports from France and Holland represented only 39 percent of the total importations from foreign countries. Still they might have given Napoleon the illusion that England was on the edge of famine.

Under these conditions, Napoleon reasoned trade might be reestablished with England while levying high duties on English goods so that this commerce could contribute to the French treasury. This was the object of the Trianon Decree of August 5, 1810, which raised the duties on all colonial products without distinction of origin from 10 to 50 percent ad valorem. Only cotton goods were excluded. The English could, therefore, export into Europe the products of their colonies and import from there the cereals that they needed. It has been said that Napoleon made a bad bargain and that he could have starved England in 1811 and have put her at his mercy. As a matter of fact, if Napoleon had forbidden the exportation of cereals from the French Empire to England, Great Britain would *not* have been starved. She would undoubtedly have increased her imports from Prussia, Sweden, Denmark, Russia, and the United States. In spite of these imports, the price of wheat rose to 116 shillings in May and in August 1810.

During this time British exports decreased greatly. Latin America was not responding to the excessive expectations of the English commercial interests. The purchasing power of the inhabitants was limited, and the revolutions from 1810 onward were beginning to slow down commerce still more. On the other hand, in England, Latin America was considered as an Eldorado. Many incompetent business men sent products that were not in demand. By 1809 the Latin America market was loaded with unsalable merchandise and, given the distance, had difficulties and delays in clearing operations. Trade between England and Latin America underwent a crisis in 1812.

Added to the crisis produced by the poor harvest of 1808–1809, tightening of the Continental Blockade aggravated the economic picture. In spite of the failure of the system, which had been obvious in the preceding years, Napoleon thought that the economic crisis that England was undergoing furnished him the right moment to strike her industry and her commerce through a tightening of the blockade. The conclusion of peace in 1809, the apogee of the *Grand Empire's* power in 1810 and 1811 allowed him to think that a stricter application of the Continental System would permit him to destroy England at last.

The annexation of Holland and of northern Germany, from Lippe to the Trave, allowed Napoleon to close the coasts more effectively. British commerce with Holland and northwest Germany broke down. Contraband traffic through Heligoland almost ceased completely during the summer of 1810. An Englishman wrote at the end of 1810: "A gentleman who arrived recently from that well-to-do island [Heligoland] assured me that from the beach to the staircases he had walked sinking to his ankles in dirty sugar and rotten coffee." It is not surprising that exports from Great Britain to Germany fell from an index of 106 in 1809 to 38 in 1810.

The English tried to recover the Baltic trade but in vain, for the French troops occupied the southwest shores of the Baltic Sea in force while Napoleon obtained by threat the seizure of British cargoes by Prussia, Sweden, and even Russia. Unfortunately, an immense convoy of more than 600 English ships was held up for several months at Göteborg by persistent south winds. When it could at last enter the Baltic, between October 5 and 12, 1810, it encountered a violent storm; 150 ships sank and an equal number were grounded on the Danish coast and captured. The others sought refuge in the ports of eastern Prussia and of Russia, where they were also seized. This was a disaster for English Baltic commerce. Cargoes valued at £7 or 8 million were lost.

The difficulties in the North and Baltic seas were not accompanied by an improvement of English commerce in the Mediterranean region. The year 1810 witnessed the greatest French expansion in the Iberian Peninsula. France occupied Andalusia and invaded Portugal again. English commerce with the Iberian Peninsula decreased appreciably; the exportations to Gibraltar and Cadiz stopped. The total value of English exports to Spain fell from £2,276,000 in 1809 to £1,207,000 in 1810. The decrease to Portugal was also considerable; the export index fell from 375 in 1809 to 285 in 1810. Only contraband trade out of Malta to Italy remained prosperous.

Commerce between Great Britain and the United States had picked up in 1809 and 1810. At the beginning of 1810 England, as we have seen, had even disposed of an enormous quantity of goods to the United States. But, abruptly at the end of 1810, thanks to a clever maneuver by Napoleon, the situation was reversed. On August 5, 1810, the French foreign minister, Nompère de Champagny, duke of Cadore, wrote to John Armstrong, the American minister in Paris, that the Berlin and Milan decrees would be revoked so far as concerned the United States and that if, reciprocally, the English did not revoke their Orders-in-Council, the United States should see that their rights were respected. In consequence, on November 2, 1810, President Madison raised all restrictions on United States trade with France and her dependencies, allowed England three months to revoke her Orders in Council, and declared that if the British orders were not revoked by February 2, 1811, American commerce with Great Britain would be interrupted. Since the British government acted slowly to annul the Orders-in-Council, and news of its revocation was received after Napoleon's concessions, a grave crisis developed between the United States and England that culminated in war, which was declared on June 18, 1812.

Between February 2, 1811, and June 18, 1812, Anglo-American commerce had diminished very rapidly. On April 27, 1811, the last ship loaded with English merchandise was admitted to the port of New York. In 1811 the United States received only 4.4 percent of the official total value of British exports compared to 17 percent the preceding year. Doubtlessly, English merchandise entered into the United States as contraband by way of Canada, but it does not seem that this traffic was very important. American exports to England were less affected. They showed, however, a decrease—one that was not significant for cotton but very noticeable for cereals. The effect on Anglo-American trade in 1811 of these events was the same as if the United States had joined the Continental System.

This crisis in British exports led to important consequences in the financial and social realm in Great Britain. In the first half of 1810 an unusual number of failures were recorded in London, primarily commercial houses specializing in exports to the Baltic region or to the Antilles. On July 7 the Brickwood Bank of London failed. Within a fortnight failures multiplied: five commission houses specializing in the export of cotton products, then a certain W. Jacob, member of Parliament and a leading exporter to South America. Several provincial banks followed the failure of the Brickwood Bank. On July 31 another London bank, the Devaynes Bank, filed its petition of bankruptcy. In August there were more important failures in London and Manchester. At the end of September the failure of the Goldsmith Bank, one of the most important of London, and frequently associated with the Baring Bank, was announced. This crash seriously hampered the state's credit, and the state bonds went down on the stock market. It became difficult to float new loans. In total, there were 1,799 commercial failures in 1810 against 1,098 in the preceding year.

The crisis naturally hampered industry. The cotton industry, which had been the most prosperous, was the first and the most severely hurt from November 1810 on. Numerous factories closed, and many workers became unemployed. The situation did not grow better in 1811. The cotton crisis was due, not to the lack of raw materials—the stacks of cotton in Great Britain were abundant at the beginning of the war with the United States— but to the insufficiency of exports. The stagnation of business extended to the summer of 1812.

The woolen industry was equally depressed during the same period. In May 1811, at Leeds, 400 workers out of 1600 were unemployed. Here, also, the stopping of exports was the base of the crisis. The situation was the same in the canvas industry. The silk industry was affected following the declines of silk imports from Europe—from 1,160,500 pounds in 1810 to only 126,500 pounds in 1811. The hosiery industry also suffered greatly.

The metallurgic industries did not escape, but they were less hard hit. Prices reached a high level in 1810, maintained themselves in 1811, but began to fall in 1812. In the autumn of that year the situation became grave. Many owners of forges had to extinguish their blast furnaces. The small metallurgy groups failed first because of the decrease of exports to Europe and the United States. Thus, the crisis of 1811–1812 touched all British industries, but it touched them unequally and at different times.

The economic crisis could not but result in grave social troubles. The workers, in effect, were the victims of a simultaneous rise in food prices (as a result of the poor harvests of 1808 to 1811) and of the reduction of salaries (descending to zero in case of unemployment) resulting from the industrial crisis. It was at the time when the price of foodstuffs was highest, salaries attained their lowest level. The misery was therefore exceedingly grave. In November 1811 a petition by weavers drew the attention of the government to the "meager and exhausted aspect" of workers, to "their clothes in tatters," to their "little children deprived of support and bare-foot." In 1812 the businessmen of Birmingham declared before Parliament that the situation of the working class was in "terrible distress . . . without precedent . . . cause of the worst convulsions."

The workers tried to obtain an amelioration of their lot. They demanded by numerous petitions to the government that it intervene so that salaries could be augmented, and aid distributed but in vain. The government as well as the House of Commons continued to support the system of economic liberalism. The workers attempted several strikes, notably the silk and cotton weavers of Scotland, at the end of 1812, but these strikes were broken. The workers resorted then to violence and destroyed the machines that they accused of being the cause of their unemployment. The outbursts were called the Luddite riots—the term being derived from Ned Ludd who in 1779 had destroyed in Leicestershire, machines used in the making of stockings. The first troubles of 1811 occurred in February at Arnold near Nottingham. A crowd of unemployed workers invaded the workshops and broke sixty looms. The uprising spread to the whole region and lasted more than a month. About two hundred looms were broken.

After several months of calm, the agitation flared again at Bulwell on November 4, when looms were again destroyed. A worker was killed by one of the manufacturers. The troubles lasted the entire month and spread even to the town of Nottingham. The Luddites ravaged the countryside, also, burned haystacks, mutilated stock belonging to magistrates and officers of the militia, and organized forced contributions in favor of the unemployed.

The local authorities asked for aid from the military: after November 15, two regiments of cavalry and three of infantry were sent to the Midlands. The government promised a reward of £50 for the arrest of every person guilty of acts of violence. These measures prevented the extension of the agitation. The factory owners announced an increase of salaries, which, little by little brought back calm, at the beginning of February 1812, in the Midlands.

Yorkshire and Lancashire became the scene of disturbances. On January 19, 1812, a factory had been deliberately burned near Leeds; each night, thereafter, masked men entered the workshops and broke the machines. The end of March to mid-April marked the high point of agitation. On the night of April 11, workers who were attacking the Cartwright factory near Liverpool were fired upon by an armed guard that the proprietor had hired. There were two deaths. This episode has been immortalized by Charlotte Brönte in her novel *Shirley.* Some days later an employer was assassinated. During the night of April 24, a mechanical loom was burned near Bolton. The presence of troops brought there, as in the Midlands, led to a rapid decrease in the number of attacks.

Parliament adopted in May and July many measures that would permit increased repression of those participating in the outbreaks. In January 1813, the assizes of York judged about a hundred guilty: seventeen were condemned to death and were hanged, eight deported.

The troubles were serious, but at all times geographically limited. However, they alarmed the British middle class, who imagined liaisons between Luddite workers, Irish revolutionaries, the radical leaders of London, and even the French government. It was rumored that a French officer commanded a Luddite band. There is no proof that the Luddities of Midlands had been in contact with those of Yorkshire or of Lancashire. The absence of concurrent timing in the attacks would indicate a total lack of communication and coordinated planning. In fact, current research finds no evidence that the Luddite movement had political aspects. The Luddite riots were struggles derived from hunger; their birth was spontaneous.

If a truly revolutionary movement had broken out at this period in England, it would have had a real chance of being successful. All favorable conditions were present—a very severe economic depression, which continued for more than eighteen months; a very great rise in prices of foodstuffs; misery of the working class; general discontent; weak government, discredited and unpopular, without any prominent personality; and a system of archaic local administration. That revolution did not break out can be attributed to the lack of revolutionary leaders. In England there were none. Previously it was noted that since 1789 all with radical leanings had been arrested, deported, pursued, and persecuted. In addition, a revolution at this time would have required an alliance between the worker proletariat and the middle class, as in France in 1789. The English middle class at this time was participating in the national political power. They were highly critical of the Luddite violence and vehemently denounced the riots. They joined the ruling class to repress them. There was not, therefore, a true revolutionary atmosphere in England. Nevertheless, Napoleon, because of the distorted reports that he received from England, could believe that this country was on the eve of revolution; he estimated that he had won the game and that he could without danger engage himself thoroughly against Russia. Thus, paradoxically, one can say that the Luddite troubles of 1811–1812 indirectly precipitated Napoleon's fall and the final victory of Great Britain.

IBERIAN AND BALKAN AFFAIRS

Napoleon was encouraged to act by the apparent decline of England's situation, but also by the impression that France's position in the Mediterranean and notably in the Iberian and Balkan peninsulas was growing stronger.

In the Iberian Peninsula, Portugal, evacuated after the capitulation of Junot at Cintra, had been reconquered in the spring of 1809. Marshal Soult had occupied Oporto, while Marshal Victor dominated the valley of the Tagus River. Nevertheless, Wellesley disembarked on April 25, 1809, prevented the junction of the two armies, and secured Coimbra, (Portugal). For this victory, he was made Lord Wellington. In 1810 the French troops of Spain occupied Andalusia (capture of Seville, February 1, 1810), and a new French army commanded by Marshal Masséna reconquered Portugal for the third time. Masséna, however, could not take Lisbon because he was stopped before the capital by fortified lines established by Wellington around Torres Vedras. At the beginning of August 1811 Napoleon had more than 360,000 men in the Iberian Peninsula. Apart from some centers of resistance, the most important of which were Cadiz and Lisbon, the entire peninsula seemed to have fallen into French hands.

The destruction of the last enemy strongholds did not appear to require much time. Also, Napoleon, who was already thinking of a war against Russia, began to recall troops from Spain. But he had overestimated his superiority. Wellington did not delay in taking the offensive, and Masséna had to retreat to Salamanca, where he yielded command to Marmont. Nonetheless, at the beginning of 1812, the French forces in Spain still numbered 224,000 men divided between five armies—that of the North, commanded by Comte de Dorsenne, then by Baron de Caffarelli, was holding the Asturias; the Army of Portugal under the orders of Marmont defended the west of Spain, from Salamanca to Badajoz; the Army of the center under Jourdan protected Madrid; the Army of Andalusia commanded by Soult was concentrated around Seville; finally the Army of Catalonia, under the orders of Suchet defended the eastern coast from Barcelona to Valencia. In spite of the evacuation of Portugal, Napoleon could justly believe in 1812 that he was master of the situation in Spain and that he could, without running great risks, direct his efforts toward eastern Europe.

In Italy, apart from the dispute with the Pope, the situation seemed reassuring. In September 1810 Murat had attempted an expedition against Sicily. A division landed on the island, but it could not maintain its position. As Murat crossed and returned through Calabria he was acclaimed. The *Carbonari* did not appear very dangerous, and furthermore, Murat had established secret contacts with them. He thought of making himself the champion of Italian unification. He spoke vaguely of this project to Napoleon when he went to Paris at the time of the birth of the king of Rome. In any case, in 1812 Napoleon had no reason to be disturbed by the Italian situation.

In the Balkans, also, the situation was such as to reassure Napoleon. Turkey had drawn close to France. In 1807 the sultan Selim III had asked Napoleon to send him French instructors for his army. It is true that the

Janissairies, considering that this was a sacrilege, rose up and overthrew Selim, who was strangled in his prison (May 1807). His successor Mustafa IV was also overthrown in August 1808, and Mahmud II, to maintain himself, had to promise the troops not to change their instruction nor their armament. Turkey had not won her war against Russia in 1806–1807. This war had been caused by the Serbs' uprising against the Turks. The Russians had supported the Serbs, but the French victory of Friedland forced Russia to conclude an armistice with Turkey at Slobodziea on August 24, 1807. War broke out again in April 1809. Two years later in 1811, there was still no decisive result. The English government feared that Russia, attacked by France, could not fight on two fronts. It intervened to bring peace between Russia and Turkey, which was signed at Bucharest only a few days before the beginning of the French offensive on May 28, 1812. At the moment when he was preparing the Russian campaign, Napoleon could legitimately believe that an important part of the Russian forces would remain immobilized in the Balkans.

THE RUSSIAN CAMPAIGN

For Napoleon, therefore, the circumstances appeared very favorable for an attack on Russia. England was crippled by a crisis, Spain was almost subdued; Russia was occupied in the Balkan peninsula. Germany appeared entirely on the side of France. Prussia had signed an offensive and defensive alliance with France on February 24, 1812, and Austria had concluded a similar one on March 14, by the Treaty of Paris. It is true that the sovereigns of these two states had secretly make known to Tsar Alexander that they would only march if constrained and forced, and that Bernadotte, royal prince of Sweden, had negotiated in secret with Russia. He yielded Finland to it in return for the promise of Norway.

Napoleon's complaints against Russia were old and numerous: the Tsar had never completely and sincerely applied the Continental Blockade; in 1809 he had encroached upon a part of Poland and had seemed prepared, if France were defeated by Austria, to overrun all of Poland. Since that time, the Tsar was still further diverted from the Continental System, and Napoleon suspected him of preparing war against France. From the Russian side, the complaints were not less numerous. The aristocracy complained of being ruined by the blockade. The Tsar reproached France for supporting Sweden and Turkey against him. Although Alexander had delayed and refused the hand of his sister to Napoleon, he had been vexed by the fact that Napoleon had in 1810, arranged the Hapsburg marriage. After Schönbrunn, he accused Napoleon of preparing war against Russia. On April

8, 1812, the Tsar had ordered Napoleon to withdraw French forces on the left bank of the Elbe, thereby clearing all French forces from Prussia and leaving Poland to Russia. The rejection of this ultimatum was the direct cause of the war. Without Napoleon's ambition and his greater willingness to take risks, the cause of friction between Alexander and Napoleon might have been alleviated, and what proved to be a disastrous campaign might never have taken place.

On June 24, 1812, after the failure of the final attempts at agreement, an army of "twenty nations and twelve languages" crossed the Nieman River. Napoleon's army against Russia numbered more than 650,000 men, half of whom came from the allied or satellite states, but there were at least 200,000 Frenchmen, and another 1,200,000 were to be called for military service. It must also be remembered that an army of 500,000 was being held in Spain in connection with the war and Napoleonic changes in the Iberian peninsula. Napoleon was thinking less of the common man who would serve in the infantry and who would have to cover vast distances on foot than on his past victories, and his confidence in his own ability to overcome all military obstacles. Napoleon did not call the Russian peasants to revolt by promising them the abolition of serfdom. The moujiks, therefore, remained faithful to the Tsar. As the French advanced they found a denuded countryside, stripped of its resources by the fleeing peasantry who followed a systematic policy of scorched earth. How to vanquish these immense deserts? How to assure the revictualing of these human masses in a country in which all resources had been voluntarily destroyed?

The timetable set by the Emperor for his Russian campaign could not be met. Napoleon was delayed at Vilna and only left on July 16–17 instead of in June. The Grand Army entered Vitebsk on July 24; it only reached Smolensk on August 7; and it finally arrived at the banks of the Moskva River on September 5. General Barclay de Tolly, who until that time had commanded the Russian army, had been criticized for his maneuver in retreat and was replaced by General Kutuzov who accepted battle. The armies met at Borodino. The battle was a French victory but one marked, as at Eylau, by great slaughter. It was a worn-out French army, already decimated by hunger and bullets, which entered Moscow on September 14, while Kutuzov's army retreated in good order to the south of the city. Napoleon had hoped that the capture of the old capital would force the Tsar to negotiate, or that at least the army could refresh itself in the largest city in Russia. Double deception: the Tsar refused all negotiation, and great fires destroyed Moscow and the immense stores of provisions that the Russians had accumulated there. Who lit this gigantic fire? The evidence is contradictory and the historians are not in agreement. Some accuse French soldiers of not having taken precautions in lighting fires in the wooden houses of the city. Count Rostopchin, governor and military commander of Moscow, blamed the French in his self-defense published after the fall of Napoleon,[2] and denied having given the order to burn the city. It may be noted, however, that when he gave his order for the Russian forces to retreat from the capital, instead of defending the city against the advancing French, he with his army took the water pumps to extinguish fires. Napoleon himself put the blame on the Russians. The French priest, Abbé Surugue, pastor of the French church in Moscow, which escaped destruction, supported Napoleon's claim.[3] Napoleon issued measures to help Russian civilians in Moscow, and to prevent looting.

The army corps that Napoleon had detached to the north while he marched on Moscow had not achieved notable success. Marshal Macdonald could not take Tiga and Marshal Gouvion Saint-Cyr marked time in the Polotsk region. In the south, Prince Schwarzenberg's Austrian corps accomplished little. Under such circumstances could Napoleon spend the winter in Moscow in a ruined city unable to live off the land, 600 miles from his bases, with very fragile lines of communication, which doubtlessly would be pitilessly cut during the winter?

After a month of hesitation, on October 19, Napoleon gave the order to retreat. He planned to withdraw by a more southern route than the road taken to Moscow, so that he could cross untouched regions in which the army could reprovision itself. But Kutuzov barred the route to him at Maloyaroslavets on October 24. Napoleon was forced to take once again the Smolensk route and cross the scene of his defeat at Borodino where the field was still covered with the dead. A week later, in November, the Russian winter set in early. Heavy snows fell and the cold was unbearable. Soon the thermometer went to below $-20°$ Centigrade ($-4°$ Fahrenheit). The retreat became a rout, and the army was nearly forced to capitulate near Borisov on the Berezina River where the army of the south, commanded by Admiral Tchitchagoff and that of the north, directed by Prince Wittgenstein, were on the point of joining to cut the Grand Army off from the road to Vilna. The Berezina was crossed thanks to the hard work of General Éblé's pontoniers, but not without 50,000 losses. On December 9 the survivors of the Russian adventure reached Vilna. Of the more than 650,000 men who had crossed the Niemen on June 24, hardly 100,000 returned to Lithuania; the remainder had disappeared.[4] Only one-fifth had

[2] Jacques Godechot, *Napoléon (Le Mémorial des Siècles),* "Relation du comte Rostopchin, pp. 315–324.

[3] *Ibid.,* "Journal de l'Abbé Adrien Surugue," pp. 301–314.

[4] See recent discussion by J. Houdaille in *Annales historiques de la Révolution française,* January–March, 1970, pp. 46–59.

been killed on the battlefield; the others had perished from hunger, from cold, from misery, and tens of thousands were prisoners.

Four days before his arrival at Vilna, Napoleon learned of an attempted *coup d'état* in Paris on October 23 to end his regime. A republican officer, General Malet, allied with members of the secret society of the *Philadelphes* and also with some royalists, who had been detained in a home for the insane, but who could easily leave the home, had tried to seize power. Malet, spread false news of Napoleon's death, formed a provisional government, obtained adherence of a part of the Paris National Guard, arrested the prefect of police Etienne Denis Pasquier, the general minister of police, René Savary, and mystified the prefect of the Seine, Nicolas Frochot. The commandant of Paris, General Hulin, one of the victors of the Bastille, had resisted, and the coup was checked. Malet and his accomplices, arrested immediately, had been judged by a military commission, condemned to death, and executed on October 29. The famous *XXIXe. Bulletin de la Grande Armée,* published in Paris in December before Napoleon's return, assured the French that the Emperor, whom Malet said had been killed, "had never been so well," but the same *Bulletin* implied defeat in Russia. The magnitude of French losses was not known until after the battle of Leipzig nearly a year later. The news of this abortive plot disturbed Napoleon. Above all he was surprised that the prefect of the Seine, Frochot, had so easily accepted the provisional government devised by the conspirators and had not once thought of recognizing the King of Rome, Napoleon's legitimate heir. Therefore, he left the retreating army December 5, after giving command to Murat, and returned in haste to Paris, where he arrived on December 18.

The departure of the Emperor aggravated the situation still more. Murat was incapable of reestablishing order in the debris of the Grand Army. The Austrians and Prussians who had not entered the forced French alliance, about-faced when they realized that destiny leaned in favor of Russia. On December 30, 1812, the Prussian general York von Wartenburg signed a convention of neutrality at Tauroggen with Russia. A month later, on January 30, 1813, Prince Schwarzenberg, commanding the Austrian corps, did the same. After these defections, demoralized remnants of the Grand Army had to abandon Poland and retire to the Oder. Prussian King Frederick William called for volunteers and convoked the *Krümpers* at the beginning of February. On February 28, he concluded an alliance with Russia and on March 16, declared war on France. Austria appeared more and more hostile to France.

Although the *XXIXe. Bulletin* had reassured the French public on the health of the Emperor, the implied losses did not quiet opposition to the continuance of the war, and only fed the rising voices of discontent.

In obscure words the municipal and general councils, the Legislative Body, and the Senate themselves appealed for peace. The moment had perhaps come to negotiate while still in fairly good condition. But Napoleon, eternal gambler, did not see it this way. He wished a new chance to try his luck, to force the hand of fate. He spent the winter in Paris, bringing all into play to prepare a new campaign that must, he thought, redress the situation.

11

THE FALL OF NAPOLEON

The Russian catastrophe was the signal awaited by all the patriots of Europe who were leading national resistance. The great movement of liberation that had been manifest in 1809 recurred, but on a scale infinitely more vast. In all corners of the Empire—in Spain, in Italy, in Germany—and on the economic front, that of the blockade, collapse was evident, while in the interior of France elements hostile to the empire regained courage, organizing, displaying themselves, and preparing openly the future regime.

THE LIBERATION OF SPAIN

Lord Wellington had retaken the offensive in 1812 after the withdrawal of troops destined for the Russian campaign weakened the French army of Spain. For four years he had fought in the Iberian Peninsula, and the English expeditionary corps had become thoroughly experienced in the type of warfare demanded by the Spanish terrain and the domestic situation. The organization of the expeditionary corps, though, was not efficient. The infantry and the cavalry were under the minister of war, but the artillery and the engineer corps were dependent on the board of ordnance, which furnished them with equipment and munitions; the officers of the infantry and cavalry still bought their ranks, while those of the artillery and engineer corps were appointed. Wellington's general staff was heavier than that of the French army but also more effective. It was composed of five groups—that of the commander in chief, which decided operations; that of the adjutant general, which prepared them; that of the quartermaster general, who organized the day's march and quarters; that of the commissary general, charged with provisioning and pay; and that of the inspector general, concerned with hospitals. Quartermaster General Murray was a remarkable organizer; he knew how to set up the stores necessary to the life of the army and the convoys of wagons or mules destined to bring the provisions. The British army, different from its adversary, did not live on the countryside. This was one of the reasons for its success. Nevertheless, Wellington could not keep his soldiers from pillaging. The information and transmission service of the army was well organized. A military telegraph system had been perfected that allowed the transmission of orders to a distance of 200 kilometers almost instantly.

The Spanish insurgents were also better organized. A central junta was again installed, at Cadiz on March 28, 1810, and was recognized by England as the legal government of Spain. The junta delegated the executive power to a council of regency (whose membership included Quevedo, bishop of Orense, Saavedra, and General Castaños) and convoked the General Cortes, which opened on September 24, 1810. The Cortes was divided between liberals—partisans of profound reforms—and conservatives. The liberals held the majority. They voted the abolition of the feudal regime, the abolition of torture, and the equality of access of all to ranks in the army. The constitution promulgated in 1812[1] was inspired both by the French Constitution of 1791 and by British institutions. The Constitution of Cadiz, as this liberal document came to be called by historians, proclaimed the sovereignty of the nation, guaranteed individual liberty and property, and declared Catholicism the state religion and allowed no other. It organized a constitutional monarchy in Spain. A unicameral legislature, the Cortes, had to meet no less than three times a year to enact laws. A constitutional commission of seven members had to supervise the application of laws and the constitution. Elections of representatives were by successive stages. The executive power was confined to the king, inviolable and sacred, and to seven ministers. A Council of State had attributes analogous to the French Council of State. Justice, too, was reorganized on the French model. There was no declaration of rights, but several rights were asserted in the text.

---

[1] A translation of the Constitution of 1812 can be found in Arnold F. Verduin, *Manual of Spanish Constitutions, 1808–1931* (University Lithoprinters, Ypsilanti, Mich., 1941).

Habeas corpus was stated in Articles 287, 290, and 300. No torture was to be used, and inviolability of domicile was guaranteed (Article 306). The right of petition to the king (Article 373) was granted, and taxation was to be proportionate to ability to pay. Military service was obligatory. The provincial administration was made uniform; councils (provincial deputations and municipal councils) were placed at the head of provinces and towns. On February 22, 1813, the Cortes abolished the Inquisition and nationalized its lands. The Constitution of 1812 rallied many liberal Spaniards, who had at first followed Joseph Bonaparte, and contributed more unanimity and effectiveness to the Spanish resistance in 1812. In 1820–1821, this constitution was in operation, then overthrown. A restoration of this constitution was henceforth the aim of Spanish liberals during the nineteenth century.

Thus, in Spain, Spanish patriots and their English allies presented good conditions, unity and efficient organization at the beginning of 1812. By contrast French armies were scattered over Spain, and their generals functioned independently. They were jealous of each other and cooperated poorly. Thus, in 1811 Soult had joined with Marmont to force Wellington to raise the siege of Badajoz, but, immediately afterward, the two generals separated, and Soult, in spite of the exhortations of Marmont, set out again for Andalusia.

Wellington profited from these divisions. He attacked in the middle of winter when the French were not expecting him. He took Ciudad Rodrigo, an important post on the Spanish–Portuguese border, on January 18, 1812, obliging Marmont to fall back on Salamanca. This enabled him to march south to capture Badajoz, (April 9, 1812) which he had vainly besieged the preceding year and where his troops had committed atrocities. Then turning to the north, he entered Salamanca on June 17, 1812, and one month later (July 22) struck Marmont a few miles south at Arapiles. The English victory at Arapiles had a profound repercussion in all Spain. This was the gravest check suffered by the French since the capitulations of Bailén and Cintra. The route to Madrid was open. King Joseph had to evacuate the capital by the Valencia route on August 10, and on the 12th Wellington installed himself in the Royal Palace. All Castile was now dominated by the Anglo-Spanish coalition. Soult, menaced on his rear, had to abandon Andalusia. After complicated movements, because of the difficult topography of southern Spain, and the action of insurgents, Soult reached Valencia only to have his troops decimated by yellow fever.

However, Wellington did not succeed in opening the way to Burgos to the north, and the French armies, grouped under the orders of Soult on the side of the Levant to the east, still represented an important numerical force: they were able to retake Madrid at the beginning of January 1813. However, on January 16 Joseph received there the celebrated Twenty-ninth *Bulletin* of the Grand Army. He then knew that he could no longer hope to receive reinforcements from France. Wellington knew this as well, and he renewed the offensive in March. The last French troops left Madrid on May 27, 1813.

While the French troops in the Levant were caught by Murray's English corps, which had landed at Alicante, Wellington was marching toward the north. On June 21, 1813, an Anglo-Spanish army of 80,000 men attacked French troops numbering only 66,000 at Vitoria in the north. Panic spread rapidly in the French ranks, and King Joseph was nearly captured. This was a total rout. On June 28, the debris of the three French armies of the North, the Center, and Portugal, recrossed the French frontier to the north of Roncesvalles. In Spain there remained only the armies of the South and Catalonia, commanded by Marshal Suchet, who fell back slowly from Valencia on Barcelona. At the beginning of November 1813, the Anglo-Spanish forces, after having taken Pamplona and San Sebastian, crossed the Bidassoa and penetrated into France.

Napoleon was furious on hearing the news from Spain. He had taken the command of troops from his brother Joseph, had given it to Marshal Soult, and had thought of negotiating with Ferdinand VII, who was still living in golden captivity at the chateau of Valençay. During the summer of 1813, Laforest, former ambassador of France to Madrid, acting for Napoleon, proposed to Ferdinand that he reascend the throne of Spain to destroy "anarchy, jacobinism, destruction of the monarchy and the republic" that the English had propagated there! After much hesitation Ferdinand, on December 8, 1813, signed with France the Treaty of Valençay, which foreshadowed his return to Madrid, granted amnesty for the *Afrancesados,* provided garrisoning the strongholds of Spain with Spanish troops instead of French, and called for the eviction by the Spanish of British troops stationed in the peninsula. Had this treaty been concluded a year sooner, it could have been of service to Napoleon in allowing him to transfer the Army of Spain to Germany. In December 1813 it was too late: Spain was lost, and its loss entailed the creation of an English front in the south of France.

AGITATION IN ITALY

In Italy the situation was much less serious than in Spain. No British expeditionary corps had been able to gain a foothold in the peninsula, and as long as Austria remained neutral, there was no great danger to fear. However, the population became more and more alienated from Napoleon for several reasons. A heavy loss in men had been sustained during the retreat from Russia. People were now fully aware ten years after the proclamation of the Italian Republic that Napoleon had no intention of satisfying the aspirations of the Italians for the unification and independence of their country. Further, the Italian Catholics were dissatisfied with the conduct of Napoleon in regard to Pope Pius VII.

The Russian campaign had been terrible for the Italians. Of the approximately 66,000 men who had been engaged, almost 40,000 disappeared. The army corps furnished by the Kingdom of Italy, alone, numbered 27,000 men at the beginning of the campaign. When it reached Germany at the end of the retreat, it did not number more than 223 able-bodied men. The losses sustained by the Italian troops in Spain and in Germany were also very high. Italians felt that these were useless losses and that all these soldiers were not sacrificed for the Italian cause. The poet Giacomo Leopardi expressed it better than anyone.

> *Sad is he who dies on the field of battle*
> *Not to defend his country or his pious*
> *Wife or his cherished sons*
> *But killed by the enemies of another people*
> *And for another, and who cannot say in dying*
> *Oh, my beautiful country*
> *The life that you have given me, I yield to you.*

The *Carbonari* became more active and more numerous in southern Italy. Certainly their program lacked clarity and precision, but they desired vaguely still, an Italy unified, independent, and liberal.

The English, who occupied Sicily, on the other hand, obliged the Bourbon king, Ferdinand IV, to promulgate a constitution, the basic principles of which had been voted on July 20, 1812, by the Old Sicilian feudal parliament. The Sicilian constitution, inspired by British and French institutions, provided for the separation of powers and a parliament endowed with legislative power—under the reservation of royal veto—having the right to vote the budget, to accuse and judge ministers. The parliament was composed of two houses—a House of Commons, of which the deputies were elected by suffrage based on property qualifications, and a House of Peers, composed of nobles and members of the clergy. Parliament had to convene each year. Individual liberty was guaranteed. The royal domain devolved on the nation in return for which the king received a civil list. The feudal regime was abolished; real payments, nevertheless, had to be redeemed.

One of the Sicilian authors of the constitution, Abbé Balsamo, felt that this constitution would attract liberal Italians, and his calculation proved right. The *Carbonari* made contact with the Sicilians to such an extent that certain historians have thought that *Carbonarism* had been introduced in Italy by the English from Sicily. In fact, if the Sicilian Constitution of

1812 exercised a great attraction for the Italians—above all after 1815, as the Cadiz Constitution did for the Spanish—it had little immediate effect. The abolition of the feudal regime in Sicily was more theoretic than real because of the lack of a substantial bourgeoisie capable of exercising power and the lack of peasants with the necessary capital to redeem the rents. The power of the Sicilian barons, therefore, remained almost intact.

Many Italian patriots pinned their hopes on Prince Eugène, viceroy of Italy, and on Murat, king of Naples. Eugène remained strongly loyal to Napoleon, but Murat listened to the leaders of the Italian party. We have seen that, invested with the command of the Grand Army on December 5, 1812, he gave it to Eugène on January 18 and had returned to Naples where he arrived on February 4 acclaimed by the population. Napoleon wrote a damning letter to Murat: "You are a good soldier on the battlefield, but away from there you have neither vigor nor character." Murat's rancor was increased by this, and he wished to present himself as champion of Italian unity to Austria and England, with whom he started negotiations. Austria restricted itself to vague oral assurances if Murat pursued unification, but the British ambassador, Bentnick, with whom Murat had an interview on the Island of Ponza, exhorted him to become the Bernadotte of Italy. Nevertheless, solicited still by Napoleon, Murat left Naples again to take a command in the Grand Army in Germany (August 1813). But he did not abandon his Italian dream and always thought of bringing about, to his profit, the unification of Italy, if circumstances permitted it.

While the liberal Italians detached themselves from Napoleon and looked toward Eugène, Murat, or Sicily, the Italian conservatives became more and more hostile to the Emperor because of his religious politics. Pius VII obstinately refused to institute the new bishops of the Empire since he had been imprisoned at Savona. A national council called at Paris in June 1811 had in vain sought a solution to this problem. Napoleon decided, therefore, to bring the Pope to France under the pretext that at Savona he was at the mercy of an English *coup de main*. On June 9, 1812, Pius VII was taken from Savona and transported to Fontainebleau, where he arrived on June 19. The Russian campaign started two days later, and it was only as a defeated man after his return to France that Napoleon had an interview with Pius VII on January 19, 1813, at Fontainebleau. Pius VII, at first firm in his refusal, ended by yielding, and he signed a text preliminary to a concordat that was to replace the one of 1801. On condition of Napoleon's recognition of papal sovereignty—without it being a question of the location of residence of the Pope—Pius VII consented to institute the newly named bishops. He also allowed the reduction of the number of dioceses in Tuscany, Holland, and the Hanseatic countries. The news of the agreement was immediately released by the press. The Emperor hoped by this to disarm Catholic opinion directed against him. In Italy "the effect was prodigious . . . they no longer spoke of conscription nor requisition, but only of the concordat."

Pius VII, however, quickly regretted having signed and refused complete execution of the agreement. Moreover, he was joined by the cardinals, the majority of whom were hostile to the new concordat. On March 24, 1813, Pius VII wrote a letter of retraction to Napoleon. Nonetheless, the *Bulletin of Laws* published the following week the Concordat as it had been ratified. Napoleon, who was about to begin the German campaign, renounced all new persecution against the cardinals of the opposition. The fate of arms dictated his conduct. Contrary to his expectation, as we are going to see, he was vanquished. Napoleon then decided to restore the Papal States to the Pope, without exacting concession (January 1814). The Pope responded that he could only receive the propositions made to him when he returned to Rome. On January 21, 1814, Napoleon decided to return Pius VII to the Eternal City, more perhaps to prevent Murat from annexing Rome to his states than to satisfy the wish expressed by the Pope. Pius VII only returned to Rome on May 24, 1814, after the fall of Napoleon. Thus, the liberation of Pius VII as that of Ferdinand VII was too late for the Emperor to derive any benefit. The treatment of the Pope and the persecution of his cardinals had been major factors in intensifying the opposition to Napoleon, not only in Italy but in the entire Catholic world.

THE GERMAN CAMPAIGN

In fact, it was not the opposition of the Catholic world but the German campaign that was the more decisive element in Napoleon's fall. The alliance between Prussia and Russia was concluded as one will remember, on February 28, 1813, and the Prussian declaration of war against France on March 16 drew in all Germany, Writers called German patriots to the "war of liberation." Ernst Arndt authored numerous patriotic brochures, the most celebrated of which was a *Catechism of the German Soldier.* Poets Karl Korner, Friedrich Ruckert, Max van Schenkendorf, Johann Uhland, and others did their best to arouse national sentiment. Public opinion to throw off the yoke of the French rose higher than the will of the sovereigns and outdistanced it. Under its pressure, Frederick William of Prussia and Tsar Alexander issued a proclamation to the Germans. They declared the Confederation of the Rhine dissolved and summoned the German princes to join them under pain of being removed as unworthy if they failed to do so. A council charged with administering occupied territories was organized with Prussian Baron Von Stein presiding. The reconquered German states were to be divided into five administrative divisions (circles), each headed by a military and a civil governor, the latter subordinate to a council of administration. It was Stein's belief that this organization would bring with it the destruction of traditional sovereignties and the realization of German unity.

Popular insurrections broke out immediately in all of the territories occupied by the French. The uprising in Hamburg on March 12 delivered the town to the Cossacks and that of March 26 allowed the Prussians to occupy the Saxon capital, Dresden, and remove the king from it. Riots took place at Oldenburg and at Hanau and in the Grand Duchy of Berg at Solingen, Elberfeld, and Remscheid. Unemployment was rampant because of the economic crisis, and it furnished the revolt with many recruits. The uprisings in the Grand Duchy of Berg were severely repressed; the captured rioters were shot, and the houses of those whom they could not take were burned. Nonetheless, their example was contagious: Mecklenburg defected; the German conscripts deserted in mass; and the French functionaries began to withdraw. However, the majority of princes of the Confederation of the Rhine remained faithful to Napoleon; to them the game did not seem finished yet. In addition, they did not have confidence in Stein, who seemed too "revolutionary" to them, and they waited for orders from Austria, who officially was still allied to France, although Schwarzenberg had abandoned the Grand Army and Metternich had made known to Napoleon that Austria would not furnish new contingents.

It seemed clear that Austria was awaiting events to choose sides. It was important, therefore, to Napoleon to defeat the Russians and Prussians quickly in order to prevent Austria's defection. Austria had offered its mediation, but she demanded as a price the return to the Treaty of Lunéville. Napoleon did not wish to grant this. At the very most, he consented to restore Illyria and a part of Galicia to Austria and to restore the king of Portugal. This was insufficient. Austria declared the alliance with France broken and proclaimed its "armed mediation" on April 14, 1813. Once more Napoleon's fate depended on the outcome of his military exploits.

Napoleon, in spite of the Russian disaster, raised a new army in France during the winter of 1812–1813. From September to April, 630,000 men were called—conscripts, those provisionally exempted, national guards, honor guards, and so forth. In addition, 540,000 rejoined so that the French army in the spring of 1813 was still composed of a total of more than one million men, of which half were in Germany. The Army of the Main (River), destined for the principal operations, alone numbered more than 150,000 men. Therefore, it had a crushing superiority over the Russian (60,000) and Prussian (45,000 men) armies. The French cavalry alone was insufficient; it had been impossible to fill the voids created by the Russian and Spanish campaigns.

The campaign in Germany began on April 28. French troops crossed the Saale River and penetrated into Saxony while the Russians and Prussians were still dispersed. Napoleon marched on Leipzig; he was attacked on the flank at Lützen on May 2. He was able to disengage himself, but at a price of losses double those of his adversaries. Nevertheless, this victory induced the king of Saxony to join the French. On May 20 and 21, Napoleon again met Russo-Prussian forces at Bautzen, on the Spree south of Berlin. It was a French victory, but the Russian and Prussian armies had not been destroyed and could retire to Silesia between the mountains of the Géants (eastern end of the Erz Gebirge) and the Oder. Russians and Prussians maneuvered the length of the Austrian frontier in the hope of drawing Metternich into their camp. Napoleon, also fearing Austrian intervention, overestimated the forces of his enemies. At the same time he was keenly aware of the depletion of his ranks because of losses sustained in the course of combat and more still from illness. Consequently, he accepted on May 29 an armistice proposed by Austria (following a suggestion that he had made on May 18). The armistice was concluded at Pleiswitz on June 4 to extend until July 20.

The armistice of Pleiswitz has been the subject of much discussion. It has been qualified as a monumental error. As soon as he appended his signature to it, Napoleon should have been aware of the folly of his action. It is improbable that he concluded it under the pressure of French public opinion. As will become evident, people began to clamor more and more vigorously for the making of peace. It is much more probable that it was the incomplete victories of Lutzen and Bautzen as well as the state of his troops that persuaded him of the necessity of a cessation of combat to reconstitute his forces. He thought that he could, at the end of July, dispatch more than 300,000 combatants to his army in Germany. He did not seem seriously to intend to conclude peace on terms close to those that Austria had proposed in April.

By agreeing to the armistice the Russians and Austrians hoped that the lull in fighting would permit Austria to complete her military preparations so that she could intervene in the best possible condition at the end of July. Actually, Metternich was still undecided about stepping in on Russia's side. He was full of the rancor of the aristocrat vanquished by the soldier of the Revolution. He mistrusted Prussian ambitions, and he feared German patriots, whom he considered revolutionaries. Lastly, he suspected Tsar Alexander's intentions, which he feared aimed at Galicia and the Balkans. Metternich, it seems, dreamed of a peace which in maintaining Napoleon in power would reinstate "the European equilibrium."

England's intervention was decisive. At the beginning of 1813 England emerged from the debilitating economic crisis that it had passed through for two years. Since the end of November, 1812, the flow of colonial foodstuffs to the mother country had increased and the cotton industry had recovered. On December 2, cotton industrialists MacConnel and Kennedy noted that the demand for cotton thread had become great and that the old supplies had almost disappeared. The news of Napoleon's disaster in Russia had released a wave of speculation. On December 14 MacConnel and Kennedy declared that prices were rising so quickly that it was impossible to fix a price that would hold for more than two or three days. The English money market advanced rapidly. Maritime commerce prospered to such a point that on December 28, 1812, the British government decided not to issue licenses for commerce with France. The rise in trade was continued in 1813. Commerce with the Baltic countries attained an unprecedented level: more than 3800 ships in each direction. In March after the Hamburg insurrection English commerce with Germany was resumed. The evacuation of Andalusia by the French also favored British commerce in the Iberian Peninsula. All this commercial movement with Europe largely compensated the losses due to the interruption of trade with the United States as a consequence of the war declared on June 18, 1812 by the United States on England.

The English political scene was also changing. In February, 1812 King George III had been officially declared insane. The Prince of Wales (the future George IV) became the regent of England. He was opposed to the pacifist Whigs, and in June 1812 replaced the inconsistent Spencer Perceval cabinet, which had been in office since 1809, with a new ministry headed by Lord Liverpool, the first lord of the treasury; Lord Bathhurst, the former minister of foreign affairs, became minister of war and of the colonies. He was replaced in the foreign office by a remarkable man Viscount Castlereagh, who had been trained by Pitt. This ministry was determined to carry on the war until the fall of Napoleon. Another objective was the return of Hanover to the royal house of England.

The British took advantage of the armistice of Pleiswitz to open negotiations with Russia, Prussia, and Austria. On June 14 and 15, 1813, the English ambassador, Sir Charles Stewart, signed a treaty at Reichenbach with the Russian and Prussian governments according them a subsidy of £ two million and in turn Prussia and Hanover were to be restored to their pre-1806 boundaries. The powers agreed not to sign a separate peace. On June 27 a second treaty of alliance was signed at Reichenbach involving England, Prussia, Austria, and Russia. Austria was to propose its mediation in favor of peace to France on the following bases: division of the Duchy of Warsaw between Prussia, Austria, and Russia; French evacuation of Illyria and of the Hanseatic departments; reconstitution of Prussia; immediate evacuation of Prussian fortresses still occupied by the French army and, if possible, the dissolution of the Confederation of the Rhine. If Napoleon rejected these propositions, the four powers would begin war against him again, and they would pursue it until the time that France abandoned Germany, Holland, Italy, and Spain. Castlereagh thought he had succeeded in what Pitt had attempted in vain in 1794 and 1799, an unbreakable alliance that would pursue a desperate struggle against Napoleon until it had attained its objective.

On the'eve of the signing of the second treaty, Napoleon had met Metternich at Dresden. Advised of the probable conditions of the coalition by the Austrian ministers, he had rejected them. In an interview on June 30, Napoleon accepted the idea that a congress of the five great powers meet at Prague but on the condition that the armistice of Pleiswitz be prolonged to August 10. He did this to stall for time.

General Caulaincourt represented Napoleon at the Congress of Prague. The emperor had instructed him to claim the reestablishment of the frontiers of 1813, but the French emissary lacked the authority to discuss the proposals and counterproposals. All propositions had to be transmitted to Napoleon, whose response did not arrive until the thirteenth of August, three days after the armistice expired.

There has been as much discussion by historians of Napoleon's role in the rupture of the armistice as of the reasons for which he had requested it. Many contend that Napoleon had been persuaded that Metternich's offers were subterfuges; the Austrian chancellor had in June 1813 but one goal: the fall of the Emperor and the reduction of France to the boundaries of 1792. However, one must remark that in sending his response after the armistice expired, the Emperor exhibited little concern about his propaganda that he desired peace, and all the appearances were against him. Thus he signified to the world that he was not concerned with establishing peace and that he desired to continue the war in the hope, evidently, of a decisive victory. In July, he had responded already to Savary, the minister of police, when he informed him of the first pacifist manifestations of French opinion: "You bore me with the need of peace." In refusing to negotiate at the Congress of Prague and in sending his response to Metternich's offers so that it arrived after August 10, Napoleon made himself fully responsible for the events to follow.

Napoleon now found himself with a changed front and one not favorable to the French. Arrayed against him were not only the Russians and the Prussians, but also the Austrians, a corps of English regulars, and even Swedish troops commanded by Bernadotte. Bernadotte wanted to annex Norway, a Danish possession, but Denmark was an ally of France and so the Frenchman who had become heir to the Swedish throne through the offices of Napoleon had deserted him and joined the Fourth Coalition. In total, there were 500,000 coalition fighting men in Germany. Against these forces, Napoleon could muster 450,000 men, but his reserves were weak and those of his adversaries considerable.

French troops concentrated in Saxony were attacked by three armies, that of Bernadotte coming from the Berlin region, that of Blücher from the Breslau district, and that of Schwarzenberg emerging from Bohemia. One might have thought that Napoleon would try the tactic that had been of such value to him in his signal success of 1796 in Italy, to strike separately each of the opposing armies. On the one hand, he was reluctant to abandon Dresden because the fidelity of the king of Saxony was doubtful; on the other, the distances to cross were two or three times greater than in Italy. Also, his army was composed of young recruits who had little training in long and rapid marches. In addition the French lacked sufficient cavalry. On August 26 and 27, Napoleon succeeded in driving back Schwarzenberg, whose advanced guards had penetrated the suburbs of Dresden, but a detachment of French under General Vandamme was captured on August 30 at Kulm (Chelm) in attempting to cut the Austrian retreat. Others of Napoleon's lieutenants likewise suffered heavy losses in the course of partial engagements. The French army diminished rapidly, while the numerical superiority of the allies increased.

The three armies of the North, Silesia, and Bohemia began again their advance before the end of September and joined forces near Leipzig on October 15. The allies drew up 320,000 men to oppose the 160,000 French. The "Battle of Nations," as it is commonly called, opened on October 16 and ended in a decisive defeat of Napoleon on October 18. The Saxons, allies of the French defected in the midst of the battle aggravating an already compromising situation. Thus Napoleon lost more than 60,000 men at Leipzig. Those who remained retreated with difficulty across Germany to the Rhine. Just before reaching there, the crippled army engaged in a bloody battle with the Austrians on October 30 at Hanau. Finally on November 2, the exhausted remainder of the Grand Army, decimated by typhus, recrossed the Rhine. The retreat from Germany in 1813 was a disaster similar to the retreat from Russia the preceding year.

All Germany to the east of the Rhine was freed except for some fortified places uselessly held by 120,000 French who resisted until Napoleon's abdication. Napoleonic Germany dismembered itself as quickly as it had been formed. The Confederation of the Rhine was dissolved and the old states recovered almost their boundaries of 1804 after negotiations with Austria, but they had to promise to help the allies in the final contest against Napoleon, which was to take place on French territory.

THE FRENCH CAMPAIGN

At the end of 1813 for the third time since 1789—as in 1793 and 1799—France was menaced with invasion on all her frontiers. Was she going to unite as in 1793 and 1799 to present the enemy with an insurmountable resistance? In truth, the situation was very different from that of 1793 and 1799. In 1793 it was the mass of the French people who rose to preserve the conquests of the Revolution—the great new principles of liberty and equality—the existence of which were still fragile and the application of which guaranteed the abolition of the condemned feudal regime and promised a happy future. In 1799 the sans-culottes had been disappointed by the failure of their demands and by the execution or arrest of their leaders. However, many still joined with the bourgeoisie to form a front against the enemy menace, whose victory would signify, doubtless, the return of the *ancien régime*. In 1814, without doubt, the majority of the French strongly adhered to the principles of 1789. They realized, though, that Napoleon was not, as they had believed in 1800, the man of the Revolution whose presence guaranteed the maintenance of its principles. He may have spread the most important of these principles to the rest of Europe, but at home he had slowly abandoned their application. Not only had he distorted the democratic regime by causing universal suffrage to disappear after 1800, not only had he abolished all liberty of opinion, not only had he removed from the chambers and councils representing local communities all possibility of expressing themselves freely, not only had he muzzled the press, but he had also brought a grave attack against equality by reinstating the nobility. Certainly, for a fraction of the peasant and worker masses Napoleon was still the son of the Revolution and was still the man who seemed to be able to oppose best the restoration of the privileges and abuse of the Old Regime. But the popular leaders who had survived the Thermidorian reaction and the persecutions of the Directory had ended by being arrested, exiled, and sometimes executed under the Empire.

From the economic point of view, the Continental Blockade and the crisis of 1811 had alienated important segments of the population. Industry had developed with the broadened market under the Empire, but it was primarily the industry of the east of France, of the regions recently annexed; the Empire, Belgium, and Rhenish Germany. In France proper the outlook was bleak. The old industry of the western and southern regions, particularly the textile industry, was gravely affected. The cotton industry lacked raw materials; the woolen industry of the south lost its outlets since the ports of the Mediterranean were tightly blockaded. The important French ports were totally inactive. Their commerce was paralyzed. Poor weather conditions, general in all Europe in 1811, added to the economic ills and provoked a general rise of prices of agricultural goods. The condition was aggravated further by licensed sales to England. Napoleon had decided to provide France with colonial products and refill the treasury via enormous customs duties. To avoid scarcity, the government had to decree measures inspired by those taken in 1793. The buying and selling of grain elsewhere than in the markets was forbidden. Merchants had to sign a preliminary declaration when their purchases were destined for other departments. The producers had to declare their stocks. On May 12, 1812, a maximum price for grain was fixed in the departments of Seine, Seine-et-Oise, Seine-et-Marne, Oise, Aisne, and Eure-et-Loir. In case of need, the maximum could be extended, but it was not because the prefects imbued with liberalism revolted against the rule. High prices did not benefit the farmers who had little grain to sell; and they certainly did not profit the consumers who had to reduce also their purchases of manufactured articles, since numerous factories had closed. As a result there was much unemployment and a wave of failures of the money-lenders and banks serving the affected industries. Thirty-seven Parisian firms declared bankruptcy, including the Bank of Simons, and the Fould Bank. In 1812 the harvest was better, but the satisfaction caused by the decrease in prices was quickly obliterated by the stupor provoked by the Russian disaster. The multiple drafting of men in 1813, the eager pursuit of draft evaders and deserters by the police, the increase of taxes, the decision to sell communal lands *(biens communaux)* to raise money, and the announcement of the defeats in Spain and then Germany aggravated dissatisfaction.

Municipal councils, councils of the *arrondissements,* and general councils formerly so laudatory to the Emperor sounded timid but significant criticisms. They refused to endorse certain expenditures demanded by the government, and they even allowed themselves to express sentiment in favor of peace. The chambers, not long ago so docile, did the same. At the end of 1813 the legislative body dared to criticize Napoleon's late response to the conditions of peace offered by Austria and vocally hoped that on the next occasion he would accept them. The deputy Laine said, in effect:

> The enemy progressed to the banks of the Rhine, offered to our august monarch a peace that a hero accustomed to so much success must have found very strange. But if noble and heroic sentiments dictated a refusal to him before the deplorable state of France had been judged, this refusal cannot be repeated without imprudence when the enemy has already crossed the frontiers of our legitimate territory. . . . [Laine denounced, in addition,] a vexacious administration, excessive taxation, deplorable methods adopted for the collection of taxes, and the worst excess yet, which the regime practiced for recruiting our armies.

The printing of this speech was approved by 225 votes against 51, but the Legislative Body was immediately adjourned. The Senate was less critical and more obsequious; nevertheless it also let its desire for peace be known.

An administration that solidly backed Napoleon perhaps could have, in spite of the rising tide of dissatisfaction and disturbances, mobilized the energy of the French against the invaders. But the administration had been modified considerably since 1808. Napoleon had replaced a great number of the revolutionaries by former nobles (self-styled rejoiners), by returned *émigrés*, by members of the old parliamentary families, by rich industrialists, or by landed property owners *(fonciers)*. Without doubt all had proclaimed their attachment to the Emperor, but this fidelity was dictated by their interests of the moment, not by their deep sentiments. In reality, many of them were tired of a dictatorship marked by perpetual war and aspired to a regime capable of coming to terms with the great European powers while maintaining the principles and the essential institutions of the Revolution. Certain of them were even disposed to accept the restoration of the Old Regime. Such men were found in the prefectorial corps. Besides authentic revolutionaries (such as the old Conventionnels, Jeanbon Saint-André at Mainz, or Chazal at Tarbes, later at Gap) after 1808 Napoleon named as prefects many former Parlement members (such as Mathieu Molé to Dijon or Arbaud-Jouques to Tarbes). Several prefects hesitated in 1814 to proclaim the conscription decided on by the Emperor. They did not approve the call to arm the mass of poor peasants and artisans. For them, the *levée on masse* should only call, as Arbaud-Jouques wrote, "landowners whose good sense, morality, age, and validity would raise no doubts of landowners interested to save their family and their goods from shame and pillage." Napoleon himself, after having decreed on January 8, 1814, the call to active service of the Parisian National Guard only armed 20,000 bourgeois guards. In fact, general conscription was only carried out in the departments of the east where the peasants knew the enemy better (the neighboring Germans) and identified them without hesitation with the counterrevolution. In the forests of Vosges the conscripts led a glorious but useless partisan fight.

In effect, the invasion of French territory had begun at the close of 1813. After Leipzig a truly "national" blaze swept through Germany. German patriots, one of whom was Joseph von Gorres, proclaimed the unification of Germany, incorporating in it the left bank of the Rhine and even Alsace and northern Lorraine. As for the Russians and the Austrians, they wished to take striking revenge for all of the defeats that they had undergone. England thought that the moment had come to establish the peace that she had meditated since 1794, the peace that would make her the major power of the world. Nevertheless, the interests of the four "Greats"—England, Russia, Austria, and Prussia—were sometimes in conflict, and a united front was not always forthcoming. This explains the tentative negotiations with France and the *mésalliances* among the allied generals that gave Napoleon unexpected opportunities of maneuver during the French campaign of 1814.

Metternich, who feared that victory would augment the power of Prussia and Russia, to the detriment of Austria, obtained from these two an agreement stating that a final offer of peace be tendered to Napoleon before the beginning of the campaign. Thus on November 9, 1813, he proposed to Napoleon that they negotiate on the basis of a France reduced to its natural frontiers, that is, to the Rhine, Alps, and Pyrenees. Napoleon received these proposals on November 15, and Caulaincourt, who had become minister of foreign affairs, accepted these "preliminaries of Frankfurt" on December 2. As in the instance of the rupture of the armistice of Pleiswitz in August, the French response arrived too late. Holland revolted against Napoleon. It had recalled the prince of Orange, and England had recognized the new government. Thus, as a consequence, it was no longer possible to guarantee France her "natural frontiers."

The sincerity of Metternich in his offer and of that of Napoleon in his late acceptance have also been much discussed by historians. It is certain that Austria, tied to England, could no longer offer France natural frontiers that Great Britain did not wish to recognize. It is more probable that Metternich wished to insure Austria's situation in Italy before the invasion of France. As Austria could not divert many troops below the Alps, it was necessary that she find an ally there. We have seen that Murat had already negotiated with Metternich in the spring of 1813. He had rejoined the French army of Germany in August, but he had left it immediately after the disaster of Leipzig. He began negotiations with England and Austria again, and on January 6 and 11, 1814, he signed treaties with these two powers. He promised to furnish them 30,000 men but they were not to fight on French soil. Murat's men were to aid Austria by fighting against Eugène, the viceroy of Italy, and to take possession of his states in return for which Murat had obtained from England and Austria a guarantee of his kingdom.

Napoleon, on his part, wished to persuade the French public that his adversaries were aggressors, and that the peace they sought would be an inglorious one for France. He hoped to raise a new army during the winter and to strike in the springtime when operations would begin. If he could get the French to back him, then he would encounter little trouble in recruiting the new army. The French were not fooled, as the reactions that we have mentioned proved, particularly the Legislative Body. Napoleon's calculation that the enemy offensive would begin in the spring was also frustrated. Under the influence of such generals as Blücher and Schwarzenberg, the allies decided to begin the offensive with all possible haste, therefore, in winter. Metternich wanted Switzerland included in the zone of operations in order to bring about a counterrevolution there, to reassert Austria's influence, and to cut France from Italy by occupying Lyon and the Alpine roads.

The offensive began on December 21, 1813. The Austrian army led by Schwarzenberg crossed the Rhine from Kehl to Schaffhausen. One corps pushed toward Geneva and Lyon while the others penetrated into France via Basel and Besançon.

At the beginning of January the Prussian army commanded by Blücher crossed the Rhine from Coblenz to Mannheim and penetrated into Lorraine pushing toward Bar-le-Duc and Saint-Dizier. The Army of the North marched much more slowly, for under the orders of its leader Bernadotte, it proceeded to Denmark, where, by the Treaty of Kiel of January 14, 1814, Bernadotte had obtained the cession of Norway. The allies, nonetheless, had 150,000 men in the northeast of France, and Napoleon could not oppose them with more than 60,000. In addition, he had to fight against Wellington between Bayonne and Toulouse and contain the Austrian corps of Bubna between Geneva and Lyon. Under these conditions there seemed little doubt of the victory of the coalition, but it was important that they agree on their goals of war before terminating operations. This is the reason why the English minister of foreign affairs, Castlereagh, hastened to the Continent.

He arrived at Basel on January 18 and had a great influence on the events about to unfold in the following months. The subsidies that the return of economic prosperity in England allowed Castlereagh to distribute abundantly gave his suggestions all the authority necessary. The money grants accorded to the allies rose from £ 3 million in 1813 to £ 5 million in 1814. In return, England obtained the concession that peace with France would be signed by common accord, that the treaty would contain no clause relative to freedom of the seas, and that the old French and Dutch colonies be annexed at least in part by England. The sovereigns of Spain and Portugal had to be restored and that of Naples indemnified. A barrier would be constructed on the frontiers of France to contain the future ambitions of that state: to the north, a kingdom of the Low Countries composed of Belgium and Holland; and to the east, Prussia (which received the left bank of the Rhine), Switzerland, and the reconsolidated Kingdom of Piedmont-Sardinia.

On January 25 Castlereagh journeyed to Langres where the future sovereign of France was discussed. The allies unanimously judged Napoleon lost, but they were not in agreement on the regime that should replace him. Tsar Alexander thought of putting Bernadotte on the throne of France, and Metternich proposed a regency in the name of Marie Louise. Castlereagh turned down these propositions and advanced the restoration of Louis XVIII, who had been living in England for five years and who seemed to be well acclaimed by public opinion. French Royalists grouped in secret societies such as the Knights of the Faith or the *Aa* organized demonstrations in favor of the return of the Bourbons. On December 3, 1813, those of Franche-Comté had made known to the Austrians in Switzerland that they were waiting for Louis XVIII; in February 1814, Lorraine rallied to the Count of Artois, who had come to Nancy, and on March 12 the mayor of Bordeaux officially proclaimed the Duke of Angoulême. The allies issued proclamations declaring that they were not making war on France, but only fighting Napoleon. These proclamations were successful in putting down any stray impulses of most of the officials to rally to Napoleon, and who henceforth were occupied with maintaining their positions under the regime to follow. By the Protocol of Langres of January 29, 1814, the allies decided to reduce France to its frontiers of 1792, and by the Treaty of Chaumont, published on March 9, they signed the general alliance against France that they had been unable to conclude since 1793. It was to be valid for twenty years and had as its objective the prevention of the maintenance of, or the return to power of, Napoleon.

While these negotiations were underway, the military scene was active. Napoleon took up a position with his army between the Marne and the Seine, between the Russo-Prussian army of Blücher in the north and the Austrian army of Schwarzenberg in the south. When one considers the imbalance of the forces, Napoleon achieved some brilliant successes. He successfully struck the Prussians at Brienne on January 29 but was overpowered by the Prussians and the Austrians at La Rothière on February 1. It seemed then that he no longer had any chance of winning. Napoleon gave Caulaincourt all powers to treat with the allies at Châtillon-sur-Seine (February 7).

In the face of their demands and the possibility again of striking the Austrians and the Prussians separately, Napoleon revoked Caulaincourt's powers and began the struggle again. On February 10 and 11 at Champaubert and Montmirail and February 14 at Vauchamps, Napoleon attacked Blücher's troops, but he did not succeed in destroying them. On February 18 he attempted to stop Schwarzenberg at Montereau. He tried to extract something from these victories by making it known that he was prepared to negotiate on the "basis of Frankfurt." The arrival of Bernadotte, who had crossed Belgium, and the exhortations of Castlereagh tightened the coalition. Blücher marched to Laon and joined his forces to those of the Army of the North. Napoleon could not dislodge these united armies from there (March 10).

In the meanwhile Schwarzenberg had begun his march toward Paris. Napoleon in a desperate maneuver tried to attack the enemy from the rear while cutting their lines of communication and so oblige them to renounce the attack on the capital. The combined allies could not be turned from their objective. On March 30 they were at the gates of Paris, which had for its defense only a small number of assorted troops. The regent, Marie Louise, the lieutenant general of the Empire, Joseph Bonaparte, and the government had fled from the city. The authorities of the capital, delivered from the fear of the Emperor, hastened to negotiate. The Senate immediately instituted a provisional government presided over by Talleyrand, who thus received the price of his treason begun in 1808. The Parisian royalists welcomed the allied troops with white flags and the Senate used this display of surrender as a pretext to decree the Emperor's downfall and to call to the throne Louis XVIII, whose ascendancy was strongly supported by England.

When Napoleon realized that his manuever had failed, he made a half turn but he was still only at Fontainbleau when, on March 30, Paris capitulated. He wished to continue to fight, but his marshals were weary. Marmont defected first. The others pressed him to abdicate. He signed his abdication on April 6, 1814. The last episode of the campaign of France was the battle of Toulouse on April 12: the two belligerents Soult and Wellington still were ignorant of the fall of Paris and the abdication of Napoleon.

The allies assigned the island of Elba to Napoleon for residence. It is located halfway between his native Corsica and the Italian coast. The fate of France was regulated by the Treaty of Paris signed on May 30, 1814. France was confined to its borders of January 1, 1792, with some small supplementary territories: Philippeville, Marienburg, Sarrebruck, Landau, Mulhouse, Montbéliard, Chambéry, Annecy, Avignon, and the Comtat-Venaissin. Of her colonies, she recovered Martinique, Guadeloupe, Guiana, the trading posts of Sénégal and of India, and the island of Bourbon (La Réunion). The fate of Europe was to be decided by a congress to meet at Vienna with the mission of isolating France and establishing a European equilibrium.

EPILOGUE: WATERLOO

The restoration of Louis XVIII in France did not bring about the restoration of the Old Regime. Louis XVIII understood that to reign over the French he had to accept the conquests of 1789 and guarantee the inviolability of the sale of the national lands. He made his acceptance clear to France when on June 4 he signed a charter to this effect. The document, officially called *La Charte,* had been prepared by the Legislative Body and the Senate of the Empire, and it was more liberal than the constitution of the year XII (1804). Nevertheless, the return of the last *émigrés,* the threats of the ultra-royalists and anti-revolutionary clergy whose leaders were members of the Knights of the Faith and the *Aa,* and disdain and superior attitude of those who had returned "in the train of the foreigner" and who "had learned nothing, forgotten nothing" soon aroused a general fear that the charter would be nullified and France would once again be subjected to a feudal regime, tithes and privileges, old administrations and forced restitution of the national lands. The acceptance of the restoration of the Bourbons in March and April 1814 was soon succeeded by distrust and fear. The old hates were aroused and resistance organized.

On the island of Elba, Napoleon waited and closely watched activities on the continent. He knew that in Vienna certain diplomats thought that he was stationed too close to the continent and considered sending him to a distant island; with the spirit of decision that he had not lost, he decided the time was ripe and made a lightning return. On March 1, 1815, he landed at the Gulf of Juan with some soldiers that the allies had left him on the island of Elba. Crossing the Alps, he rallied republican peasants. At Laffrey, near Grenoble, he fired the soldiers who had been ordered to arrest him with enthusiasm for his cause, and a little further on Colonel Labédoyère came to join him at the head of his regiment. From that time on "the eagle flew from steeple to steeple to the towers of Notre Dame."

Napoleon returned, carried more by the spirit of the Revolution which he seemed to incarnate in the eyes of his adversaries, the Bourbons, than by the memory of the last years of the Empire. To maintain himself and to group the mass of the French against the new, menacing coalition, he had to ally himself with the Jacobins who were now called the liberals. Napoleon did not dare to do so. Prisoner of the bourgeoisie who had installed themselves in power and who feared above all a return to the social politics outlined by the sans-culottes in 1793 and 1794, Napoleon was forced to install a political regime resembling that which Louis XVIII had begun. The enthusiasm of March 1815 deflated quickly and confidence disappeared. The *Acte additionel* to the imperial constitution was the *Charte* issued by Louis XVIII with the addition of universal suffrage, electoral colleges, hereditary nobility in the Senate. This modified constitution was approved by only a little more than a million and a half citizens out of 6 or 7 million electors.

The allies had decided—by virtue of the Pact of Chaumont that they would unite to bring about the downfall of Napoleon and would not sign a separate peace—to fight Napoleon and to concentrate their armies in Germany and the Low Countries. Napoleon rapidly raised an army and crossed the Belgian frontier at its head on June 15. Although conscripts had been called up, the nucleus of the fighting forces were soldiers who had campaigned with Napoleon. On June 16 he struck the Prussians at Ligny. But two days later, he met at Waterloo an army of English, Dutch, Belgians and Hanoverians—96,000 men commanded by the victor of the Spanish war, Wellington. On Napoleon's side, he started the battle with only 74,000 troops. He almost achieved victory, for the allied commands were poorly coordinated. He was on the verge of opening the road to Brussels near by, when Blücher's Prussian corps came to support the British who were yielding. "Victory changed camp" and soon, in spite of the heroism of the Old Guard, it was a debacle for the French. Napoleon lost 30,000 men and 7500 prisoners.

Napoleon returned to Paris and was forced by the Chambers to abdicate a second time. The "Hundred Days" were over. He went to Rochefort with the intention of embarking for the United States, but an English cruising ship was on the lookout for him. He made the decision then to surrender "to his oldest and most constant enemy." The British government decided to deport him to Saint Helena in the middle of the South Atlantic, far away from the scenes of his former glory and from which he could not escape. There, for six years, Napoleon patiently built his legend. He portrayed himself as the liberator of peoples, constructor of nationalities, and unifier of Europe. This legend would have more influence on the history of Europe than the reign of Napoleon himself. The entire history of the Continent from 1830 to 1870 would be profoundly marked by it.

After the departure of Napoleon, Louis XVIII returned, and the Allies, after a second invasion of French territory, imposed on France conditions more severe than the preceding year. The second Treaty of Paris of November 20, 1815, deprived France of Philippeville, Marienburg, Sarrelouis, Sarrebruck, Landau, and Savoy. The road to Paris by the valley of the Oise was dangerously exposed. France also had to pay an indemnity of war of 700,000 million francs and be subject to occupation by allied troops for three years.

For France, the imperial adventure terminated in national disaster. However, the Empire had consolidated and extended to the entire western world the essential principles of the Revolution.

12

EUROPE IN 1815

THE INTERNATIONAL SCENE

One impact of the Revolutionary and Napoleonic Wars was illustrated by the settlement agreed upon at the Congress of Vienna. Territorial boundaries were not restored to what they had been in 1789. Although peace respecting France had been signed with Napoleon in 1814, the allies realized that the clock could not be turned back to the beginning of the wars, and therefore, an international congress was called to meet at Vienna, the capital of Austria, the most consistent opponent of Napoleonic rule on the Continent. Although the work of the Congress was interrupted by Napoleon's "Hundred Days," its sessions continued, and after ten months, the final terms were signed on June 9, 1815.

Liberal historians of the nineteenth century severely criticised the Vienna settlement because it essentially ignored national sentiments aroused during the Revolutionary and Napoleonic era. Too much weight was given to a statement of the Prince de Ligne, a Belgian at the Congress, that the "Congress dances but does not work." Writings of Frederik von Gentz, secretary to the Congress, about the daily activity have negated his implications. In addition, the fact that there was no general European war until 1914 led to a reappraisal of the accomplishments of the Congress of Vienna. There was much display and pomp at Vienna, but while court festivities were attended by heads of states, prime ministers or chief delegates, their staffs continued work behind the scenes. Since all independent states attended, it was necessary to negotiate many treaties, bilateral and multilateral. Although there were jealousies and conflicting claims among the great powers and the lesser ones, agreement was reached by all after nine months of arduous work.

The problem of Napoleonic France was dealt with in the first and second treaties of Paris, arranged by the victorious allies. The work of the Congress of Vienna involved building peace for the rest of Europe. Talleyrand arrived in Vienna in September as a representative of the restored Bourbon France, but he was not admitted to the sessions with acknowledgement of an equal voice for France until January 9, 1815. In the interim, while negotiating with the representatives of the Big Four — Great Britain, Austria, Prussia, and Russia — Talleyrand defended vociferously the rights of the other signatories of the first Peace of Paris — Spain, Portugal, Sweden, and the lesser principalities of Germany. By so doing, he succeeded not only in reducing the role of the big four victors, but of gaining a voice for France and the lesser states. Although a plenary session of all delegates to the Congress was scheduled for October 1, 1814, it was postponed, and no plenary planning session was ever held. The Big Four served in all their dealings as a steering committee, but they did not dominate the gatherings as they had originally intended. All states that had felt the impact of the Napoleonic Wars and Napoleonic rule made their voices heard.

The principle of legitimacy, one of the three basic tenets embodied in the various treaties of 1815, appears to have been proposed by Talleyrand. Whatever changes of side Talleyrand had made since 1789, his own interests coincided with that of the opposition, and often furthered the interest of France. His advocacy of legitimacy was also defensive of France — not the France of Napoleon — but the France of many centuries and of 1815. France was to be ruled by Louis XVIII, the returned Bourbon. The principle of legitimacy applied elsewhere led to the restoration of Ferdinand VII in Spain, Ferdinand IV (now I) in the Kingdom of Naples (including Sicily), the House of Savoy-Sardinia in Piedmont, the house of Este at Modena, the house of Lorraine-Hapsburg in Tuscany — all areas where Napoleon had placed his relatives. In some areas, this principle was not applied, such as the assignment of the Duchy of Parma for life to the ex-empress Marie-Louise. Milanese territory was returned to Austria. Venezia was not restored as a republic, but annexed to Austria. The Papal Estates were restored to the Pope.

Although Napoleon had greatly reduced the number of states in Germany by consolidation of many small ones, especially in the Rhineland,

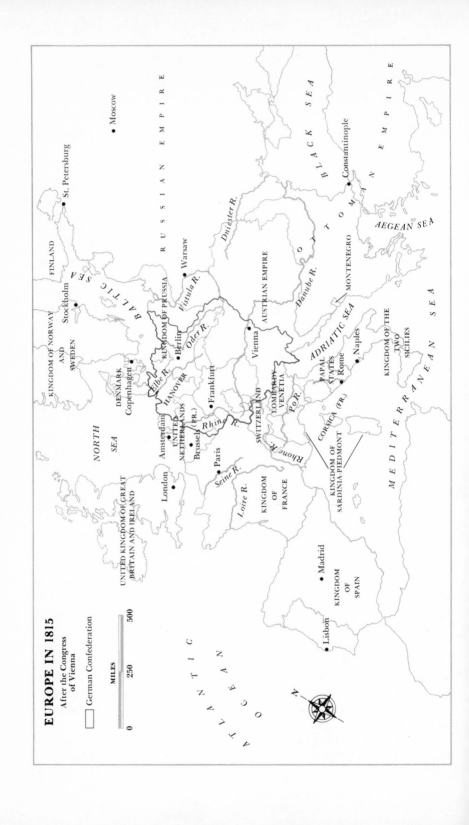

EUROPE IN 1815

After the Congress
of Vienna

German Confederation

MILES
0   250   500

UNITED KINGDOM OF GREAT BRITAIN AND IRELAND

London

ATLANTIC OCEAN

Lisbon

Madrid

KINGDOM OF SPAIN

KINGDOM OF FRANCE

Paris

Seine R.

Loire R.

Amsterdam

UNITED NETHERLANDS

Brussels (PR.)

Rhine R.

Rhône R.

SWITZERLAND

NORTH SEA

Copenhagen

DENMARK

HANOVER

Frankfurt

Elbe R.

Berlin

KINGDOM OF PRUSSIA

Oder R.

Vistula R.

Warsaw

KINGDOM OF NORWAY AND SWEDEN

Stockholm

FINLAND

BALTIC SEA

St. Petersburg

RUSSIAN EMPIRE

Moscow

Dniester R.

Danube R.

AUSTRIAN EMPIRE

Vienna

LOMBARDY VENETIA

Po R.

PAPAL STATES

Rome

KINGDOM OF SARDINIA-PIEDMONT

CORSICA (FR.)

KINGDOM OF THE TWO SICILIES

Naples

ADRIATIC SEA

MONTENEGRO

OTTOMAN EMPIRE

BLACK SEA

Constantinople

AEGEAN SEA

MEDITERRANEAN SEA

N

and other states in the former Holy Roman Empire were made satellite kingdoms or principalities, he had not dethroned their rulers in all cases. A new Germanic Confederation came out of the Congress of Vienna, composed of forty states (the Holy Roman Empire had included more than 300), including Hohenzollern West Prussia but not East Prussia, and the German-speaking part of the new Hapsburg Austrian Empire including Bohemia, but not Hungary, Austrian Poland, Italian and Dalmatian possessions. Prussia was enlarged by the annexation of a part of Saxony and Swedish Pomerania and the confirmation of the second and third partitions of Poland. Hanover, crown land of the British royal house since George I became king of England in 1714, had been a part of the Kingdom of Westphalia during Napoleon's changes in west Germany. It became a separate kingdom in 1815 although it remained under England until 1837.

A second principle underlying arrangements made at Vienna was compensation. If a victor lost some territory, it was rewarded with other territories. In the case of Great Britain, she acquired Ceylon and the Cape of Good Hope, former Dutch possession, Trinidad from Spain, Heligoland from Denmark, Malta from the Knights of Saint John who had been ousted by the French and then the French by the English, and a protectorate over the Ionian Islands in the Adriatic Sea. Britain had already been confirmed by the second Treaty of Paris in the possession of the former French colonies: Mauritius, Tobago, and Santa Lucia. These territories, most of which would increase British overseas dominions, were a reward for her seapower against Napoleon and her financial and military aid to the Continent.

The Dutch asked the House of Orange to return, and William I, son of William V, who had lived in England, was confirmed as ruler of the United Netherlands by the Treaty of Paris and then of Vienna. Since Holland had lost Ceylon and Cape of Good Hope to England, it was compensated by the union with the former Austrian Netherlands. Both these areas had once been Spanish possessions, but Holland had won its independence, which was recognized by Spain at the Peace of Westphalia in 1648. The Spanish southern area, which was to become Belgium in 1839, had been transferred to Austria in 1713 (Peace of Utrecht). When the Directory took over the administration of the area, it was organized into French departments. Whatever national sentiment that had begun to develop was ignored at Vienna, and now, instead of Vienna, it was to be governed from The Hague and Amsterdam. Denmark, who had been forced to cooperate with the Continental System, lost Norway to Sweden. This was compensation for the loss of Finland to Russia. The Napoleonic Grand Duchy of Warsaw and the Polish territory involved in the partitions of 1772, 1793, and 1795 were not restored as an independent country, but confirmed to the three partitioners, Russia, Austria, and Prussia. Russia gained in addition a part of the area around Warsaw, which had been annexed by Prussia in the

Third Partition, and with other Polish territory set up a Polish kingdom with a constitution but under the jurisdiction of Russia. This concession to the Poles did not satisfy Polish nationalists. In 1830 they attempted a revolution that failed. Russia then retracted its concession and ruled Poland directly from Saint Petersburg. Poland did not again become independent until after World War I.

The third principle of international politics followed by the Congress of Vienna was the creation of buffer states, or guarantees, in order to secure future peace. The annexation of Belgian territory to Holland was a measure of assurance against further aggression northward by France. Annexation of Bessarabia by Russia was an assurance against Turkey, which had been supported by France. The Confirmation of the Kingdom of Piedmont-Sardinia was both a safeguard against France in north Italy and against expansion westward of Austria.

The two measures taken at Vienna that lasted longest were not concerned with boundaries or dynasties, but arrrangements growing out of the revolutionary and Napoleonic era. The issue of natural boundaries accentuated the importance of rivers and their control, and the Napoleonic campaigns had increased their significance. The new boundaries in central Europe could not erase historic developments of diverse states along the borders of the rivers. A general agreement was drawn up to establish an international system for rivers touched by several states. A code for the regulation of traffic was drafted and a commission to enforce it set up. The Scheldt, the Rhine, and the Danube came under the commission's administration. There were to be no tolls, and navigation was to be free to all people. Concepts of a paper blockade and the doctrine of continuous voyage were being formulated, and the right of search and seizure was being further developed, along the lines of Britain's concern for freedom of the seas.

The second measure was a step taken to prohibit slave trade. Both England and the United States had already abolished such trade by their own national laws (1807 and 1808, respectively). Britain would not look with favor on Spain, Portugal or France gaining by this. While the Congress of Vienna denounced the slave trade, it could not get an international agreement to an immediate abolition. Instead it recommended to the signatories of its final agreement that they abolish the slave trade by law. After the Spanish Latin American colonies won their independence and after abolition of the slave trade by European countries by 1836, such trade died out except for smuggling. Although the French Revolution had abolished slavery in 1793, Napoleon reinstituted it in connection with the rebellion in Saint Domingue. The declaration of independence of that colony as Haiti in 1804 and its recognition ended the French role in slavery on the island.

It was also in response to the long period of wars, the many coalitions, and the desire for peace that Alexander I of Russia proposed the Holy Alliance. Although this proposal was suspect to Castlereagh and Metternich, it merely stated peace as a common concern of Christian rulers and promised consultation in case of the prospect of war. The alliance was open to signatures of all independent European states, and in fact, all but the papacy signed and promised forbearance and cooperation. Since Turkey was not a Christian state, it was not invited to sign. This declaration of collective security, combined with the Quadruple Alliance (whose members were also members of the Holy Alliance and whose original purpose was to prevent further aggression by France) became an instrument to maintain the status quo established by the Congress of Vienna and to suppress liberal movements within states. Although in actuality the Holy Alliance existed only through the Congress of Verona of 1822, it may have strengthened the concept of a concert of Europe, which prevailed until the 1850s, and was revived from time to time until a league of all nations was established after World War I. The concept, however vague, is at the base of movements toward European union since World War II.

From the foregoing treatment of the peace settlement of 1815, it may appear at first that its major features were a return to conditions before 1789—restoration and legitimacy. However, the two principles were not applied universally. Napoleon claimed, at Saint Helena, that he aimed to build a federation of Europe. His measures, his revocation of them, and his establishment of members of his family in many areas of western Europe, together with his system of satellite and allied states, were not viewed in the same light by the non-French peoples as by Napoleon. Great Britain, always his enemy, and the neutral states whose trade he had interfered with and consequently exerted corresponding pressures on internal conditions, were not prone to look to a unification of Europe under French hegemony. Many actions of Napoleon indicated a prime role for himself and for France in any unity of Europe. Napoleon underestimated, as did many rulers after 1815, the force of national sentiment unleashed by revolutionary ideology and strengthened in the fight to defeat Napoleon.

National sentiment in France, which began in 1789 with the unity of those desiring liberal reforms, developed along two avenues after emigration began. The *émigrés* were ready to invade France to bring about a return of the Old Regime. The revolutionaries, on the other hand, were ready to defend the reforms of the Revolution and the French soil upon which these reforms and new institutions were applied. With the declaration of war against Austria and Prussia, the two forces clashed. One force defended French soil against invasion, and the other backed invasion by foreign powers supporting the *émigrés* and the monarchy. After the execution of

Louis XVI revolutionary nationalism supported the Republic. French armies won victories beyond the former French borders, and began to establish regimes that introduced some of the changes of the French Revolution in the name of liberty and equality. Fraternity meant all those peoples cooperating with the French regime. French armies, at first under revolutionary leaders and then under Napoleon, aroused national sentiment against their former rulers, and, at least in Italy, Napoleon gave Italians hope that he would bring about unification.

After the change in France from the Consulate to the Empire, the successive policies of Napoleon appeared less interested in national aspirations than in the promotion of the Emperor's own power, with the aid of his numerous family. Napoleon took the throne of Holland away from Louis Bonaparte when Louis appeared to defend the national interests of Dutch trade against the Continental System, and the early hope of a Kindom of Italy ruled by an Italian changed to a title for Napoleon and for his son (king of Rome). In other areas instead of elevating a national to head the region Napoleon assigned his brothers or his marshals to former principalities or crowns. The wars of liberation of 1813, 1814, and 1815 aroused national sentiments among intellectuals and the middle class, which had not held office or benefited by Napoleonic rule, and these sentiments were to survive in the nineteenth century despite the settlement of Vienna.

THE INSTITUTIONAL BALANCE SHEET

Although certain features of the pre-1789 Europe reappeared after 1815, the international scene was certainly not the same. It was modified in several ways, and the origins of these modifications could be traced to the events of the preceding twenty-five years in France. Institutions within states bore strong evidence of influences from the eighteenth century *philosophes,* from the Revolutionary decade, and from the Napoleonic period. A written constitution was one of the most prominent examples of French influence. Throughout Europe such a document setting forth the principles governing a state not only was accepted but became a must for all governments.

Many states were granted written constitutions inspired by the ideas of the *philosophes,* whereas prior to the French Revolution, only the United States possessed a constitution of this type. The Congress of Vienna declared with respect to Germany: "There will be a regime of assemblies of estates," which allowed one to suppose the existence of a constitution of the German Confederation. Almost all of the constitutions established in 1815 had been influenced by new ideas propagated by the French Revolution and Imperial France. Some were also inspired by English constitutional principles, which had been popularized not only by Montesquieu and Voltaire but above all by the treatise of the Swiss jurisconsult Jean Louis Delolme, a refugee in England during the Revolution and author of *Constitution of England.* The constitution of the United States had also exerted a certain influence.

In France, in spite of the Restoration, the Charter, while "granted" by Louis XVIII, continued the Revolutionary tradition. It was, moreover, more liberal than the Napoleonic constitutions. The constitution of the new Kingdom of the Netherlands presented many analogies with the French Charter, but in contrast to the Charter, it had not been "granted" but debated by an assembly of "notables." This constitution organized a strong executive power, confided to a king, and a legislative power given first to one chamber then to two, an "upper" house composed of members named for life and a "lower" house of elected deputies. The two chambers discussed bills presented by the king, international agreements requiring the exchange or cession of territories, and peace treaties. They voted the budget with the reservation, however, that fixed and regular expenditures were voted for ten years: only extraordinary expenditures were the object of annual deliberation.

In 1812 the Cortes of Cadiz had voted a constitution inspired by English institutions and by the French Constitution of 1791. In the same year Sicily had also received a very similar constitution drafted under the influence of the British minister, Lord William Bentinck. The constitutions accepted by the countries at war with France should have continued after the fall of Napoleon, but Ferdinand VII in Spain and Ferdinand I in Sicily abolished them as soon as they thought the forces backing the constitutions were vanquished. The enforcement of these constitutions became from that time onward the fundamental demand of the revolutionary parties and secret societies. In 1815 there was no longer any constitution in force in Italy or in the Iberian Peninsula.

In Switzerland the "long diet" voted a constitution that was ratified by the cantons on September 9, 1814, but this constitution only provided, as under the former regime, an assembly of ambassadors of the cantons. Each canton possessed, moreover, its own particular constitution, but these were much more impregnated by the institutions of the old regime than by revolutionary principles. Alexander I granted the Kingdom of Poland a constitution more liberal than the Polish Constitution of May 3, 1791 (approaching in certain regards the French constitution of 1791) for the powers of the Diet were broader but less democratic. In fact, the landed nobility enjoyed a privileged status there. Certain provisions of this constitution recalled the constitution of the Grand Duchy of Warsaw; others even resembled the Declaration of the Rights of Man of 1789, but they were rapidly violated.

In Germany, in spite of the promises of the Final Act of the Congress of Vienna, the king of Prussia and the emperor of Austria refused to give their subjects a constitution. In 1814 of all the German states, only the little Duchy of Saxe-Weimar retained its constitution. Nevertheless, in 1817 the sovereigns of Baden and of Bavaria each granted their subjects one and the king of Württemberg imitated them in 1819. These four constitutions showed traces of the political ideas of the *philosophes*.

In Scandinavia, Sweden and Norway already possessed constitutions. That of Sweden, dating from 1809, did not copy the French model. Rather it was inspired by the ideas of Montesquieu and Delolme. In Norway on November 4, 1814, Bernadotte, now ruling Sweden and Norway, accepted a constitution voted by an assembly convoked for the purpose. Like the Swedish constitution it was influenced not only by Delolme, but also by the French Constitution of 1791. As in the latter, the separation of powers was very distinct. Suffrage was very broad, while elections were organized by "classes" (officials, burghers, peasants).

In conclusion, the European constitutions of 1814 that had been most profoundly influenced by the Revolution were those of France, the Low Countries, Sweden, and Norway. In Europe as in Central and South America, the revolutionary party had as its primary objective, after acquiring power, the establishment of a constitution based on the Great Principles spread abroad in the world since 1770.

The word *constitution* had, in fact, an explosive character. No basic distinction was drawn between constitution and revolution. But that was not true of institutions. Many of those that had been created and diffused by revolutionary and imperial France were so rational, and hence so superior to those that had preceded them, that the restored sovereigns did not hesitate to preserve or to imitate them. Thus the Napoleonic Council of State (*conseil d'état*) had been imitated by Tsar Alexander I under the influence of Speransky before it was incorporated in the constitutions of the Netherlands and Poland.

However, it was particularly in the countries that had formed part of the *Grand Empire* that institutions of French origin had taken root. The division into departments imposed by France had been preserved under the name of provinces in the Kingdom of the Netherlands, *arrondissements* became districts, prefects became governors, and subprefects became district commissioners. The general councils were transformed into provincial estates, elected by three "classes"—nobles, townsmen, and the rural population. In Switzerland the canton of Vaud, created by the revolution of 1798, was retained, but the former department of Mont Terrible, where French was spoken exclusively, was attached to the French- and German-speaking canton of Bern. In Spain, on the contrary, the prefectures created by Joseph Bonaparte disappeared, and in Italy there remained little trace of the Napoleonic departments.

The French judicial system, which was a very logical organization, was preserved in full in France. In Belgium and in Italy the assize courts lost their jury. The purchase of judicial offices was even reconstituted in the Kingdom of Naples. In Poland, however, the justices of the peace and the hierarchy of courts imported by the French were preserved.

Like the tribunals, the Napoleonic codes had been diffused throughout the *Grand Empire*. After the dismemberment of the empire, they were maintained in many states—in the Low Countries, although Netherlandized by Corneille Felix Van Maanen; in the Duchy of Parma, where the Criminal Code was rendered milder; in the Kingdom of Naples; in Rhineland Prussia; in various smaller German principalities; in the Polish provinces belonging to the Grand Duchy of Warsaw. Even where they were suppressed, the Napoleonic codes exercised influence on the legislation that replaced them. Their influence was even felt in the United States. The first Civil Code of the state of Louisiana was greatly influenced by the Napoleonic Code.

Under the Directory, the Consulate, and the Empire, Fouché reorganized the French police, and his organization was retained by the returned Bourbons after 1815. The Netherlands patterned the administration of general police on the French model. Many Italian and German states, as well as Sweden and Norway, established a ministry of police in imitation of imperial France. The police practices of the Restoration, in their action against the liberals, were often inspired by Fouché's methods.

In financial matters, the system of direct taxes created by the Constituent Assembly and the organization of their collection worked out by the Directory and the Consulate were generally admired. This system was based on equality before the tax collector and could not be put into effect except where fiscal privileges had been abolished. The French tax system was preserved in the Low Countries in its entirety until 1822, at which time it was slightly modified. For Old Regime taxes that were predominantly indirect levies, the Cortes of Cadiz substituted two direct taxes on the French model, one on land and the other on industry and commerce. These were levied from 1812 until 1814 and from 1820 to 1822. In Italy the Duchy of Modena preserved the French fiscal system even though its sovereign was one of the most reactionary in Italy. It was the same in Rhineland Prussia. In Poland the financial organization of France had not been wholly applied. Licenses of the French type remained side by side with the salt monopoly borrowed from Prussia. In Sweden the tax privileges of the nobility were suppressed between 1789 and 1809.

Following the example of England and the United States, the French Constituent Assembly had decided that the legislature should vote the budget. This principle was more or less applied until 1814. It then became one of the fundamental articles of the French Constitution (the Charter) and of the Constitution of the Netherlands. But in most of the Italian states, in the Germanies, and in Poland a budget promulgated by the administration was substituted for a budget voted by a legislature. The financial accounts in France were verified by a Cour des Comptes instituted in 1807, and which succeeded a Commission of National Accounting dating from 1790. This fiscal court was copied in the Netherlands, Sweden, and in certain German states.

As for a state bank, France had not originated such an institution: the Bank of France imitated the Bank of Amsterdam and the Bank of England. The Bank of France did serve as a model for others. In 1814 a Netherlands Bank was created, in 1822 a *Société Générale de Belgique,* and at Naples in 1818 a Bank of the Two Sicilies was organized on the same model.

The changes in the fiscal systems of the various states were linked to economic changes. The modifications produced in the rural economy by the more or less complete abolition of the feudal regime have been mentioned. In the realm of industry, the French Constituent Assembly had hesitated to proclaim the freedom of labor. It had suppressed the guilds but maintained, as under the Old Regime, the prohibitions against workers associations, coalitions (unions), and strikes. In the Kingdom of the Netherlands, similar legislation was maintained in principle, but certain guilds were reconstituted. In Spain the Cortes of Cadiz had abolished guilds, but Ferdinand VII authorized them again. In Italy the guilds were reestablished in the Kingdom of Sardinia. In the Germanies guilds survived in Prussia and in Austria, but they remained suppressed in the Rhineland and in certain smaller states. In Poland only a certain number of corporate bodies were authorized in 1816. In Scandinavia, although guilds were not forbidden, they declined rapidly after 1815. Strikes, unions, and journeymen's associations (compagnonnage) were, as in France, forbidden throughout Europe.

The suppression of customs barriers within states had begun even before 1789. The most noteworthy example was Tuscany. The movement accelerated during the revolutionary and imperial periods and led to the creation of customs agreements between states, notably the Zollverein in the Germanies. The metric system spread between 1792 and 1814 and was adopted little by little. By 1814 it was used in the Netherlands, Rhineland Prussia, and several Italian states.

The French army, which had been almost always victorious from 1792 to 1812, naturally served as a model for Europe. At first, it was the organization of recruitment—universal military service—that was imitated and adopted in Prussia, and in Sweden after 1814. The opportunity for everyone to rise to officer rank was maintained in the Netherlands, for instance, although national discrimination in favor of the Dutch was substituted for social discrimination. In Spain Ferdinand VII reinstituted the requirement that proofs of nobility be produced in order to become an officer. In practice, in the Germanies and in Sweden only nobles became officers. The organization of French military education was even copied in the United States, where the military academy of West Point, founded in 1802, was inspired by the School of Military Engineering of Metz. After 1815 numerous French officers emigrated to the United States, where they introduced certain French institutions to the American army.

The secularization of the Church and its subordination to the state, applied in France from 1792, was adopted only in countries divided between different religions. This was attenuated by the concordats concluded with the Pope. The French Concordat of 1801 served as a model for similar agreements signed after 1815, in Italy by Sardinia, the Two Sicilies, Lombardy-Venezia, Lucca, Tuscany, Modena and Parma; in the Germanies by Bavaria, the smaller Catholic states, Prussia, Hanover, Württemberg, Baden, the two Hesses, Saxony, and the free cities of Frankfurt, Bremen, and Lübeck. The Helvetic Confederation also concluded a concordat as did the tsar for the Kingdom of Poland. Only Austria and Spain among the Catholic states refused to sign treaties of this kind.

The concordats specified the rights of Catholics and often recognized Catholicism as the state religion. Civil registration of births and deaths and civil marriage were maintained in France and in the Netherlands. Except in France, the Netherlands, Switzerland, and the United States, Jews lost their civil and political rights. Regarded as allies of the Revolution, they were often subjected to humiliating, discriminatory measures.

Before the Revolution, in Catholic countries social welfare and education were in the hands of the Church. The Revolution made these services public, in France and in almost all of the countries of the *Grand Empire.* Despite the concordats, they often remained so. In the Netherlands, the welfare offices, organized under the French regime, were preserved. Welfare remained in great part a charge of the state in Sardinia, the Two Sicilies, Tuscany, and even the Papal States. In Rhineland Prussia the hospitals retained their French-style organization. In Poland welfare councils similar to the French offices were created in 1817. On the other hand, in Switzerland and in Spain there remained nothing of the welfare organizations created under the influence of France.

As for education, its secularization was often expanded in those countries whose peoples professed several religions. The French-style universities created by Napoleon in 1808 did not succeed in eclipsing the older German or Italian universities, but the example of a secular university was followed in the United States, where Jefferson created the University of Virginia in 1820. Under the Empire, a University of Warsaw was organized in Poland and one at Brussels in Belgium, to which were added universities at Ghent, Liège, and Louvain. The secular French *lycées* were effective producers of bureaucrats and army officers, and hence were preserved in the Netherlands and the Rhineland.

Thus, in the domain of institutions, even political, the Revolution had been relative, and more of the changes survived by example or by adoption during the period than the rulers after 1815 were aware.

THE SOCIAL BALANCE SHEET

Social and economic landmarks in the sweep of history have not always corresponded with political developments. Although social conditions have been profoundly influenced by political events and changes, social modifications have often been extended over longer periods and without the sharp crises of the political and international scene. Since the French Revolution and the Napoleonic period covered a long period of war in Europe, the first question to be asked of the social balance sheet is the effect on population. In the period 1789 to 1815, did the riots, the civil rebellions, and the foreign wars depopulate Europe? What happened to the class structure that prevailed during the *ancien régime* in Europe?

POPULATION[1]   Wars of the twentieth century, the shrinking of the potential of future agricultural production, and the cry of many people for a higher standard of living, have led to a new, or rather renewed, interest in population statistics. It was in 1798 that Malthus published his pessimistic essay, based upon population growth of the eighteenth century, and there is a neo-Malthusianism in many quarters today. Governments have always been interested in the numbers of subjects, and then of citizens, in connection with taxation, and once conscription is introduced, in the numbers of men for the army, the navy, and recently, the air force. Historians today are dissatisfied with older appraisals of population and are asking more questions about population growth. Marcel Reinhard, Ernest

---

[1] On demography, see *Rapports, XIIe Congrès international des sciences historiques*, vol. I, pp. 450–573 (Vienna, 1965) and *Rapports conjoints* (Paris, 1966), 50 pp; G. S. Graham, "European Balance of Power at the End of the Napoleonic Wars"; Lewis Hertzman, "Change and Continuity in Western European Society. . . . , 1815–1848"; A. Z. Manfred, "Idées sociales et politiques en 1815"; A. L. Narochnitzki, on the Continental Blockade, with special reference to Russian participation. See also J. Godechot and S. Moncassin, *Démographie et subsistances en Languedoc du XVIIIe au début du XIXe siècle*, (Paris, 1965). A. Meynier, *Une Erreur historique. Les morts de la Grande Armée et des armées ennemies* (Paris, 1934); J. Bourgeois-Pichot, "L'évolution générale de la population francaise depuis le XVIIIe siècle," *Population*, October–December, 1951, pp. 635–662.

Labrousse, Albert Soboul, Jacques Godechot, and others have been engaged with their students in much new research for the period 1770 to 1815, and as this text goes to press, an issue of the *Annales historiques de la Révolution française,* January–March, 1970, contains three articles on demography for the period, pointing up some reasons for unreliability of statistics hitherto utilized, pointing new ways of using them and of filling gaps, but J. Dupâquier, J. N. Biraben and J. Houdaille, do not contradict the general increase in population.[2]

The latest research indicates that the European population continued to grow between 1770 and 1815, but the growth varied according to the country. It should be remembered that war and revolution did not take place continuously over the entire period in any one country. European population increased from 160 million around 1770 to about 210 millions in 1815. Certain states already possessed a well-organized statistical service to record population data, while others did not.

France was, without dispute, the nation most affected by the Revolution and Napoleonic Wars, yet its population had not ceased to grow, rising from 24 million in 1770 to 30 million in 1815. In this period, however, although the rate of marriages increased, the birth rate decreased. If, therefore, the population increased, it was due to the lowering of the mortality rate at the same time that the birth rate tended to be stabilized. Movement of the French population is well known for the revolutionary era because of the periodic censuses, at first sporadic but regular during the Napoleonic

---

[2] See papers given by these Frenchmen and papers by Graham, Hertzman, Manfred, and Narochnitski on the *Bilan du monde en 1815, XIIe. Congrès international des sciences historiques,* (Vienna, 1965); *Rapports,* vol. I, pp. 450–573, (Vienna, 1965); *Rapports conjoints,* (Vienna, 1966). See also, Marcel Reinhard and André Armengaud, *Histoire générale de la population mondiale* (Paris, 1961); and Marcel Reinhard in *French Society and Culture since the Old Regime,* edited by Evelyn M. Acomb and Marvin L. Brown, Jr., (New York: Holt, Rinehart and Winston, 1966). The Commission d'histoire économique et social de la Révolution Française has been publishing yearly brochures containing monographic material on population as well as other social and economic problems. *Annales historiques de la Révolution francaise,* January–March 1970: J. Dupâquier, "Problèmes démographiques de la France napoléonienne," pp. 8–29; J. B. Biraben, "La statistique de population sous le Consulat et l'Empire," pp. 30–45; J. Houdaille, "Le Problème des pertes de guerre," pp. 46–62. Dupaquier emphasized the importance of conscription and war losses. He then pointed out shortcomings of existing statistics. Biraben, while praising the work of Reinhard, also points up shortcomings of imperial statistics. Houdaille, by a sample for which good records exist, and a check by statistical methods, arrived at a figure of losses between Meynier and Taine. In pointing out the gaps and limitations of the statistics of the Consulate and Imperial periods, these three indicate further research to be done on the ratio of men versus women, age level, immigration and emigration, dead versus wounded.

era. The substitution of civil registration in 1792 for former parish records and the preservation of these *états civils* enables the historian to trace fairly accurately the movement of population. The records indicate the rise in the marriage rate, stimulated by laws that exempted married men from military service. The greatest number of marriages coincided with the heaviest conscription: 1794, 1795, 1809, 1813.

The absolute number of births grew, but the fertility rate diminished. The mean number of births per one hundred marriages was 476 about 1780, whereas it was only 318 about 1810. An increase in the number of marriages corresponded with a decrease in births, which, without doubt, was voluntary. The rate of reproduction in 1815 would not have been higher than 107.5, or just enough to assure a slight increase of population. This figure was maintained until the end of the nineteenth century, and gave the movement of French population its individual characteristic. If there was an increase, it was due to the decrease in the mortality rate. It should be remembered that little of the fighting, except the Vendéen War was on French soil until 1814-1815. Only about 40,000 persons were victims of the Terror, and to man his armies, Napoleon relied on an increasing number of soldiers from other countries, especially from 1812 on. If there had been a large emigration during the Revolutionary decade, many had returned after the Napoleonic amnesty; the total number of *émigrés* has been estimated to be from 129,000 to 150,000.[3] Their exodus would affect Revolutionary population figures, and increase that of France in the Napoleonic period, but the increase from 1780 to 1815 still stands.

Figures of war losses, according to Meynier, give an overall number of 1,300,000 deaths between 1792 and 1815, an average of 70,000 per year. Houdaille, in the most recent study, revised this figure downward to 916,000, tentatively, by allowance for returned prisoners but without counting naval losses.[4] One suspects that the figures varied within the period, and were higher for 1806 to 1807, when the bloody battles of Eylau and

[3] For statistics on the Terror, see Donald Greer, *The Incidence of the Terror during the French Revolution* (Harvard University Press, Cambridge, 1935). Despite criticisms of his statistical method by Richard Louie in the *French Historical Studies,* Spring, 1964, pp. 381–387, Greer's main conclusions stand, have been accepted by French historians of the field, and no contradictory evidence has yet been provided. Donald Greer used a similar method for his *The Incidence of the Emigration during the French Revolution* (Harvard University Press, 1951).

[4] A. Meynier, *op. cit.,* who estimated losses for the period 1800–1815 as 1 million. Houdaille by his sampling, made allowances for the return of soldiers and especially prisoners of war, but emphasized the heavy loss of young men born between 1793 and 1795. A note written by M. Reinhard, p. 62, relative to a statement purported to have been made by Napoleon while viewing the dead on the field of Eylau (a very bloody battle) that "one night in Paris would repair all these losses" raises the question of authenticity of the statement, and indicates that the Parisian birthrate would not have justified this statement.

Friedland occurred, and for 1812–1813, when both the retreat from Moscow and the Iberian campaign took heavy toll, than for other years. Despite these heavier losses, there still appeared to be an increase of population by 1815. Therefore, one can only conclude that the increase in the over-all population statistics would have been far greater without war.

Few other countries of Europe have provided the caliber of population studies that the French historians have for France. Some of the European countries, particularly England, and parts of Germany also underwent in this twenty-five year period large population movements as a result of the Industrial Revolution and attendant urbanization, with masses of inhabitants moving to manufacturing towns around factories. The population of England was scarcely 7 million in 1770. By 1815, it surpassed 11 million. This increase was essentially due to an increase in the birth rate, but it was also affected by a decline of the death rate. The large amount of manpower needed for Napoleonic armies and the prosecution of the continental wars was not required for England's naval defense. It was only in the last few years before 1815 that a sizeable British army was employed in the Peninsular War and the final defeat of Napoleon. That England needed sailors was evidenced by the use of impressment, which led to the embroilment with the United States, but had England adopted a form of conscription, the situation might have been different. In any case, since England had established her primacy on the sea by 1805, the mortality rate in the navy was relatively low. The increase of the British population, manifested earlier in the eighteenth century and continued through 1815, seems to have been brought about by increasing urbanization, the lowering of the marriage age, the diffusion of smallpox vaccination, and the improvement of social assistance. The upheavals of the Revolutionary and Imperial epoch had, in accelerating the Industrial Revolution, a favorable effect on the demographic evolution. The Continental Blockade, with attendant food shortages, especially in 1795, 1805 (before the real blockade) and 1812, seem not to have affected the growth. According to Marcel Reinhard,[5] English demography, in its long run development was no longer dominated by the food supply at the time that Malthus was proclaiming its role. After 1815, emigration caused a slackening in the growth.

Belgium, Holland, Bohemia, and Hungary, whose boundaries remained stable within the twenty-five year period, and for which reliable studies are available, all showed a growth in population of approximately 1 million — an increase of one eighth for Hungary, one third for Belgium and Bohemia, and double for Holland.[6]

---

[5] Marcel Reinhard, *Rapports,* vol. I, Vienna, 1965. Cited on p. 230, fn. 1.

[6] Belgian population increased from 2,900,000 in 1784 to 3,500,000 in 1815; that of Holland from 985,000 to 2,000,000 in the same period; that of Bohemia from 2,300,000 in 1772 to 3,200,000 in 1812; for Hungary, from 7 millions in 1787 to 8,260,000 in 1815.

Norway (Danish territory until 1815) and Sweden showed a relatively stable population rate (794,000 inhabitants in 1789 and 907,000 in 1815). There was a fall in the birth rate and a slight increase in mortality rates, despite neutrality in the Napoleonic Wars.[7] Both Italy and Spain, theaters of warfare, also showed a stagnation of population growth; in both cases a higher birthrate was offset by an increased death rate.[8] Statistics for the Iberian Peninsula are less satisfactory than for the other countries cited.

Lack of adequate studies of population sources for the remainder to Europe permits only tentative conclusions. The large number of states in Germany before 1789, the changes in boundaries during the Napoleonic period, and the partitions of Poland must be taken into account when discussing their populations. For Germany, studies have been made for Bremen, Cologne, and Nuremberg. Despite a high mortality rate, an increase in population was indicated in those cities,[9] but no precise figures can be given.

Although it is known that the population of Russia more than doubled in the period under consideration,[10] despite 700,000 dead from the wars, registration records of births, marriages and deaths are lacking. It is not possible to assess the extent that the acquisition of large parts of Poland, Finland in 1815, and Bessarabia may have played in Russian population statistics.

The evolution of the Finnish population resembled that of Scandinavia. On Poland, a good documentation exists, parish records and census figures, but it is difficult because of the variations in the frontiers of Poland as a result of partitions and Napoleonic changes, to compare the figures. It would appear that there was a considerable increase, and even the economic crisis of 1812, when the mortality rate increased, does not seem to have changed the general evolution.[11]

Present studies of population show that nearly half a century of internal troubles and foreign wars scarcely modified the demographic evolution of the Western world. If wars, riots, and economic crises increased the death rate, these were compensated for by an augmentation of the population due

---

[7] Norway's population rose from 794,000 in 1789 to 907,000 in 1815, — the birth rate fell from 328 in 1790 to 271 in 1814, but the mortality rate increased from 223 to 249 between the two dates. Sweden showed a similar development.

[8] Population in the Italian peninsula, whose statistics are not entirely dependable, increased from about 16 millions in 1770 to 18.5 millions in 1815. There was a great increase in mortality rates in 1801 and 1804 (a rate of about 300).

[9] High mortality rates were recorded for Bremen and Nuremberg in 1795, 1800–1803 for Cologne, 1806 for Bremen, 1812–1814 for Cologne.

[10] From 20 millions in 1770, Russian population increased to 50 millions in 1815.

[11] From 7 millions in 1787, the increase in Poland was to 8,260,000 in 1815, explained by a high birth rate despite a high mortality.

to the Industrial Revolution, which tended to decrease mortality and to increase births, except in France. The new demographic pattern—a low birth rate and death rate caused by a better standard of living, improvement in nutrition, and the progress of medicine—would prevail in nineteenth century France. This pattern developed in much of Europe in the twentieth century. It must be remembered that war in the late eighteenth and early nineteenth century did not involve the large percentage of manpower available for fighting that the twentieth-century world wars have required. Only where conscription was adopted was the ratio of fighting men to the entire number of males increased with a probably perceptible effect on male mortalities.

To what extent was the growth of population the consequence in western and central Europe of urbanization (that is of migrations) and to better records in the cities than in the rural areas? Why had the population of Russia appeared to increase so markedly on its immense plains? Did this have a relationship to the persistence of serfdom in that country? To answer these pertinent questions, historians must uncover more salient facts. Nevertheless, there appears to be one well-established conclusion that can be made for Europe and America: the period from 1789 to 1815 had not been a demographic catastrophe, on the contrary, it was a period of population expansion.

SOCIAL CLASSES[12]   The same era produced a profound transformation of society. In the countries where feudalism had been declining in the two or three centuries prior to 1789, new social structures had developed slowly. When the French Revolution began, the society of all coun-

---

[12] On social conditions, see in particular Arthur Goodwin, *The European Nobility in the Eighteenth Century* (London, 1953). See also Umberto Marcelli, "La crisa economica e sociale di Bologna nel 1796: Le prime vendite dei beni ecclesiastici (1797–1800)" *Atti e Memorie della Deputazione di storia patria per le provincie di Romagna,* vols. III and IV, 1953–1954, and *La vendita dei beni ecclesiastici a Bologna e nelle Romagne, 1797–1815* (Bologna, 1961); Renato Zangheri, *Prime ricerche nulla distribuzione della proprieta fondiaria nella pianura bolognese, 1789–1835* (Bologna, 1957) and *La proprieta terriera e le origini del Risorgimento nel Bolognese,* vol. I, *1789–1804* (Bologna, 1961); I. Delatte, "La vente des biens nationaux en Belgique," *Revue d'histoire moderne,* 1940, pp. 44–51; R. Devleeshouwer, *L'arrondissement du Brabant sous l'occupation française, 1794–1795* (Brussels, 1964); R. de Felice, *La vendita dei beni nazionali nella Repubblica romana del 1798–1799* (Rome, 1960); J. Cl. Wiedman, *Le déclin et l'abolition du régime féodal dans le royaume de Naples* (Toulouse, 1958); P. Villani, *La vendita dei beni dello stato nel regno di Napoli, 1806–1815* (Milan, 1964) and "Giuseppe Zurlo e la crisi dell'Antico Regime nel regno di Napoli" in *Il mezzogiorno tra reforme e revoluzione* (Bari, Italy, 1962); Adeline Daumard, *La Bourgeoisie parisienne de 1815 à 1848* (Paris, 1963) and E. P. Thompson, *The Making of the English Working Class* (London, 1964).

tries of Europe could be divided into roughly three classes and in most there was a declining mobility upward. The three groups were the clergy, the nobility, and the third estate or common people. The third estate was in turn, divided into an urban upper and lower class (artisans) and a rural lower class, with various gradations of peasants, free and unfree. The volume, *The European Nobility in the Eighteenth Century*, edited by Arthur Goodwin, indicated variations in the social composition by country, but in all countries a clerical and legal aristocracy with privileges existed. The aristocracy was based on land holding and hereditary privileges associated with long tenure.

The Revolution took steps to destroy privileges associated with the feudal regime; wherever French armies were victorious, social reform was undertaken. The destruction of so-called feudal society had been more or less complete, according to the country, by the time Napoleon fell. In its place appeared a "capitalist" society more or less marked. The stage of development of the capitalist society depended primarily on the degree of economic evolution of the particular state. The social transformations brought about by the Revolution and the Imperial regime throughout Europe were so profound that it appeared impossible to the governments taking over in 1815 to restore the old social order.

In the social transformations, one must distinguish a double current. On the one hand, there is the abolition of the so-called "feudal regime," which had divided society into privileged and unprivileged orders and on the other, the substitution for the old orders, of classes organized according to socio-economic criteria, founded on a new regime of property and of business.

THE DESTRUCTION OF THE FEUDAL REGIME[13]   The feudal regime, as we have seen in Chapter 9, was a complex social system. Here, we are first concerned with the effect of its suppression or transformation on social

---

[13] The author, Jacques Godechot, here uses the term "feudal regime" in an inclusive sense of the Old Regime social and economic institutions, including privileged classes, the Catholic Church with its properties and its tithes, the seignorial regime with its serfdom, peasant services and payments. This system was based upon land holding and hence wealth measured in revenues from land, whereas the institutions that were emerging from the Revolution and Napoleonic era would be classes, some wealth inherited from the earlier system, but now more than ever based on revenues from industry, commerce, as well as agriculture and extractive industries (lumber, mines). The new wealthy became capitalists in the modern sense when they derived their chief revenues from investments rather than a mutual labor system of the seignory. Of interest also is the entire issue of *Annales historiques Révolution française,* April–June, 1969, on the abolition of feudal regime in Europe. See introductory note in the *Annales* by Jacques Godechot. The articles on the various parts of Europe confirm Godechot's text.

classes. Serfdom was abolished in France in 1789, in Belgium by Joseph II and during the French occupation and in Holland in 1795. In 1798, serfdom was abolished in the Rhineland, and in 1808 in Westphalia, Berg, Frankfurt and Bavaria. It had been abolished under enlightened despotism before 1789 in Baden, but in the remaining areas of the former Holy Roman Empire, serfdom continued to operate, to some degree. It was during the reform period in Prussia, before the war ending in the Peace of Tilsit that serfdom was abolished, but indemnification of the landlord was made difficult. Attempts of Joseph in Austria failed, and his laws in Bohemia in 1781 and Hungary in 1785 ended serfdom but judicial power and administration of the landlord over the peasant remained. Feudal institutions did not disappear completely in the Austrian Empire until after 1848.

Serfdom disappeared in North Italy, but in central and southern Italy (Naples), high rates of indemnification of landlords (1809) and their hostility to change led to reinstitution of their power after 1815. Although Spanish serfdom was abolished in 1811, it reappeared after 1815 and only disappeared after 1837.

In the Duchy of Warsaw some reforms were instituted by the Napoleonic regime in 1809, but after the renewed partition of Poland in 1815, peasants in the Austrian section were liberated at the same time as Austria, but not until 1861 in Russian Poland. Serfdom declined in Prussian Polish provinces, gradually, as in Prussia proper.

Whereas serfdom disappeared in the greater part of Europe as a result of the French Revolution and Napoleonic periods, seignorial dues and jurisdiction were in some areas abolished without indemnity, and in others were redeemable by the peasantry. By 1815, personal privileges had disappeared in France, Belgium, Holland, North Italy, Berg, Frankfurt, the Hanseatic principalities, Lucca, Massa, Carrare and Tuscany, and to a large extent in Switzerland, but in all other areas they were made redeemable. Redemption was made very difficult in Bavaria, and restored in 1815 to the Papal States. Seignorial privileges were maintained in Württemberg, Baden and Poland, and in any areas where serfdom survived. Tithes were abolished in France and areas annexed to France, in north Italy, only small tithes in Switzerland, and they were made redeemable in Frankfurt. Tithes prevailed after 1815 in the Papal States.

The generalization is valid that in Western Europe serfdom disappeared or was considerably attenuated in the Revolutionary and Napoleonic period, and surviving seignorial dues made redeemable. In areas where Napoleon introduced the Codes, feudalism tended to disappear. However, as one proceeds eastward, serfdom survived in some cases until 1848, and indemnities sometimes even longer.

The countries that were able to maintain their independence during the revolutionary epoch underwent, nevertheless several social upheavals.

In England, the seventeenth century revolution had already abolished feudal tenures. There remained, at the end of the eighteenth century, only a few vestiges of the feudal regime, and their suppression after 1815 was accelerated by the French example. In Prussia, serfdom had been abolished as we have seen in 1807, and the peasants were permitted to own land. The lord, however, preserved intact his jurisdiction over the peasants and dues and forced labor were maintained. Prussia was one of the least socially developed states in central Europe. Austria, too, lagged in social development.

PROPERTY OWNERSHIP   It is incontestable that in all of western Europe, and in the greater part of central Europe, laws transformed the feudal societies into modern ones. Modernized social conditions after 1815 permitted access of the peasant and the worker to property ownership. Did economic reality correspond with the liberalized legislation? Was the division of landed property transformed during the Revolutionary epoch to the profit of the most disadvantaged of social groups?

To give a categorical and precise answer to such a question is difficult because of the lack of sufficient studies for most countries. Only a few regional monographs are available, and it would be impossible to generalize from these. Nevertheless, they do permit some understanding of the probable nature of the shift in property ownership.

In France, for the department of the Nord, Georges Lefebvre established[14] that the clergy who owned about 20 percent of the total land in 1789 owned virtually none by 1799. The property of the nobility fell from 22 percent of the total to 12 percent in the same period, that of the bourgeoisie increased from 16 to 28 percent, and peasant property rose from 30 to 42 percent. What was the evolution of ownership from 1800 to 1815? We do not know, but a study of 5 or 6 thousand communes for the Napoleonic cadastre might throw light on the problem. Nevertheless, the fragmentation of landed property seems to have continued and the peasants profited from it. It is also certain that in the imperial era, the Church began to reconstitute landed property, and that the nobility also attempted to regain possession. Not all *émigré* lands were sold. In the department of the Nord, of the 30,000 hectares of noble lands that had been sold, 7,000 had been re-

---

[14] The original edition of Georges Lefebvre's *Les Paysans du Nord pendant la Révolution francaise* (Paris, 1924) contained extensive footnotes and supporting material, but this volume has long been out-of-print. The Bari, Italy, edition of 1959 omitted the footnotes. Lefebvre's volume was a definitive study of the peasantry in one region and has served as a model of research for all studies made since then. Only two other works of comparable stature have appeared since Lefebvre, Paul Bois, *Les paysans de l'Ouest,* a study chiefly of the Sarthe, and P. de Saint-Jacob, (Paris, 1961), on the peasants of northern Burgundy.

purchased by their former owners by 1815. The great majority of peasant proprietors, even with acquisitions, did not have large enough holdings from which to make a living. To maintain themselves and their families, they had to rent or sharecrop additional farms, acquire small farms *(Métairies)*, augment their incomes by employment in small scale industry in their homes.[15]

As in France, the lands of the Catholic Church were confiscated and sold as national property in Belgium, the Rhineland, Piedmont, and the Cisalpine Republic. Such sales began in 1796 according to terms that were advantageous for purchase by the bourgeoisie, particularly in Belgium and in the Rhineland.

In the plains of the Po, north central Italy and central Italy, sales of land benefitted chiefly the bourgeoisie, holdings of clergy and noblemen declined, but the great majority of peasants remained sharecroppers. They had merely changed masters. In the Po River plains, trusts and lands held in *mainmorte* hindered rapid changes of ownership and division. In the Bologna area, bourgeois property doubled between 1789 and 1804, and increased further by 1835, while aristocratic property decreased in the same period. In the Papal States, the *latifundia* (large estates) prevailed, and the clergy owned three-fifths of the lands as of 1796. Sales made in 1798 and 1799 were annuled in 1800. A study of the sales shows that if the sales had been maintained, they would have profited primarily the bourgeoisie.[16] Clergy and Nobles also retained a hold on two-thirds of the land in the Kingdom of Naples.[17] Although peasants redeemed slowly payments against seignorial fees, they were unable to buy land, but there was no distribution of public lands and communal lands to aid them. Where State lands were sold, the sales profited the nobility and the bourgeoisie; in the province of Salerno, the bourgeoisie bought 61 percent of the alienated lands and the peasants only .021 percent (three purchasers out of 292). The social structure of the Kingdom of Naples did not modify. The great landed estate continued to dominate in north and central Italy; its proportion remained at 72 percent

---

[15] This phrase implies the domestic system of putting out in the countryside spinning, weaving, etc., thereby providing more of the article, but without the requirement of the guilds being met. Studies comparable to that of Georges Lefebvre are needed for many other areas of France, before the picture of France as a whole will be clear.

[16] R. de Felice, *La vendita dei beni nazionali nelle Repubblica romana del 1798–1799,* Rome, 1960.

[17] J. Cl. Wiedman, *Le declin et l'abolition du régime féodale dans le royaume de Naples,* D.E.S., Toulouse, 1958; P. Villani, *La vendita dei beni dello Stato nel Regno di Napoli,* 1806–1815 *(Studi e ricerche de storia economica italiana nell eta del Risorgimento,* Milan, 1964); Id., "Guiseppe Zurlo e la crisi dell 'Antico Regime nel regno di Napoli," in *Il Mezzogiorno tra reforme e revoluzione* (Bari, 1962).

during the entire period. The bourgeoisie were more dynamic in the administration of their properties than the nobility. It was the bourgeoisie who developed the cultivation of rice.

The domination of the large estate was true in central and eastern Europe, to the east of the Rhine, and even more so to the east of the Elbe. Great landed aristocratic estates were preponderant before 1805 and they continued to dominate in 1815. Bourgeois property was negligible there, especially in Prussia and Poland.

The abolition of serfdom resulted in the creation of a landless peasant proletariat. A class of peasant proprietors appeared only in certain regions, such as Saxony, Silesia, and Pomerania. The abolition of the judicial framework of the "feudal" regime led to a modification of the division of landed property, and hence, of the social structures only in parts of western and central Europe.

THE TRANSFORMATION OF SOCIAL STRUCTURES   Under the Old Regime in Europe, there had been a social structure of "orders" and decreasing mobility, but the Revolutionary and Napoleonic period profoundly influenced this social organization. The Emperor himself preferred intermediary corps, councils, groups such as Montesquieu had defended. While the new classes based upon a capitalistic society emerged, it was the introduction of the Civil Code that gave scope to classes. The more or less profound modifications introduced in the codes of the different countries are an index of a slight development of the new classes and above all, of the bourgeoisie which was to be the principal beneficiary of the Civil Code.

The Bourgeoisie   In France before the Revolution, the French bourgeoisie included a relatively small percentage of the population and was composed predominantly of government officials below the top ranks, wholesale and retail merchants, as well as the professions, lawyers, doctors and an aristocracy of a few crafts. During the period from 1789 to 1815, not only did the ranks of the bourgeoisie increase, but also its composition changed. Businessmen and industrial leaders now were predominant, followed by government officials and members of the liberal professions. Only for Paris are figures available that permit a statistical breakdown of the categories of this upper middle class in 1815 and after. Industrialists formed 54 percent, functionaries and members of the liberal professions 24 percent; rentiers (those living from property or other investments) and absentee owners, 22 percent.[18]

---

[18] Adeline Daumard, *La bourgeoisie parisienne de 1815 a 1848* (Paris, S.E.V.P.E.N., 1963). See also *Annales historiques de la Révolution française,* January–March 1790.

Jean Tulard, in an article "Problèmes sociaux de la France napolé-onienne," in the *Annales historiques de la Révolution française* of January–March 1790 (pp. 135–160) asserts that the important capitalists were merchants rather than industrialists and that the Continental Blockade in 1810 had stimulated speculation among bourgeoisie that had already been important during the Old Regime, such as the Périers. In an age of inflation and risks at sea, they had found purchases of nationalized lands a sure investment, as well as a means to rise in the social scale. Napoleon drew his functionaries from proprietors, *rentiers,* wholesale merchants, and the law professions including notaries. Although they could hope for promotions, and some few for ennoblement, Napoleon preferred to win the old nobility to loyalty to the Empire by promoting them in his service. One may note, however, the development of a caste of functionaries. If ennobled, there was a lag in the nineteenth century in being fused with the old nobility after 1815. Napoleon did award the Legion of Honor to some of the functionaries drawn from the bourgeoisie.

Outside of France there is no exact information. It is certain that the numerical importance of the bourgeoisie diminished progressively as one crossed Europe from west to east. In England, on the other hand, the bourgeoisie was very powerful, thanks to the development of commerce and industry. The English bourgeoisie was separated from the aristocracy only by weak barriers, which were frequently opened. As a matter of fact, the members of the upper bourgeoisie had access frequently to the peerage. The social classification, in spite of the theoretical maintenance of the old hierarchies, was in reality founded on wealth, and not on birth. A study of the Grand Duchy of Warsaw shows that the bourgeoisie in 1810 occupied only a minimal place.[19]

The Landed Aristocracy The power of the landed aristocracy was almost the inverse of the bourgeoisie. In France and in Belgium, it lost all its former privileges. Even in 1815, neither the returned *émigrés* nor the new Imperial nobility had special privileges. In addition, the nobles who emigrated lost a part of their landed fortune, which passed to the bourgeoisie and to the peasants. In 1815, the noble who still enjoyed the prestige of his title and of the influence due to the lands that he still held, found himself more and more in conflict with the bourgeoisie. In England, the nobility retained the honorific privileges of their class, but here, too, the noble often found his position challenged by the bourgeoisie who now

---

[19] According to statistics given by Godechot without identifying the book or article from which they were derived were: in 1810, the Duchy counted 200 financiers, 4000 manufacturers, and about 5000 merchants. The exporters of grain and cloth dominated the manufacturers, whose business was on a small scale.

rivaled him as a landlord. However, the great prestige of the English nobility continued and its voice in the House of Lords dominated Parliament.

In Germany, the gradations of the landed aristocracy are numerous between the left bank of the Rhine, where the situation was the same as in France, and Prussia where the Junker preserved almost intact all his rights and privileges. In the Grand Duchy of Berg and the Kingdom of Westphalia, privileges were abolished in 1809, and marriages were authorized between nobles and commoners. Nevertheless, the aristocracy retained its predominance unimpaired. In Bavaria the constitution had proclaimed the abolition of the *stände* (orders), and civil equality, but in fact, only fiscal privileges disappeared. A *matricule* or register of the nobility was established, and its prestige was consolidated by certain obligations, which, if ignored, would result in being stricken from the rolls of the nobility. Here seignorial justice was regularized, but maintained. In Württemberg and in Baden, the nobility lost its monopoly of landed property, but in Baden it preserved its inherited (entail) estates and those held in trust. In Saxony the nobility continued to be exempted from taxes.

The Polish nobility were a special case. Its ranks were very numerous, more than 300,000 persons, 7 percent of the population of the Grand Duchy of Warsaw. It was divided into a poor nobility, which formed the great majority and from which were recruited the functionaries and the intelligentsia, and a landed aristocracy of magnates, who were very rich but few in number. These magnates kept their properties, public charges, and their influence. Moreover, the Constitution of 1807 granted the Polish nobility a special legal status. It elected sixty of the one hundred members of the Chamber of Nuncios (the deputies); the forty others representing the communes could be chosen among the bourgeoisie, but they were, in fact, often nobles. In 1811 only 17 percent of the deputies were commoners. However, because of the peculiar structure of the Polish aristocracy, the nobles of the middle rank gradually made common cause with the magnates, while the lesser nobility, more and more pauperized, furnished most of the leaders for the national and revolutionary movements.

In the countries not touched directly by the revolutionary expansion, the landed aristocracy maintained its privileges and its preponderance and showed itself to be fiercely hostile to the Revolution, even when it was personified by Napoleon. Austria and Russia strongly resisted French influences. The impact of French rule in Spain was only temporary. Spanish nobles retained their privileges and estates after 1815.

Opposed to the dominant classes, the rural and urban masses, except for several brief periods, remained submissive. They profited from the new influences in varying degrees according to the regions of revolutionary uprisings.

The Peasants   In France the peasants rose in mass in 1789 to obtain the abolition of the feudal regime. They sought the suppression of seignorial rights and tithes as well as fiscal equality. By July 1793 their demands had been met. Henceforth, their energies were directed at preserving the results rather than advancing further changes. This is why they rallied *en masse* to Bonaparte in 1800, and they became firm supporters of order. During the Empire period, on the other hand, a breach developed in their ranks and gradually widened. On the one side were peasant proprietors who owned enough land to support themselves and their families. On the other side were the peasants who, possessing only small parcels, had to rent additional land or hire themselves out as part-time agricultural laborers in order to make a living. Since their employment was seasonal and uncertain, their lot was improved very little by such labor. The increase of the rural population, important in France under the Empire, and the subdividing of inheritance facilitated by the Civil Code, further increased the mass of poor peasants. However, the continued increase of grain prices and the relative scarcity of labor due to conscription, produced by 1815 an amelioration of the standard of living of the peasants. After 1817, the trend was reversed: the decrease in the price of cereals at that date and the presence of a surplus labor force aggravated the lot of the poor peasants, many of whom migrated to the cities and the developing industrial centers.

In Great Britain, the rise of heavy industry drained the countryside. There was a movement to the cities also in Belgium and the Rhineland. On the right bank of the Rhine few changes affected the status of the peasantry. In the Kingdom of Westphalia, the prefects promoted the division of communal lands and the abolition of the right of common pasturage in order to hasten the disappearance of forced labor (*contraint par sole*), theoretically abolished by law. In Bavaria this was also abolished and the division of family tenure made possible. These measures had had, by 1815, only feeble results. On the right bank of the Elbe, the peasants, freed from serfdom but deprived of their land, formed an immense agrarian proletariat who did not abandon the soil until much later.

The Urban Workers   There is less information about the urban working class than any other social class of the period. We begin to know only for France, England, Belgium, the Rhineland and the Sarre. In France, there were journeymen, apprentices, and day wage earners employed in French towns in 1789, but after the disappearance of the guilds, the Loi Le Chapelier prevented them from organizing for mutual benefit. The sans-culottes were drawn from this group, augmented by small scale shopkeepers, but at the same time, the artisans were the dominant group. The urban worker, as a sans-culotte, played an important role politically for a time in the sectional governments during the Terror and also in the Jacobin Club, if he could afford the club membership fee.[20] They held lower civilian office, and by universal suffrage could be elected to the National Convention and to town government. They were also a prominent element in Revolutionary armies and in civilian industry.[21] Much less is known about this segment of the population during the Napoleonic period. Workers undoubtedly continued to serve in the army, and to be employed in urban industry, but they had lost their independent political role completely. By 1815 their economic status had changed little from that of the sans-culottes of 1793. The working class was still a mixture of wage-earning workers, of former master craftsmen, and of more or less independent shopkeepers. On the average, the number of employees per enterprise in 1807 would not have exceeded three. The number of salaried Parisian wage earners in the same year reached 130,000; with their families they constituted 300,000 to 400,000 persons, more than half the population of the capital.[22]

Edward P. Thompson[23] has provided information about the formation of the British urban working class. It was concentrated in the textile region and in the "black country" of the north and northwest. The industrial Revolution, accelerated by the Napoleonic Wars and the Continental Blockade, attracted workers to textile towns by the relatively higher wages and the regularity of employment. Parliamentary investigations prior to factory legislation in the 1830s, revealed that working conditions were bad, hours long, security safeguards lacking and that the overcrowding in cities led to slum living conditions, already existent but aggravated after 1815. In Europe the core of proletarian workers formed in the regions of industrialization around Ghent, Antwerp, Cologne, Aix-la-Chapelle and Saabrücken.

The working class was as diverse within its ranks as the peasantry. Neither formed a self-conscious class, in 1789, nor in 1815. Each might be concerned with the struggle for existence, but each was busy with his own affairs and knew little or nothing about the other group. Military service

[20] Crane Brinton, in his *The Jacobins* (New York, 1930), made a study of the membership of the Jacobin Clubs throughout France, and showed that they must have had some property to be able to pay the membership fees. In other words, the Jacobins were not the scum, vagabonds, thieves that Taine and other historians had made them out to be.

[21] Richard Cobb, *Les armées révolutionnaires* (The Hague, 1961, 2 vols.); Albert Soboul, *The Parisian Sans-Culottes and the French Revolution 1793–1794* (Oxford University Press, 1964). This is a short translation of his thesis, *Les Sans-Culottes parisiens en l'an II.*

[22] Adamard, *op. cit.;* Marcel Reinhard, "La population des villes: sa mesure sous la Révolution et l'Empire," in *Population,* 1954, pp. 279–288; Soboul, *op. cit.*

[23] E. P. Thompson, *The Making of the English Working Class,* (London, Z. V. Gollancz 1964).

may have brought urban and rural workers together during the Revolutionary and Napoleonic Wars, but there is no evidence that this developed class consciousness.

THE ECONOMIC BALANCE SHEET

If the period of revolutions and wars from 1770 to 1815 had not notably affected the demographic rise of Europe and America, had it not at least slowed their economic growth? While the statistics known are difficult to compare and too often few in number and imprecise, nonetheless, they do permit us to draw up an economic balance sheet in 1815.[24]

AGRICULTURE   Agriculture still dominated the European economy, even in the most industrialized country, England. The price curves that can be drawn for each of the countries of Europe demonstrate the consistency of agricultural prices, even in times of crisis. Most of the food crises had for their origin weather phenomena of a continental order and thus, had produced uniform price rises throughout the Continent.

France still remained essentially an agricultural country. We possess precise and almost complete market prices of grain for the period for France. They show that the rise of the price of wheat, begun in the eighteenth century, continued and even accelerated in the Napoleonic period. The price of bread in Paris reached an all-time high on July 14, 1789— it was the highest level of the century to date; a comparable rise took place in 1795 and even greater rises in 1802–1803, 1812, and 1817. This last year marked, moreover, the highest point of the entire nineteenth century. From 1780 to 1817, the price of wheat rose 55 percent.

It is very difficult, however, to establish for all of France from 1789 to 1815, price curves for the other agricultural products, but their rise is certain. Without being able to evaluate with accuracy the rate of this rise, we know that it was without doubt about 50 percent. Belgian prices rose to a greater extent than French prices, and Dutch prices still more, about 100 percent.

---

[24] See reports from the Twelfth Congress in Vienna, cited on p. 230, footnote 1, especially Ernest Labrousse, *Rapports.* See also F. Crouzet, "Bilan de l'économie britannique pendent les guerres de la Révolution et de l'Empire, *Revue historique,* 1965, fasc. 475, pp. 71–110; F. Dreyfus, "Bilan économique des Allemagnes en 1815," *Révue d'histoire, économique et sociale,* 1965, pp. 434–464; A. Z. Narochnitzki, in *Rapports conjoints, op. cit.;* Von Finckenstein, *Die Entwicklung der Landivertschaft in Preussen und Deutschland 1800 bis 1930,* 1960; B. Grochulska, "Sur la Structure économique du duché de Varsovie," *Annales historiques de la Révolution française,* 1964, pp. 349–363.

In England, the price of cereals led all others. Cereals experienced a considerable rise, but in England the peak was reached in 1812, not in 1817 as in France. The price of wheat rose very rapidly before 1800. Then its rate of acceleration became more moderate, but the total rise was double that attained in France, since it reached 106 percent. When comparing France and England, one must take into account the inflation in England from 1804 onward. Nevertheless, the corrections to compensate for the inflation that one can bring to the price curve of English wheat would not result in a rise inferior to that of the French curve. The prices of the other agricultural commodities followed the price of wheat and also rose more than French prices.

In Germany, also, the price of cereals rose throughout our period of study, but the maximum was reached in Berlin, Hamburg, and Vienna in 1806, undoubtedly influenced by Napoleon's resumption of war on Prussia. The rise seemed to be, on an average, in the neighborhood of 40 percent.

The price of cereals in Poland followed the German pattern, reaching a maximum in 1806. At Danzig the price of wheat had almost doubled during the revolutionary period. For Russia statistics are lacking, but reliable indices show that there had been a rise with two peaks, one between 1804 and 1806 and the other between 1812 and 1817.

A similar evolution is found in southern Europe. The price of wheat doubled in Portugal between 1787 and 1812, and the price of other agricultural commodities followed. In Spain it was in 1817, as in France, that the maximum price of wheat was recorded, and it was the same in Italy. Thus, the revolutionary and imperial epochs coincided with a rise of long duration of agricultural prices, of which the maximum varied from 50 percent to 100 percent according to the country of which grain was the staple.

What was the cause of this rise? Decrease of the quantities produced or increase of consumption? There is only meager evidence concerning the quantities produced. Thus, we know that in England the production of wheat increased 50 percent between 1780 and 1820 and that of potatoes even more. For France there exists no overall data before 1815. Nevertheless, an increase seems to be certain, but it is not possible now to ascertain if it was proportionately the same as that of the population. For Germany, even less information is at hand. Certain historians estimate that in the Prussia created by the Congress of Vienna, the production of cereals, of potatoes, and of livestock remained stationary between 1804 and 1816. Polish production should have followed the same evolution except for sheep raising. For Mediterranean Europe, statistics on prices and production are practically nonexistent. Only an increase in the production of wine in Italy and Spain is certain.

The little information that is available for Europe does permit one to presume an increase of agricultural production. One might think so since, with the exception of Spain, devastated by war for four years, the population increased considerably, and it follows that the populace would not have suffered undernourishment. One can generalize also that one of the causes of the rise of agricultural prices was an increased demand brought about by demographic pressure, that the increase in production did not keep pace with the population rise, and that waste was inevitable in periods of revolution and war.

INDUSTRY   Because of the Industrial Revolution, there is no doubt that industrial production made a great leap forward, above all in England, and to a lesser extent in France, Belgium, and Germany. For this information there are precise figures. In England the gross value of cotton production rose from £ 4 million in 1781 to £ 30 million in 1817. Concerning wool, the statistics are less complete, but figures for production of carded wool textiles in the West Riding of Yorkshire, showing an increase of 78 percent between 1788 and 1815, can be assumed to be representative of the industry as a whole. The net value of production in the entire United Kingdom rose from £ 3,400,000 in 1770 to £ 7,500,000 in 1823. It was the English textile industry that was the most dynamic of the country, and as a consequence, of the world.

The metallurgic industry also experienced great progress. British production of cast iron increased from 68,000 tons in 1788 to 325,000 in 1811. That supposes a considerable increase in the production of coal. Although there is little exact information on this subject, it is estimated that coal production rose 75 percent between 1792 and 1815. The price of these different industrial products, in contrast with the agricultural prices, had increased only slightly in the twenty-five year period.

In France industrial production had risen, but it had been restrained, especially for cotton products, by the blockade. The statistics for industrial production are vague, but it seems justifiable to fix the over-all increase of French industrial production between 1781 and 1821, at 25 percent, aside from building construction and artisanal activity. Industrial prices also climbed, although undoubtedly less than the prices of agricultural commodities.

For Germany the increase seems to have been more marked than in France. Industrial production seems to have risen by 30 percent between 1800 and 1820, while the increase in France had only been 18 percent during the same period. The increase occurred essentially in the production of coal, cast iron, and textiles. Because of a lack of general statistics, it is impossible to give, as in the case of England, valid figures for all of Germany. Some regional statistics were compiled. For example, in the Ruhr Valley, the production of coal rose from 60,000 tons in 1770 to 388,000 in 1815; in Silesia from 20,000 tons to 30,000. In Saxony the number of spindles for spinning cotton was 13,200 in 1806 and 283,000 in 1814. The great jump here was a direct result of the blockade. There was a pronounced decline in the years following the collapse of the *Grand Empire*. Belgium was, from the point of view of industrial evolution, halfway between Germany and France.

The east and the south of Europe were infinitely less industrialized, and only fragmentary evidence concerning industry is available. It is certain that the textile industry made great progress in Russia, but much less so in Portugal, Spain and Italy. Material on the other basic industries in these areas of the Continent is so meager that not even presumptions can be ventured.

This investigation has shown that during the Revolutionary and Imperial period, the industrial growth of the eighteenth century continued and even increased. Had the blockades restricted or accelerated the increase? It seems that they had sometimes disturbed it, but never halted it. At the international level, cotton, metallurgy, and mining had continued to experience a rapid advance. If industrial prices rose proportionately much less than agricultural prices, in contrast the quantities produced increased in very superior proportions. The national revenue had increased, without any doubt, in the majority of the countries of Europe, and in the United States too, more rapidly from 1770 to 1805, than from 1805 to 1817. In effect, the reversal of the trend began to make itself felt in 1806 in Germany, in 1809 in the Iberian Peninsula, and in 1817 in France and Great Britain. Nevertheless, it seems established that in spite of revolutions, wars, and blockades, the economic growth was marked in Europe, and North America as well, from 1770 to 1815. What Ernest Labrousse wrote about World War II could apply as well to our period: "The longest since the Thirty Years' War, the most costly up to the Great War, Europe (and America) had in the end increased their stock of men, of products and of capital."[25] What social group had profited above all from the economic growth and the accumulation of capital? The reply to this question is even more complex according to whether the Revolution has overturned the social structures more or less profoundly in the different states.

COMMERCE   Among the consequences of the Revolutionary and Napoleonic eras on economic development was the primacy of Great Britain in world trade. The defeat of Napoleon on the seas, the dislocations of trade under the Continental System, and the growth of English industry during the previous twenty-five years, resulted as of 1815, in a strong British merchant marine, the reopening of European markets, and the develop-

---

[25] Labrousse, "Les éléments d'un bilan économique. La croissance dans la guerre." *Rapports, XIIe Congrès, op. cit.,* vol. 1, p. 494.

ment of world-wide trade with the Americas and the Far East. Not until the end of the nineteenth century, did Great Britain begin to find a competitor, in German commerce, and the real challenges came essentially in the twentieth century after two world wars. The expansion of Britain's colonial empire as a result of acquisitions of territories during the Napoleonic Wars, confirmed and added to the 1815 settlement, was a further factor in the expansion of British commercial markets.

After 1815, conflict arose in England between the landed aristocracy, who had brought about the Corn Laws of that year, (a tariff on the import of agricultural products), and English industrialists and merchants, who saw an end of the surviving Navigation Acts and laissez-faire as necessary to commercial expansion. The Navigation Acts were repealed gradually, and the last of the Corn Laws were finally repealed in 1846. Free trade increased the headstart that Britain enjoyed in commerce in 1815.

France remained essentially protectionist, and so did much of continental Europe, but the Revolutionary and Napoleonic periods had at least eliminated internal customs barriers. Steps to end tariffs between states of the German Confederation preceded political unification in Germany, but in Italy were simultaneous with the stages of national unification.

The Austrian Empire had a customs union among the diverse nationalities that made up its empire, but levied tariffs against foreign imports. The loss of the colonies in the New World rendered Spain's elaborate mercantilism unnecessary and a dead letter. The impact on Portuguese trade was less severe, in part because of continued trade with England under earlier trade treaties and because of trade with the colonial empire.

Holland (united with Belgium) suffered from Napoleonic rule, but after 1815 it gradually developed its commerce. She conducted a lucrative carrying trade with the rest of Europe and increased trade with her Far Eastern possessions. Holland did not seriously challenge Britain.

It took a long time after 1815 for Russia, the Balkans under Turkish rule, and Turkey herself (in the process of losing territory in the nineteenth century) to rebuild their trade. The tremendous growth of Greek trade in the twentieth century could not be foreseen in 1829 when Turkey recognized the independence of a part of present-day Greece.

The developments of trade and its tremendous expansion in the second half of the nineteenth century were primarily influenced by the Industrial Revolution and the development of transportation; this growth overshadows the influence of the Napoleonic period on commerce in the immediate post-1815 period.

13

CULTURE IN THE
AGE OF NAPOLEON

Culture, even less than social and economic conditions, does not develop by the same sharp crises and periods as the political world. Historians of culture have tended to write in terms of whole centuries. The Enlightenment was a development characteristic of the eighteenth century, but some of its features began before 1700, and some of its effects carried over after 1789. The new political forms and ideas of liberty and equality of the Revolution era, with their accompanying social and economic changes did influence cultural developments. They exerted a fourfold influence: in respect to the contributors along cultural lines, their ideas, their techniques, and cultural institutions. The cosmopolitanism of the eighteenth century and the idea of human progress carried over in the revolutionary era in the effort to spread French institutions, with an emphasis on the "rights of man"—all mankind—and the hope of universal happiness and well being. In their enthusiasm, the French revolutionaries tended to ignore the differences of past history and national status of the governments and peoples to whom they directed their missionary efforts. Thereby, they unwittingly laid a background for the development or an intensification of national sentiment, depending on the area.

The French revolutionaries attacked the Roman Catholic Church in its secular power; they also continued the secularization of life and thought that had been going on for two centuries. For a time, at least, they substituted a new morality or intensified the teaching of strict Christianity in respect to virtue and the duties of citizens. Republican ideals derived from antiquity and the Neoclassicism of painting, sculpture, drama, and some poetry were a marked change from the paintings of Watteau, Boucher, or from Choderlos de Laclos' *Les Liaisons dangereuses*. The sentimentalism and preromanticism of the eighteenth century were transformed, and the groundwork for Napoleon and the nineteenth century laid.

From 1799 until 1815 Napoleon exerted a marked influence on cultural development,—on its basic ideas, and manifestations, public taste, and the interaction of French culture and that of other areas of Europe and the Muslim world, at least in Egypt. Napoleon appreciated cultural achievements. We have already noted his desire to have a traveling library of literary and historical works and his concern for education. The breadth of his interests will emerge in connection with cultural developments of his age. There are many evidences that he did not concentrate exclusively on military affairs. Napoleon sometimes manifested contrary tendencies. It may be well to remember that he was a self-made man, with a desire for ostentation to prove himself the equal of others born to the purple and an occasional appreciation of bigness rather than quality, such as his statement in the Council of State in 1806, "Nothing is beautiful unless it is large. Vastness and immensity can make you forget a great many defects."

PHILOSOPHICAL THOUGHT AND RELIGION

No great French *philosophes* comparable to Voltaire, Montesquieu, and Rousseau were propounding their ideas during the revolutionary decade and Napoleonic era. Except for Condorcet—the philosopher of human progress, who lost his life in the Terror because of his political affiliations, and indeed it was while he was in prison that he wrote his great work on human perfectibility—the period 1789 to 1815 in France was rather one of application of the ideas of the Enlightenment and pragmatism than of abstract thought. At the same time in England David Hume's more radical ideas about the nature of man exerted an influence, and Immanuel Kant, the great philosopher who never left his home town of Königsberg in East Prussia, nevertheless, had written many works challenging the rationalism of the eighteenth century. His *Critique of Pure Reason* had been published in 1781, and practically all of his works had appeared before 1799, but his idealist philosophy was felt especially in Germany in the Napoleonic period and extended on into the nineteenth century. His influence on Romantic literary works was exerted during and after the Napoleonic era. Napoleon is reported as saying in 1804, the same year as the death of Kant, "The prince arch chancellor was discussing with the Emperor a metaphysical point of Kant's. But the Emperor settled the question by declaring that Kant was obscure and that he did not like him; and he brusquely left the prince." Was this really ignorance on Napoleon's part or his keen practical mind?

The French were the leaders in many cultural lines, but it was the Germans who led in the nineteenth century in philosophical thought. Johann Fichte had perhaps, in this epoch, more influence on German national spirit than on philosophy. His earliest work, after his study of Kant's philosophy, was published in 1792, *Critique of All Revelation,* which Kant himself praised and which led to Fichte's appointment to the chair of philosophy at the University of Jena. In 1799 he moved to the University of Berlin. In the next year he published his best known philosophical work, *Fundamental Principles in the Whole Theory of Science.* Fichte rejected the idealism of Kant, and by means of an idealistic dialectic, constructed his metaphysics and philosophy of man's knowledge. During the reform and revival period of Prussian history, as it reacted to the Napoleonic Wars, Fichte became a leader of the German patriotic spirit and through his teaching exerted a great influence on German youth. His *Theorie de Science* was written in 1794. In 1807 and 1808 he exalted Germany in his *Address to the German Nation,* and his historical lectures aroused pride in Germany's past greatness.

Hegel also taught at Jena and from 1816–1818 at Heidelberg. In 1818 he succeeded Fichte as professor of philosophy at Berlin. Hegel constructed a complete philosophy of the universe. Already in 1807 he had published *Phenomenology of Mind* and in 1812–1816, *Science of Logic.* In the next year came his *Encyclopedia of Philosophical Knowledge.* Hegelian dialectic was to exert a great influence in the nineteenth and twentieth centuries. In putting into value the oscillations of history that passed from thesis to antithesis to produce a new synthesis, Hegel led in two nineteenth-century currents: nationalism and Marxism. His belief in a *Zeitgeist* (spirit of the times) exerted tremendous influence on German intellectuals. For a period, he thought that Napoleon embodied the contemporary spirit but became disillusioned as Germany suffered from Napoleonic pressures. Hegel was substituting for Newtonian method and science, an idealistic logic, but his writings tended to emphasize the logic rather than the idealism.

A Christian revival began in the Napoleonic period. The short period of atheistical worship during the Terror and Jacobin puritanism were discredited. Napoleon's own attitude toward religion was purely practical, in respect to the teaching of morality and good citizenship—embodied in the

Imperial Catechism — and also in respect to a church that was subservient to the state. It was in 1802 that Chateaubriand published his *Le Génie du Christianisme*, and *Les Martyrs* (1809) which were to exert a profound influence at first outside France, but later, on Catholics in France. The first work influenced not only the intellectual and emotional attitude toward Christianity, but also, by its literary form, the development of Romantic literature. Napoleon had appointed Chateaubriand as French legate to the Pope in Rome, and then as the French representative to the Republic of Valais. The assassination of the duke d'Enghien estranged Chateaubriand, and he lived in exile until the return of the Bourbons in 1814,

In 1799, when Pope Pius VI died in exile at Valence, the members of the French Directory believed that he would not have a successor. Nevertheless, Pius VII was elected. He improved the situation of the Roman Catholic Church in France by signing the Concordat of 1801. The restoration of 1814 seemed to mark the triumph of the Roman Catholic Church.

This triumph had, however, both a positive and a negative aspect. On the positive side, there had been the purification of the Church by a return to primitive poverty. In many countries, notably in France and in the Germanies, the Church had lost its wealth. Although the clergy tried to reconstitute their property, particularly for the benefit of the religious orders, they lived in relative poverty. There was no comparison between the revenues of a French bishop in 1815 and those of a Cardinal de Rohan or of Archbishop Loménie de Brienne on the eve of the Revolution. On the other hand, if the priests were not rich, they were not miserable either, as some of them had been in 1789. Thanks to the salary paid by the state in France, they could exercise their ministry in a suitable manner. One no longer found the scandalous gulf that had separated the parish priests and the bishops under the *ancien régime*. The call to the Christian life was spiritualized and henceforward it attracted those who sought to serve rather than to gain personal profit. In the greater part of Europe the tithe was suppressed and the Church, disengaged from feudalism, could devote itself to the tasks that were peculiarly its own and for which it was fitted. Thus was consummated within the Church the rupture between the social structure of the *ancien régime* and the structure of the nineteenth-century Church.

There was also a negative side. The Church had a tendency to believe that the counterrevolution had triumphed thanks to its theoreticians. The works of the Abbé Barruel, of Louis de Bonald, of Joseph de Maistre, and of their disciples were considered by the Roman Curia, by the greater part of the bishops, and by numerous priests as fundamental works whose ideas ought to prevail. The Revolution, whose flames the Church feared might return, was attributed to a conspiracy of Satanic and Masonic forces. The economic, social, and political causes were misunderstood or ignored. The

Church did not wish to admit the great change that was in the process of being accomplished in the civilization of the West. The gulf between the Church and the Revolution was deepened instead of being filled in. Certainly, Pius VII and Cardinal Consalvi, his secretary of state, who had lived through the revolutionary epoch, who had resisted Napoleonic Caesaro-Papism, and who understood the distinction between fundamental forces, and temporary and superficial appearances, attempted to resist this current. However, they encountered a powerful opposition which triumphed when they had disappeared from the scene. This opposition was to lead the Church to the encyclical *Quanta Cura* and to the *Syllabus of Errors* and to accentuate the divorce between itself and lay society.

Even when one considered the traditional tendencies of the Old Regime in certain countries—regalism of the Courts, episcopalism of the bishops, and antipapal Jansenism—the theocratic and ultramontane current still seemed to have prevailed. The liberal Catholicism of Father Lamennais was derived from ultramontanism, but in general this movement became conservative. It was also frequently accompanied by a renewal of mysticism that bordered on occultism. Alessandro di Cagliostro had been exposed as a charlatan and died in prison in 1795. The role of Emanuel Swedenborg in this period, Friedrick Schleiermacher, both Protestants, Novalis, and Zacharias Werner all need further study for their mystical Romanticism. Protestantism and the Hebrew faith did not manifest, wherever these faiths were practised, a marked reaction to ideas and events of the Revolutionary and Napoleonic era. In France the grant of citizenship to people of all faiths was never retracted, but the advocacy of the equality of all before the state had been forged by prerevolutionary persecution. Where Protestantism was the state church, Napoleonic campaigns tended to exert an influence similar to that on Catholicism—curtailment of church wealth. Neither the Protestants of Holland nor of the Protestant cantons of Switzerland opposed Napoleon as Protestants. These areas produced no important religious thinkers at that time.

POLITICAL THOUGHT

Eighteenth-century philosophers had inspired French revolutionary constitutionalism, the concept of popular sovereignty, equality before the law, ideas of justice, the rights of man, all of which culminated in the first French Republic. The defense of these ideas is not found in treatises of political science during the arduous days of the Revolution, but rather in the debates of legislatures and the oratory of representatives of the period. Pamphlets were published, but in France there was no time to sit down and write a long defense of any of the democratic ideas and practices being implemented. When Napoleon took over on 18 Brumaire, Year VIII (1799) and established the Consulate, some of the principles of the Revolution were written into the Codes; but as time went on, and especially during the Empire, Napoleon's own political ideas were put into operation. The more democratic institutions, such as the plebiscite, were misused to bolster his power. The constitutions set up legislative institutions in such a way that Napoleon gained the essential initiative. Furthermore, he virtually controlled all appointments, both civil and military. Napoleon wrote no works on the theory of imperial power or dictatorship. His *Mémoirs* dictated at Saint Helena were a self-justification and later contributed to the Napoleonic legend. One may say that the whole period from 1789 through 1815 was one of experimentation in the political field, experiments often inspired by the Enlightenment or improvised to meet the emergencies or the malfunctioning of eighteenth-century theories. Many of the constructive and successful ideas were incorporated in the Codes, and hence became a part of the permanent legacy of the period. The form of the executive might change, but administrative institutions and a permanent civil service helped to perpetuate ideas of liberty and equality.

In 1815 the world was tired of war, and concepts of liberty and equality were being modified. But many intellectuals such as Byron, regretted that the great hopes for republics had collapsed. The spectrum of political ideas on the political stage from the extreme right to the extreme left was infinitely varied.

The partisans of theocracy, Louis de Bonald and Joseph de Maistre, seemed to triumph with the Restoration, but the ultraconservative character of their theories prevented them from being applied. Both, as defenders of the divine origin of monarchy and papal authority, became spokesmen of the traditionalist thought of the Restoration era and may have bolstered the defense of conservatives of the restored Bourbon rule. In Germany Karl Ludwig von Haller, in his *Restauration der Staatswissenschaft* (*Restoration of Political Science*), also made himself the champion of monarchical and clerical absolutism. In areas where reaction was strongest in 1815, such as Spain, the revival of an autocratic monarchy was more a response to opposition of foreign rule embodying revolutionary ideas than a conscious operation of absolutist theory. However, the censorship and the very active state police of all the more autocratic regimes after 1815 copied Napoleonic models. The principle of legitimacy and the authority of the state passed into law through the intermediary of the historical school of law in Germany with Friedrich Karl von Savigny and his group.

The more liberal ideas of the Revolutionary decade continued to be diffused by the opponents of reaction and conservatism, and were the basis of the thinking and oratory of nineteenth-century liberals and the passwords of many of the revolutionaries of 1830 and 1848, in France and elsewhere in Europe. Ideas of national political unity drew from Revolutionary sources but were intensified by liberation movements against Napoleonic rule.

LITERATURE

During the decade of the Revolution in France, writers popular before the Revolution continued to be read and their plays given. Voltaire's *Henriade* was harmonious with ideas of monarchy and of religious toleration. Some of his plays based on classical themes, notably *Brutus,* that were critical of absolutism and arbitrary power, continued to be performed. Beaumarchais' *Marriage of Figaro,* satirical of the French court although the scene was laid in Spain, was no longer presented after the abolition of the nobility, and works based on monarchy and privileges fell into disuse.

Political prose held sway, and journalism took tremendous strides. Many new papers started publication, some ephemeral sheets, but others continuing until Napoleonic censorship. The *Moniteur Universel* was first published in November 1789. It soon became virtually the official paper of the first two revolutionary legislatures. Other newspapers that became important influences on public opinion were Jacques Pierre Brissot de Warville's *Patriote Français,* Bertrand Barère de Vieuzac's *Point du jour,* Jean Paul Marat's *L'Ami du Peuple,* and Jacques René Hébert's *Père Duchêne.* The last two were more radical, and their language was that of the lower-class citizen of Paris. There were, however, so many newspapers, not only in Paris but in the large provincial towns too, that Gérard Walter required a volume of nearly 600 pages to inventory them.[1]

The *Moniteur* gave full coverage of the news, with extensive publication of legislative debates through the Terror. Its pages reported international news, the scene in Paris and the provinces, notices of books, occasional reviews of plays, poems, and patriotic songs, and a list of plays being given in the many Parisian theaters. Few of the plays written between 1789 and 1795 are performed today. They were topical, glorified the ordinary citizen, preached patriotism, used comedy more often than tragedy, and often drew their themes from antiquity. More theater was accessible to more people than ever before.

Already during the spring of 1794 when Robespierre was at the height of his power, censorship was reintroduced. He realized that with widespread illiteracy, the theater was a potent means of education for the spread of

---

[1] Gérard Walter, *Catalogue des journaux révolutionnaires (1789–1799),* Paris, Bibliothèque Nationale, 1943.

ideas of liberty, equality, and patriotism.[2] Censorship was exercised against plays that cast aspersions on Jacobin leaders, the Republic, and the ideals of the Revolution or favorable to monarchy, the privileged classes and the Old Regime. An official censor removed lines from the play in advance of presentation, if considered undesirable, even if the play as a whole was not forbidden. Audiences themselves acted as censors. Sometimes they protested lines or acting when either was considered to be used to convey derogatory criticism of a popular leader or a revolutionary situation. Revolutionary audiences were quick to interpret scenes of antiquity with overtones of contemporary situations. Some theaters were closed and a few playwrights and actors imprisoned because of the productions they presented. On the promise to avoid criticisms of the Republic, they were usually released. Newspapers were censored, and pamphleteers were required by law to sign their publications. They were thus made responsible for what they said rather than to be allowed the freedom of the anonymity of the early Revolution.

Censorship became stricter under the Directory, but François Eve and Joseph Aude were making a parvenu fishwoman, Madame Angot, so popular that they and their imitators wrote many plays built around her as the heroine. During the Napoleonic period an even stricter censorship, with some arbitrariness of execution, developed. Napoleon's own taste in theater was conventional. As already indicated, the number of Parisian newspapers was reduced to four, and plays were censored for anything derogatory first of the Consulate and then of the Empire. Opposition to Napoleon was censored at the same time that Napoleon used propaganda to promote Napoleonic institutions and ideas and loyalty to himself.

In creative literature the taste for Neoclassicism continued, fostered by Napoleon himself. The beginnings of Romanticism, dating back to the sentimentalism of Rousseau and Diderot, developed during the Revolution; and nineteenth-century Romantic literature flourished from the literary advances of the Napoleonic era. There has been much controversy on the meaning of Romanticism. No one author, no one painter combined all features that have been recognized as different from the Classicism or Neoclassicism of the Revolutionary and Napoleonic periods. Among its outstanding characteristics was an appeal to the imagination and the emotions rather than to the philosophic intellect and rationalism. The appeal to the emotions led to new techniques—in literature, to a rich vocabulary and a revolt against classical rules of composition; in painting, the use of

---

[2] See Beatrice F. Hyslop, "The Theater during a Crisis: The Parisian Theater during the Reign of Terror," *Journal of Modern History*, December, 1945, pp. 332–355.

bright colors, realism of the emotions. Romanticism led to different subject matter too. Idealization of the Middle Ages vied with contemporary themes and events. There was less use of the Greek and Roman classics and characters. Just as the characters of the new Romanticism showed passion, so the emotions of the reader or the viewer of art were aroused. A further characteristic of Romantic writers and artists was a *mal de siècle,* a pessimism as contrasted with the optimism of progress held during the Enlightenment. There was a new appreciation of nature, not the placid scenes or mere background of classicism—a Watteau, a Boucher, or a Fragonard— but the turbulent nature of the Alps or other mountains, cascading streams, storms at sea. There was appreciation of flowers, birds, landscapes for their own sake. The Egyptian campaign may have stimulated an interest in Egyptian and Turkish themes. The Muslim world replaced China for exoticism and for contrast with the Christian world.

Whereas French had been the chief language of the Enlightenment, national languages developed during the Romantic era. In 1810, in spite of the occupation of three fourths of Europe by the French, the French language was less universal than in 1750. In the interior of the French Empire the measures of coercion taken by Napoleon to make French obligatory in the newly annexed departments of Holland, some of Germany and Italy, provoked by reaction, an increased use of national languages. In the vassal or allied countries there was no serious attempt to implant French, but the presence of French troops and functionaries and the importation of French expressions also provoked, by a sort of defensive instinct, the purification and development of local languages. As French armies advanced, the French language receded. In the "occupied" states masterpieces of the native literature were produced. These works, sprung from the new Romanticism, appealed in general to popular traditions and forces of the past. They put into relief the original characters of each people and were totally opposed to the simplifying and unifying classicism.

Individualism was also a feature of Romanticism. Heroes and heroines were often rebels against their society. In this respect, Romanticism prepared the background of the revolutions of the nineteenth century in the political field and challenged the restoration of privileged orders after 1815 in the social field. Freedom was a keynote of Romantics, whether in the individuality of their thought or in the methods of conveying them.

At first poetry was the chief vehicle of Romantic literature. André Chénier is often considered the forerunner of Romantic poetry in France. He was discovered by Chateaubriand. Chénier's most famous poem was *La jeune captive,* written about a young woman in the same prison where Chénier was imprisoned in 1794 after his arrest for his political views. Both became victims of the Terror, and the poem about the emotions and life of the young woman appealed to any who had suffered or feared the Terror.

The poem breathed some of the *mal du siècle* of the later period. After disillusion based upon the divergence between ideals and expectations for the common welfare *(bonheur commun)*, drawn from the *philosophes*, there had been the Terror, then military dictatorship and perpetual wars of the Consulate and Empire. The great French Romantic poets—Alfred de Vigny, Alfred de Musset, Victor Hugo, Alphonse de Lamartine—were growing up under the Napoleonic regime, but their best known works postdated that regime. Benjamin Constant, in his *Adolphe* (1816) reflected some of the *mal du siècle,* and combined philosophical tradition with cynical bourgeois materialism. Today it is difficult to understand the success that Constant enjoyed at the end of the Imperial period: it was due essentially to his devotion to property, which was real, and for his enthusiasm for liberty, which was perhaps less sincere. His concept of both property and liberty was their strictly individualistic form. He contributed, thereby, to nineteenth-century liberalism some of its theoretical foundation.

Romanticism often chose themes from the Middle Ages. It was a good age for the nobles, but not for the serf. The medieval times as constructed by the Romantics had never existed, but they frequently wrote about knighthood and chivalry. Chateaubriand looked back to early Christian times and the Middle Ages. Madame de Staël's *De l'Allemagne* (1810) used Tacitus and German medieval times, with praise for this German past in contrast to more recent times. Her writing on Italy also painted the greatness of Italy's past tradition.

Romanticism started earlier in England than in France. The Lake poets had written their most famous poems before the Revolution. The lines of William Wordsworth in praise of the fall of the Bastille are famous, although the early enthusiasm for French liberty was dimmed. William Blake had written his best poems before 1800. Byron, Keats, and Shelley took up the Romantic torch and published their best poems between 1810 and 1825. Sir Walter Scott, after having published such poems as *The Lay of the Last Minstrel* (1805), *Marmion* (1808), *The Lady of the Lake* (1810), and *Rokeby* (1813), made his name with his first historical novel in 1814, *Waverley. Ivanhoe* came out in 1819 and *Quentin Durward* in 1823.

In Germany the *Sturm und Drang* (storm and stress) period of Schiller and of Goethe's early writing was largely published before Napoleon came to power, but the residence of both of these literary luminaries in Weimar from 1798 until 1805 was a rich period for German Romantic literature. Schiller's trilogy on *Wallenstein* came out in 1800, and his *Wilhelm Tell* in 1804. The latter was and remains a powerful plea against tyranny. Goethe occupied some of this same period in scientific investigation, but he was also working on his great masterpiece. The first part of *Faust* was published in 1808, the second, not until 1832. Goethe started his autobiography,

Dichtung und Warheit, in 1811 but modified it after 1815. One may note changes in his attitude toward the French Revolution, the Napoleonic Wars, and the reputation of the later Napoleon. These German writers no longer used French as Frederick the Great had, and their patriotism or nascent German national sentiment inspired them to reject French influence. Johann Gotfried Herder had already appealed to German patriotism. Now, Clemens Brentano, Ludwig von Arnim, the brothers Jacob and Wilhelm Grimm, Adelbert von Chamisso, Heinrich von Kleist and Ernest Theodor Hoffman were producing their major works, inspired by national traditions and legends. Between 1810 and 1820 appeared Brentano's *The Journal of a Voyage of a Student,* Chamisso's *The Marvelous History,* the *Tales* and *Myths* of the Grimm brothers, and Hoffman's *Pot of Gold.*

In Italy, Vittorio Alfieri, born in Piedmont but who lived most of his productive life in Florence, had at first been enthusiastic about the French Revolution, but he turned from it. In 1799 he published a bitter diatribe against France in *Misogallo.* Although he died in 1803, he had lived long enough to see the changing attitudes of the French "liberators" of Italy and to become a forerunner of the *Risorgimento,* the cultural movement that prepared national spirit for unification. Alessandro Manzoni made his literary debut in 1815 with his *Sacred Hymns* and Giacomo Leopardi his in 1817.

While Adam Mickiewicz, Polish patriot, was glorifying the national idea in Poland, Alexander Pushkin did the same in Russia. A Greek literary revival preceded the formation of a secret society (Philikè Hetairia or Society of Friends) in 1814, aiming to win independence from Turkey.

Indeed, Romanticism had not yet triumphed in 1814. The literature of the eighteenth century was still very popular in cultivated circles. Voltaire and Rousseau were reprinted in France and translated in foreign countries. In England the vogue for Rousseau had never been greater than it was after 1815. The *Encyclopédie* of Denis Diderot and Jean le Rond d'Alembert was the great reference work. If the Restoration began to turn from Classicism and the Revolutionary spirit, it was certainly not in order to return to the old formulas but to adopt the new tendencies of Romanticism. The latter, which marked a return to a legendary past, was allied to the spirit of the Restoration because it was at the same time an exultation of the national sources of inspiration and a struggle against French influence and the rationalism on which the Revolution had aspired to build a new world. The partisans of legitimacy favored the feudal and monarchical past. Although the Napoleonic period engendered Romantic origins in France and on the Continent, and stimulated English Romanticism, the full flowering of Romanticism was after 1815.

In contrast to the *mal du siècle* literature, Utopian Socialism was also born in the Napoleonic period. This movement composed of different schemes for human regeneration, all had in common, however, a belief in progress and the perfectibility of man—concepts of the Enlightenment. Like Rousseau, Buonarotti, and Babeuf, its proponents wished to overthrow existing society or to remodel it on new foundations. The three leaders of this type of thought had expressed their essential ideas before 1814. Henri de Saint-Simon had published as early as 1802 his *Letters of an Inhabitant of Geneva to his Contemporaries;* in 1813, his *Memoir on the Science of Man* and his *Work on Universal Gravitation.* During the Restoration, he worked on his *Industrial System,* which was published in three volumes (1820–1823). It was in 1808 that Charles Fourier finished his *Theory of the Four Movements.* In England Robert Owen passed from philanthropic ideas applied at New Lanark to his first really socialist ideas.

THE ARTS

A Neoclassicism in the arts replaced the eighteenth-century style of Rococo and sentimental imagination during the Revolution and remained strong during the Napoleonic era. The Church of the Madeleine, the Vendôme Column, the Arc du Carrousel, and Arc de Triomphe exemplify the classical models. The Madeleine was begun under Louis XV but continued by Louis XVI. The Vendôme Column commemorating Napoleon's victories over Austria was erected in 1805. The two arches were begun by Napoleon, also to celebrate his victories, but were not completed until the 1830s. Public buildings and museums in other countries also turned from the overornate Rococo style to the simplicity of Greek column, pediment, and only slightly tilting roof.

Painting illustrates *par excellence* the Neoclassical style. On the eve of the French Revolution, Jacques Louis David had created a furor by his exhibit of the *Oath of the Horatii.* The heroism of the Horatii, who overthrew the tyrant Tarquinius and the stark simplicity of representation intensified the challenge of liberty in the viewer. In the early Revolution David's *Oath of the Tennis Court,* later his dramatic picture of the death of Marat, and his many designs for public ceremonies in honor of some hero or great event in the Revolution were inspired by classical ideas and forms. David has been called the "pageant master of the French Revolution."[3] One might think that some of the designs for the altar used for the *Fête of the Federation,* commemorating on July 14, 1790, the capture of the Bastille, had been friezes borrowed from antiquity. While David was busy bringing about the end of the exclusive privileges of the former Academy,

---

[3] David L. Dowd wrote a book about David which he titled *The Pageant-Master of the French Revolution* (Lincoln, Nebr.: University of Nebraska Press, 1948).

and fought for the rights of fellow artists during the Revolution, he became an art dictator himself. He continued in this role for most of the Napoleonic period. His early representation of Napoleon on horseback crossing the Saint Bernard Pass into Italy may have idealized his model (it has been said that Napoleon rode a mule), but it does not make a hero of him. This painting may also be cited for some of the nascent Romanticism that emerged despite his Neoclassicism. His painting of *The Coronation of Napoleon* and Josephine was realistic in the detail of the background and of the personal portraits of the participants (except Napoleon's mother who was not present), but the atmosphere is that of the pomp and circumstance of Augustan Rome. More will be said of this picture in the last chapter.

There was a classic simplicity to much of the portraiture of this period. Romantic painting, born in the studio of David, began to be shown in the *Plague Victims of Jaffa,* exhibited by Antoine Jean Gros in the Salon of 1804. Incidently, this picture glorified Napoleon, who visited the victims and was not afraid to touch them. Theodore Géricault and Eugène Delacroix revealed the basic features of the new school with the *Raft of the Medusa* and *Virgil Conducting Dante to the Underworld.* Although the proportions of the figures in the first painting were the classical proportions, the subject of a contemporary shipwreck was presented so graphically that one knows the sea will swallow up the emaciated, shipwrecked figures on the raft before they can be rescued. The second, while combining antiquity and the Middle Ages, would arouse the fear of Hell by its coloring as well as its symbolic figures. Although both of these painters were producing in the 1820s and represent the fully developed Romantic school, Jean Auguste Ingres, pupil of David continued to carry on the Neoclassical style.

In Spain Francisco Goya had reacted as early as 1807 against the Classicism of David and his followers. His portraits of the Spanish queen and king and of Godoy were revolutionary in their realism and color, but his most famous composition, depicting the execution of Spanish rebels by Napoleonic soldiers on the *Dos de Mayo,* or his *Tre de Mayo,* is only surpassed in its patriotic appeal and the horror of war by Pablo Picasso's *Guernica* of the twentieth century. John Constable painted placid landscapes in England. The Italian schools of painting had declined since 1700. Romanticism would only emerge later in Germany.

Sculpture is prone to change more slowly than the other arts, perhaps because marble dictates to some degree the style. Winckelmann had given an impetus to the use of classical statuary in the 1770s, and the career of Antonio Canova spanned the end of the Old Regime to 1822. He used classical subjects, and his treatment was less that of the great Greek period of the fifth to fourth century B.C., but more of Hellenistic Greece. Canova's renown overshadowed any other sculptors of the period.

In costume and interior decoration, the Empire gave its name to a particular style. Just as external architecture was inspired by classical models, so also were interiors. Pilasters and straight lines in furniture replaced the curves of the Rococo. The trappings of monarchy, the *fleur-de-lis,* and the symbols of feudalism became taboo. At first the union of the three orders had been depicted in cartoons, engravings, and even on china, but then, when the privileged classes had turned against the Revolution, the sans-culotte as a workman or a soldier was used, with his long trousers and his liberty cap. David's portrait of a woman of the common people was a far cry from a Madame Lafarge. Powdered wigs were no longer worn (except by Robespierre). The egg and dart, walls of Troy, laurel leaves, and other designs of antiquity appeared on furniture, on works of art, on costumes. The Napoleonic bee replaced the *fleur-de-lis.* The Empire style of dress with the high waistline was inspired from antiquity. A great deal of new building was done by Napoleon, which gave work to architects, builders, and interior decorators. The Sèvres porcelain factory became again the great producer of costly ceramics, using classical lines, and the Gobelin Tapestry Factory wove tapestries glorifying episodes of Napoleon's rule.

During his campaigns Napoleon after a victory required the defeated, especially in Italy, to send works of art to Paris, where many were exhibited in the Louvre. The famous bronze horses, brought by the Venetians in the Fourth Crusade from Constantinople to Venice's San Marco were placed on the top of the Arc du Carrousel in Paris, but they were returned to Venice after 1815. The peregrinations of these famous horses were not over, but they may be seen today again over the doors of San Marco cathedral in Venice. It was unfortunate that horses of French troops were stabled in the refectory of Santa Maria della Grazia in Milan, where the famous *Last Supper* by Leonardo da Vinci was painted in fresco on the end wall. This was not a command of Napoleon but an error of judgment of a subordinate. However, there is no evidence that he was punished for this. Fortunately, the painting is high enough on the wall that no basic damage was done to it. There will be no attempt to indicate here how many of the present treasures of the Renaissance period or of the great period of Spanish painting may have been kept in the Louvre after 1815. In any case, the Louvre became a public gallery and remains one of the richest collections in the world for all periods and types of art.

MUSIC

The music of Mozart and Hayden had set the styles of opera, orchestra, quartette, and piano in the eighteenth century. Mozart's *Marriage of Figaro,* based upon Beaumarchais' play, was given in Paris in the early

Revolution and the premier of his *Magic Flute,* so frequently considered to be influenced by the ritual and ideals of Free Masonry, was given in Paris in 1793. Gluck's *Armide* was also popular in that period. Popular songs, however, with new words to old folk tunes were sung by the common people. Rouget de Lisle' *The Marseillaise,* was sung on all public occasions, and other patriotic music was composed by André Grétry, Etienne Méhul, François Gossec, and others.

It was in Germany, however, that Romanticism would most forcefully displace Bach and Mozart. As in literature and art, Romantic music revolted against the classical harmonies, rhythms, and forms. Melodic content still prevailed, and even predominated in the works of Schubert, Schumann, and Chopin—the great Romantics whose works postdate 1815. Beethoven composed his *Appassionata* in 1804, and had intended to dedicate his *Heroic Symphony* to Napoleon but withdrew this honor after the battle of Austerlitz. His best work had been composed before 1815, after which there was a confused period with personal troubles and adjustments to his deafness, but his *Ninth Symphony* comes later. Weber, Rossini, Donizetti, Bellini, whose works are still heard today, either began their careers during the Napoleonic period or derived inspiration from the changing styles and tastes for the musical expansion of the nineteenth century. Many composers heard between 1789 and 1815 are seldom heard today. If their music is played at all, it is chiefly in their own country. They have been overshadowed by the great names already mentioned or the Brahms, Berlioz, Wagner, and Verdi of the later nineteenth century.

SCIENCE

The sciences had taken giant leaps forward in the eighteenth century. Newtonian science had spread to other countries and sparked new research both by its principles and its method. Count George de Buffon, the natural scientist, Carl Linnaeus, the botanist, Joseph Priestley and Antoine Laurent Lavoisier, chemists, had done their major work before the French Revolution. During the Revolution mathematics, chemistry, astronomy, and physics were advanced by Gaspard Monge, Lavoisier (until he was executed for his Old Regime role as "farmer-general"—tax collector), Priestley (until molested for his liberal support of the French Revolution), Pierre de Laplace, Luigi Galvani and Alessandro Volta. Nicolas Leblanc advanced experiments on soda. In Paris the former *Jardin de Roi* became a Museum of Natural History, open to the public, but also a research center.

During the supremacy of Napoleon, this work in science was carried further. Monge, who had published his *Traité de géometrie descriptive* in 1799 and founded the École polytechnique in Paris, developed his work in geometry, and Laplace, after publishing his *Système du monde*, continued it with *Mécanique celeste*. In these works he developed rational mechanics and expounded a system of the universe. Georges Cuvier, who began with botanical studies at the Museum of Natural History, changed to anatomy and published his *Anatomie comparée* (1800–1805). He continued his research and his teaching. In recognition for his great contributions to the study of comparative anatomy, he was elected to the Institute and awarded the Legion of Honor. His productive life continued well after 1815. The Chappe brothers (Claude and Ignace) but especially Claude, invented the first form of telegraph which was used by Napoleon in his campaigns.

While Napoleon possessed a great admiration for science and wanted it taught in the schools, he was more concerned with applied science than with pure theory. He had, of course, studied much mathematics in military school as a young man, but he applied his knowledge to artillery rather than to theories alone. Further development of the balloon had taken place after the first successful ascension by the Mongolfiers in the 1780s. In 1808 a proposal was made by a Monsieur L'Homond to General Clarke, the minister of war, and relayed to Napoleon, to provide a fleet of one hundred balloons big enough to carry in each 1000 men with food and munitions and even twenty-five horses. L'Homond believed that such equipment would enable Napoleon to invade England from the air. Napoleon had dissolved the balloon corps existing when he came to power, and L'Homond's proposal did not receive consideration. Napoleon must have lacked confidence in an airborne invasion. It was more than a hundred years later that air power would play a crucial role over the English Channel.

Napoleon also seems to have had a low opinion of the medical profession, which probably explains why he did so little to improve the medical and health services of his army. In 1806 he made the following statement to the Council of State: "Medicine is not an exact and positive science but a science based on conjecture and observations. I would have more confidence in a physician who has not studied the natural sciences than in one who has." In the same year, Napoleon prescribed a treatment to General von Wrede: "You must tranquilize your mind: this is the best way to cure the body." Napoleon himself was an excellent psychologist in his understanding of the power of mind over matter, in his discipline in the French army, and in his own self-discipline. He enjoyed good health most of his life, without resort to doctors. Only a strong physique could have undertaken the tremendous campaigns and constant mental activity that he did. He believed that constant activity was good for one's health.

Medicine and pharmacy had shown progress in the eighteenth century, especially with the introduction of vaccination, but no marked improvements were made during the period from 1789 to 1815.

It was in 1793 that the National Convention authorized the establishment of the metric system, but wars prevented the undertaking of measurements and the perfecting of the system. It was not until the Consulate that it became mandatory to use one uniform standard of weights and measures based on tens. Introduced in all French departments and those organized on foreign soil, the metric system gradually replaced other systems in the nineteenth century.

Chevàlier de Lamarck, in his *Philosophie zoölogique* published in 1809 and John Playfair's *Illustrations of the Huttonian Theory of the Earth*, defending the work of James Hutton, prepared the way for Darwinism much later in the nineteenth century.

John Dalton advanced his atomic theory in 1808. Karl J. Gauss did extensive work in mathematics and electricity as did Alessandro Volta and A. M. Ampère in the investigation of magnetism and electricity in the Napoleonic period. The contributions of these eminent men, though, were more appreciated later. The work of scientists, like social and economic change, does not tend to change at a specific date or fit the particular political period.

The Napoleonic period that had remade the map of Europe, conducted wars against coalitions of European powers, spread some ideas and institutions of the Revolutionary era, and saw a virtual dictatorship in France, was nevertheless, a period of cultural developments. The *Grand Empire* left a profound mark on civilization.

There was an Empire style in the arts. Literature, while it lacked liberty carried a trace of the Empire when it attached itself to dying classicism, as well as in Romanticism, making its first appearance. While Europe tended to unify by the reduction of its political division and the adoption of regimes more or less inspired by the Revolution, in the domain of literature, diversification increased. As a result of the heritage of the Revolution, the peoples of Europe had received the idea of "nation," which led to the awakening of nationalisms (the word only appeared after 1850). Nationalism manifested itself in language. Although French spread at first with French armies, by 1815 a reaction against the use of French had arisen, and national languages were promoted. Culture had been cosmopolitan in the eighteenth century; the age of Romanticism developing out of the Napoleonic era demonstrated national differences in the cultural developments.

Paris had been the center from which the Empire radiated, and it remained the chief city of arts and letters throughout the nineteenth century. Only after 1870 could Vienna, Rome, or Berlin offer some competition, but not one could display the European character of Paris. London and English culture had never been a center of European culture. While Germany and Austria produced more outstanding musical composers in the nineteenth century than France, and Germany was the homeland of famous philosophers, France excelled in literature and art, and vied in the field of science with all others. Paris was truly the world capital during the French Revolution and Napoleonic era.

14

NAPOLEON: THE MAN AND THE LEGEND

Although glimpses of Napoleon the man have been given in the foregoing pages, it is well to examine more closely what type of man he really was. It is appropriate to review the character of this obscure, second son of a minor, poor, noble family of Corsica who rose to dominate the whole of Europe and even parts of the world outside.

It is difficult to use Napoleon's works in his own handwriting for source material since Napoleon's handwriting is one of the most illegible of history. Fortunately for historians, Napoleon dictated many of his dispatches and letters, and hence, only his signature may appear in his own handwriting on the document. His brief letters to Josephine, Marie Louise, and many to the various members of the Bonaparte family were in his own hand. Although Maximilien Vox claims that there is much spurious material ascribed to Napoleon that undoubtedly influenced his own times and past historians, Vox has not yet written a definitive critique in this respect.[1]

---

[1] Maximilien Vox, *Correspondance de Napoléon: Six cents lettres de Napoléon de travail, 1806–1810,* (Paris, 1943), provided an extensive criticism of prior partial editions of Napoleon's letters as well as of the complete edition, but did not then indicate the ways in which the picture of Napoleon would have to be revised on the basis of his research and interpretation of the same correspondence.

The most important sources for a Napoleonic biography have been his *Mémoirs,* dictated at Saint Helena, but, as we shall see, these contributed to the legend and must be compared with memoirs of those around him during his exile and the memoirs of the many ministers, officers, friends, and foreign contemporaries of the Napoleonic period in order to derive a true portrait of the man. Some memoirs were not published until the late nineteenth century and even the twentieth, as for example, the memoirs of General Caulaincourt, who was a virtual military secretary to Napoleon and accompanied him on the Russian campaign, and remained with him until after Waterloo. Such volumes are invaluable to correct earlier beliefs about Napoleon, but a distinction must be made between what Napoleon's contemporaries knew and what has come to light since his death. His voluminous correspondence was not known at the time, except to the recipient and possibly his or her entourage, unless published. The correspondence is invaluable in the delineation of his character. Napoleon's contemporaries tended to judge him by the published record, his *Bulletins de la Grande Armée,* circulated to friend and foe, and avowedly propagandist. His enemies were prone to judge him by his acts, rather than his words, which often seemed contradictory or to carry a veiled meaning.

THE MAN

Although Napoleon was only fifty-one at his death, he lived a full life touching every facet of his times. For a genuine portrait of the man, both words and deeds must be reviewed. Only a critical examination of Napoleon's own statements and those of his contemporaries, and by a careful analysis of the official papers, can one arrive at a more valid portrait. An appraisal of Napoleon the man emerges with greater clarity by dividing his life into several periods: (1) his birth in 1769 until 1795; (2) 1795 through 1804, (3) 1804 through 1811, the zenith of his power, (4) 1811 through his fall, 1815, and lastly the exile at Saint Helena and the Napoleonic Legend.

Until 1793, Napoleon Bonaparte was more a Corsican than a Frenchman, even though he received military training in French military schools. His participation in Corsican affairs engaged much of his attention. The young Napoleon was closely attached to the Bonaparte family. His strong feeling for his family and the family recognition of his leadership emerged very early in his life. After the death of his father in 1785, when he was only sixteen, Napoleon rather than his elder brother Joseph took the greater responsibility for the impecunious, large family. Even while at school in France, he took an active role in family matters. By contrast, the consuming ambition that was to be an outstanding trait in later life had not as yet come to the fore. Modern psychologists look back on Napoleon's youth and underline his strong attachment for his mother. This is a thread that runs throughout his life—admiration for and attention to the opinion of Madame Mère. After he was in a position to spend money freely, he showered her with gifts, and when he became emperor, he assigned her an honored place at his court. He also looked after his brothers and sisters, but also used them for his own ambitions. Filial devotion contrasted with the repudiation of many others who failed to do his bidding—including his brothers and sisters.

During the first two years of the Revolution, Napoleon took long leaves of absence from his military assignments to visit Corsica, to work for the island's independence as well as supervise family affairs. In the struggle for independence of his birthplace, Napoleon eventually broke with Pasquale di Paoli, the liberation leader, with whom his father had quarreled. Napoleon came to favor integration with France, not independence. The break with the partisans of Corsica dates from 1793 when Paoli and his followers condemned the Bonaparte family and they fled to Toulon from their native land, in fear of their lives from followers of Paoli. Napoleon was by now the recognized leader of the Bonaparte clan.

In the same year as his "exile" from Corsica, Napoleon found time to write about his political views in a work entitled *Le Souper de Beaucaire* in which he favored a strong central government and spoke against the separation of outlying provinces. *Le Souper* revealed his Jacobin ideas. His previous youthful novels and this pamphlet reflected the prevailing sentimentalism of the era. The plots as well as some of the characters, some scholars contend, were autobiographical and sometimes portraits of his contemporaries.

When he landed at Toulon, he had to put such intellectual pursuits as writing and extensive reading, aside for the time being. He rejoined the French army and rapidly rose to the rank of artillery commander in the Army of the Midi. In this capacity he was called in to suppress insurgents in Paris on 13 Vendemiaire, Year IV (October 5, 1795), shortly before the final sessions of the National Convention. The next day he wrote to Joseph Bonaparte, "At last it is all over." After recounting the plot and the measures to suppress the uprising, Napoleon ended with the comment, "As usual, I haven't had a scratch." He came to have great confidence in his destiny, which gave him courage to face the enemy in battle. There was no mention of the famous "Whiff of grapeshot" in his letter, but this was the occasion. Napoleon was second in command to Barras, who was soon to become a director and who was useful to Napoleon more than once in the Directory period.

Thermidoran society, after the "republic of virtue" of the Robespierre period, was notoriously dissolute. Napoleon seems to have entered into it particularly after meeting Josephine de Beauharnais, widow of General Beauharnais and on intimate terms with Barras. Napoleon's low estimate of feminine character may have begun to develop at this time. Napoleon had had mistresses before, but he seems to have been genuinely in love with Josephine. He married Josephine on March 9, 1796, on the eve of the Italian expedition, before he had made his reputation. His love letters to her during the Italian campaign before she joined him in Italy after his victories, appear exaggerated today, but they did show his emotion, which, naturally, he would not include in military reports. During the Egyptian campaign he learned of Josephine's infidelities, and after his return to France and a stormy exchange, they patched up affairs. Josephine was invaluable to him in some of the background negotiations to win loyalty for the change from the Directory to the Consulate, and her social graces helped to build the atmosphere and style of the period. Napoleon showed, even before the Empire, a normal married man's desire for offspring, but when he became emperor, this desire was magnified by his personal ambition and his wish to have a natural, legitimate heir. Although Josephine had had two children by Beauharnais, Eugène and Hortense, she was unable to give Napoleon a child. His divorce in 1809 was motivated by *raison d'état* (reason of state) rather than personal sentiment. Malmaison remains to this day the symbol of his affection for Josephine.

This second period we have denoted began with the Directory and extended to the establishment of the Empire, 1804. Napoleon refused an appointment to suppress the uprising in the Vendée, but accepted the command of French forces fighting Austria in Italy. Until then he had essentially fought against Frenchmen. Even at Toulon Frenchmen predominated in the land forces. The Italian campaign was to challenge all his military abilities. In a relatively short time he transformed a defeated, disorganized, poorly fed and clothed rabble into the superb fighting force that began to win victories against superior numbers. His victories in north Italy enabled him and his army to live off the rich plains of Lombardy. In Italy Napoleon showed his mastery of strategy. He knew how to employ effective surprise of the enemy to gain victory. He also displayed his understanding of the psychology of the common soldier. His own fearlessness and that of some of his officers stimulated the courage and bravery of his soldiers. He proclaimed to the army on April 26, 1796, "Soldiers, in fifteen days you have won six victories . . . But you have done nothing yet, since there remains much for you to do". He had promised his tattered army food and clothing, and he had delivered the goods. Their morale changed as drastically as their physical condition, and few soldiers left for home or deserted. Napoleon continued to win victories. It was at this time that Napoleon began to be preoccupied with *gloire*.

Even before the end of the Italian campaign, he took upon himself the task of negotiating armistices and peace treaties, ignoring orders from the Directory and going beyond them. By 1797, when he returned to Paris after the signing of the Treaty of Campo-Formio, he was no longer a figure to be ignored.

Napoleon's idea of combating England, not by direct invasion of the British Isles, which he declined to lead, but by striking at English power in the Mediterranean via Malta and Egypt indicated a willingness to take great risks. His ambition could not be satisfied with some subaltern post in Paris. The Egyptian expedition, which the Directors were willing to approve since they thought they would then rid themselves of a troublesome general, popular because of the Italian victories, was conceived by Napoleon without full realization of the influence of naval power on a campaign so remote from France. To be sure, the French fleet had not yet sustained the losses it was to suffer at Abukir Bay and later at Trafalgar, but Napoleon at no time was the master of sea strategy comparable to that of land defense. The undertaking of the Egyptian campaign indicated the beginning of the overconfidence in Napoleon's character that would be his ultimate undoing.

During his occupation of Egypt, Napoleon introduced reforms in the Egyptian government, that indicated his administrative initiative and his ability in civil organization as well as in military organization. He declared himself a Muslim during his stay in Egypt, and at least one of his generals, Menou, converted to the Muslim faith. Napoleon was more concerned for the practical effect of religion than for theological and spiritual inspiration. In the planning of the Egyptian campaign Napoleon had made provision for a group of archeologists to accompany his army. One of the permanent contributions of Napoleon to world civilization was a by-product of this cultural interest. It was Napoleon's archeologists who discovered the Rosetta Stone now in the British Museum. Its decipherment by Jean Jacques Champollion-Figeac, has enabled the world to read Egyptian hieroglyphics. Napoleon's interest in enhancing French cultural resources was shown by his acquisitions for the Louvre during the Italian and Egyptian campaigns. Although the Egyptian expedition was really a defeat of the French army, the French did not know this for some time. Napoleon, master of propaganda, had sent glowing bulletins about lesser victories, and when he returned to France, leaving administration and campaigning to his generals, he was known as the victor of Italy and of Egypt.

Napoleon's appraisal of his own importance to France and increased ambition applied not only to the military sphere but also to the political arena. The establishment of the Consulate in 1799 after the overthrow of the Directory (18 Brumaire) placed him at the center of the French government. He was still loyal to certain ideas of the Revolution. In establishing republics in Italy, he had been carrying out the Propagandist Decrees of 1792. He saw to the appointment of leaders favorable to the French influence. The republics and satellite states assured a background for further victories against France's enemies who had formerly controlled the territory. At home in France Napoleon continued to show loyalty to the Republic while moving to subordinate other officials and organs to the First Consul.

His increasing ambition was shown in the setting up of the Life Consulate (1802), which was only a stepping stone to emperorship. The *coup d'état* of 18 Brumaire had been a resort to illegal force, but Napoleon made it "legal" by holding a plebiscite after the change to the Consulate had been effected. Napoleon's concern for outward appearances and his recognition of masking his personal ambitions were revealed in the semi-legal steps by which the Consulate was transformed to the Life Consulate, with a second resort to the plebiscite for approval of the change.

The greatly increased "yea" vote demonstrated the belief of the common Frenchman that Napoleon could bring peace and prosperity to France. The Treaty of Amiens had been signed in March and the war of the Vendée was brought to an end in May. Napoleon had already promulgated the Concordat of 1801 with the Pope, again an augury at the time of peacemaking and of the healing of wounds from the revolutionary period. General Leclerc appeared to gain peace in Saint Domingue, although in the same month, May 1802, Napoleon declared the maintenance of slavery in the French colonies very probably desired by the plantation owners but a cause of the ultimate loss of the West Indian colony and a step back from the principles of self determination of 1790 and of equality of 1793. Napoleon had said to the Council of State on May 1, "It is not as general that I govern, but because the nation believes that I have the civil qualifications to govern." Eight days later, the plebescite ratified the change to Life Consul for Napoleon, which he interpreted as a manifestation of popular sovereignty. Some of his contemporaries and historians did not view this measure as a democratic consultation of the French people.

Another attenuation of the principle of equality was the organization of the Legion of Honor. Although Napoleon's idea was to honor individuals of merit, the awards proved to be one means of creating loyal followers and of rewarding successful generals and a by-product was the creation of an elite corps. Soon after, an imperial nobility with honorary status was created, but without privileges as under the Old Regime. Nevertheless, its members too were set above the people as an elite. Nearness to Napoleon when he dispensed favors, was as valuable as it had been at the court of Louis XIV.

The third period from 1804 to 1811 was the era of the *Grand Empire*. Once Napoleon had the title of emperor, again ratified by plebiscite (by an overwhelming vote but a much higher number of nays), his love of adulation, his impatience with limitations, and his glory in the outward signs of wealth were all manifested in the imperial court that he set up. Napoleon's love of ostentation had been revealed on numerous occasions. In 1801, he had a saber made using the huge Regent diamond and other small ones. The ceremony of his coronation (December 2, 1804) in Notre Dame Cathedral, for which he required the presence of the Pope although Napoleon himself placed the crown on his own head, had all the ceremonial pomp and regal trappings associated with the *ancien régime,* as the canvasses of Jacques Louis David depict. The imperial court came to rival that of any of those of Austria, Russia, England.

The imperial style developed at Napoleon's court, through his patronage, and that of officials, generals, and their families surrounding Napoleon. Already before he was emperor, we have seen him building up the Louvre as a great art gallery by the requisitions of paintings from defeated Italian cities. His encouragement of writers and scientists also manifested itself by the establishment of prizes. Despite his many absences on campaigns, Napoleon built up the imperial court and culture, which has been an important part of the heritage of France from the Napoleonic regime.

Napoleon's ideas of grandeur carried over into his views on architecture and his physical surroundings. An elegant court required the correct setting—a beautiful capital city. The kings of France since Louis XIV had lavished their wealth upon Versailles, but during the French Revolution and Napoleonic era Paris became increasingly the nation's leading city. The revolutionary regimes had had no time to clear the narrow streets or construct new buildings and so turn the city into an imposing capital of the Republic. Napoleon undertook the task. He constructed new bridges across the Seine, built the Church of the Madeline on the right bank, and erected the imposing Arc de Triomphe and Arc du Carrousel as well as the Vendôme Column. The Paris of today, however, is the city more as it was transformed during the second Empire, when Napoleon III, inspired by his uncle's work, set out to complete the beautification.

Artists, craftsmen, architects, builders were undoubtedly busy after the declaration of the Empire, reconstructing and constructing the outward signs of the imperial regime, and bringing the Empire style into being.

Tapestry makers, upholsterers, wall paper manufacturers, ceramists, furniture designers—all the arts of interior decoration flourished for a period during the Empire, both because of change of styles, the wealth from Napoleonic conquests, and the impetus given by the Emperor himself.

The fine arts were all used during the Empire to glorify Napoleon and to provide a grandiose setting for the imperial court. Painting was outstanding. Jacques Louis David became the imperial court painter, and continued the Neo-classical style that he had developed on the eve of and during the Revolution. He began to show, however, some Romantic features. Napoleon commissioned him to paint four pictures related to the celebration of the coronation in 1804. The one of *The Coronation of Napoleon* himself can be discerned from sketches (see the illustration on page 79 and preliminary

The Coronation of Napoleon, by Jacques Louis David. The artist made sketches of the famous persons attending the coronation. Note the imperial background. Napoleon, although he wished the Pope to be present, crowned himself. (The Louvre. Photo from Giraudon)

designs). The final canvas of *The Coronation* depicts Napoleon crowning himself, with the Pope seated behind him and Josephine kneeling. It portrays the new pomp and circumstance of the imperial court, and is impressive for its size, its portrayal of individuals participating in the scene, and its setting. Later, David painted pictures for the marriage with the Archduchess Marie Louis, and his *Distribution of the Eagles by Napoleon I* (the standards topped by eagles were symbols of military bravery and victory) combined a dramatic public ceremony with artistic qualities of design and color. David drew several sketches for each of his big canvasses before choosing the final design. David's *Napoleon in his Study*, portrayed the emperor with a self-satisfied smile. Gérard's representation of the victory of Austerlitz glorified Napoleon the general, but his portrait of Napoleon the Emperor wearing all the velvet and ermine of majesty represented Napoleon the ruler rather than Napoleon the man. Baron Gros was another famous portraitist of Napoleon. His picture of Napoleon at Arcole, depicts the young, lean Napoleon leading his troops across the bridge, when he miraculously escaped death. A portrait of Napoleon as consul in a red velvet coat pointing to a long sheet of paper on which his accomplishments have been written, and Napoleon and the cholera victims of Jaffa are among Gros' best known paintings.

Several painters designed portraits with Napoleon holding his right hand inside his waistcoat. The use of this position by different painters has led some to ask whether Napoleon had a deformed or injured hand. This was not the case. Some portraits reveal both hands, and hence, this was a pure convention of the artists. The battle scenes were painted later, for the most part. Napoleon would never have allowed the *Retreat from Moscow* by Meissonier to have been displayed, had it been a contemporary painting. Meissonier painted this famous canvas after he had been an eyewitness of the Prussian siege of Paris, 1870–1871, which afforded the opportunity to the artist to see gunfire, retreating troops, the wounded, and snow. As Meissonier painted the scene, Napoleon is on horseback with his head high and his staff seconding him, and the lines of the soldiers in the background are orderly—an idealized version of the disorder, hardships, and deaths that Napoleon revealed in his own military dispatches, but not in the *Bulletin de la Grande Armée*. Napoleon would have wanted only his victories painted for his contemporaries and for posterity to view.

The painters and engravers who found favor with Napoleon produced works that glorified Napoleon at court and with his army. Although there were numerous other painters who "immortalized" the emperor, Napoleon preferred David. When in 1810, the Institute awarded a prize that Napoleon had established, to Girodet rather than to David, Napoleon cancelled the award. The emperor was also displeased that Canova, the famous sculptor of the classical style of statuary of the period, did not receive recognition at the time.

Despite his steps during the Consulate to build up public education, he did less for primary education than for the education of an elite through lycées and the *Grandes Écoles*. He recognized, however, that a high degree of illiteracy persisted and, therefore, promoted theater for the common people, as had the Terror. Opera and theater were among the frequent distractions for Napoleon when he was in Paris, and even to some degree on his campaigns, after victory. Henri Lecompte, an historian of the theater has provided a list of all the operas and plays that Napoleon attended.[2] Something of his taste may emerge from references to this list. The tragedies he saw most frequently were: *La Phèdre*, ten times; *Iphigénie en Aulide, Andromaque, Oedipe*, nine times each; and *Le Cid*. Of comedies, he saw *La Gageur Imprévu* eight times; and *L'Epreuve nouvelle* and *Le Legs*, both of the Revolutionary repertoire, seven times each. Napoleon only attended a performance of Beaumarchais' *Le Mariage de Figaro* three times. The custom of one-act curtain raisers that dramatized contemporary events was illustrated by *Victoire de Marengo*, by B. Bonnet-Bonneville, given at Lyon during Napoleon's passage through the city after that battle.

Napoleon heard two operas four times each, *Alceste* and *Ossian ou Les Bardes*, both by French composers, but perhaps because of his Corsican origin, he appeared to prefer Italian opera. *Lodoiska*, by Cherubini, which had been popular during the Revolution, was performed seven times. Two other operas that have dropped completely out of sight seem to have been particular favorites of Napoleon if the number of times attended is a criterion: *Le Cantatrici villane*, ten times, and *Griselda* seven times. This contrasts with only one performance of Mozart's *Marriage of Figaro*. In serious drama and opera, Napoleon seems to have preferred themes based upon antiquity, which was also the source of inspiration for much interior decoration of the Empire Period and of Imperial symbolism.

The emperor's taste also made itself felt in respect to ballet. Various troupes performed for his pleasure. In a letter February 13, 1810 to M. Remusat, prefect of the palace, who arranged for the programs, Napoleon expressed disapproval of operas and ballet based upon "Holy Scripture: such things should be left to the Church." He also advised in the same letter that in the future all programs be submitted to advance censorship and permission for performances. "The ballet *The Rape of the Sabine Women* is based on history: that is more what we want. Mythological and historical

---

[2] See L. Henry Lecomte, *Napoléon et le monde dramatique*, (Paris, 1912), appendix.

ballets may be given, but never allegorical ones." At the end, in speaking of four new ballets that he wished to be danced, he suggested a second historical one, "but one more appropriate to modern conditions than *The Rape of the Sabine Women*." This episode had been the subject of one of Jacques Louis David's great paintings after his release from house arrest following the fall of Robespierre.

Napoleon had already displayed his talent for effective propaganda. As time elapsed, his use of laudatory statements about himself became more obvious and less subtle than earlier. Censorship of the press was stricter, at the same time that Napoleon set up newspapers and bulletins aimed to publicize his action and his military victories. He took pains to prevent the publication of adverse information, and losses in battle were minimized. Napoleon impressed the common Frenchman with monuments, museums, processions and parades glorifying the Emperor.

Although war had been renewed against England, the consequences of the naval warfare were not immediately felt by the ordinary French citizen. A plot against Napoleon had been squelched with suddenness and ruthlessness by the arrest, summary trial, and immediate execution of the duke of Enghien. There was no time for self-defense or any real investigation of the complicity of the duke. Safeguards against punishment of the innocent that had been written into the law and defined in the codes, were ignored. Napoleon was as ready to break law, if he saw fit, as he was to observe some outward semblances of legality, such as the plebiscite ratifying the Empire. Evidence of dictatorship had appeared from time to time before the Empire, but it was to increase as all branches of civil government as well as the army and navy came under Napoleon's direct command.

Fouché, former Terrorist, was appointed minister of the police of the imperial regime as strong and as obedient to Napoleon as the army was to him. Discipline replaced liberty, and the Criminal and Penal codes reintroduced heavier penalties than were in effect during the Revolution, with the exception of execution for treason.

Napoleon, as the empire grew and reached its zenith in 1810–1811, began to take more risks and was increasingly unwilling to brook opposition to Napoleonic power at home and abroad. His ambitions had already expanded. Had Napoleon given England fewer reasons to suspect his continental ambitions and been more willing to conciliate the Malta affair, England would not have declared war in 1803, ending the only period of peace France had enjoyed since 1792 or would again enjoy until after 1815. Napoleon's victories at home as well as abroad had fed his ambition, and he had no doubts whatever that he could continue to defeat one enemy at a time and dominate the whole of Europe while bringing about the defeat of England on the sea. After Trafalgar, he merely changed his method of bringing about the defeat of Britain. England had likewise exhibited overconfidence in her ability to overcome Napoleon when she broke off further negotiations by a declaration of war. England had traditionally prevented any one power from dominating the Continent, and had upheld a balance of power. In 1803, her own national interests dictated the renewal of war.

After the battle of Trafalgar, instead of invading England, despite elaborate plans for this, Napoleon hurried to campaign against Austria. From then, through 1809, his great land victories over Austria, at Ulm, Austerlitz, Wagram, and others, over Prussia at Jena and Auerstadt, and the combined forces of Prussia and Russia at Eylau and Friedland, brought him to the zenith of his power on the Continent, despite the less successful attempts to defeat England by the Continental System. His annexation of conquered territory, and independent republics set up earlier, and then exaction of obedience to the restrictions of the Continental System, requisitions and conscription, began to turn portions of these subject peoples, satellite kingdoms and even allies against him. Napoleon's marriage with Marie Louise, daughter of the oldest reigning house in Europe, the Hapsburgs, appeared to reassure his preeminence in Europe. In 1810, he had made peace with Austria, leading to the marriage, peace with Prussia and Russia at Tilsit; his brother Joseph held the throne of Spain, Louis of Holland, Jerome of Westphalia, and Murat, husband of Napoleon's sister, Caroline, was king of Naples. Should Napoleon not have been satisfied with this preeminent power? For about a year, he enjoyed his new domestic scene, his court and internal affairs, but the prosecution of the Continental System led him to new annexations, a break with Russia and trouble in the Iberian peninsula. New coalitions began to form, with England always a key member, and the French alliance with Russia was broken off.

While increasing conscription, stricter censorship and the levying once again of indirect taxes, Napoleon had been remaking the map of Europe, recruiting larger contingents from satellite and allied countries, requiring large indemnities—measures that aroused nascent or latent national sentiment against French domination. He became more censorious of the conduct of his sisters and other relatives. For the Emperor, the welfare of France came first; thus he tended to ignore the welfare of other parts of his empire. His attitude is illustrated by a letter to Prince Eugène, son of Josephine and viceroy of Italy, on August 23, 1810, in which Napoleon is complaining about raw silk from Italy going to England, and wants it diverted to France (for the Lyon silk industry): "My first principle is France first. . . . So make this your motto too—France first." In this same letter, Napoleon voiced his overconfidence: "If I were to lose a great battle, a million men —nay, 2 million men of my old France would flock to my banners." Perhaps earlier, he would not have even suggested the loss of a battle!

Napoleon also became more dictatorial toward the Pope. He had been stretching the clauses of the Concordat of 1801 even beyond the Organic

Articles, and in 1809 after his excommunication by the Pope, Napoleon had the pontiff removed from Rome to Savona. There may have been some Gallicanism in Napoleon's action, but it was motivated more by his desire to dominate religion as well as secular affairs. On January 5, 1811, Napoleon instructed Count Bigot de Préameneu, minister of public worship, to have published a statement of the Pope's refusal to invest certain appointees, the text of the papal bull of excommunication and "the freedom that he (the Pope) enjoyed at Savona and the way he abused it"! Napoleon's conviction that his temporal authority, even in relation to Church matters, superceded that of papal authority and that all Church officials were to bow to his direction is evident in a letter to the governor general of the Transalpine departments, Prince Borghese, beginning with the statement: "The Pope has taken advantage of the liberty I allowed him at Savona to sow rebellion and disorder amongst my subjects." He went on to accuse the Pope of obstinacy and treachery. Napoleon defended himself to the French ecclesiastical committee in March 1811, in which he accused the Pope: "he has not merely attacked my authority; he has attacked the authority and welfare of the churches within the Empire." And later, in the same letter, "I am aware that one should render unto God the things that are God's. But the Pope is not God." Such statements indicate an imperious tone that Napoleon would not have used either in 1801 when the Concordat was signed, or for some time thereafter. While proceeding with force against the temporal power of the Pope and even against the symbols of the Pope's headship of the Roman Catholic Church, Napoleon urged attendance of divine worship and restored the elaborate ceremony of the mass in the Cathedral of Notre Dame. This was the side of religion that he believed necessary for the common people which, with the *Imperial Catechism*, tied religion to loyalty to Napoleon. The baptism of his infant as King of Rome, in full pomp on June 9, 1811, not only provided Napoleon with the legitimate heir he had desired, but had implications also for papal power, which however, because of the fall of Napoleon never eventuated.

A younger Napoleon and one whose ambitions had not blinded him to the greater and greater strain of battle would never have undertaken the Russian campaign. He should have learned from the bloody battles of Eylau and Friedland on the Prussian plains that the vast distances to be covered to overcome Russia would overtax his supply lines as well as require long marches for his foot soldiers. Already in 1811, Napoleon was preparing mentally for renewal of war, for he asked M. Barbier, his librarian, in December of that year, for the best books on Russian topography, and volumes on Charles XII of Sweden's campaigns in Poland and Russia. In a large measure, the Russian hard winter had been responsible for the Swedish defeat, but this forewarning did not deter Napoleon whose original campaign plans called for the defeat of Russia before winter set in. One wonders what the future history of Europe might have been if Napoleon's ambition had not driven him to overlook the great distance of Moscow from Paris, more than 3000 miles, and the tremendous problem of logistics this entailed! A younger Napoleon with a more controlled ambition, might have recognized that there were no longer unlimited resources of military manpower and that half his army was composed of units from satellites and allies whose loyalty could not always be assured. Napoleon was thinking less of the French people than of his own "gloire." His self-conceit warped his judgment.

Even earlier, Napoleon had tended to blame on his enemies the breaking of international law. This was the case in the issuance of the Berlin and Milan decrees of the Continental System. When Allied armies began to invade France, Napoleon accused them of atrocities against French civilians. He recommended publicity be given to eye-witness reports of such incidents as a means to stimulate patriotism in the defense of France. In a note to Prince Cambacères, he complained against reports of the minister of police that Napoleon was a "peace lover." He then stated, "I do want peace, but not a dishonorable peace, nor one which will force me within three months to take up arms again." Later in the same letter, he asserts that "No one is fonder of peace than I am." Here is a part of the beginning of the Napoleonic legend—that Napoleon stood for peace. Napoleon practically repeated the same words to General Caulaincourt, who had accompanied him to Russia in January 1814. In another letter to Caulaincourt a month later, Napoleon complained of the treatment of women as well as men civilians by the Allied invading forces. He claimed to have seen the atrocities himself after the passage of the enemy. A letter from Nogent, to the quartermaster-commissioner (also February 1814) sounded as if the retreating French soldiers who had obtained provisions during campaigns outside France, were having difficulty living off the land of Frenchmen, and were meeting opposition by their own countrymen. Napoleon still gave commands to make severe examples against random offenders in order to assure order, rather than terror.

If Napoleon appeared callous about army losses and too sure that all Frenchmen would rise and fight in his defense, he began to be aware that the imperial treasury was not inexhaustible. All along he had given careful attention to expenditures and collection of taxes. Already in August 1811, he gave instructions to General Duroc, grand marshal of the palace to cut down on expenditures for his wardrobe. Among the items were 48 waistcoats and breeches and 48 vests. All were to last three years. Among the miscellaneous items were scents, eau de cologne and a reducing mixture (Napoleon gained weight after 1809 when until 1812 he was more at court in Paris than on campaign). The following November, he was complaining of Josephine's extravagance. In the same month in a letter to Count Mollien, who was in charge of the treasury, he wanted to know if there was not some way to bring larger sums into the imperial treasury from gambling houses in Paris. In March 1812 Napoleon was asking that soup kitchens be set up to remedy food shortages suffered by the poor. He asked how 10 million francs could be raised to help the poor but did not suggest cutting the millions being spent on the army and on the court. There were overtones of "tax the rich" in many of his letters. In February 1813 he suggested economies in meals and also in the staff to serve them during his campaigns, thereby cutting expenses. Economy would not be the rule for the celebration of Emperor's Day on August 10, 1813, however. Twenty sous were to be distributed to each soldier, a *Te Deum* sung, and officers were to dine outdoors with their men. It would sound as if there were no shortage of gunpowder, for 100 gun salutes were to be fired after each toast, nor a lack of funds to pay for the salvos. Economic crisis intensified Napoleon's problems at this period.

Napoleon's affection for Marie Louise and gratitude for the heir she bore him dotted his official correspondence. There is a small volume by Frédéric Masson, entitled *Napoléon chez lui* which highlights the man and his family and his preoccupations as head of a household. Napoleon as a father, husband, lover, and a famous brother of Bonapartes, was a more vulnerable human being than his military dispatches, his civilian orders, or the propaganda picture of himself, which he took care to circulate, made him out to be. According to Metternich who observed him while Austrian ambassador to France, Napoleon was charming at home or in a small gathering, but overbearing and ill at ease at court.[3] Yet Napoleon created his court and surrounded himself with his appointed officials and officers. His pride in his son was reflected in a letter to the duke of Cadore written February 19, 1814. Marie Louise had sent Napoleon a portrait of the king of Rome in Polish costume. Napoleon expressed regret that the costume was not that of the French National Guard. He suggested, however, that if such a picture labeled "I pray to God for my Father and for France" could be engraved and circulated within forty-eight hours, "it would have an excellent effect."

Napoleon had early displayed his psychological understanding to win loyalty of his soldiers to make sacrifices and to undergo hardship. His terse reports of victory to the Directory contributed to Napoleon's reputation in the Italy campaign for the glory of France. His mastery of propaganda began to show itself in the Egyptian campaign when he minimized or suppressed losses, and publicized small victories. Upon his unexpected return to France, he was known as the hero of Italy and of Egypt. This publicity contributed to the collapse of opposition to the coup d'état of 18 Brumaire, and the plebiscites he sponsored on the consulate and the change to the Empire, despite manipulation, indicated the conviction of a great era for France under Napoleonic rule.

---

[3] Jacques Godechot, *Napoléon (Le Mémorial des Siècles),* "Napoleon vu par le Prince de Metternich," pp. 227–228, 236–237.

Statements about history to his minister of education, and the censorship of the press showed an increasing control of public opinion, by the publication of news favorable to Napoleon and suppression of opposition or even criticism. His reputation for invincibility spread, and was in large measure justified up to 1812, but increased control of news, especially with regard to the disaster in Russia, left the ordinary Frenchman ignorant of the real situation. The *Bulletins de la Grande Armée* published only what Napoleon wanted to be known. The Emperor of Austria recognized the psychological value of news bulletins slanted toward French victory and Napoleonic invincibility, but Napoleon's enemies were less skilled in propaganda. They had not consulted the citizenry on action, but only their close advisers and they did not follow the French Emperor's example.

In a letter to Francis I of Austria, on September 9, 1812, two days after the battle of Borodino, Napoleon asserted that Russian losses had been 40,000 to 50,000 men, whereas the Grand Army suffered only 6,000 to 10,000! When the retreat from Moscow began, however, he was acknowledging to his commanders and in official reports to the French government the disorganization of his retreating army, the necessity of foraging for supplies, and heavy losses. He advised his commanders to take measures to avert desertion and disorderly conduct.

When Napoleon could no longer wage successful warfare and had to sue for peace, he blamed the allies for delays and refusals of his peace offers. He was particularly bitter against England. His hostile opinion of England manifested early in his career, had not changed; but rather it had increased. After Waterloo, Napoleon hoped for magnanimity of the English but did not obtain it, his Anglophobia increased at Saint Helena.

An injustice is done to Napoleon if one studies only one facet of his character or career. He was a many-sided person, a man of great intelligence, boundless energy, and comprehensive interests. His reorganization of France, his financial measures, his educational institutions, his religious policy, and above all his codes lived on in spite of his defeat. This legacy revealed Napoleon the statesman as well as the warrior. Although there was opposition and some criticism of the first Empire and its head, the imperial censorship and police kept them in check, or from being publicized until after 1814 and 1815. There was no concerted opposition to Napoleon, and it was rather the vilification of Napoleon by the Allies and the Bourbons restored to power that led to acquiescence in the new regime.

THE LEGEND

Albert Sorel, author of the monumental volumes on *Europe and the French Revolution*, once said that there are always two histories—what happened and what people believed to have happened. Even before the fall of Napoleon, a Napoleonic legend began to take form. As a result of the 1969 celebrations of Napoleon's birth, the legend may be developing further.

As early as 1809, Lewis Goldsmith, an Englishman,[4] who derived some of his information from Talleyrand, wrote a bitter denunciation of Napoleon as a bloodthirsty man, the "ogre of Corsica." In his two-volume work, *Napoleon in Caricature* (1910), Alexander M. Broadley reproduced or described the derogatory cartoons appearing in France, but much more frequently in England and the conquered countries. Many of these were as much a distortion of reality as was the Napoleonic propaganda. Following the fall of Napoleon, the Bourbons hoped to win support of the French people for their regime by publications of this sort about Napoleon. One of the first was *De l'état de la France sous la domination de Napoléon Bonaparte* by Louis André Pichon. The best known work was probably Chateaubriand's *De Buonaparte et des Bourbons.* There were books depicting Napoleon as a constant warrior, who disregarded public welfare. His muzzling of the press resulting in the silence or exile of such writers as Benjamin Constant, Frederic Schoell, Alfred Beauchamps, and others, was emphasized. These portrayals of Napoleon came to be known as the black legend.

Napoleon himself was the greatest contributor to the Napoleonic legend. During his rule, he had taken great pains to publicize a favorable image of himself. His writings at Saint Helena reinforced the legend already begun, and tried to counteract the "black legend." The first edition of Napoleonic memoirs, entitled *Manuscrit de Sainte-Hélène* appeared in 1817. Although attributed to Napoleon, it is believed that the real author was Auguste Marmont, Madame de Staël, or a friend of hers. Napoleon dictated his genuine memoirs at Saint Helena, and the *Mémoirs* by Emanuel Las Cases, transcribing many conversations with Napoleon in exile, painted Napoleon as he wished to be known. These volumes, translated into many languages, made a fortune for their author. The breadth of topics of conversation revealed Napoleon's wide reading, his comprehensive intelligence, his humanitarianism, his concern for all people as against rulers, but soft-pedaled his tyrannical measures, his ambition and his incessant military campaigns. The undesirable side of his rule was attributed to his enemies. The Napoleonic legend took form: Napoleon the successful warrior, peacemaker, statesman, giant of his age.

Memoirs by those who shared Napoleon's exile at Saint Helena began to appear soon after Napoleon's death in 1821. Dr. Barry O'Meara, Madame Albine de Montholon, and much later, Henri Bertrand and Gaspard Gourgaud revealed their mutual jealousies, but also much about Napoleon. These volumes described Napoleon as a liberal, propagator of the reforms

---

[4] Godechot, *op. cit.,* pp. 358–394.

of 1789—the heir of the French Revolution. All these authors credited him with measures for liberty and equality and for the abolition of the feudal regime and depicted him as the restorer of order after the civil wars of the revolutionary period. This idealized picture contained some truths, but ignored both the work started during the revolutionary decade and the more dictatorial rule of Napoleon after 1810. Las Cases emphasized the human qualities of Napoleon. The other Saint Helena memoirs did criticize some of his measures, such as censorship and conscription. The authors either seemed unaware of the contradictions with their praise of Napoleon or ignored them in their over-all favorable portrait. After reading these memoirs, one should read the account by Sir Hudson Lowe,[5] the English commander at Saint Helena, of his relations with Napoleon. He did not have an enviable task, and Napoleon and his companions did not make it an easy one. Even his attempts to help were misinterpreted and rebuffed.

Albert Guérard, in his volume on Napoleon III, summed up the contributions of Saint Helena writings to the growth of the Napoleonic legend:

> With his unique sense of strategy, he had massed his forces on two points: that he was a martyr, and that he was a martyr for democracy. Neither claim was wholly true; but both, especially in combination, were extremely effective. . . . Napoleon remembered that he was democracy incarnate only after the legitimate sovereigns had outlawed him. . . . But, as all hope of a second return faded away, he saw that his one chance before posterity was to pose as the champion of the people. . . . Thus he shaped his own myth, not as a proud conqueror, but as the organizer of a free Europe assuming leadership in a united Europe. In this new perspective his fall appeared the defeat, not of tyranny, but of the Rights of Man.
>
> Such was the gospel that was preached by the Saint Helena writers, Gourgaud, O'Meara, Las Cases. . . . It spread in all directions, to the bourgeoisie and to the poets; the masses were the last to be affected.[6]

These same works presented Napoleon as an agent for peace. If he waged war, it had been forced upon him by perfidious enemies. If the Consulate justified this picture, his many subsequent campaigns and policies that brought on renewals of war had been neutralized by his propaganda on French *gloire*. Civilians with grievances, disgruntled office holders, military officers dismissed, draft-dodgers, deserters, were silent opponents. In view of widespread illiteracy in rural areas and a controlled press, it may well be

---

[5] See Godechot, *op. cit.,* pp. 395–424. This volume also gives appraisals of Napoleon drawn from the writings of Don Manuel Godoy, Sir Walter Scott, and William Ellery Channing.

[6] Albert Guérard, *Napoleon III, an Interpretation* (Cambridge, Mass.: Harvard University Press, 1943), pp. 30–31.

that the French peasants knew very little about the Napoleonic Wars, except as conscription affected a given locality or until the invasion of French soil in 1814, when those in the fighting areas had to cope with retreating French armies as well as foreign invaders. Ten years of building up the greatness of Napoleon and the Empire, with its outward pomp and circumstance created a favorable image that was only changed in some degree by the Bourbons and the Allies who hoped to win the French people over to the new order by blackening Napoleon. The people were confused, more than convinced. They failed to rise in opposition, but some of the leaders who had served Napoleon, such as Talleyrand, who brought about the restoration, did.

Some writings of the restoration period, other than those emerging from Saint Helena, began faintly to voice sympathy for Napoleon. Pierre Jeanne de Béranger's poems in 1818 *Champs d'Asile* written before Napoleon died and one celebrating the evacuation of French territory by the allies after France had complied with the reparations clauses of the second Treaty of Paris might arouse nostalgia for the great days of the Empire. But far stronger sympathy for the former emperor is aroused by Béranger's poems written in 1821 as a part of *Le Cinq Mai* (about an old soldier stopping at Saint Helena at the time of the death of Napoleon), *Le Vieux Drapeau,* and *Le Vieux Sergeant.* Histories of the Revolutionary and Napoleonic periods published in the 1820's rehabilitated the Revolution and to a similar degree the Napoleonic era: Louis Adolphe Thiers published in 1825, 1827, and François Mignet, in 1824.

The Napoleonic legend which began before the fall of Napoleon, and was augmented by writings from Saint Helena and by other writings during the Restoration era, received new impetus during the reign of Louis Philippe after 1830. Louis Philippe hoped to gain support for his own regime by measures reviving the age of Napoleon. He had Napoleon's statue put back on the top of the Vendôme Column, from which it had been removed during the Restoration, and in 1840 he had Napoleon's remains removed from Saint Helena and held a grandiose ceremony for their burial in the rotunda of the Hotel des Invalides in Paris. He also completed the Arc de Triomphe, begun by Napoleon. Although the arch aimed to commemorate Napoleonic military greatness, the sculpture most often reproduced from its pictured history is the one representing the French Revolution François Rudé's *Marseillaise,* rather than Napoleon. The location of the tomb of the unknown soldier of World War I under the arch has led to other associations in the twentieth century than those linked with Napoleon.

The Versailles Palace had been neglected for some time. Louis Philippe converted it to an historical museum, dedicated to France's greatness, but more associated with royalty than with the Revolution and Napoleon. During the French Revolution, the Pantheon (Church of St. Geneviève) had been a hall of fame, but the church was restored during the Restoration. Louis Philippe again secularized it, and the Pantheon remains to this day a hall of fame at first, of the revolutionary era, now of all French history.

At the same time that Louis Philippe contributed to the Napoleonic legend by these moves, he appeared to have checkmated Louis Napoleon's bid to revive the empire. Son of Louis Bonaparte and of Hortense de Beauharnais, Josephine's daughter, Louis Napoleon lived in exile in Germany and Switzerland. He trained in the Swiss army and participated briefly in *Carbonari* efforts in Italy, and wrote sympathetic letters to Polish patriots. Louis Napoleon was thoroughly convinced that a return of Napoleonic rule would promote the prosperity and grandeur that France enjoyed during his uncle's regime. In 1836 at Strasbourg Louis Napoleon made an unsuccessful attempt to return to France but when the soldiers and inhabitants failed to come to his support, he slipped back across the Swiss border.

In 1839, on the eve of a second attempt to gain power, Louis Napoleon published a pamphlet, *Les Idées napoléonniennes.* Although he aimed to win support for himself, the volume praised Napoleon I and renewed the legend that Napoleon favored liberty, equality, order, prosperity, and peace. Near the end of the pamphlet, Louis Napoleon said "In conclusion, let us repeat, the Napoleonic Idea is not one of war, but a social, industrial, commercial idea, and which concerns all mankind."

In 1840 Louis Napoleon made his second attempt at Boulogne near the statue Napoleon erected in connection with the invasion of England that never materialized. This time, Louis Napoleon was arrested and imprisoned in the chateau of Ham in the north of France. No one would have predicted at that time that he would be elected president of the second French Republic eight years later. During his imprisonment at Ham, Louis Napoleon received visitors and carried on a wide correspondence, building his own legend, but he was no more satisfied to remain there than his uncle had been at the island of Elba. When in 1845 Louis Philippe refused to allow Louis Napoleon to visit his dying father, despite a promise to return, Louis Napoleon took matters in his own hands and escaped disguised as a workman. His absence was concealed until evening, when it was too late to prevent his crossing the Channel to England. The Napoleonic legend was not dead, but took on a new lease of life, carefully intertwined with the growing legend of Louis Napoleon.

The greatness of Napoleon I was constantly in the background of Louis Napoleon as he campaigned for the presidency in 1848 and also when by a *coup d'état* he established the Second Empire in 1852. Although Victor Hugo had contributed to the memory of Napoleon I, in 1830, by his poem *Les Chants du crespuscule,* in which he compared the bravery of the revolutionary generation of 1830 with that of their fathers in Napoleon's army, Hugo became the bitter enemy of Louis Napoleon. His long poems, written in exile on the Channel Islands, *Le Châtiment* and *Napoléon le petit,* built up the uncle by comparison with the nephew. The Imperial Court of Napoleon III, his foreign policy, and many domestic policies were inspired by or interpretations of Napoleon I's regime. The beautification of Paris stemmed from the work of Napoleon I. The Paris of today with its grand boulevards, associated with the work of the Baron Haussmann, comes in large part from changes made during the Second Empire. Memoirs of Napoleon were published, documents edited, and paintings of his battles hung in the salons of the Second Empire.

It is not necessary to trace the subsequent development of the Napoleonic legend, but a few highlights would serve as a background of the bicentennial celebration of Napoleon's birth in 1969. It was inevitable that there be an eclipse of the legend after the fall of the Second Empire in 1871, but there was much less detraction from Napoleon I than from his nephew. Despite the establishment of the Third Republic, there were more memoirs of the Napoleonic era, and such accounts as the *Notebooks of Captain Coignet,* who retired to civilian life after Waterloo, romanticized the Grand Empire. Coignet remembered only the bravery of Napoleon, his admiration for his general and not the hardships and dangers of the campaigns. Edmond Rostand's *L'Aiglon* — the name given to Napoleon's son — first performed in 1900, included a scene where the young son, prisoner in Austria, recited to his tutor all of Napoleon's battles. The role of l'Aiglon was made famous by Sarah Bernhardt. This play is still given each year and attended by hordes of school children as well as adults; thus, the legend is kept alive.

The romanticized painting, "Retreat from Moscow", by Meissonier has already been mentioned. Toulouse-Lautrec's famous lithograph of Napoleon on horseback, with a French marshal and a Muslim behind him, also contributed to the legend.

Ever since the First Empire, the training of French army officers has included a thorough study of Napoleonic battles. Although weapons have changed, lessons can be learned from his successes and his defeats. Napoleon's reputation as one of the great warriors of history will go down in history with those of Alexander the Great and Julius Caesar, both of whom Napoleon greatly admired.

The year, 1969, may revive the Napoleonic legend or even bring to light new features of it. As a part of the bicentennial of the birth of Napoleon, public celebrations, historical colloquia, and expositions were organized in France. Four exhibits of note were held in Paris, one at the Grand Palais, which depicted *La Gloire,* one at the Bibliotheque Nationale built around the Napoleonic legend (and its refutation), one at the Archives Nationales, *Napoleon tel qu'en lui-même,* and one at the Museum of the Legion of Honor, *Napoleon et la Légion d'honneur.* In other parts of France there were appropriate ceremonies and additional exhibitions. Outside

Paris, there was a new, augmented exhibit at Malmaison, Josephine's residence; there were two in Ajaccio, the capital of Corsica, and one on the Ile d'Aix, in the west of France, where Napoleon stayed until he went to Saint Helena. These exhibits all capitalize on the diverse activity and rich life of the Emperor of the *Grand Empire* and his era. The most spectacular was that at the Grand Palais and the one that probably impressed the general public the most. On view were the huge portraits, original texts of proclamations, treaties, and correspondence, that are France's legacy. The elegance of the court was conveyed by the furniture, tableware, objects of art, costumes, jewelled swords and imperial necklaces, rings, and bracelets. The contrasts with life in present-day France may have created a new longing for the *gloire* of the First Empire.

Ever since the Napoleonic period, there have been defenders and detractors of the Corsican-born leader. One of his best known defenders is Louis Madelin, who argued his case in many volumes. Historians of the revolutionary decade have been critical of Napoleon; they assert that he betrayed his early loyalty to the ideals of the Revolution. Historians from other countries have usually been less complimentary to Napoleon than his fellow Frenchmen, especially those from countries that suffered conquest during his era. Some, however, have recognized his role in bringing to an end the old regime in their country and his role in laying the groundwork for their country's modern transformation.

Is the picture of Napoleon drawn by his Russian enemy, Count Rostopchin, a fair appraisal of the French Emperor?

> Napoleon was in my eyes a great general after his campaign in Italy and Egypt, benefactor of France when he stemmed the French Revolution during the Consulate; a despot dangerous for Europe as soon as he made himself emperor; insatiable conqueror until 1812; man drunk with Glory and blinded to fortune as soon as he undertook the conquest of Russia; a genius defeated at Fontainbleau and Waterloo; and at Saint Helena, a Jeremiah prophet.[7]

This portrayal was by a contemporary, an enemy of Napoleon. In the words of Jacques Godechot, "The legend is, however, tenacious. The Napoleon who is popular today is the Napoleon of the legend rather than the Napoleon of history."

---

[7] Godechot, *op. cit.*, from Mémoirs of Rostopchin, p. 323.

Bibliography

BIBLIOGRAPHICAL NOTE

There is a wealth of primary source materials in French and foreign archives and libraries, and well over 200,000 books have been written about Napoleon and the Napoleonic period.

With respect to the primary sources, see Jacques Godechot, *L'Europe et l'Amérique à l'époque napoléonienne* (Paris, 1967), pp. 16–19, which cites the principal collections, series at the Archives Nationales, other French deposits of archives, and notes about collections outside of France. Anyone studying Napoleon should read the extensive critique of published editions of Napoleon's memoirs and correspondence given by Maximilien Vox, *Correspondance de Napoléon: Six cent lettres de Napoléon de travail, 1806–1810* (Paris, 1943). He casts doubt upon the authenticity of many letters ascribed to Napoleon. See also *Revue de l'Institut Napoléon.*

Two recent issues of the *Annales historiques de la Révolution française* have provided additional information of value to the social and economic material on the Napoleonic era. The issue of April–June 1969 treated the disappearance of serfdom outside of France. The entire issue of January–March 1970 is devoted to the Napoleonic period. In each issue specialists have written the articles. Jacques Godechot gave an overview of Napoleonic retention and modification of changes started during the Revolutionary decade.

COLLECTED BIBLIOGRAPHIES

Davois, Gustave, *Bibliographie napoléonienne française jusqu'en 1908*, 3 vols. (Paris, 1909-1911).

Geyl, Pieter, *Napoleon For and Against* (New Haven, Conn.: Yale University Press, 1945).

Godechot, Jacques, *L'Europe et l'Amérique à l'époque napoléonienne* (Paris, 1967). For reference to laws, minutes of legislative bodies, administrative texts, and newspapers, see pp. 22–24.

Kircheisen, Friedrich M., *Bibliographie des Napoleonischen Zeitalters*, 2 vols. (Berlin, 1902); published in French as *Bibliographie du temps de Napoléon*, 2 vols. (Paris, 1908–1912); published in English as *Bibliography of the Times of Napoleon*, 1 vol. (London, 1902).

Stewart, John Hall, *France, 1715–1815, A Guide to Materials in Cleveland* (Cleveland, Ohio: Western Reserve University Press, 1942).

PRIMARY SOURCES

WRITINGS OF NAPOLEON

Early Works

Clisson et Eugénie, in *Le nouveau fémina* (Paris, 1955).

Le Souper de Beaucaire (Paris, 1793).

Masque prophète, le comte d'Essex, ed. by Frédéric Masson (Paris, 1895).

Memoirs

Mémoires pour servir à l'histoire de France sous Napoléon, écrits à Sainte-Hélène, sous la dictée de l'Empereur, par les généraux qui ont partagé sa captivité et publiés sur les manuscrits entièrement corrigés de sa main, 6 vols. (Paris, 1823–1825); 7 vols. (London, 1823–1824); published in English, 7 vols. (London, 1823–1824). For various shortened forms and excerpts see listings in John Hall Stewart, *France, 1715–1815*.

Correspondence and Miscellaneous Collections

The Bonaparte Letters and Despatches . . . from His Private Cabinet, 2 vols. (London, 1846).

The Confidential Correspondence of Napoleon Bonaparte with His Brother Joseph, Sometime King of Spain, 2 vols. (New York, 1856).

Correspondance de Napoléon Ier publié par l'ordre de l'Empereur Napoléon III, 32 vols. (Paris, 1858–1870).

The Corsican (Boston: Houghton Mifflin Company, 1910). Selections of documents and sources.

Lettres de Napoléon à Josephine . . . et à sa fille, 2 vols. (Paris, 1833).

Lettres inédites de Napoléon à Marie Louise, 1810–1814, ed., Louis Madelin (Paris, 1935); published in English (New York, 1935).

Unpublished Correspondence of Napoleon I Preserved in the War Archives, ed. by Ernest Picard and Louis Tuetey (Paris, 1912); published in English, 3 vols., trans. by Louise S. Houghton (New York: Duffield and Company, 1913).

Bourgeat, Jacques, *Lettres à Josephine* (Paris, 1941); published in English, trans. by Henry F. Hall (London and New York, 1901).

de Brotonne, L., *Lettres inédites de Napoléon Ier (an VII–1815)* (Paris, 1898).

Chuquet, A., *Inédits napoléoniens*, 2 vols. (Paris, 1913–1919).

———, *Ordres et apostilles de Napoléon, 1799–1815*, 4 vols. (Paris, 1911–1912).

Herold, J. Christopher, *The Mind of Napoleon* (New York: Columbia University Press, 1955).

Lecestre, L., ed., *Lettres inédites de Napoléon Ier (an VIII–1815)*, 2 vols. (Paris, 1897).

Masson, Frédéric, *Napoléon, manuscrits inédits*, 2d ed. (Paris, 1908).

Roy, Claude, *La Vie de Napoléon racontée par Napoléon* (Paris, 1955).

Thompson, J. M., *Napoleon Self-revealed* (New York: Houghton Mifflin Company, 1934).

Tulard, Jean, *Proclamations, ordres du jour, bulletins de la Grande Armée* (Paris, 1965).

Vox, Maximilien, *Six cent lettres de Napoléon de travail, 1806–1810* (Paris, 1943). The editorial note about the authenticity of prior collections is indispensable.

WRITINGS OF PERSONS WITH NAPOLEON AT SAINT HELENA

Antomarchi, Francesco, *The Last Days of Napoleon*, 2 vols. (London, 1826). The author was a doctor who attended Napoleon at Saint Helena.

Bertrand, Général Henri Gratien de, *Cahiers de Sainte-Hélène*, 3 vols. (Paris, 1949–1958).

Bourrienne, Louis A. F. de, *Mémoires de M. de Bourrienne, . . .* , 10 vols. (Paris, 1829); published in English, 3 vols. (Edinburgh, 1830); 4-vol. ed. in 2 (London, 1836); 4 vol. ed. (New York, 1891).

Forsyth, W., *History of the Captivity of Napoleon at St. Helena*, 3 vols. (London, 1853).

Gourgaud, Général Gaspard, *Journal de Sainte-Hélène*, 2 vols. (Paris, 1944); published in English as *The St. Helena Journal of General Baron Gourgaud*, trans. by Sydney Gillard (London, 1932).

Las Cases, Emmanuel, Comte de, *Mémorial de Sainte-Hélène*, 8 vols. (Paris, 1832); there is another undated 4-vol. edition; published in English as *Memoirs of the Life, Exile and Conversations with the Emperor Napoleon*, 4 vols. (London, 1825); 4 vol. ed. (Philadelphia, 1823).

Lowe, H., *Histoire de la captivité de Napoléon à Sainte-Hélène, d'après les documents officiels et les manuscrits de Sir Hudson*, 4 vols. (Paris, 1854).

Marchand, Comte, L. J. M. de, *Mémoires de Marchand, premier valet de chambre de l'empereur*, 2 vols. (Paris, 1952–1955).

Montholon, Général Comte Charles, *Récits de la captivité de l'empereur Napoléon*, 2 vols. (Paris, 1847).

O'Meara, B. E., *Napoleon in Exile*, 2 vols. (London, 1822).

CORRESPONDENCE OF NAPOLEON'S RELATIVES

Bonaparte, Jérome, *Mémoires et correspondance du roi Jérome et de la reine Catherine*, 7 vols. (Paris, 1861–1866).

Bonaparte, Joseph, *Mémoires et correspondance politique et militaire du roi Joseph*, 10 vols. (Paris, 1854–1858).

Bonaparte, Lucien, *Lucien Bonaparte et ses mémoires, 1775–1840*, edited by Henri F. T. Jung, 3 vols. (Paris, 1882–1883); published in English as *Lucien Bonaparte and his Memoirs* for 1792-Year VIII (New York, 1836).

Josephine, Empress, *Mémoires et correspondance de l'impératrice Josephine* (Paris, 1820).

Marie Louise, *The Private Diaries of Marie Louise, Wife of Napoleon I*, ed. by Frédéric Masson (London, 1922).

See also Stewart, *op. cit.*, pp. 299–301 for biographies of Elisa, Caroline, Pauline, and Napoleon's mother Letitia.

MEMOIRS OF OTHER PROMINENT CONTEMPORARIES

Caulaincourt, Armand de, *Mémoires* . . . , 3 vols. (Paris, 1933); vol. 1 published in English as *With Napoleon in Russia* (New York: Grosset & Dunlap, Inc., 1935); an additional volume has been published as *No Peace with Napoleon* (New York: William Morrow & Company, Inc., 1936).

Constant, Louis C. W., *Memoirs*, 4 vols. (London, 1896). The author was Napoleon's head valet.

Fouché, Joseph (Duc d'Otrante), *Mémoires*, 2 vols. (Paris, 1824); published in English, trans. by C. Knight (London and New York, 1825).

Godoy, Alvarez, *Memorias*, 2 vols. in Spanish (Madrid, 1908–1909); published in French in 4 vols. (Paris, 1836); published in English, 2 vols. (London, 1836).

Metternich-Winneburg, Prince Clemens de, *Mémoires*, 8 vols. (Paris, 1881–1886); published in English in 5 vols. (New York, 1880–1882).

Staël-Holstein, Baronne de, *Mémoires*, undated edition, Paris; published in English (London, 1821).

Talleyrand-Périgord, Charles, *Mémoires*, 5 vols. published by the Duc de Broglie (Paris, 1891–1892); published in English, trans. by R. Ledos de Beaufort (New York, 1891–1892).

SECONDARY WORKS

GENERAL REFERENCES

Aulard, Alphonse, et al., *Napoléon*, vol. IX of E. Lavisse and A. Rambaud, *Histoire de France* (Paris, 1917).

Bruun, Geoffrey, *Europe and the French Imperium, 1799–1814,* (New York: Harper & Row, Publishers, 1938).

Cambridge Modern History, vol. IX, *Napoleon,* A. W. Ward et al., eds. (London: Macmillan & Co., Ltd., 1906).

Droz, Jacques, *Histoire diplomatique de 1648 à 1919,* 2d ed. (Paris, 1959).

Fugier, R., *La Révolution française et l'empire napoléonien,* vol. IV, *Histoire des relations internationales* (Paris, 1954).

Gaubert, H., *Conspirateurs au temps de Napoléon Ier* (Paris, 1962).

Gershoy, Leo, *The French Revolution and Napoleon,* 2d ed. (New York: Alfred A. Knopf, 1964).

Godechot, Jacques, *La Contre-Révolution* (Paris, 1961).

———, *Napoléon et l'Europe à l'époque napoléonienne,* Clio series (Paris, 1967).

Goodspeed, D. J., *Napoleon's Eighty Days* (Boston: Houghton Mifflin Company, 1965).

Gottschalk, Louis, *The Era of the French Revolution, 1715–1815* (Boston: Houghton Mifflin Company, 1929).

Herold, J. Christopher, *The Horizon Book of the Age of Napoleon* (New York: Harper & Row, Publishers, 1963)

Hobsbawm, E. J., *The Age of Revolution, Europe from 1789 to 1848* (London: Weidenfeld & Nicholson, Ltd. 1962).

Holtman, Robert B., *The Napoleonic Revolution* (Philadelphia: J. B. Lippincott Co., 1967).

Kircheisen, F. M., *Napoléon I, sein Leben und sein Zeit,* 9 vols. (Munich, 1911–1934); published in English in 1 vol. as *Napoleon the First,* trans by Henry St. Lawrence (New York: Harcourt, Brace & World, Inc., 1932).

Lefebvre, Georges, *Napoléon,* vol. XIV of *Peuples et civilisations* (Paris, 1965); published in English in 2 vols.: *From Brumaire to Tilsit,* trans. by Henry F. Stockhold (New York: Columbia University Press, 1968), and *From Tilsit to Waterloo,* trans. by J. E. Anderson (*idem,* 1969).

Lucas-Dubreton, J. *La France de Napoléon* (Paris, 1948).

Madelin, Louis, *Histoire du Consulat et de l'Empire,* 16 vols. (Paris, 1936–1954); published in English in 2 vols.: *The Consulate and the Empire,* trans. by E. F. Buckley (New York, 1932–1933).

Mistler, Jean, ed., Vol. I, *Un Général de fortune,* Vol. II, *La Conquête du pouvoir* (Lausanne, 1969).

The New Cambridge Modern History, vol. IX, C. W. Crawley, ed., *War and Peace in an Age of Upheaval, 1793–1830* (London: Cambridge University Press, 1965).

Pariset, G., *Le Consulat et l'Empire,* vol. III of *Histoire de France contemporaine* (Paris, 1921).

Pinkney, David H., *Napoleon: Historical Enigma* (Lexington, Mass., D. C. Heath and Co., 1969).

Six, G. *Les généraux de la Révolution et de l'Empire* (Paris, 1947).

Sorel, A., *L'Europe et la Révolution française,* 8 vols. (Paris, 1885–1904).

Thiers, L. A., *Histoire du consulat et de l'Empire, faisant suite à l'histoire de la Révolution française,* new ed., 21 vols. (Paris, 1845–1874); published in English in 20 vols.: *History of the Consulate and the Empire of France under Napoleon,* trans. by D. Forbes Campbell (London, 1893–1894); 12 vol. ed., trans. by D. Forbes Campbell and John Stibbing (Philadelphia, 1893–1894).

Thiry, J., *Napoléon Bonaparte,* 16 vols., originally published 1800-1808, 1814–1816 (Paris, 1946–1964).

Villat, L., *La Révolution et l'Empire,* vol. II (Paris, 1936).

BIOGRAPHIES OF NAPOLEON

Aubrey, Octave, *Napoléon* (Paris, 1936), published in English as *Napoleon, Soldier and Emperor,* trans. by Arthur Livingston (Philadelphia: J. B. Lippincott Co., 1938).

Bainville, Jacques, *Napoléon* (Paris, 1931), published in English, trans. by Hamish Miles, (London: Jonathan Cape, Ltd., 1932; Boston: Little, Brown & Company, 1933).

Castelot, André, *Bonaparte,* vol. I; *Napoléon,* vol. II (Paris, 1969).

Driault, E., *La vraie figure de Napoléon* (Paris, 1928).

Fournier, Auguste, *Napoleon I. Eine Biographie,* 2d ed., 3 vols. (Vienna, 1904–1906); English edition, Edward Bourne, ed., *Napoleon I: A Biography* (New York: Henry Holt, 1903).

Godechot, Jacques, *Napoléon* in "Le Mémorial des Siècles" (Paris, 1969). Text and excerpts from Metternich and other contemporaries.

Markham, Felix, *Napoleon* (New York: The Macmillan Co., 1963).

Masson, Frédéric, *Napoléon et sa famille,* 13 vols. (Paris, 1897–1919).

Masson, F. and Biagi, G., *Napoléon inconnu,* 2 vols. (Paris, 1895).

Rose, J. Holland, *Life of Napoleon I* (London: Macmillan & Co., Ltd., 1902; New York: The Macmillan Company, 1901–1902).

Stendhal, *Vie de Napoléon* (Paris, 1876); pub. in English as *The Life of Napoleon,* trans. by Richard N. Coe (London: Rodale Books, Inc., 1956).

Tarlé, E., *Napoléon,* orig. Russian ed. (Warsaw, 1937); published in French, trans. by Charles Steber (Paris, 1937); published in English, trans. by John Cournos (New York: Knight Publishers, Inc., 1937).

Thompson, J. M., *Napoleon Bonaparte, his Rise and Fall* (London: Oxford University Press, 1952).

Vox, Maximilien, *Napoléon* (Paris, 1959); published in English, trans. by Maurice Thornton (London and New York: Grove Press, Inc., 1960).

BIOGRAPHIES OF NAPOLEON'S CONTEMPORARIES

Aubrey, P., *Monge* (Paris, 1954)

Bertaut, J., *Marie Louise* (Paris, 1940).

Brinton, Crane, *The Lives of Talleyrand* (New York: W. W. Norton & Co., Inc., 1936).

Castelot, André, *Le Fils de l'Empereur* (Paris, 1962); published in English as *The King of Rome*, trans. by Robert Baldick (New York: Harper & Row, Publishers, 1960).

Chambrun, Marie de, *Le roi de Rome* (Paris, 1941).

Cole, Hubert, *Josephine* (New York: The Viking Press, Inc., 1963).

Connolly, Owen, *Gentle Bonaparte: A Biography of Joseph, Napoleon's Elder Brother* (New York: The Macmillan Co., 1968).

Decaux, Alain, *Letizia* (Paris, 1949).

Garnier, J. P., *Murat, roi de Naples* (Paris, 1959).

Geer, Walter, *Napoleon and His Family*, 3 vols. (New York: Coward-McCann, Inc., 1927–1929)

Guillemin, H., *Madame de Staël, Benjamin Constant et Napoléon* (Paris, 1959).

Hautecoeur, L., *Louis David* (Paris, 1954).

Knapton, E. J., *Empress Josephine* (Cambridge, Mass.: Harvard University Press, 1963).

Labarre de Raillicourt, D., *Louis Bonaparte* (Paris, 1963).

Lucas-Dubreton, J., *Murat* (Paris, 1944).

Madelin, M., *Fouché, 1759–1821*, 2d ed. (Paris, 1955).

Nabonne, Bernard, *Bernadotte* (Paris, 1946).

———, *Pauline Bonaparte* (Paris, 1963).

Oddie, E. M., pseud. (Elinor May O'Donoghue), *Marie Louise*, Empress of France, Duchess of Parma (New York: Charles Scribner's Sons, 1931).

Reinhard, Marcel, *Le Grand Carnot*, vol. II (Paris, 1952).

Saint-Marc, P., *Le maréchal Marmont, duc de Raguse* (Paris, 1957)

Stirling, Monica, *A Pride of Lions. A Portrait of Napoleon's Mother* (London: Collins, Sons & Co., Ltd., 1961).

Tarlé, E., *Talleyrand* (Moscow, 1958).

Turquan, J., *Caroline, soeur de Napoléon* (Paris, 1954).

———, *Elisa et Pauline, soeurs de Napoléon* (Paris, 1954).

Warner, Oliver, *The Life and Letters of Vice Admiral Collingwood* (New York: Oxford University Press, 1968).

Wright, Constance, *Daughter to Napoleon*, Hortense (New York: Holt, Rinehart & Winston, Inc., 1961).

NAPOLEON AND EUROPE

Acton, Harold, *The Bourbons of Naples* (London: Metheun & Co., Ltd., 1956).

Anderson, E. N., *Nationalism and the Cultural Crisis in Prussia* (New York: Holt, Rinehart & Winston, Inc., 1922).

Arcola, M., *Los Origines de la España contemporanea*, 2 vols. (Madrid, 1959).

Askenazy, S., *Le Prince Joseph Poniatowski, 1763–1813* (Paris, 1923).

Berengo, Marino, *L'agricultura veneta dalla cadute della Repubblica all'unità* (Milan, 1963).

Botzenhart, Manfred, *Metternichs Pariser Botschafterzeit* (Munster, 1967).

Carlsson, E. T. Hojer, *Den Svenska utrikenspolitikens historia*, vol. III (Stockholm, 1954).

Chorley, Patrick, *Oil, Silk and Enlightenment. Economic Problems in 18th Century Naples* (Naples, 1965).

Clauders, Anna C., *American Commerce as Affected by the Wars of the French Revolution and Napoleon* (Philadelphia: Kelley Publishers, 1932).

Connelly, Owen, *Napoleon's Satellite Kingdoms* (New York: The Free Press, 1963).

Coquelle, P., *Napoléon et l'Angleterre* (Paris, 1904).

Criault, E., *Napoléon et l'Europe*, 5 vols. (Paris, 1910–1927)

Dard, E., *Napoléon et Talleyrand* (Paris, 1936)

Devleeshouwer, R., Droz, J., Dufraisse, R., and Haak, J. *Les Pays sous domination française, 1799–1814* (Paris, 1968).

Dunan, M., *Napoléon et l'Allemagne* (Paris, 1942).

Ford, G. S., *Stein and the Era of Reforms in Prussia, 1807–1815* (Princeton, N.J.: Princeton University Press, 1922)

Fugier, André, *Histoire des rélations internationales*, vol. IV, *La révolution et l'Empire napoléonien* (Paris, 1954).

————, *Napoléon et l'Espagne*, 2 vols. (Paris, 1929–1930).

————, *Napoléon et l'Italie* (Paris, 1947).

Geoffrey de Grandmaison, Charles Alexandre, *L'Espagne et Napoléon*, 3 vols. (Paris, 1908–1931).

Grochulska, Barbara, "La structure économique du duché de Varsovie," *Annales historiques de la Révolution française,* July–September, 1964 pp. 349–363.

Halecki, O., ed., *The Cambridge History of Poland* (London: Cambridge University Press, 1941).

Handelsmann, Marceli, *Napoléon et la Pologne* (Paris, 1909).

Haumant, E., *La Formation de la Yougoslavie* (Paris, 1930).

Heckscher, E. F., *The Continental System* (Oxford: Clarendon Press, 1922).

Heriot, Angus, *The French in Italy* (London: Chatto & Windus, Ltd., 1957).

Kohn, Hans, *Prelude to Nation-States* (Princeton, N.J.: D. Van Nostrand Company, Inc., 1967).

Langsam, W. C., *The Napoleonic Wars and German Nationalism in Austria* (New York: Columbia University Press, 1930).

Lebel, G., *La France et les principautés danubiennes* (Paris, 1955).

Lemmi, F., *L'età Napoleonica* (Milan, 1938).

Lobanov-Rostovsky, A., *Russia and Europe, 1789–1825* (Durham, N.C.: Duke University Press, 1947)

Lovett, Gabriel H., *Napoleon and the Birth of Modern Spain*, 2 vols. (New York: New York University Press, 1965).

Lyon, E. W., *Louisianian French Diplomacy* (Norman, Okla.: University of Oklahoma Press, 1933).

Madelin, L., *Le Rome de Napoléon, la domination française à Rome de 1809 à 1814* (Paris, 1904).

Maurois, A., Chastenet, J., Huyghe, R., and Dunan, Marcel, *Napoléon et l'Empire*, 2 vols. (Paris, 1968).

Mowat, R. B., *Diplomacy of Napoleon* (London: Edward Arnold & Co., 1924).

Mylonas, G., *The Balkan States, An Introduction to Their History* (Washington, D.C.: Public Affairs Press, 1947).

Nowell, Charles E., *A History of Portugal* (New York: Van Nostrand-Reinhold Books, 1952).

Pingaud, A., *La domination française dans l'Italie du nord, 1790–1805*, 2 vols. (Paris, 1914).

Puraye, P., *Liège sous l'Empire* (Paris, 1954).

Puryear, V. J., *Napoleon and the Dardanelles* (Berkeley, Calif.: University of California Press, 1951).

Richardson, A. E., *Georgian England . . . 1700–1820* (London: B. T. Batsford, Ltd., 1931).

Robert, A., *L'idée nationale autrichienne et les guerres de Napoléon* (Paris, 1933).

Roessler, H., *Oesterreichs Kampf um Deutschlands Befreiung . . . (1805–1815)*, 2 vols. (2d ed., Vienna, 1947).

Rogger, H., *National Consciousness in Eighteenth Century Russia* (Cambridge, Mass.: Harvard University Press, 1960).

Rota, E., *Il problema italiano dal 1700 al 1815* (Milan, 1938).

Seeley, J., *Life and Times of Stein. Germany and Prussia in the Napoleonic Age*, 3 vols. (London, 1879).

Shanahan, William O., *Prussian Military Reforms, 1786–1813* (New York: AMS Press, Inc., 1945).

Sorel, A., *L'Europe et la Révolution française,* 8 vols. (Paris, 1885–1904)
Srbik, H. von, *Metternich, der Staatsmann und der Mensch,* 2 vols. (Munich, 1925).
Tarlé, E., *Le blocus continental et le royaume d'Italie* (Paris, 1928).
Tommila, Paivio, *La Finlande dans la politique européenne en 1809–1815* (Helsinki, 1962).
Vandal, Albert, *Napoléon et Alexandre I,* 3 vols. (Paris, 1891–1896).
Van Houtte, J. A., et al., *Algeemene Geschidenis der Nederlanden,* vol. IX of a 12-vol. ed. (Utrecht, 1956).
Von Finckenstein, *Die Entwickling der Landwirtschaft in Preussen und Deutschland, 1800 bis 1930* (1960)

POLITICAL INSTITUTIONS

Bourdon, Jean, *La Constitution de l'an VIII* (Rodez, France, 1941).
———, *La réforme judicaire,* 2 vols. (Rodez, France, 1941).
Brisset, Jacqueline, *L'adoption de la communauté comme régime légal dans le Code Civil* (Paris: Presses Universitaires Françaises, 1967).
Chevallier, J. J., *Histoire des institutions politiques de 1789 à nos jours* (Paris, 1952).
Durand, Charles, *L'exercise de la fonction législative de 1800 à 1814* (Aix-en-Provence, 1955).
———, *Études sur le Conseil d'État napoléonien* (Paris, 1949).
———, *Le fonctionnement du Conseil d'État napoléonien* (Gap, France, 1955).
Garaud, M., *Histoire générale du droit privé française de 1799 à 1804* (Paris, 1953).
Gobert, A., *L'opposition des assemblées pendant le Consulat, 1800–1804* (Paris, 1925).
Godechot, Jacques, *Les Institutions de la France sous la Révolution et l'Empire* (1st ed., Paris, 1951; enlarged ed., Paris, 1968).
Regnier, J., *Les Préfets du Consulat et de l'Empire* (Paris, 1913).
Schwartz, Bernard, ed., *The Code Napoleon and the Common-Law World* (New York: New York University Press, 1956).
Thiry, J., *Le Sénat de Napoléon, 1800–1814* (Paris, 1932).

WARFARE

Camon, Général, *Quand et comment Napoléon a conçu son système de bataille* (Paris, 1935).
Chandler, David G., *The Campaigns of Napoleon* (New York: The Macmillan Company, 1966).

Desbrière, E., *Projets et tentatives de débarquemenì aux îles britanniques,* 3 vols. (Paris, 1901).

Dodge, T. A., *Napoleon, A History of the Art of War, from the beginning of the French Revolution to Waterloo,* 4 vols. (Boston: Houghton Mifflin Company, 1904–1907).

Dupont, M., *Napoléon et ses grognards* (Paris, 1945).

Glover, Richard, "The French Fleet, 1807–1814," *Journal of Modern History,* September, 1967.

Heckscher, E. F., *The Continental System* (Oxford: Clarendon Press, 1922).

Mackesy, P., *The War in the Mediterranean* (London: Longmans, Green & Co., Ltd., 1957).

Mahan, Alfred T., *The Influence of Sea Power upon the French Revolution and Empire,* 10th ed., 2 vols. (Westport, Conn.: Greenwood Press, Inc., 1968).

Maine, René, *Trafalgar: Napoleon's Naval Waterloo,* trans. by R. Eldon and B. W. Robinson (New York: Charles Scribner's Sons, 1957).

Masson, Philippe and Muracciole, José, *Napoléon et la Marine* (Paris, 1968).

Melvin, F. E., *Napoleon's Navigation System* (New York: Appleton-Century-Crofts, 1919).

Oman, Sir Charles, *Studies in Napoleonic Wars* (London: Metheun & Co., Ltd., 1929).

Oman, Carola, *Napoleon at the Channel* (New York: Doubleday & Co., Inc., 1942).

Parker, Harold T., *Three Napoleonic Battles* (Durham, N. C.: Duke University Press, 1944).

Rodger, A. B., *The War of the Second Coalition* (Oxford: Clarendon Press, 1964).

SOCIAL CONDITIONS

Population

Bourgeois-Pichat, J., "L'évolution générale de la population française depuis le XVIIIe siècle," *Population,* 1951, pp. 635–662.

———, "Note sur l'évolution générale de la population française depuis le XVIIIe siècle," *ibid.,* 1952, pp, 319–344.

Godechot, J. and Moncassin, S., *Démographie et subsistances en Languedoc du XVIIIe au début du XIXe siècle,* "Commission d'histoire, économique et sociale de la Révolution" (Paris, 1965).

Meynier, A., *Une erreur historique. Les morts de la Grand Armée et des armées ennemies* (Paris, 1934).

Pouthas, Charles H., "L'évolution démographique du département du

Nord pendant la première moitié du XIXe siècle," *La Revue du Nord,* 1954, pp. 331–339.

———, *La population française pendant la première moitié du XIXe siècle* (Paris, 1956).

Reinhard, M., "La statistique de la population française depuis le XVIIIe siècle," *Population,* 1950, pp. 103–120.

———, "La population des villes: sa mesure sous la Révolution et l'Empire," *Population,* 1954, pp. 279–288.

Reinhard, M., and Armengaud, André, *Histoire générale de la population mondiale* (Paris, 1961).

Rapports, XIIe Congrès international des sciences historiques, vol. I, pp. 450–573 (Vienna, 1965).

Religious Problems

Anchel, R., *Napoléon et les Juifs* (Paris, 1928).

Bindel, V., *Le Vatican à Paris, 1809–1814* (Paris, 1942).

Constant, L. M. J., *L'Eglise de France sous le Consulat et l'Empire, 1800–1814* (Paris, 1928).

Daniel-Rops, Henri, *L'Eglise des révolutions* (Paris, 1960).

Dansette, A., *Histoire réligieuse de la France contemporaine,* vol. I (Paris, 1948).

Latreille, A., et al., *Histoire du catholicisme en France,* vol. III (Paris, 1962).

Leflon, J., *Monsieur Emery,* vol. II, *L'Eglise concordataire et impériale* (Paris, 1947).

Léonard, E. G., *Histoire générale du protestantisme,* vol. III (Paris, 1964).

Poland, Burdette, *French Protestantism and the French Revolution* (Princeton, N.J.: Princeton University Press, 1957).

Walsh, H. H., *The Concordat of 1801* (New York: Columbia University Press, 1933).

General Social Conditions

Broc, Vicomte de, *La vie en France sous le Premier Empire* (Paris, 1895).

Bruhat, J., *Histoire du mouvement ouvrier français,* vol. I (Paris, 1952).

Daumard, Adeline, *La bourgeoisie parisienne de 1815 à 1848* (Paris, 1963).

Dolléans, E., *Histoire du mouvement ouvrier* (Paris, 1936).

Francastel, A., *Le style empire, du Directoire à la Restauration* (Paris, 1939).

Le Poittevin, G., *La liberté de la presse depuis la Révolution, 1789–1815* (Paris, 1900).

Pernoud, Régine, *Histoire de la bourgeoisie en France,* vol. II (Paris, 1962).

Robiquet, J., *La vie quotidienne au temps de Napoléon* (Paris, 1942);

published in English as *Daily Life in France under Napoleon* (London: Allen & Unwin, Ltd., 1962).

Thompson, E. P., *The Making of the English Working Class* (London: V. Gollancz, 1964).

Vidalenc, *Les émigrés français, 1789–1825* (Paris, 1965).

Walter, G., *Histoire des paysans de France* (Paris, 1963).

Weiner, Margery, *The French Exiles, 1789–1815* (London: Murray, Ltd., 1960).

ECONOMIC CONDITIONS

Clough, Shepard B., *The Economic Development of Western Civilization* (New York: McGraw-Hill, Inc., 1959).

Crouzet, F., *L'Empire britannique et le blocus continental, 1806–1813*, 2 vols. (Paris, 1958).

Deutsch, Harold C., *The Genesis of Napoleonic Imperialism* (Cambridge, Mass.: Harvard University Press, 1938).

Festy, O., *L'agriculture sous le Consulat* (Paris, 1952).

———, "Les enquêtes agricoles en France de 1800 à 1815," *Revue d'histoire, économique et sociale*, 1956, pp. 43–59.

Fohlen, Claude, *Histoire générale du travail*, vol. III (Paris, 1961).

Higby, C. P. and Willis, C. B., "Industry and Labor under Napoleon," *American Historical Review*, LIII, 1948, pp. 465–480.

Jouvenel, B. de, *Napoléon et l'économie dirigée. Le blocus continental* (Paris, 1943).

Lacour-Gayet, J., *Histoire du commerce*, vols. III and IV (Paris, 1951–1952).

Levasseur, E., *Histoire du commerce en France*, vol. II (Paris, 1912).

Pares, R., "The Economic Factors in the History of the Empire," *Economic History Review*, 1937, vol. VI, pp. 119–144.

Payard, M., *Le financier Ouvrard, 1770–1846* (Paris, 1958).

Sée, H., *Histoire économique de la France*, vol. II (Paris, 1942; 2d ed., 1951).

Stourm, R., *Les Finances du Consulat* (Paris, 1902).

Thurot, H. and Brousse, P., *Le Consulat et l'Empire*, part of *Histoire Socialiste* (Paris, 1905).

Viennet, Odette, *Napoléon et l'industrie française; la crise de 1810–1811* (Paris, 1947).

THE FALL OF NAPOLEON

Artz, Frederick B., *France under the Bourbon Restoration, 1814–1830* (Cambridge, Mass.: Harvard University Press, 1931).

Browning, O., *The Fall of Napoleon* (London, 1907).

Delderfeld, R. F., *The Retreat from Moscow* (New York: Atheneum Publishers, 1967).

Ferrero, G., *The Reconstruction of Europe* (New York: W. W. Norton & Company, Inc., 1941).

George, H. B., *Napoleon's Invasion of Russia* (London, 1899).

Nicolson, A., *The Congress of Vienna* (London: Metheun & Co., Ltd., 1946).

Ponteil, F., *La chute de Napoléon Ier et la crise francaise de 1814–1815* (Paris, 1943).

Rath, R. John, *The Fall of the Napoleonic Kingdom of Italy* (New York: Columbia University Press, 1941).

Sweet, P. R., *Friedrich von Gentz, Defender of the Old Order* (Madison, Wis.: University of Wisconsin Press, 1941).

Webster, C. K., *The Congress of Vienna* (London: Thames & Hudson, Ltd., 1934).

EUROPE IN 1815

Bilan du Monde en 1815, Comité International des Sciences historiques, XIIe Congrès (Vienna, 1965); *Rapports conjoints* (Paris, 1966). Reports by G. S. Graham, Lewis Hertzman, A. Z. Manfred, and A. L. Narochnitzki.

Bertier de Sauvigny, G., *La Restauration* (Paris, 1955); published in English as *The Bourbon Restoration,* trans. by Lynn M. Case (Philadelphia: University of Pennsylvania Press, 1966).

Dreyfus, F.-G., "Bilan économique des Allemagnes en 1815," *Révue d'histoire, économique et sociale,* 1965, pp. 434–464.

Gulick, Edward V., *Europe's Classical Balance of Power* (Ithaca, N.Y.: Cornell University Press, 1955).

Kissenger, Henry A., *A World Restored* (Boston: Houghton Mifflin Company, 1957).

CULTURE IN THE NAPOLEONIC PERIOD

Artz, Frederick B., *From the Renaissance to Romanticism* (Chicago: University of Chicago Press, 1962); the book does not include a treatment of science; see chap. VI and the bibliography.

Aulard, Alphonse, *Napoléon Ier et la monopole universitaire* (Paris, 1911).

Bayard, Emile, *Le style empire* (Paris, n.d.).

Charpentier, John, *Napoléon et les hommes de lettres de son temps* (Paris, 1935).

Crosland, Maurice, *The Society of Arcueil: A View of French Science at* the Time of Napoleon I (Cambridge, Mass.: Harvard University Press, 1967).

Dowd, David L., *The Pageant-Master of the French Revolution* (Lincoln, Nebr.: University of Nebraska Press, 1948).

Droz, Jacques, *Le Romantisme allemand et l'État: Resistance et collaboration dans l'Allemagne napoléonienne* (Paris, 1966).

Gontard, M., *L'enseignement primaire en France . . .* (Paris, 1959).

Hall, A. R., *The Scientific Revolution, 1500–1800: The Formation of the Modern Scientific Attitude* (Boston: Beacon Press, Inc., 1954).

Hautecoeur, L., *L'art sous la Révolution* (Paris, 1953).

————, *Histoire de l'architecture classique en France,* vol. V (Paris, 1953).

Lanzac de Laborie, Léon de, *Paris sous Napoléon;* vol. VII, *Le théâtre francais;* vol. VIII, *Spectacles et musées* (Paris, 1905–1913)

La Sizeranne, Robert de, Réau, Louis and Saunier, Charles, *L'art et les artistes sous Napoléon* (Paris, 1821).

Lecomte, L. Henri, *Napoléon et le monde dramatique* (Paris, 1912).

Lelièvre, P., *Vivant Denon* (Angers, 1942).

Mason, S. I., *Histoire des sciences* (French ed., Paris, 1956).

Moreau, Pierre, *Le romantisme* (Paris, 1932).

Taton, R., *Histoire générale des sciences* (Paris, 1958).

Vuillermoz, E., *Histoire de la musique* (new ed., Paris, 1955).

Weill, Georges, *Histoire de l'enseignement secondaire en France* (Paris, 1921).

MODERN INTERPRETATIONS

Andrews, G. G., *Napoleon in Review* (New York: Alfred A. Knopf, 1939).

Broadley, Alexander M., *Napoleon in Caricature,* 2 vols., (London, 1910).

Clough, Shepard B., et al., *The European Past,* vol. I (New York: The Macmillan Co., 1964).

Dowd, David, *Napoleon, Was He the Heir of the French Revolution* in "Problems in World Civilization" (New York: Holt, Rinehart and Winston, Inc., 1957).

Geyl, P., *Napoleon, For and Against* (New Haven, Conn., Yale University Press, 1949).

Gooch, Brison D., *Interpreting European History,* vol. I (Homewood, Ill.: Dorsey Press, 1967).

Holtman, R. B., *Napoleonic Propaganda* (Baton-Rouge, La., Louisiana State University Press, 1950).

Kohn, Hans, *The Age of Nationalism, The First Era of Global History* (New York: Harper & Row, Publishers, 1962).

Maccunn, Francis John, *The Contemporary English View of Napoleon* (New York: The Macmillan Company, 1914).

CATALOG OF EXHIBITS, 1969

Archives Nationales, *Napoléon tel qu'en lui-même* (Paris, 1969); 143 pp. with illustrations.

Bibliothèque Nationale, *La Légende napoléonienne* (Paris, 1969); 83 pp. with illustrations.

Ministère d'État, Affaires Culturelles, *Grand Palais* (Paris, 1969); 224 pp. with illustrations.

Musée Nationale de la Légion d'Honneur, *Napoléon et la Légion d'Honneur* (Paris, 1968); over 100 pages with illustrations and advertisements.

Carlo Maria Buonaparte (1746

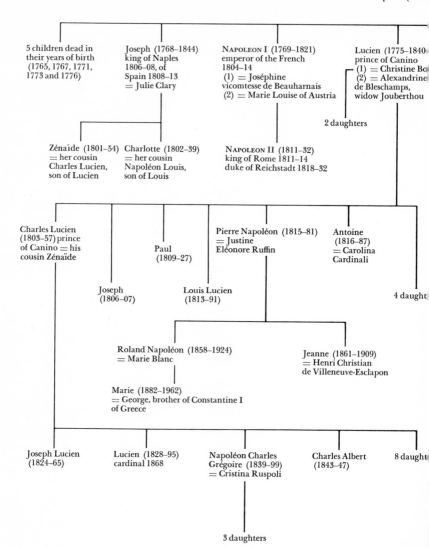

5 children dead in their years of birth (1765, 1767, 1771, 1773 and 1776)	Joseph (1768–1844) king of Naples 1806–08, of Spain 1808–13 = Julie Clary	NAPOLEON I (1769–1821) emperor of the French 1804–14 (1) = Joséphine vicomtesse de Beauharnais (2) = Marie Louise of Austria	Lucien (1775–1840 prince of Canino (1) = Christine Bo (2) = Alexandrine de Bleschamps, widow Jouberthou

2 daughters

Zénaïde (1801–54) = her cousin Charles Lucien, son of Lucien

Charlotte (1802–39) = her cousin Napoléon Louis, son of Louis

NAPOLEON II (1811–32) king of Rome 1811–14 duke of Reichstadt 1818–32

Charles Lucien (1803–57) prince of Canino = his cousin Zénaïde

Paul (1809–27)

Pierre Napoléon (1815–81) = Justine Eléonore Ruffin

Antoine (1816–87) = Carolina Cardinali

Joseph (1806–07)

Louis Lucien (1813–91)

4 daught

Roland Napoléon (1858–1924) = Marie Blanc

Jeanne (1861–1909) = Henri Christian de Villeneuve-Esclapon

Marie (1882–1962) = George, brother of Constantine I of Greece

Joseph Lucien (1824–65)

Lucien (1828–95) cardinal 1868

Napoléon Charles Grégoire (1839–99) = Cristina Ruspoli

Charles Albert (1843–47)

8 daught

3 daughters

*The Bonaparte family gave several names to each child; the table gives the name by which the person known in history. The names of daughters are included only if they are important historically. No attempt been made to show the complicated descendance from Caroline through Prince Murat. There is living a m heir from a male line: Prince Joachim Murat, born in 1944 through the eldest branch; Pierre, born in 19 through another male descendant; and Achille, born in 1956 through a third. The head of the house descend through the male line, as required by the Salic Law for rulers of France. Through marriage the Bonapa descendants are related to many royal houses and important noble families.

Further details can be derived from genealogical tables in: *Encyclopaedia Britannica* (1965 edition) vol. p. 901, and *Napoléon I, Le Consulat et l'Empire,* Éditions de la Tourelle, in the Collection "Les Grandes Da Historiques de France."

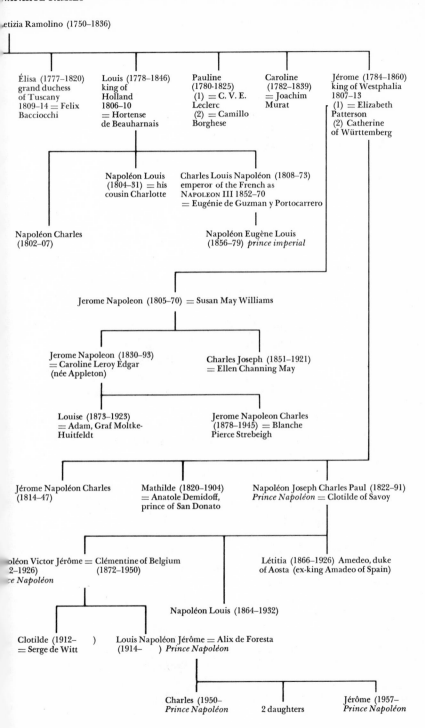

etizia Ramolino (1750–1836)

Élisa (1777–1820) grand duchess of Tuscany 1809–14 = Felix Bacciocchi

Louis (1778–1846) king of Holland 1806–10 = Hortense de Beauharnais

Pauline (1780-1825) (1) = C. V. E. Leclerc (2) = Camillo Borghese

Caroline (1782–1839) = Joachim Murat

Jérome (1784–1860) king of Westphalia 1807–13 (1) = Elizabeth Patterson (2) Catherine of Württemberg

Napoléon Louis (1804–31) = his cousin Charlotte

Charles Louis Napoléon (1808–73) emperor of the French as NAPOLÉON III 1852–70 = Eugénie de Guzman y Portocarrero

Napoléon Charles (1802–07)

Napoléon Eugène Louis (1856–79) prince imperial

Jerome Napoleon (1805–70) = Susan May Williams

Jerome Napoleon (1830–93) = Caroline Leroy Edgar (née Appleton)

Charles Joseph (1851–1921) = Ellen Channing May

Louise (1873–1923) = Adam, Graf Moltke-Huitfeldt

Jerome Napoleon Charles (1878–1945) = Blanche Pierce Strebeigh

Jérôme Napoléon Charles (1814–47)

Mathilde (1820–1904) = Anatole Demidoff, prince of San Donato

Napoléon Joseph Charles Paul (1822–91) Prince Napoléon = Clotilde of Savoy

oléon Victor Jérôme 2–1926) ce Napoléon

= Clémentine of Belgium (1872–1950)

Létitia (1866–1926) Amedeo, duke of Aosta (ex-king Amadeo of Spain)

Napoléon Louis (1864–1932)

Clotilde (1912–) = Serge de Witt

Louis Napoléon Jérôme (1914–) Prince Napoléon

= Alix de Foresta

Charles (1950– Prince Napoléon

2 daughters

Jérôme (1957– Prince Napoléon

Chronology

1769	August	(Aug. 15) Birth of Napoleon at Ajaccio, Corsica
1779	January	Collège d'Autun
	May	École militaire de Brienne
1784	September	École militaire de Paris
1785	October	Rank of second lieutenant; attached to artillery corps of regiment of La Fère at Valence
1786–1790		Various absences in Corsica and some service in France
1791	January	Rejoins his regiment
	September	Absence again
1792	January	Adjutant major to National Guard in Ajaccio; then second lieutenant colonel
	May	Journey to Paris to justify his role in revolt in Ajaccio
	October	Returns to Corsica
1793	May	Bonaparte family is banished from Corsica by Paoli and moves to southern France
	June	Napoleon rejoins his regiment at Nice
	July	Sent against Marseille federalists
	September	Commander of artillery; sent to Toulon
	October	Chief of his battalion
		Adjutant general, chief of brigade
	December	Successful capture of Toulon
		Brigadier general of Army of the Midi
1794	March	Commander of artillery in the Army of Italy
	August	Accused of complicity with Robespierre; dismissed from army; rejoins army
1795	June	Refused appointment as general of infantry in the Army of the West

	August	Attached to topographical bureau of the Committee of Public Safety
	October	(Oct. 5) Barras names Napoleon in charge of suppression of Paris insurrection of 13 Vendémiaire
		General of division of the Interior
		(Oct. 26) Commander of the Army of the Interior
1796	March	(Mar. 2) Commander in chief of the Army of Italy
		(Mar. 9) Marries Josephine de Beauharnais
		Leaves for campaign in Italy
	May	(May 10) Battle of Lodi
		Armistice between Napoleon and Sardinia
	June	Armistice with Pope at Bologna
	August	Treaty of San Ildefonso between France and Spain
	October	Creation of Cispadine Republic
		Directory forbids importation of English goods
		The French subdue Corsica
	November	Battle of Arcola (Italy)
		Death of Catherine II of Russia; accession of Paul I
1797	January	Battle of Rivoli
	February	Mantua capitulates
		Battle of Cape Saint Vincent
		Treaty between France and the Pope at Tolentino
	April	Preliminary peace of Leoben
	May	Creation of New Republic of Venice
	June	Creation of Ligurian Republic
	July	Creation of Cisalpine Republic; annexation of Cispadine Republic to it
	September	(Sept. 4) *Coup d'état* in Paris of 18 Fructidor, Year V
	October	Treaty of Campo-Formio with Austria
	December	Congress of Rastatt
		Death of Frederick William II of Prussia; accession of Frederick William III
1798	February	Creation of the Roman Republic
	March	Creation of Helvetic Republic
	April	Napoleon made general in chief of the Army of the Orient
	May	Napoleon sails for Egypt
	June	Napoleon captures Malta
	July	The French occupy Alexandria
		Battle of the Pyramids
	July–September	Napoleon reorganizes Egypt at Cairo
		Landing of French expedition in Killala Bay (Ireland)
	August	Battle of Abukir Bay (French defeat by England)
	December	France declares war on Kingdom of Naples

1799	January	Second Coalition
		Creation of Parthenopean Republic (from Kingdom of Naples)
		Bonaparte invades Syria
	March	Austria declares war on France
		Napoleon at Jaffa
	March–May	Siege of Acre
	June	(June 18) Conciliar *coup d'état* in Paris of 30 Prairial, Year VII
	July	Napoleon defeats Turks at Abukir Bay
	August	Napoleon sails from Egypt
	September	Battle of Zurich
	October	Napoleon lands at Frejus and journeys to Paris
	November	(Nov. 9–10) *Coup d'état* of 18 Brumaire. Establishment of the Consulate
	December	Constitution of the Year VIII. Napoleon made First Consul
		Amnesty in the Vendée
1800	March	Pius VII becomes Pope
	May	Napoleon crosses Great Saint Bernard
		Malta surrenders to English
	June	Battle of Marengo (against Austria)
	August	Union of England and Ireland
		Commission appointed to draw up Code
	October	Treaty of San Ildefonso (Spain cedes Louisiana)
	December	Battle of Hohenlinden (won by General Moreau)
		Armed neutrality of the North
		(Dec. 24) Abortive attempt to assassinate Napoleon, rue Saint-Nicaise
1801	February	Treaty of Lunéville between France and Austria
		Armistice with Kingdom of Naples
	March	Resignation of Pitt in England
		Left bank of Rhine annexed to France
		Assassination of Paul I. Accession of Alexander I of Russia
		Commercial treaty with Naples. Peace between France and Naples
		Duchy of Parma annexed to France
	April	Nelson defeats Danish fleet at Copenhagen
	May	Toussaint L'Ouverture issues constitution for Saint-Domingue
		Cisalpine Republic becomes Italian Republic
		Act of Malmaison

	July	Concordat of 1801 between Pius VII and Napoleon
	August	Surrender of French army in Egypt
	September	Reorganization of the Batavian Republic
		French forces evacuate Egypt
	October	Peace between France and Russia. Commercial treaty
		Constitution of Holland
		Peace with Portugal. Commercial treaty
1802	January	Napoleon elected President of the Italian Republic
	February	General Leclerc arrives in Saint-Domingue
	March	Treaty of Amiens between France and England
	April	Concordat of 1801 promulgated with Organic Articles
	May	End of the War of the Vendée
		Partial amnesty to *émigrés*
		Senate votes to make Napoleon first consul for life
		Educational reforms begun
		Establishment of the Legion of Honor approved
		Reestablishment of slavery in colonies
	June	Capture of Toussaint L'Ouverture by General Leclerc
		Commercial treaty with Turkey
	August	Constitution of the Year X accepted. Napoleon becomes First Consul for life. Plebiscite
		Republic of Valais, controlled by France
	September	Annexation of Piedmont
		General insurrection in Saint-Domingue
1803	February	Napoleon mediates in Switzerland
		Diet of the Holy Roman Empire issues Recess
	March–April	Reorganization of the Holy Roman Empire
		Anglo-French negotiations over Malta
	April	Law against labor associations strengthened
		Purchase of Louisiana by the United States
		Bank of France chartered for fifteen years
		England declares embargo on French and Dutch trade
	May	England declares war on France
	September	Fifty-year alliance between France and Switzerland
1804	January	Cadoudal plot against Napoleon
	February–March	Arrest of conspirators
	March	Execution of the Duc d'Enghien
		Civil Code (Code Napoléon) promulgated
	April	Pitt prime minister in England again
	May	The first French Empire created by Constitution of the Year XII
		Plan to invade England
	May–June	Execution or imprisonment of leaders of Cadoudal plot

	July	First awards of the Legion of Honor
		Fouché becomes minister of police
		Napoleon makes tour of military inspection
	October	Napoleon returns to Saint-Cloud
	November	Pope Pius VII arrives in France for coronation
	December	(Dec. 2) Coronation of Napoleon as Emperor in Cathedral of Notre Dame
		Franco-Spanish Alliance
		Spain declares war on England
1805	January	Creation of the Grand Cordon of the Legion of Honor
		Levy of 60,000 conscripts
	March	Napoleon reorganizes Batavian Republic
		Napoleon is offered crown of Kingdom of Italy
	May	Napoleon is crowned king of Italy at Milan
	June	Genoa and Ligurian Republic annexed to France
		Prince Eugène de Beauharnais (stepson of Napoleon) is made viceroy of Kingdom of Italy
		Lucca placed under Elisa Bonaparte and husband
		Napoleonic Code extended to Italy
	June–July	Establishment of Confederation of the Rhine
	July	No celebration of Bastille Day
		Naval battle at Cape Finisterre
		Austria joins Third Coalition (England-Russia)
	August	Napoleon drops idea of invasion of England
	September	War renewed against Austria
	October	Capitulation of Ulm to the French
		(Oct. 20) Defeat of French fleet at Trafalgar
	November	French capture Vienna
		Treaty between Prussia and Russia
	December	Napoleonic victory at Austerlitz
		Treaty of Schönbrunn with Prussia
		Treaty of Pressburg with Austria. End of Holy Roman Empire
1806	January	Death of Pitt
	February	Napoleonic order to construct Arc de Triomphe
		Neapolitan Bourbons flee to Sicily
	February–March	Peace talks between England and France
	March	Formation of the Grand Duchy of Berg (Murat and Caroline Bonaparte, rulers)
		Joseph Bonaparte, king of Naples
	May	British Orders-in-Council blockading the Continent from Brest to the Elbe River
		Batavian Republic suppressed
	June	Louis Bonaparte, king of Holland

July	Creation of the Confederation of the Rhine. Jerome Bonaparte made king
August	Francis II, emperor of the Holy Roman Empire, renounces this title and becomes Francis I, emperor of Austria
	Metternich sent by Austria as ambassador to France
October	War between France and Prussia, after Prussia's ultimatum
	Battles of Jena and Auerstädt
	French forces capture Berlin
	Duke of Saxony adheres to Confederation of the Rhine
November	Berlin Decree (Continental Blockade)
	Armistice between France and Prussia
	French army enters Warsaw
December	Venice added to Italian Kingdom
	Dalmation provinces taken from Austria, under Napoleon
	Napoleon arrives in Warsaw
1807 January	British Order-in-Council prohibiting trade between French ports and French colonies
February	Battle of Eylau
March	Siege of Danzig
April	Alliance between Prussia and Russia
May	Surrender of Danzig
June	Battle of Friedland
July	Peace treaties of Tilsit with Prussia and with Russia
	Creation of Grand Duchy of Warsaw
August	Alliance between Denmark and France
September	England bombards Copenhagen and captures Danish fleet
	Denmark adheres to Continental System
October	The English leave Copenhagen with Danish fleet
	Portugal declares war on England but secretly signs treaty with England
	Reorganization of Prussian government under Stein
November	England issues Order-in-Council that all ships must touch in England for license before proceeding to the Continent
	Russia declares war on England
	Prince-Regent and his family of Portugal sail for Brazil
	The French enter Lisbon
December	Milan Decree (Continental System)
	French Commercial Code and Code of Civil Procedure
	Abolition of the slave trade by England

		United States Congress passes Embargo Act
1808	February	French government established in Lisbon
		French troops enter Rome
		French army invades Spain
	March	United States adopts Non-Intercourse Act
		Spanish revolts. Ferdinand welcomed in Madrid
		The French enter Madrid
		Consistories for Jewish communities in France
		Tuscany annexed to French Empire
		Pope Pius VII excommunicates Napoleon
		University of France organized
	April	Bayonne Decree
	May	(May 2–3) Dos de Mayo revolt in Madrid; suppression
		Napoleon annexes Urbino and Ancona to Kingdom of Italy
		Parma and Plaisance annexed to France
		Pope forbids bishops to obey French government
		Charles IV abdicates (Spain)
		Revolts in southern Spain
	June	Joseph Bonaparte made king of Spain and General Murat replaces him in Naples
		Spanish insurrection
	July	Capitulation of Dupont at Bailén (Spain)
	August	Joseph and the French evacuate Madrid
		Wellesley and English troops land near Lisbon
		Wellesley (future Lord Wellington) defeats Junot at Vimiero
		Convention of Cintra between Napoleon and English for French evacuation of Portugal
	September	Military treaty between France and Prussia
		Ancona and Urbino added to Kingdom of Italy
		Conscription of 160,000 approved by the Senate
	September–October	Congress of Erfurt between Napoleon and Alexander I
	October	Napoleon in Weimar; meets with Goethe
		Renewal of Franco-Russian alliance
		English army enters Spain. Napoleon leaves for Spain
	November	Napoleon commands French army in Spain but places Soult in charge
		French victories in Spain
		The English withdraw to Portugal
	December	Napoleon enters Madrid. Seizures from Spanish treasury
		French Criminal Code

		Murat and Caroline Bonaparte become rulers of Kingdom of Naples
1809	January	Call for 100,000 conscripts
		Battle at La Coruña; England withdraws from Spain
	February	Napoleon captures Saragossa after siege
	March	Declaration of Austria against France
		The French invasion of Portugal
		Forced abdication of Gustavus IV of Sweden
		Sweden allies with Russia and adheres to Continental Blockade
		Accession of Charles XIII (Sweden)
	April	Austria declares war on France
		Uprising in the Tyrol
	May	Napoleon captures Vienna
		Napoleon annexes Papal States
		French bombardment of Pressburg (Bratislava)
	June	Annexation of Rome to France
		Pope excommunicates Napoleon
	July	Wellesley expels Soult from Portugal
		Arrest of Pope at Ancona
		Battle of Wagram
	July–September	British Walcheren expedition
	October	Treaty of Schönbrunn-Vienna with Austria
	December	Napoleon divorces Josephine
		Illyrian provinces annexed to French Empire
1810	January	Treaty between France and Sweden
	February	Contract for marriage of Napoleon and Marie Louise (House of Hapsburg) signed at Paris and Vienna
	March	Rambouillet Decree (Continental System)
	April	(Apr. 1) Civil marriage between Napoleon and Marie Louise at Saint-Cloud
		(Apr. 2) Religious marriage at the Louvre
	May	United States Congress passes Macon Bill
	July	Napoleon annexes Holland to French Empire, deposing Louis
	August	Masséna invades Portugal
		Introduction of Code Napoléon in Poland
		Inauguration of the Vendôme column
		Trianon Tariff (Continental System)
		Bernadotte becomes king of Sweden
	September	Cortes meets in Spain
	October	Fontainebleau Decrees (Continental System)
		Sweden declares war on England

	December	Napoleon annexes Hamburg, Bremen, and Oldenburg (town) to French Empire; also Republic of Valais
		Russia breaks with Continental System
		French Penal Code promulgated
		Italian Tyrol added to Kingdom of Italy
1811	January	Kingdom of Westphalia, Grand Duchy of Berg, and Duchy of Oldenburg annexed to Empire
	March	Birth of son of Napoleon and Marie Louise, Napoleon II, King of Rome
	March–April	Masséna retreats in Spain
	April	Dalmatia organized into 9 departments
	October	Peasant land ownership reformed in Prussia
	November	Suppression of riots in England
	December	120,000 conscripts
1812	January–April	British advance in Spain
	January	Catalonia annexed to France (4 departments)
		Napoleon demands troops from Prussia
		Napoleon demands troops from Austria
	April	Secret Swedish-Russian Alliance
		Ultimatum by Alexander I (Russia) to France
	May	Coalition of England, Sweden, Russia
		Treaty of Bucharest between Russia and Turkey
	June	The Pope transferred to Fontainebleau
		United States declares war on England
		Napoleon begins invasion of Russia
	July	Wellington captures Salamanca
	August	Smolensk evacuated by Russians. Koutouzov made general-in-chief of Russian armies
		Wellington captures Madrid
	September	Battle of Borodino
		(Sept. 14–19) Capture and occupation of Moscow by Napoleon
		Call of 137,000 men
	October	(Oct. 19) Retreat from Moscow begins
		Abortive *coup d'état* led by Malet in Paris
		Execution of Malet and his accomplices
	November	Battle of Berezina River
	December	Napoleon leaves the Grand Army; reaches Paris December 18
		Constitution established in Spain
1813	January	Concordat of Fontainebleau
		Renewed conscription. Anticipation of class of 1814
		Punishment of English rioters

February	Marie Louise designated as regent
	Alliance between Prussia and Russia. War on Napoleon
April	Austria breaks alliance with France
	Napoleon leaves Paris to head French army
May	Battles of Lützen and Bautzen. The French evacuate Dresden and Leipzig. Napoleon reenters Dresden
	French withdraw from Madrid
June–August	Armistice of Pleiswitz; Congress of Prague
	Grand Alliance against Napoleon
June	Battle of Vitoria (Spain); French army retreats to France
	Napoleon refuses Austrian mediation
August	Austria declares war on France
	Battle of Dresden; Prussian retreat
October	Battle of Leipzig (Battle of the Nations). French forces retreat
	The French surrender strongholds in Spain
November	Frankfurt Declaration of the Allies
	French army retreats across Rhine
	Prince of Orange returns to Holland
December	Allies announce plan to reduce size of France
	Treaty of Valençay providing for return of Ferdinand to Spain

1814	January	Treaty of Kiel
		Allies invade France. Protocol of Langres
		Pius VII returns to Rome
	January–March	Napoleon fights defensive battles, some victories, some defeats against Allies
	February	Wellington captures Bayonne
		Failure of conferences at Lusigny for armistice
	March	Treaty of Chaumont between Allies. Battle of Laon
		Comte de Provence declared Louis XVIII
		(Mar. 30) Allies enter Paris
		(Mar. 31) Capitulation of Paris
	April	Senate deposes Napoleon. Recalls Louis XVIII
		(Apr. 6) Abdication of Napoleon
		Soult surrenders Toulouse. Armistice with Wellington
		Treaty of Fontainebleau
		Napoleon's farewell to the Imperial Guard
		Napoleon to be granted rule over island of Elbe
	May	(May 3) Louis XVIII enters Paris
		(May 4) Napoleon lands on island of Elbe
		The Pope arrives in Rome
		First Peace of Paris

	June	Louis XVIII grants the Charter *(La Charte)*
	September	Congress of Vienna begins
	December	Treaty of Ghent between United States and England
1815	January	Treaty of Vienna between Allies
	February	(Feb. 26) Napoleon leaves Elbe
	March	Napoleon lands in France
		(Mar. 20) Napoleon enters Paris; beginning of the Hundred Days
	April	Allies united to defeat Napoleon
		Additional Act to Imperial Constitition
	May	Treaties of Congress of Vienna on future boundaries and status of Europe; adopts declaration against slave trade
	June	(June 18) Battle of Waterloo
		(June 22) Abdication of Napoleon in favor of Napoleon II
	July	Louis XVIII reenters Paris
		Napoleon surrenders to English (Captain Maitland); leaves France for Saint Helena
	September	Foundation of the Holy Alliance
	October	Napoleon arrives on Saint Helena
	November	Second Treaty of Paris; Quadruple Alliance
1818		France admitted to Quadruple Alliance
1821	May	(May 5) Death of Napoleon

THE NAPOLEONIC LEGEND

1832	Death of Napoleon II in Austria
1836	Louis Napoleon's abortive coup at Strasbourg
1839	Louis Napoleon publishes *Les idées napoléoniennes*
1840	Napoleon's ashes brought to the Hôtel des Invalides in Paris
	Louis Napoleon's coup at Boulogne and imprisonment at chateau of Ham
1845	Louis Napoleon escapes from Ham and goes to England
1848	Louis Napoleon elected president of Second French Republic
1851	Louis Napoleon to be president for ten years
1852	Louis Napoleon becomes Emperor Napoleon III after a *coup d'état*
1870	Franco-Prussian War; capture of Napoleon III by the Prussians; overthrow of Napoleon III
1969	French celebrations of birth of Napoleon I

Index